Evolutionary Principles of
Human Adolescence

LIVES IN CONTEXT
Mihaly Csikszentmihalyi

Evolutionary Principles of Human Adolescence

GLENN E. WEISFELD
Wayne State University

BASIC
BOOKS

A Member of the Perseus Books Group

Lives in Context

Copyright © 1999 by Basic Books, A Member of the Perseus Books Group

Published in 1999 in the United States of America by Basic Books, 10 East 53rd Street, New York, NY 10022.

Library of Congress Cataloging-in-Publication Data
Weisfeld, Glenn, 1943–
    Evolutionary principles of human adolescence / by Glenn E. Weisfeld.
        p.   cm — (Lives in context)
    Includes bibliographical references and indexes.
    ISBN 0-8133-3317-2 (hardcover). — ISBN 0-8133-3318-0 (pbk.)
    1. Adolescent psychology.   2. Psychology, Comparative.   I. Title.
II. Series.
    BF724.W35   1999
    305.235—dc21   98-45153
                                                                          CIP

10   9   8   7   6   5   4   3   2   1

For Carol and Miriam

Contents

Tables and Illustrations

Photos

Acknowledgments

For their assistance in this project, thanks are extended to: Mihaly Csikszentmihalyi, Catherine Murphy, Michelle Baxter, Jennifer Chen, Kevin MacDonald, Nancy L. Segal, Michele K. Surbey, Leslie Ziegenhorn, Miriam Weisfeld, Carol Cronin Weisfeld, Lisa Wigutoff, Joan W. Sherman, Mimi Zeiger, Amy L. Martinez, and my students. I also thank the psychology faculty and administration of Goldsmiths' College, University of London, for hosting the sabbatical during which I wrote the first draft of the book.

Glenn E. Weisfeld

Adolescent Chimpanzee. Watercolor by Miriam Weisfeld.

1 The Biological Approach

Generalizing About People

The study of adolescent behavior has traditionally concentrated on individual and cultural differences. Textbooks on adolescent psychology typically describe historical trends in drug use, social-class differences in academic achievement, and age differences in contraceptive use. These studies of diversity provide important practical information, and they confirm the point that human behavior is highly variable. However, they tell us little about the essence of adolescent behavior and development; they provide us with few, if any, general facts. Moreover, there is no assurance that the knowledge these studies impart will hold even for the same population a few years later, let alone for other adolescents abroad in the world. They fail to provide us with a general model of human adolescence.

Science is based on generalization. The sciences have established general laws to explain natural phenomena—the ideal gas laws, principles of chemical reactions, atomic theory, natural selection, and so forth. Logically, a science should first describe general phenomena before exploring variations and exceptions. In fact, variability is of little initial interest, except insofar as it illumines the general case, as, for example, when variability is introduced by experimentation. Thus, the aim of a science is to generalize—to reduce multiple instances to a single rule. And in studying behavior, not only *can* we generalize about people—we *must* (Crawford, 1989).

To derive general laws of behavior, we must initially focus on general findings. In the case of adolescence, that means establishing facts about this life stage that hold across time and distance, not just in a particular society. In other words, it is necessary to view adolescence as a developmental stage in our entire species and to study it as a biological phenomenon. However, this does not mean we should ignore the role of culture and other aspects of experience. Rather, we must integrate biological factors with the current environmentalist approach to the study of human development. Many adolescent psychologists explain almost every observation in terms of the environment, and they limit the role of biology to causing the bodily (but seldom behavioral) changes of puberty. This stance is no longer compatible with the facts, and it leaves us with only a limited understanding of the complex phenomena of adolescence.

Uniting Psychology with Biology

There is a certain logic to studying behavior from a biological perspective. Psychology is the study of behavior, and behavior is a property of living organisms. It follows, then, that psychology is properly a branch of biology, and indeed it is often defined as such (e.g., Drever, 1964; Michel & Moore, 1995).

More compellingly, irrefutable evidence exists regarding the major role played by genes in human behavior. We humans share 98.4 percent of our genes with our closest relative, the chimpanzee, whose behavior obviously has a major genetic basis. Many of these genes pertain to the nervous system—more than to any other bodily system—so genes surely affect human behavior. They shape our general, specieswide behavioral characteristics, as well as close to half of all individual variation. The general characteristics include many behavioral capacities, such as learning, cognition, sensation, perception, and movement.

In recent years, many insights have been gained into the biological roots of human behavior (Segal et al., 1997), and it is becoming increasingly difficult to ignore advances in the neural sciences, endocrinology, ethology, sociobiology, behavioral genetics, and physical anthropology. Many psychologists now recognize that human social behaviors such as sex, aggression, pair bonding, altruism, and parental behavior are not simply products of human culture; they occur in other species as well. Also, recent work by evolutionary anthropologists reveals that the chimpanzee possesses quite elaborate traditions, or culture (McGrew, 1992; Wrangham et al., 1994). This research renders obsolete any simplistic distinction between humans as cultural and animals as biological beasts. Furthermore, in humans, many of these behaviors are affected by hormones, just as they are in other species.

In light of these realities, it would seem appropriate for developmental psychology to be integrated further with biology and the related natural sciences (G. E. Weisfeld et al., 1997). This would require a wholehearted acceptance of the central theory of biology—evolutionary theory. The unique contribution of the evolutionary approach to the study of behavior is its attention to the adaptive value, or biological function, of an evolved trait. Evolutionary analysis allows one to identify the "why" of specieswide traits.

The goal of this book is to apply evolutionary analysis to the study of human adolescence. General characteristics of adolescents will be described, and the possible adaptive value of these universals will be discussed. A number of important questions will be addressed, including: Why does competitiveness increase at adolescence? Why do the sexes differentiate so markedly? What are the functions of the various changes in body and behavior at puberty? Why do these changes follow the sequence they do? Why does parent-adolescent conflict occur? What are the functions of puberty rites?

But taking a biological view of adolescence does not mean ignoring or minimizing the role of culture and other aspects of experience. Evolutionists readily acknowledge that genes interact with experiential factors: These scientists are not genetic determinists. Indeed, our abilities to learn, speak, and transmit culture are themselves evolved capacities that enhance fitness in our species. But evolutionists argue that individual and cultural variation is not idiosyncratic or random; rather, they contend, experience usually interacts with genes in ways that enhance an organism's fitness. For example, pubertal maturation is usually slowed by harsh environmental conditions and accelerated by propitious ones, promiscuity varies with the availability of suitable mates, and economic factors influence the age of attaining adult social status and the amount of child care performed by fathers.

Evolutionists appreciate the fact that a great deal of valuable data about adolescent behavior has been gathered by psychologists and other scholars over the years. However, they believe that these data can sometimes be explained by evolutionary analysis, thereby rendering them more meaningful and global. The point of this book is to suggest evolutionary principles for integrating such facts and concepts.

A final reason to focus on the biological aspects of adolescence is to balance our knowledge of psychological factors in behavior. Most students and lay readers are quite familiar with phenomena such as learning, memory, perception, attitudes, and cognition. This book is based on the assumption that the reader already grasps general psychological facts and concepts and seeks to complement that information with an appreciation for the role of biological factors.

Introduction to the Biological Approach

The rest of this chapter will provide background on the biological approach to the study of human behavior. The biological approach is employed by researchers who call themselves ethologists, sociobiologists, behavioral ecologists, and evolutionary psychologists. All espouse Darwinism—evolution by natural selection—although there are slight differences in emphasis and methodologies among these scholars. Ethologists, for instance, emphasize naturalistic observation aimed at identifying the basic, evolved behaviors of the species under investigation. Human ethologists study spontaneous human behavior that is likely to exemplify the universal, evolved behaviors of our species—the human **ethogram**, or the inventory of the basic behaviors of our species. But human ethologists also use questionnaires and other methodologies to study evolved behaviors.

The biological approach stresses the adaptive functions of specieswide traits. It addresses the often fascinating question of why a particular behavior or other system works as it does, how it aids survival and reproduction. In this way, we can learn *why*, for example, a pubertal change occurs, not just *how* and *when* it occurs. By taking function (**ultimate causation**) into account, we can add another dimension to the traditional concerns of psychologists regarding questions of ontogeny (developmental change) and mechanistic (**proximate**) causes. Complete knowledge of a behavior requires us to understand all of these interrelated aspects of it (Tinbergen, 1963a). In the example just mentioned, knowledge of the sequence of pubertal changes would be rather meaningless without appreciating why that particular sequence evolved.

Unlike some other theories of behavior, Darwinism is very highly regarded as a scientific theory. It is a clear, simple, powerful theory that explains myriad facts about all aspects of human and animal behavior, physiology, and anatomy. It is not merely a cognitive theory or a personality theory. Perhaps most important, the notion of evolution through natural selection is not merely speculative. It is as factual as the law of gravity, and it is accepted by all reputable biologists.

The evolutionary, or biological, approach has some drawbacks, however. It is foreign to most students of behavior. In fact, some misconceptions about the biology of behavior must be overcome before most psychology students can appreciate its lessons. Also, this approach requires a certain amount of general knowledge in several fields of biology, including primatology, anthropology, neuroscience, and physiology. Consequently, the first several chapters of this book will be devoted to providing information on the biocultural background of human adolescence. Many of the examples used will refer to adolescence and young adulthood, but not until after the first quarter of the book will adolescence be dealt with exclusively.

The biological approach is challenging, especially to those with a weak background in biology. However, many students find it rewarding, and almost all agree that it offers a new and powerful perspective to which they have not been exposed.

Basic Issues

To study behavior biologically, some basic issues and common misconceptions must be addressed. First, what are **evolved behaviors?** An evolved behavior or anatomical trait is one that was selected by evolution. It was adaptive for the animal during its phylogenetic past, even if it is no longer adaptive today. Presumably, some complex of genes exists on the animal's chromosomes to help mediate each evolved trait. These genes arose by random mutation and conferred a selective advantage on their bearers that surpassed the advantage of other variants.

Next, it is necessary to understand why the members of a species resemble one another. Because all members of a given species experienced much the same evolutionary habitat and underwent similar selection pressures, they closely resemble each other genetically. For most purposes, we may assume that all members of the same species possess the same genetic complement, or **genome** (neglecting sex chromosome differences). Individual and population genetic differences do exist, but the commonalities of the species—in our case, of the human family—far outweigh such differences.

Those traits that do vary across populations within the same species—that is, local variants—may reflect genetic differences. For example, populations that evolved in cold regions, such as the Inuit, tend to be rather stout (Logue, 1991). It is this genetic variability, arising by random mutations, upon which natural selection operates.

But population differences may also reflect differences in experience. Styles of weaving, for instance, vary around the world, presumably because of differences in training. But individuals may also differ because of an interaction between genes and environment. Thus, people who grow up at high altitudes with little oxygen develop special respiratory efficiency. Apparently, the lungs develop differently in different environments, as though nature has endowed us with multiple developmental options (Crawford & Anderson, 1989).

One objection to the evolutionary approach is that it is improbable that any single gene would be responsible for the development of a specific trait—say, hunting. This is indeed true; no one gene could mediate a behavior as complicated as hunting. But this does not mean that a complex of genes for hunting could not have evolved. Since humans were hunters for millions of years, it is certain that selective pressure favored individuals with genes for good eyesight, ability to orient in space, arm strength, and so forth. As with anatomical and physiological traits, behavioral traits are usually influenced by multiple genes (**polygeny**). Further complicating things, most genes have multiple effects on various bodily systems, which is known as **pleiotropy**. Thus, a single gene might make the pancreas work better but the liver work worse. If a gene is, on balance, better than any others that have appeared through random mutations, it will be selected for. However, the resulting organism and species are bound to have some imperfections.

Some skeptics acknowledge that genes influence human behavior during infancy but believe that once the child begins to speak, the effects of culture "swamp" those of genes. There are some strong arguments against this view.

First, the brain continues to differentiate in gross anatomical terms throughout maturation, so genes continue to mold behavior. General myelination of the association areas continues beyond 15 years of age, and cerebral lateralization is not completed until puberty (Kolb & Whishaw, 1990). These structural changes are bound to have some influence on behavior; if they did not, they would not have evolved.

Second, there is the issue of **heritability**. The heritability of a trait is the proportion of observed variance that is due to genetic differences across individuals. For personality traits, cognitive capacities, and even attitudes and beliefs, heritability is between 0.3 and 0.5 (Plomin,

1994; J. R. Harris, 1995). This means that individuals differ behaviorally almost as much because of genetic differences as because of different environments. In fact, the heritability of behavioral traits is about as high as that of anatomical traits. Moreover, the high heritability of psychological traits holds true for adults as well as children. In general, the heritability of cognitive and personality traits does not decline over maturation, contrary to what would be expected if experience swamped genetic differences (Scarr & McCartney, 1983). In fact, the heritability of IQ is greater for adults than for children. Despite the accumulation of experience and exposure to culture through language, *genes contribute to individual differences in behavior as strongly in adolescence as in infancy.*

Third, genes and environment operate interactively throughout development, from conception to death. This is the notion of **interaction**, a basic principle on which developmental psychologists agree. For example, a mother's smoking during pregnancy—which influences the intrauterine environment of the fetus—can affect her baby's birth weight, so environmental factors are important even in **congenital** conditions (those present at birth). And genes can be turned on long after birth, as when they orchestrate the changes of puberty or bring on Huntington's chorea, a neurological disease with an onset around age 35 or 50. Thus, culture does not neutralize biology, even in adulthood.

Another common misconception is that culture and biology are mutually antagonistic in their effects on behavior. If the biological and the cultural programs were antagonistic, neither would operate smoothly and the fitness of the organism would suffer. It is far more likely that the capacity for language and other essentials of human culture evolved to supplement the preexisting biological program, to aid us in fulfilling our adaptive needs. For example, cooking and other cultural practices of food acquisition and preparation aid us in meeting the biological need for nutrition.

The notion of culture acting to suppress biological tendencies is especially strong in adolescent psychology. An early psychoanalyst with some erroneous ideas about evolution, G. Stanley Hall, wrote an influential book on adolescence (Hall 1904) that described this life stage as a drama in which culture tries to suppress biological urges. Although perhaps true in some instances, this view is generally incorrect. *Culture and biology collaborate to direct our behavior along adaptive lines.*

Another example of this sort of collaboration is seen in incest avoidance. Many primates besides humans develop sexual aversions for siblings and other close relatives to which they have been frequently exposed during maturation. Humans seem to have retained this biological tendency, which, of course, reduces inbreeding for us, too (Daly & Wilson, 1983), and we have added a cultural taboo against incest (varying somewhat from society to society in regard to which sexual relationships are forbidden). Culture and biology generally cooperate for the good of the organism.

Confusion also arises about the relation of learning to genetic influences on behavior. Learning shapes human behavior profoundly. But learning does not depend completely on environmental experience; it is mediated by evolved brain structures, too. Animals' brains vary in their capacities to learn, perceive, and move. Each species is adapted to adjust to change in its particular habitat. It is *prepared to learn* what it needs to learn—to migrate, to hide, to hunt, and so on.

In fact, every human behavior and every human action represents an interplay of genetic and environmental factors—the doctrine of interactionism. There is always a genetically programmed brain, and always an environmental context and history. Each of these can vary and thereby affect the behavior. No behavior is completely determined by genes or environment: Both environment and genes are indispensable, and they intertwine to produce every behavioral action. In a sense, therefore, the nature-nurture distinction is meaningless; neither can operate without the other (Anastasi, 1966).

For this reason, biologists avoid speaking of genetic determinants (although they are often accused of doing so). Instead, they refer to genetic, evolved, or biological *influences* or *bases*—or, for the sake of simplicity—*evolved behaviors*. Even a behavior such as feeding, which obviously has an evolved basis, is influenced by environmental factors such as past diet, food presently available, and modeling. And even an imprinted, fixed response such as a duckling following its mother is influenced by environmental factors, especially exposure to the mother. Ironically, it is the environmentalists who are being determinists if they ignore any suggestion of genetic influences on human behavior.

Because of their familiarity with phenomena such as imprinting, evolutionists generally believe that behavior results from interactions of genes and environment. They acknowledge that no behavior is completely determined by genes and that, therefore, environmental intervention is always possible in theory. In fact, the more that is known about the genetic aspects of a trait and how they interact with experience, the easier it ought to be to intervene somehow to alter the outcome of the trait. (For example, understanding the metabolic basis of phenylketonuria (PKU) made it easier to devise a dietary treatment for this genetically based condition, which results in mental retardation if left untreated.) Consequently, the biological approach is emphatically not a fatalistic one. Rather, it is a realistic approach to the study of behavior as it exists. If genes influence some behavior, then the more we know about how this occurs, the more effectively we should be able to intervene if we so choose.

Identifying Evolved Behaviors

Any behavioral act results from some interplay of genetic and experiential influences. Therefore, all behaviors are both genetically and environmentally based. There is no point in trying to distinguish genetic from environmental behaviors.

But there is indeed a point to identifying *evolved* behaviors—those that were selected by evolution and were adaptive. A bear's genes and training may allow it to ride a bicycle, but this is not a specieswide, evolved, adaptive behavior. But the bear's sleeping through the winter is. Bears will exhibit this behavior under natural environmental conditions.

Charles Darwin's theory is mainly concerned with the functional analysis of evolved traits. To study behavior functionally, we must begin by identifying a specieswide, evolved behavior for analysis. An evolved behavior is identified by controlling for variable environmental influences and seeing if the behavior still occurs. If it does, then it cannot have been caused by variable environmental influences (such as imitation or parental instruction). Utilizing this principle, Darwin himself (1872/1965) devised several specific research strategies for identifying an evolved behavior (G.E. Weisfeld, 1982).

1. One such research strategy is the *social isolation* of an animal from early life, the so-called deprivation experiment. If such an animal nevertheless exhibits a given behavior, social learning cannot have been responsible. Observations of so-called wild children are our only ethical means of using this technique on humans, and some of the rare accounts of wild, or feral, children have been extremely enlightening (e.g., Shattuck, 1980). For example, Victor of Aveyron,

who survived in the woods until he was captured in adolescence, exhibited a capacity for moral indignation when Itard, his teacher, deliberately mistreated him as an experiment (Malson, 1972).

2. A related research strategy is to study *handicapped individuals*. Congenitally blind children, for instance, smile, so smiling cannot depend on observational learning. It may depend on other aspects of experience, but social acquisition can be ruled out, leaving natural selection for the trait as a strong possibility.

3. Another method for identifying evolved behavior is to *study newborns*. Because newborns have had little opportunity to acquire behaviors by observation or practice, whatever they do probably reflects specific biological programming. Sex differences as well as traits seen in both sexes can be tested for an evolved basis in this way. A sex difference in smiling emerges quite early in infancy (Freedman, 1979).

This method can yield false negatives, however. If a behavior or sex difference does not emerge until, say, adolescence, this does not necessarily mean that environmental factors trigger it. Perhaps pubertal hormones are responsible.

False positives can also occur. If the behavior is congenital, genes need not be responsible. A prenatal environmental factor may be involved, such as the mother's consumption of alcohol leading to mental retardation in her child.

4. One of the most important means of identifying the evolved core of human behavior is *cross-cultural research*. Most behaviors that occur universally despite the enormous variability of cultural influences are probably evolved. It is very unlikely that a given practice became universal by arising in a single culture and then diffusing to all other human populations. After all, there are hundreds of cultures, some of them extremely isolated by linguistic and geographic barriers. It is much more likely that the practice arose before humans spread around the globe and was retained because it continued to be generally adaptive for human beings. Speech is universal and obviously adaptive to humans no matter what their way of life. Vocabulary, by contrast, varies across cultures and therefore is not an evolved trait. Thus, the same reasoning is applied to human traits as was illustrated by the bear example mentioned earlier. Specieswide traits are usually evolved, but local variants may or may not be.

5. Another method is to *test for phylogenetic continuity*. If we share a trait with our primate relatives, it probably has an evolved basis. This is true of behavioral traits as well as anatomical and physiologi-

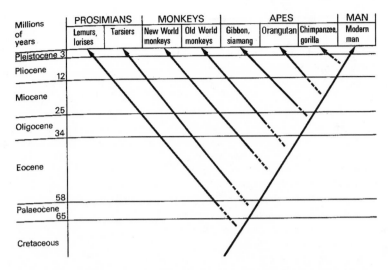

Millions of years	PROSIMIANS		MONKEYS		APES			MAN
	Lemurs, lorises	Tarsiers	New World monkeys	Old World monkeys	Gibbon, siamang	Orangutan	Chimpanzee, gorilla	Modern man
Pleistocene 3								
Pliocene 12								
Miocene 25								
Oligocene 34								
Eocene 58								
Palaeocene 65								
Cretaceous								

Figure 1.1   Establishment of Homologies, or Phylogenetic Continuity. If a trait appears in humans and, say, marmosets (a group of New World monkeys) but not in apes, which are closer human relatives, then homology between the trait in marmosets and humans is not established. There is no common ancestor of humans and marmosets that could have passed the trait on to both but not also to the apes. Source: Passingham (1982). Reprinted by permission.

cal ones. However, this test can give false negatives, too, since every species has some evolved traits that it does not share with its relatives. For example, humans have speech, but our closest relatives do not.

Another caution is that a gap in the phylogenetic tree between ourselves and the other species that exhibit a trait negates the test. Continuity must be unbroken so that the trait can be traced to a common taxonomic ancestor. If a distant primate relative such as the marmoset exhibits pair bonding but a closer relative such as the chimpanzee does not, then no **homology** (evolutionary connection) exists between pair bonding in marmosets and humans (see Figure 1.1). Table 1.1 illustrates primate taxonomy, so the reader can weigh the likelihood of homology for behaviors that we share with various simian relatives. The closer the relationship, the more likely it is that a common trait is homologous.

6. Another research method is to seek a **specific physiological basis** for the behavior. If a particular neural structure mediates the behavior,

TABLE 1.1   Taxonomy of the Primate Order

Suborder Prosimii
  lemurs, lorises, bushbabies, pottos, galagos, tarsiers, sifakas
Suborder Anthropoidea
  Infraorder Platyrrhini (New World monkeys)
    Family Callitrichidae
      marmosets, tamarins
    Family Cebidae
      capuchins, owl monkeys, howler monkeys, sakis, titi monkeys, squirrel monkeys, spider monkeys, woolly monkeys
  Infraorder Catarrhini (Old World simians)
    Superfamily Cercopithecoidea (Old World monkeys)
      guenons, patas monkeys, mandrills, mangabeys, baboons, geladas, macaques, Celebes black ape, langus, colobus monkeys
    Superfamily Hominoidea (apes and humans)
    Family Hylobatidae (gibbons, siamang)
    Family Pongidae (great apes)
      orangutan (*Pongo pygmaeus*), gorilla (*Gorilla gorilla*), common chimpanzee (*Pan troglodytes*), bonobo (*Pan paniscus*)
    Family Hominidae (hominids)

Note: The New World monkeys are distinguishable by their widely spaced nostrils, which open laterally, and by the prehensile tails that many possess. The nostrils of Old World monkeys tend to be widely separated and to open frontally.

this suggests that evolutionary pressure has fashioned the structure and its behavioral function. Similarly, if some hormone seems to trigger a certain behavior, then the neural structure on which the hormone acts probably has an evolved basis (and so does the behavior). For example, testosterone increases aggression at maturity in many species, and so this increase in aggression has an evolved basis. Demonstrating the effects of pubertal hormones on human behavior has been a fruitful means of identifying evolved features of adolescence.

But the neural structure or hormone must be highly specific for the behavior. The motor cortex mediates typing in some people and piano playing in others. No one-to-one correspondence exists between the structure and a specific behavior, so no evolved behavior has been demonstrated. Of course, our present inability to identify the precise neural pathway involved in a given behavior does not mean we won't be able to do so in the future. In fact, progress in neuroscience is proceeding very rapidly. The amygdala of the brain, for instance, is now known to register the emotional tone of perceived facial expressions, so we seem to have an evolved capacity for these discriminations (LeDoux, 1994).

7. Finally, a related method is to *look for stereotypy*. If a behavior takes a more or less fixed form from its first appearance, this suggests the operation of a specific neural mechanism that has evolved to mediate the behavior. Human facial expressions are a good example of **fixed** (or **modal**) **action patterns** in our species. Similarly, a consistent onset of a behavior, such as an increased interest in infants that is seen at puberty, suggests an evolved basis. So does sensitivity to a particular stimulus, or **releaser** (e.g., fear of the dark).

These are the main methods for identifying evolved human behaviors. They should be used cautiously and in conjunction with one another, since none is infallible. In the case of some traits, such as the sex difference in aggressiveness, the evidence derives from several of these research strategies and is conclusive. But for other traits, more research is needed.

However, there is no reason why we should be more hesitant to entertain a biological hypothesis than an environmental one, as has sometimes occurred. Biological knowledge is subject to misuse, but so are psychological concepts, some of which, after all, have provided the basis for the use of torture, for advertisements to promote smoking, and for propaganda techniques designed to instill hatred. The accepted standards of evidence and statistical significance should be applied uniformly and objectively.

Note that no mention has been made of research that seeks to demonstrate an environmental contribution to a given behavior. This is because no one doubts that environmental factors influence every behavior, and usually these environmental factors include socialization factors. The question of interest is whether there is *also* an evolved basis to a sex difference or other trait. Demonstrating that there is a cultural or other environmental influence on a behavior tells us nothing about the coexistence of an evolved basis. For example, the many demonstrations of cultural influences on sex differences carry no implications for the nature-nurture issue with respect to these behaviors. If, however, the possibility of cultural acquisition is ruled out, as by showing that the trait is universal, then an evolved basis is likely.

Determining the Function of an Evolved Trait

Once a trait that appears to be evolved is identified, its function can be examined—that is, the "why" question can be addressed. However, traits that are not evolved need not be and should not be analyzed in terms of evolutionary function. *Rare traits are not typical of the species, and therefore, they are not likely to be evolved and adaptive.* Biologists are under no obligation to demonstrate the function of a rare trait even if it is genetically based; it can merely be regarded as arising from a mutation. Pathological traits are generally rare (usually occurring in far less than 1 percent of the population) because their genetic bases are selected out as fast as they appear. Since, by definition, pathological traits reduce biological fitness, they need not be explained functionally.

Problems for evolutionists arise only if a trait is widespread and appears to detract from fitness. One then wonders why individuals possessing the trait are not being selected out more rapidly. For example, male homosexuality seems to be more prevalent than would be expected for a trait that obviously lowers reproductive fitness. Accordingly, biologists are perplexed about why this behavior is so prevalent (Savin-Williams, 1987). But this is an issue of the evolutionary significance of homosexuality, not a serious challenge to the theory of evolution.

Functional analysis also need not be applied—and should not be applied—to cultural practices that are widespread in a population but are unlikely to have evolved. For instance, modern health measures such as pasteurization may increase biological fitness but cannot have evolved, since they are too recent. Evolution takes many generations, so the concept of biological function should be reserved for traits that truly arose through natural selection.

Thus, evolved traits need not still be adaptive in modern society. *Our genes equipped us for the hunter-gatherer, small-group existence* that we pursued for 99 percent of our hominid existence. They have had virtually no time to adjust to agricultural society (which is just 10,000 years old), let alone industrialization. Therefore, when we contemplate the adaptive value of a given human trait, we must consider our species's natural habitat: Stone-age settlements on the African savanna. Our human nature equipped us for a foraging existence, and because of the slow pace of evolution, we are stuck with those features.

The biological concept of function is a nice and clear one. An evolutionary explanation must show how the behavior in question raises the individual's fitness. A functional explanation must show how the behavior enhances feeding, defense, reproduction, or some other biological exigency. Reaching a new cognitive stage, achieving self-fulfillment, communicating with others, releasing energy, and other such psychological notions are not, in themselves, functional explanations in biological terms. In some cases, such achievements may lead to fitness dividends, but it is more to the point to identify the crucial aspect of the behavior that enhances fitness. Biologists seek to reduce their functional explanations to tissue needs whose utility is obvious. All tissues need to feed, be hydrated, remove waste, reproduce, protect themselves, and so forth.

Dissipating energy is definitely *not* an acceptable evolutionary explanation, since organisms evolved to conserve metabolic energy (the **law of economy**) and hence minimize the need for food. In some cases, an animal may raise its fitness by using energy to defend, attack, or flee, but the benefits come from the behavior itself rather than from burning calories. Humans are the only joggers in the animal kingdom.

How does one identify the function of an evolved trait? This is not mere speculation, or a just-so story. Speculations are proposed, but they are then tested by comparative analysis. This is done by identifying the environmental or social condition that characterizes those species that exhibit the behavior, and by figuring out how those species benefited from the behavior. For example, the behavior of **biparentalism**—both parents aiding in the care of offspring—is found in species with relatively helpless young, such as birds and primates. Biparentalism tends to be absent from species with young that are born or hatched relatively mature and self-reliant. A plausible functional explanation of biparentalism, then, is that the efforts of both parents are needed in order to give the offspring a good chance of survival.

Another example is the function of testis size. Large testes in primates are associated with the promiscuous, or multimale, breeding system, so this trait probably functions to aid sperm competition to fertilize females (Short, 1981). That is, if a female is inseminated by multiple males, then natural selection will favor the copious production of sperm. This example shows that the quantitative variation of a trait across species—not just its presence or absence—can be analyzed functionally.

As these cases illustrate, the function of a trait is usually analyzed by considering its phylogenetic distribution. Analogously, an epidemiologist isolates the cause of an epidemic by identifying the victims. But other aspects of an evolved behavior also offer clues about its function. As mentioned earlier, the "how," "when," and "why" questions about a given evolved trait are interrelated. For example, development offers hints about function, since a behavior must suit the animal's level of maturation. Thus, a behavior that emerges at adolescence must be understood in terms of other developmental events occurring at that stage. Similarly, the internal and external elicitors of a behavior help elucidate its function. For example, the Moro response, by which a newborn grasps with its arms and legs, is elicited by falling and other dangers, and obviously functions to hold the caretaker tightly.

Sometimes, the function of a trait is obscure, especially if the trait is found only in humans, thus preventing comparative analysis. However, the notion that most specieswide traits are (or were) adaptive is taken as a general principle by biologists. Just because current knowledge in a field is incomplete does not invalidate its theoretical basis. As knowledge expands, the adaptive value of more and more traits is established. For example, additional adaptive advantages to breast feeding are discovered practically every year. There is now evidence that breast-feeding familiarizes the infant with the foods that the mother eats, so that after weaning, the infant will seek these foods, too (Bartoshuk & Beauchamp, 1994). Virtually every human anatomical trait has a known function; analogously, every specieswide behavioral trait is likely to be adaptive, too.

Another way to test a functional hypothesis is by direct experimentation. One famous example was provided by Tinbergen (1963b), the Nobel-winning ethologist, who speculated that black-headed gulls remove the eggshells of their hatchlings from the nest because the inside of the shell is shiny and attracts predators. He tested this hypothesis by gluing the eggshell fragments into the nests of some gulls. Sure enough, these birds suffered greater predation than the controls.

Confusion exists about the proper level on which to explain the function of a given behavior. Many people believe that fitness is considered in terms of the consequences of the trait for the species. This is an incorrect level of explanation for most purposes. Rather, the advantage for the individual is paramount.

Consider what would happen if a certain animal went about helping other members of its species at some cost to itself. It would be at a competitive disadvantage compared with the selfish recipients of its help. It would leave fewer descendants, and its altruistic tendency would die out. Thus, the evolutionary advantage of a trait must be considered in terms of its consequences *for the individual* that possesses it, not for the whole group affected by it. This notion of **individual selection** is accepted by modern evolutionists, as opposed to the discredited notion of **group selection**. Thus, when contemplating the adaptive advantage of an evolved behavior, one must ask how the trait affects the individual's fitness.

Why, then, do the members of a species resemble each other genetically, if they are subject to individual selective pressure? They are alike because they live in the same habitat and need similar traits. Mutations are always arising, but they tend to be harmful and hence are selected out. However, a beneficial mutation will spread through the population and become standard. As a result, the commonalities of a species reflect the operation of individual selection. Each common trait is advantageous for its bearer.

How is biological fitness measured? Both survival and reproduction are required to pass on one's genes; survival alone is not enough, no matter how long a given animal lives. Consequently, fitness is usually defined as reproductive success, or lifetime number of offspring. But the number of grandoffspring is a still better measure.

Yet another complication was fully appreciated only in recent years. W. D. Hamilton (1964) pointed out that an animal can help to pass on its genes by aiding its relatives' reproductive success. This phenomenon, **kin altruism**, is quite common in the animal kingdom. We call it *nepotism* when it occurs in humans (L. *nepos,* "grandson" or "nephew"). Naturally, the closer the relative, the greater the effect, so that animals and people favor close relatives over distant ones. Because of Hamilton's work, biologists now take kin altruism effects into account when defining fitness. This expanded concept is called **inclusive fitness**. It includes one's individual reproductive success plus the reproductive success of kin that results from one's aid, taking into account closeness of kinship.

Summary

Science seeks to establish generalizations about natural phenomena. But adolescent psychology has instead emphasized variability. This has resulted in a field devoid of basic theory and even of general observations about adolescents. Given the raft of important research on behavior being conducted by biologists and other evolutionists, it would seem timely to begin to integrate adolescent psychology into biology and the other natural sciences. This would require identifying general adolescent behaviors that occur everywhere and that will presumably endure indefinitely. Members of the human species share 99 percent of their genes, so there are probably quite a few human universals in behavior. Further underscoring the importance of genes in human behavior is the fact that almost half of the individual differences in behavior are due to genetic differences. This fraction does not decline through development; (see previous discussion).

The classical approach of ethologists to the study of behavior is to identify the basic, evolved behaviors of a given species and to analyze them functionally. Evolved behaviors and sex differences in adolescence have been identified mainly by cross-cultural, cross-species, and sex-hormone research. As will be shown in later chapters, quite a few universals of human adolescence exist, largely because of the far-reaching effects of hormones on behavior. Once these specieswide behavioral elements are identified, they can be analyzed functionally, developmentally, and mechanistically so that a complete, integrated understanding of the behaviors can be gained. The biological function of an evolved trait refers to its contribution to the individual's inclusive fitness, rather than to the survival of the group. Evolved traits are analyzed functionally by delineating their distribution in the animal kingdom and then testing hypotheses to explain that pattern of prevalence.

Analysis of the evolved features of adolescence should go a long way toward explaining this life stage (see Bogin, 1994). If we can begin to understand why adolescents behave as they do—often despite the urgings of their elders—we can perhaps work more cooperatively with them in addressing individual, family, and societal needs.

In adopting an evolutionary perspective, we need not minimize the importance of learning and culture, or the contributions of mainstream adolescent psychologists. To the contrary, evolved and learned behavioral tendencies usually conspire to guide the organism toward the fulfillment of its biological needs. Shaped by genes and experience, behavior tends to be adaptive for the individual during the evolution of the species.

2 Motives

The principal goals of this book are to describe the nature of human adolescence and to arrive at valid conclusions about adolescent traits. Of course, many people have formed their own casual conclusions about adolescents. Indeed, since classical times, adolescents have been a source of great interest—or, perhaps more accurately, concern. Aristotle's (McKeon, 1941) view of youth is often quoted in textbooks on adolescence: He found youth to be impulsive, irascible, sexually unrestrained, facetious, companionable, charitable, and fond of victory and self-confident yet prone to bashfulness. Throughout much of Western history, adolescents have been viewed with suspicion, and they have often been seen as a badly behaving lot likely to flout social conventions. Much of the impetus for studying adolescence seems to have come from societal concern with "problem" behaviors that may erupt at this stage, such as delinquency, drug abuse, and out-of-wedlock births. This may help to account for the conventional emphasis on variability rather than general facts in the study of adolescence.

The "problem" behaviors of adolescence are matters of *motivation*. Likewise, Aristotle's characterization of youth is cast in terms of motivational, or temperamental, traits. What seems to interest most people about adolescents is their motivation—what they do and why. We wonder why some adolescents are well behaved and others are troublesome, what normal adolescent behaviors are, how to motivate adolescents to do what adults want them to do, and so forth. In this chapter, a case will be made for emphasizing motivation in the study of human behavior, and some concepts about motivation will be introduced.

The Importance of Motives

As argued in Chapter 1, individual differences in behavior are important, but it is more basic to ask which behaviors all humans exhibit.

This fundamental question has not interested most social scientists schooled in the learning theory tradition. Some anthropologists have claimed that human behavior varies so much across individuals and cultures that one literally cannot generalize about people. Yet it is obvious that all normal people eat, avoid pain, sleep, aggress, seek companionship, avoid boredom, become afraid, and so on.

As these examples indicate, many specieswide human behaviors are motives, or emotions. In fact, these behaviors—our motives—comprise the basic, whole-body behavioral tendencies of human beings. Psychology is said to have skipped the descriptive phase with which most sciences begin (Timbergen, 1963a; Charlesworth, 1986, 1992), for it never defined the basic elements in observable behavior. These basic behaviors seem to be the motives.

In a biological perspective, the main units of observable behavior—the elements of the ethogram of a given species—appear to be its motives. Most of the observable behaviors that animals exhibit consist of motivated behaviors, such as feeding, courtship, aggression, and care of offspring. These behaviors may be guided or modified by perception, learning, and cognition, but motivated behaviors are fundamental in a descriptive sense.

The functional importance of motives is revealed by taking a comparative perspective. In many species, motivated behaviors are fairly fixed actions triggered by various releasing stimuli in the environment. Learning may be of little importance, much less cognition. For example, a frog may reflexively lap up a flying insect in an invariant, stereotypic fashion. In mammals, learning and cognition can modify the triggering and the form of a response, but the basic response—usually called a motive, or instinct—still exists to satisfy some particular biological need. No organism lacking a set of motives appropriate for its environment would have evolved, no matter how much it learned or understood. Natural selection weeds out animals on the basis of their actions, not their knowledge.

This is not to deny the importance, the biological adaptiveness, of cognition and learning. But a comparative, evolutionary view of behavior indicates the primacy of motives, not cognition or learning (G. E. Weisfeld, 1997b). Motives come first in the evolution and development of behavior. A newborn has little capacity for learning or cognition yet behaves well enough to survive. An anencephalic newborn will survive for a time even without a cerebral cortex as long as the subcortex is intact and can mediate feeding, breathing, sleeping, and other motives. Later, the cerebral cortex in a normal child becomes very important in organizing and refining behavior, but the cortex still serves the subcortex—the seat of motivation—rather than the reverse. In essence, our planning and memory and learned skills are recruited to serve the imperious subcortex. Likewise, the cortex is temporarily shut down during coma, anesthesia, and shock in favor of the vital subcortical structures. If the situation were reversed—if the subcortex were subordinate to the cortex—then one would expect that the cortex would have grown progressively larger and the subcortex relatively smaller in primate evolution. But in fact, both divisions of the brain grew apace in primate evolution; the cortex did not dwarf the subcortex at all, even in humans (Russell, 1994).

What Motives Are

What, then, are motives? Simply put, they are the voluntary actions of an animal. They are the basic behavioral tendencies of an organism that help it to survive and reproduce. Virtually every whole-body, voluntary behavior can be said to be motivated. This excludes only reflexes, perceptions, cognitions, and neutral sensations—and many of these other processes play a role in motivated behavior, as will be explained.

Motives are specieswide and hence evolved; they are standard equipment for the species. Moreover, no normal member of the species will acquire any motive that other members lack. Motives are not learned; we only learn when to experience a given motive and how best to fulfill it. For example, we have all learned that electric shocks can be painful and to avoid electric shocks by keeping electrical appliances away from water. But we did not have to learn to dislike the pain of an electric shock. If we were to maintain that shock avoidance is a learned motive, then we would have to recognize thousands of other learned motives. It seems far more parsimonious to recognize, in this example, fear as an evolved motive rather than myriad learned sources of fear.

Confusion often arises regarding the terms *motivation* and *emotion*. One might argue that a behavior (such as feeding) that lacks prominent expressional and autonomic components is a motive but not an emotion. But then we are faced with the problem of differentiating emotions from motives, which seems a difficult and even pointless task, especially given the common etymology of the two terms (both from *movere*, L., "to move"). In fact, no solid basis exists for distinguishing between motives and emotions, drives and emotions, or biological motives and so-called learned motives (G. E. Weisfeld, 1997b). Furthermore, these distinctions tend to obscure the commonalities between these supposedly contrasting entities. All human motives are characterized by affects and overt behaviors; all motives are governed by both internal "drives" and external factors; and all motives are evolved (and hence biological) and yet are modifiable by learning. Therefore, in this book, the terms *motive* and *emotion* will be used more or less interchangeably.

Motives possess the following aspects, or facets (Scherer, 1984). All motives include **overt behaviors,** the observable actions that an animal takes. All are accompanied by **affects,** at least in humans—pleasant or unpleasant feelings that prompt certain overt behaviors.

Like all other evolved traits, all motives exhibit several other facets. All motives show a typical **developmental pattern;** they may be present from birth to death or only for a limited time in the life span. There is always a biological **function** for the motive and for each of its facets, as well as a **phylogenetic distribution** of the motive: Certain species have found it adaptive, and others have not. All motives have mechanistic **causes**—genetic, neurological, environmental, or hormonal. Among the important causes are internal and external stimuli. Some of the external stimuli are prepotent (unlearned) releasers of the motive, and others are learned. For example, rancid odors are prepotent releasers of disgust, whereas a rat may learn an aversion to a food that has made it nauseated.

The preceding facets are properties of all motives. Other facets are not always present; these will be mentioned next. Some—but not all—motives are accompanied by changes in the activity of the viscera—**autonomic adjustments** that enhance the efficiency of the overt behavior. For instance, anger is typically accompanied by sympathetic arousal—fast heartbeat, increased respiration, and so on. Some motives are characterized by **emotional expressions,** as seen when an infant expresses its needs to a parent in order to solicit care. Facial expressions are well developed in the primates, whereas other animals communicate mainly by means of general bodily movements. Lastly, emotions differ in their characteristic **cognitive features.** For example, when we are afraid, our thinking is impulsive and quick, which is ideal for reacting quickly in emergencies but not desirable for solving complex problems that require time.

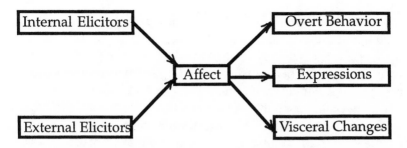

Figure 2.1 Simplified Model of the Activation of an Emotion. An internal elicitor, such as low blood sugar, or an external one, such as a dangerous stimulus, triggers the experience of a particular affect, mediated by the limbic system and hypothalamus. These structures, in turn, stimulate an appropriate overt behavioral response and, sometimes, expression via various motor structures, as well as visceral and hormonal adjustments via the autonomic nervous system and pituitary gland. Note that direct involvement of the neocortex is not part of the ancient, general vertebrate system for motivated behavior. For further discussion, see LeDoux (1994) and G. E. Weisfeld (1997b).

Figure 2.1 presents a simplified model of how some of these facets interact in behavior. Stimuli from inside and outside the body give rise to an affect. Experience influences our interpretation of internal and external stimuli and hence the arousal of affect. Once aroused, this affect disposes us to act in some way; a feeling is of no use unless it leads to adaptive behavior. Whether and exactly how we act in a particular situation depends largely upon our experience, that is, our learning and cognition. An affect may also prompt appropriate changes in the internal organs (autonomic adjustments) or emotional expressions. Once we execute an appropriate behavior, such as eating, our affective state changes, usually in the direction of pleasure. This feedback allows us to learn how to satisfy our needs.

How Can the Basic Human Motives Be Identified?

The study of motivation has led philosophers and psychologists to try to identify the basic human motives. The lists of motives, or emotions, they developed have differed widely, largely because of disagreement about the distinguishing property of a motive. Which of these facets is the definitive one? How shall we identify the basic human motives—by their autonomic components, their overt behaviors, or what other characteristic?

Some investigators, such as Ekman (1973), have favored emotional expressions as the defining characteristic of a motive. Ekman has identified eight apparently universal human emotional expressions: anger, fear, surprise, disgust, interest, happiness, sadness, and contempt (Ekman & Friesen, 1986). People exhibit and interpret these facial expressions similarly around the world. The universality and stereotypic form of these expressions constitute strong evidence that they are evolved and hence are facets of basic human motives.

However, as previously mentioned, some motives (such as hunger) seem to have no specific emotional expression, so if we define motives by their expression, we will omit some of them. Moreover, certain expressions, notably those of happiness and sadness, accompany many different overt behaviors and hence are too vague to serve as identifying characteristics of specific motives. Thus, this method will not yield a complete list of the discrete human motives, although it does provide important guidance for compiling such a list.

Another possible defining criterion is autonomic adjustments. However, since many motives lack a distinctive visceral profile, this method, too, will miss many of them. It is sometimes claimed that emotion is characterized by physiological arousal, but some emotions are accompanied by reduced activity, such as drowsiness and fatigue. These motives, like those with mild autonomic changes, are likely to be missed if one emphasizes this facet.

A more plausible, comprehensive criterion for defining motives might be their overt behaviors. All motives give rise to overt behaviors; otherwise, there would be no reason for them to have evolved. However, it may be difficult to distinguish between major and minor overt behaviors; for example, chewing and swallowing subserve eating. Also, a single motive can give rise to many different overt behaviors. A bear, for instance, may feed by means of numerous overt behaviors. This is an especially serious problem in the case of primates (including ourselves), whose behavior is highly flexible. Moreover, the same overt behavior can stem from different motives: Eating can be done for nourishment or to be sociable.

Mechanistic causes, especially neural pathways, often furnish useful information for delimiting our motives. For instance, different overt forms of attack in mammals seem to involve different neural pathways, thus suggesting that what we call aggression actually includes several different motivational systems. However, the mapping of the brain is still too incomplete to provide a comprehensive inventory of the motives.

A case can be made for relying mainly on affects for identifying the basic human motives (G. E. Weisfeld, 1997b). Affects occur in every motive, and they occupy a central position in motivated behavior (see Figure 2.1). Moreover, affect is the most distinguishing feature of emotion. Unlike overt behaviors, affects are not directly observable; however, humans can report their own affects with apparent accuracy, at least in simple situations. Affects are quite distinct from each other, and there seems to be a manageable number of them. Moreover, affects correspond closely with recognizable biological functions, such as hunger and feeding, fear and escape, drowsiness and sleep. For these and other reasons, many evolutionists have chosen to identify human motives primarily by their affects and secondarily by their functions and other facets (cf. Darwin, 1872/1965; McDougall, 1923; Tomkins, 1962; Pugh, 1977; Izard, 1977).

Affects goad the organism into action and then guide its actions once it is mobilized. Thus, when a hungry animal is prompted to eat by internal tissue factors and begins to feed, it is rewarded affectively. When nothing more is to be gained by continued feeding, it is satiated and ceases to feed. The organism need not be aware of what it is attempting in terms of biological adaptiveness; it only needs to act in ways that raise its fitness. *Affects have evolved as signposts to guide us in the general direction of survival and reproduction.* As we heed them—and we really have no choice in the matter—we will perform actions that have generally been adaptive in our evolutionary past.

A Working List of the Basic Human Motives

The following is my working list of the basic human motives, or emotional modalities (G. E. Weisfeld, 1997b). To reflect the main criterion of the list, I have used terms that refer to affects, or feelings, rather than to overt behaviors, functions, or some other facet. Nevertheless, each emotion presumably has a function, phylogenetic history, overt behavior, developmental pattern, and set of causes, and each may (but need not) have distinct autonomic components, emotional expressions, and cognitive aspects.

1. tactile pain and pleasure
2. hunger
3. thirst
4. tasting
5. smelling
6. disgust
7. fatigue
8. drowsiness
9. sexual feelings
10. loneliness
11. interest/boredom
12. beauty appreciation
13. music appreciation/noise annoyance
14. humor appreciation
15. pride/shame
16. anger
17. fear

Some of the modalities (such as 1, 4, 5) are actually composites of several physiologically discrete affects. They are combined for purposes of simplicity. Thus, there is a certain arbitrariness to the list. As another example, whole-body behaviors that are mainly reflexive, such as air hunger and elimination feelings, have been omitted here, although other researchers have included them. The basic composition of the list is, however, not completely idiosyncratic; it is similar to those of Pugh (1977), McDougall (1923), and others of a biological bent. The list is meant to be comprehensive (that is, to exhaust the domain of human affects) but to have no overlap, or redundancy. Sometimes, of course, we experience **blends** of more than one affect simultaneously, but these blends are not basic.

A number of general properties of emotions can be identified. Some of these modalities are exclusively positive in valence, or polarity (e.g., 14), and some are only negative (6, 17). Most of the rest are both, even if the emotion term refers to only one end of the scale. In addition, each emotion has a certain priority, or threshold. For example, an animal will usually protect itself from danger before it engages in most other motivated behaviors. But there is a certain efficiency in completing what one has begun, so that we do not repeatedly interrupt an ongoing activity to reorder our priorities. Also, the strength of motivation increases as we near the payoff, as in sexual behavior. Another general principle is that we adjust our expectations so as to continue to be motivated and fulfill all of our needs. Thus, dog food will look good to a starving man. Similarly, a good student will not be satisfied with a B grade. Also, one modality may inhibit or facilitate another. For example, fear inhibits sexual arousal, whereas flavorful food enhances hunger.

The function of most of these modalities is readily apparent. Many can be reduced to immediate tissue needs. For instance, tasting, smelling, and disgust guide our selection of foods to ingest. The aesthetic emotions are somewhat puzzling but can be understood as drawing us to environmental conditions and stimuli that have generally been conducive to fitness. This is supported by the observation that people around the world seem to prefer landscapes that resemble the primordial savannas of hominid evolution (Eibl-Eibesfeldt, 1989).

The possible functions of modalities 9, 10, 11, 14, 15, and 16 will be discussed in Chapters 3 and 4. These largely social motives are very important in adolescence.

Because these motives seem to occur universally, this model applies to humans in general. It also allows us to explain individual differences in temperament, by simply assuming that some individuals will be more, say, irritable or gluttonous than others. The reason may be genetic or environmental. The motivational differences among people are probably even more important than the cognitive differences, and they at least must be acknowledged. This is especially true of sex differences in motivation, as explained later in the book.

Vicarious Emotion

All of these modalities can be experienced either directly or vicariously. Our capacity for experiencing an emotion vicariously allows us to imagine the feelings that accompany a particular hypothetical situation. This means that we can anticipate the affective consequences of future actions, partly on the basis of our ability to relive—not just recall—the affects that accompanied past events. Often, we even experience the autonomic changes and emotional expressions of the imagined emotion.

Our ability to experience emotions vicariously also allows us to empathize with others; that is, we can imagine how someone else's experience must feel. This helps us to assist others, including our children. Primates' sensitivity and flexibility as parents seem to depend upon this capacity to understand the needs of others and to invent novel ways of addressing these needs. Humans and other primates may not have a distinct parental motive or group of motives. Instead, we seem to possess a general capacity for empathy (see Chapter 3).

Thus, the capacity for vicarious emotion allows us to imagine many past and future situations and hence to anticipate the consequences of a given course of action for ourselves or others. Many of life's pleasures and pains are experienced vicariously—daydreaming about a great triumph, identifying with a heroine, recalling a vacation, regretting a remark, anticipating a bath, or having a nightmare. These recollections probably help us to learn from past mistakes and successes. Drug-induced euphoria can also be considered as vicarious emotion; the drug acts on the brain's pleasure centers.

Fearing a future event seems to constitute a special, compound type of vicarious emotion. We imagine the unpleasant event; this constitutes what we might call the vicarious emotion of dread. We might anticipate feeling ashamed, in which case we experience a twinge of shame vicariously. If we fear being in a hot room, we imagine the specific discomfort of excessive heat. If we fear bodily injury, however, we experience not only vicarious pain but also fear itself (modality 17).

Development of Motivation

This list of motives refers to mature (adolescent and adult) affects. Our affective life changes from birth to old age in ways that make adaptive sense. At each stage of life, qualitative and quantitative changes occur in our emotions. Motives develop and, sometimes, disappear as the need for particular behaviors changes over the life span. These motivational changes are probably more important than cognitive developmental changes, so some of them will now be mentioned.

In newborns, the sucking drive is present, and it is a modality distinct from hunger; babies suck even on nonnutritive objects such as pacifiers (Pugh, 1977). The sucking motive, like the sucking reflex, drops out later on, when hunger is sufficient to ensure feeding. Contact comfort, a type of tactile experience, is also prominent in babies. In addition, repetitive vestibular stimulation (passive bodily movement sensed by the inner ear) is apparently highly pleasurable to primate infants, so that they seek to be carried about by their parents and are not left behind. Thus, babies enjoy gentle, rhythmic rocking or bouncing, as provided by cradles, rocking chairs, piggyback rides, ponies, carousels, and so forth.

In infants and young children, fear of prepotent stimuli, such as darkness, falling, noises, and strangers, is prominent. Fear of strangers and bonding to parents regulate social contacts. As learning proceeds, increasingly complex stimuli become less fearsome and more interesting. Children are very curious and spend much time in perceptual, motoric, and linguistic play. In older children, peer play is a prominent activity.

Between ages 2 and 3, the child becomes sensitive to feelings of pride and shame, and first exhibits blushing (Darwin, 1872/1965; Stipek, 1995). Rivalry, or dominance contests, occur spontaneously, especially between boys (Omark et al., 1975). Children also compete to improve their abilities, and they can be readily rewarded or punished by a word, tone of voice, smile, or frown. Accordingly, learning through imitation and instruction is enhanced.

At puberty, the appetite increases to fuel the growth spurt. New sexual and amorous feelings emerge, along with intense interest in sex and love. Pride and shame become more profound, for reasons that will be discussed later. In this the healthiest period of life, the discomfort and fatigue of illness are comparatively minor. Many sex differences in motivation as well as in cognitive abilities emerge at this time, so that it is hard to generalize about adolescents without noting their sex.

Among the elderly, sensitivity to heat, cold, and fatigue increases and sensitivity to smells decreases. Sexual motivation declines. Fear of injury (fright) increases.

This sketch of developmental changes in emotion is intended to be illustrative, not comprehensive. It is meant to suggest that, just as motivation is the key for understanding behavior, changes in motivation are the essence of behavioral development.

Development of Cognition and Learning

Most current theories of development do not emphasize motivation, however. Rather, they stress cognitive changes and learning. Cognitive development does take place, of course. As they get older, children improve in problem solving. At adolescence, starting around 11 or 12 years of age, some children begin to solve problems that require an orderly, systematic testing of all possible solutions. Before this, children test solutions haphazardly. For example, the problem might be to discover which 2 of 7 chemicals make yellow when poured together. Someone who tests all the possible combinations systematically (1 with 2, 1 with 3, 1 with 4, etc.) is said to have used **formal operational reasoning**. Someone who tries pairs of chemicals at random has not.

Piaget claimed that formal operations are characteristic of adolescence. The attainment of this cognitive period is currently the leading psychological explanation for the development of adolescent behavior. Yet only about 60 percent of college-educated people ever reach this cognitive stage (Neimark, 1975), so most people never do, even in the West. In traditional cultures, scarcely anyone reaches this stage, as defined by standard tests, although for important and highly specialized tasks, such as tracking animals, systematic thinking may be employed. Through childhood, cognitive development does seem to follow the Piagetian periods around the world, but at adolescence, the theory breaks down as a cross-culturally valid description. Thus, formal operations can hardly qualify as a general characteristic of human adolescents. The potential for formal operations, so-called emergent formal operations, is claimed to be universal. But a mere potential to exhibit a trait would seem to be a weak basis for a general theory of behavior.

There are other problems with the concept of formal operations aside from its limited applicability to adolescents. For instance, even in Western populations, cognitive development proceeds smoothly rather than in the stagelike fashion predicted by Piaget (Steinberg, 1996). Those adolescents who achieve formal operational ability and can solve problems by systematically testing alternatives reach this capacity slowly and unevenly, and they frequently do not apply it consistently. People do not abruptly get the hang of formal operational thinking and proceed to use it consistently even if they do belong to the minority who acquire it at all. Lastly, Piaget provided no clear explanation for how one progresses from one stage to the next. Perhaps research linking neural changes to cognitive development will help us to confirm or refute Piaget's notions. Along these lines, Diamond (1991) has provided evidence for the neural basis for the maturation of the capacity for object permanence. This capacity unfolds through the maturation of the dorsolateral area of the frontal lobes in rhesus monkeys.

Still, there is no denying that abstract reasoning ability steadily improves through childhood. This capacity, also called **fluid intelligence**, reaches its peak at the end of adolescence, around age 20 in the West (Steinberg, 1996). And it makes adaptive sense for the brain to

be at its peak of cognitive ability at the time of reproductive maturation. If the peak came later, then ability to reason as an independent
adult would be delayed. If it came earlier, less time would have been
available for the maturation of these cognitive powers. For the same
reason, the body reaches its peak strength and efficiency early in maturity (see Chapter 9). This improvement in cognitive powers contributes greatly to the adolescent's growing social and technical competence.

Piaget's theory of formal operations was extended by Elkind
(1978), who postulated the existence of various manifestations of typical adolescent thinking. The **imaginary audience** involves being so
self-conscious that one believes oneself to be the center of everyone's
concern. The **personal fable** entails believing oneself to be absolutely
unique and exalted, so that others cannot possibly understand one's
feelings. The personal fable also supposedly includes believing that
one is destined for great things and is invulnerable to disaster. Several
researchers have been unable to confirm Elkind's prediction of a rise
in these various manifestations of so-called adolescent egocentrism,
and there are additional problems with these two concepts (Steinberg,
1996). For example, it makes no adaptive sense to expect any
psychosis-like cognitive deficits to arise at adolescence. Adolescents
are very concerned about their social acceptance, but they do not actually experience a thought disorder whereby they believe that everyone else is obsessed with them.

Perhaps Elkind's interpretation can be salvaged by simply observing that adolescents become increasingly competitive, for reasons to
be discussed in Chapter 5. Maybe the belief in one's future greatness
and invulnerability simply reflects this heightened competitiveness
and self-confidence, as well as the reality that adolescents are very
healthy and resilient. That is, perhaps these changes at adolescence, to
the extent that they actually exist, represent emotional, not cognitive,
adjustments. This interpretation might also explain the increase in
risk taking at adolescence, especially in boys (Steinberg, 1996; see
Chapter 9). Competitiveness and self-confidence might lead to underestimation of the risks of defeat or injury.

Like Piagetian theory, learning theory does not seem very helpful
in understanding the unique features of adolescence or any other
stage of development. As explained in Chapter 1, the influence of experience apparently doesn't swamp that of genes as development proceeds. Moreover, learning occurs in similar ways throughout develop-

ment, so there is nothing qualitatively distinctive about learning during adolescence and hence not much of a basis for a theory of adolescence. This is not to deny the importance of learning and cognition for explaining individual differences throughout the life span.

Summary

Adolescents' motivated behaviors have been of concern throughout recorded Western history. Despite the traditional emphasis on learning and cognition in U.S. psychology, motivation may be conceptually more fundamental for the analysis of observable behavior.

Human motives, or emotions, are whole-body, voluntary behaviors that occur in all cultures. They include a distinct affect, an adaptive behavioral tendency, and internal and external elicitors. They may also include a characteristic expression or pattern of visceral changes. These facets make up the emotion complex, but the most characteristic factor for identifying an emotion may be its affect. A list of emotions based mainly on affects is proposed to provide a common terminology for examining the elements of human adolescent behavior. Emotional life in adolescence is characterized by the appearance of the sex drive, mature pair bonding, and increased hunger as well as pride and shame.

Theories of adolescent development that are grounded in cognitive developmental theory or learning theory have serious shortcomings, even though they are helpful in describing individual and age differences. Likewise, psychoanalytic theories, not reviewed here, have been criticized as vague, untestable, convoluted (P. H. Miller, 1993), and inconsistent with evolutionary theory or with the existence of cross-cultural variation.

An evolutionary theory centered on emotional development may offer some advantages over these more traditional theories of adolescent development. An emotions model would seem particularly well suited to explaining the profound behavioral sex differences that are observed at adolescence. Incidentally, sex differences in motivation presumably limit our ability to imagine vicariously the feelings and inclinations of people of the opposite sex. We cannot really put ourselves in their shoes, so they remain somewhat bewildering.

3 Social Motivation

The main questions about adolescents that interest most people involve social motivation. Yet social motives are poorly understood compared with more solitary motives, such as hunger, thirst, sleep, and pain. To characterize social motivation in adolescence, it is necessary to examine human social motives in some depth. In keeping with the evolutionary approach of this book, functional considerations will be emphasized.

Sexual Feelings

Sex is obviously a very important aspect of behavior from an evolutionary viewpoint. It is sometimes asserted that there is no threat to the animal's health if sex does not occur. But health and survival are biologically pointless without reproduction. No matter how long an animal survives, its genes will not be propagated without reproduction, and fitness is consequently measured as reproductive success. On the emotional level, we would expect an animal whose reproductive imperative was constantly thwarted to be quite distressed or even desperate.

If, as has been suggested, contemporary psychology downplays the importance of sex, then our understanding of adolescence and young adulthood will be especially impoverished. As everyone who has passed through puberty recalls, sex and romance become extremely important during adolescence. One study found that sex and money were the most frequent subjects in the daydreams of college men and women—even in the conservative United States of the 1950s (Shaffer & Shoben, 1956). Accordingly, much of this book will be devoted to the topic of sexual behavior.

Presumably because of its direct relevance to biological fitness, sexual behavior is very complex. For one thing, sexual feelings interact with several other emotional modalities. Sex evokes the emotion of interest because biologically important matters tend to elicit attention. Sexual arousal can be interrupted by anger or fear. A sexual or amorous conquest makes us proud; a rejection causes shame.

Sexual feelings can be pleasant or unpleasant. The desire for sex presumably is unpleasant for animals that must be stirred to locate and secure a sex partner. For instance, an estrous rat is **proceptive,** actively seeking sex, because during estrus she must locate males that may be quite distant. It is not sufficient for her merely to be **receptive** to any males that appear. In general, however, it is the male animal whose sex drive is more intense, for theoretical reasons that will be explained in Chapter 5.

The evolved basis of many aspects of sexuality has been amply established. The human sexual motive is clearly primed and regulated by hormonal changes, as described in Chapter 9, and many universal aspects of this motive have been demonstrated (Daly & Wilson, 1983). Young women flirt by using similar facial expressions across cultures (Eibl-Eibesfeldt, 1989). Certain bodily features, such as a small waist-to-hip ratio in women (Singh, 1995) and a square jaw in men (Keating, 1985), are specific sexual attractants. Incest avoidance is universal. And copulation involves stereotypic releasers, autonomic changes, and fixed action patterns, including a distinctive vocalization during orgasm (also recorded in chimpanzees—Symons, 1979). Finally, the neural basis of sexual behavior is being elucidated with some success. As Symons argued, if sexual behavior were completely flexible, the individual's biological fitness would be hostage to the vagaries of experience and the manipulations of others.

Loneliness

Loneliness is a form of distress relieved by contact with people in general or with particular individuals. Social isolation is unpleasant, but no amount of general social contact can compensate for the loss of a particular loved one. Affinity for a particular individual (**monotropy**) occurs in many species. Members of some highly social species, especially the primates, seem to need several different types of relationship. In humans, these include filial, parental, romantic, friendship, and general kin relationships. For adolescents of both sexes, loneliness is associated with distance from parents as well as with having few close friendships, especially with girls (Santrock, 1996).

Perhaps each of these bonds should be regarded as a separate emotion. However, their similarities may outweigh their differences. All of these bonds show a similar consummatory response of approach with visual or tactile contact. Attraction is focused on the face (Money & Ehrhardt, 1972), which is consistent with the highly individualized nature of these relationships. Other distinctive features of the other person, such as the voice, may also take on special appeal. These social bonds tend to be mutual; if they were not reciprocal, contact would be less consistent. The social proximity that loneliness prompts sets the stage for other behaviors to come into play, such as care of offspring; there is no direct biological payoff to mere proximity. In ring doves, for example, proximity of the mate helps to trigger sexual and parental behaviors, such as nest building (Lehrman, 1961). Lastly, in animals and humans, prolonged separation brings increasing distress and prompts efforts at reunion. If separation is permanent, lassitude or depression ensues and is followed by gradual emotional recovery if the animal survives. Reunion often causes intense interaction, which may function to strengthen the bond. The basis for these similarities in various social bonds may be a common origin in the maternal instinct (McDougall, 1923). Each of these forms of relationship will now be described.

1. Gregariousness, or **sociality,** tends to occur in species that are vulnerable to predators. Animals in groups can protect themselves from predators by relying on each other for signs of danger and for collective defense. As terrestrial primates with little anatomical weaponry, humans are a highly social species. Moreover, humans cooperate for many purposes in addition to defense. Accordingly, we are distressed by prolonged social isolation.

We seem to enjoy social contact and to benefit from it physiologically as well as behaviorally. Benign social contact can lower indicators of stress, such as the level of the stress hormone cortisol. Lonely people tend to have poor immune system activity, a sign of stress, and hence are susceptible to disease (Buck, 1988). Even pet ownership can lower one's heart rate (Hoyenga & Hoyenga, 1984).

However, excessive social contact can be overwhelming. Visitors can fatigue a hospital patient, and crowding induces physiological signs of stress in animals, apparently by increasing the frequency of social contact rather than because of lack of space (Gray, 1987). In one study, the number of people per room was positively correlated with the amount of family violence, with social class taken into account (Gove et al., 1979).

2. **Attraction to kin** occurs widely in the animal kingdom. Social groups are often made up of relatives, who tend to aid each other where possible. As explained in Chapter 1, natural selection tends to favor altruistic behavior directed toward kin. Furthermore, it has been suggested that the behavioral mechanisms that lead to kin recognition and kin altruism extend to unrelated individuals who resemble us, which woupld help to explain the preference for similarity in friendships, as well as ethnic solidarity and discrimination.

3. **Coalitions** between nonkin occur between animals in some species, and take various forms. Play partnerships, grooming partnerships, and fighting coalitions are prominent in many of the terrestrial primates. We usually refer to such dyads as friendships when they occur in our species. Juvenile primates are often attracted to older individuals of the same sex; perhaps the latter serve as models. In many primate species, groups of same-sex adults are frequently observed; this occurs in most human societies (Katz & Konner, 1981).

4. If mated animals stay together beyond the time necessary for conceiving their young, then the relationship is a **pair bond**. The pair-bond relationship allows the male and female to cooperate in caring for their offspring. Pair bonding has evolved in species in which the young are born or hatched in a quite helpless state and therefore need the efforts of both parents to survive (see Chapter 1). We are such a species, and this pattern of pair bonding and biparentalism—marriage, in human terms—is found in all cultures. In general, single parenthood is a difficult undertaking that entails many developmental risks to the child, as has been amply confirmed (e.g., Amato, 1993).

The affect underlying the pair-bonding motive will be referred to here as **amorousness,** or **romantic love,** for lack of a more appropriate term that would also refer to the same tendency in pair-bonding animals. This affinity is partly sexual, but the evidence suggests that something else is also involved. For one thing, sexual attraction is not always confined to the mate, especially in males, so the sexual emotion can readily disrupt a pair bond (Symons, 1979). Sex can occur without love, and love can occur without sex. These two emotions are distinguished in our species by the fact that sex is evoked by various bodily features, whereas amorousness is mainly aroused by the face (Grant, 1976). Also, the behavioral goal, or consummatory response, of sex is coitus, whereas for love, it is proximity and reciprocated favorable attention.

However, sexual attraction doubtless enhances romantic love. The nexus of these two distinct emotions is indicated by their developmental course. In childhood, amorous infatuations often occur toward a member of the opposite sex. Typically, attractive children receive more of this attention (Grant, 1976). Other aspects of the mature form of amorousness are also observed, including gift giving, hugging, and jealousy. If it is not prevented, sexual play also occurs in childhood. The sex-play partner is as likely as not to be some child other than the object of the infatuation. It is not until puberty that the individual of love interest becomes the object of particular sexual interest, too (Money & Ehrhardt, 1972).

Once this point in the development of amorousness is reached, amorousness does not change qualitatively. An adolescent is capable of experiencing "true love," even if the partner is a poor choice for a spouse. In fact, the first love affair is often reported to be the most intense that the person ever experiences (Money & Ehrhardt, 1972).

The capacity for amorousness is universal (Grant, 1976; Jankowiak & Fischer, 1992). It occurs even in societies in which marriages are arranged—ideally, between the bride and groom once they are married but also sometimes extramaritally. Thus, the notion that romantic love arose in the Middle Ages with the troubadours is, well, romantic; see Photo 3.1.

Amorousness is monotropic; in other words, being romantically in love with more than one person at a time is very rare (Money & Ehrhardt, 1972). Thus, interest in a new partner usually cools one's interest in an old one. Intense infatuation seldom lasts more than 2 years, perhaps to prevent parents from being so obsessed with each other that they neglect their baby. This may help to explain the cross-national finding that divorce peaks 3 to 4 years into marriage (Fisher, 1989).

Behaviorally, amorousness prompts not only mutual approach but also respect for (overrating of) the other person, and mutual aid. The amorous couple help each other as well as their common offspring, so the fitness of all three parties is enhanced.

It is natural that possessiveness, or **jealousy**, characterizes this relationship, for anything worth having is worth defending. Accordingly, many pair-bonding species exhibit jealousy. For example, a male hamadryas baboon keeps his mates close by biting them when they stray and by repelling intruding males. Since jealous behavior seems to evolve in animals as one means of retaining exclusive mating opportunities, it probably has an evolved basis in our own species, too.

Photo 3.1   Ancient Egyptian Couple. Photo by Carol C. Weisfeld.

It may be exaggerated to a pathological degree in certain individuals, but jealousy is fundamentally adaptive. It does not seem to reflect a distinct affect, and so it is not listed as a basic emotional modality in Chapter 2. Jealousy seems to represent some combination of anger, fear, loneliness, sexual frustration, and shame. It apparently is an evolved tendency to respond to the possibility of mate loss with various defensive behaviors.

Research on monogamous mammals such as the prairie vole has implicated two pituitary hormones in pair bonding. Oxytocin seems to prompt the female to bond to a single male, and in males, vasopressin enhances pair bonding, repulsion of intruding males, and defense of offspring (Insel & Carter, 1995). Oxytocin is released at orgasm in rodents and humans, and vasopressin rises during men's sexual arousal. Thus, a possible hormonal explanation for the relation between sex and pair bonding, including jealousy, is emerging; also see Chapter 9.

5. In species that exhibit parental care, prolonged separation usually motivates the offspring and parent to rejoin each other. This **parent-offspring bond** can be said to be maintained by parental and filial affinities. In the great apes as well as humans, this bond is usually maintained up to adolescence and even beyond. Deprivation of this bond has widespread and long-term physiological and behavioral sequelae for mammals (Fernald, 1992).

In most vertebrates, parental behavior is highly fixed, or stereotypic. The presence of a particular animate or inanimate stimulus releases the appropriate parental behavior in the responsive, hormonally primed mother (Fleming, 1990; Harper, 1981). For example, a pregnant lioness will pull out the fur around her nipples, exposing them for suckling. She obviously does this without foreseeing its advantages but merely because this fur becomes uncomfortable during pregnancy. And mammalian mothers' eating the placenta and birth membranes (**placentophagia**) seems to be triggered by salt deprivation. Placentophagia and licking the newborn serve multiple purposes: providing the dehydrated and desalinated mother with fluid, sodium, and perhaps needed hormones; drying and warming the newborn; stimulating waste elimination by the newborn; and ridding the nest of the odoriferous placenta, which would otherwise attract predators and microbes (Coe, 1990). Very little learning or cognition seems to be involved in these stereotypic parental behaviors. Nature seems to have recruited various preexisting parental emotions (such as hunger, interest, and tactile feelings) to serve filial needs. Further, each maternal behavior (such as assuming the nursing posture, retrieving errant young, maternal aggression, and nest building) is mediated by different neural pathways—although all such maternal behaviors are hormonally primed (Numan, 1990).

Figure 3.1   Chimpanzee Mother Removing Cinder from Infant's Eye. Watercolor by Miriam Weisfeld.

In the large mammals, especially carnivores and primates, parental behavior is less fixed and more variable and cognitively complex (Fernald, 1992). The mother seems to respond less rigidly to specific releasers and more innovatively to nonspecific calls of distress by the offspring (Coe, 1990). She seems to be motivated to relieve these signs of distress out of empathy, the vicarious experiencing of the offspring's displeasure. For example, a chimpanzee mother was observed to remove a cinder from her infant's eye, an act that required her both to comprehend the source of distress and to be motivated to intervene (Figure 3.1). Similarly, when a hamadryas baboon was delivering her infant next to a cliff edge, a male who was observing the process rushed forward to rescue the newborn dangling over the edge by its umbilical cord (Hrdy, 1981). Obviously, no behavior as unusual as this could have been selected for specifically in evolution.

Primate mothering still retains some hardwired behaviors, such as placentophagia and nursing. However, it is likely that maternal hormones prime the mother to be especially responsive to the releasers of these specific behaviors and to the distress of her infant. Primate mothers also benefit from observation and experience in caring for their offspring. Thus, primate maternal behavior is shaped by hormones, releasers, learning, cognition, and vicarious emotions.

A baby can provide many profound parental pleasures, but a baby in distress disturbs people greatly. A crying infant increases sympathetic tone in male and female children and adolescents (Frodi & Lamb, 1978). An infant who cries frequently or shows other signs of abnormal development thus can be an aversive stimulus much of the time. Premature infants and those with various congenital anomalies tend to have aversive cries. Blind infants or those with Down's syndrome are judged to be less expressive and less rewarding, and they elicit less stimulation from parents and others. Difficult or less attractive infants evoke inferior care (J. R. Harris, 1995). Likewise, a healthier twin received more positive maternal stimulation at 8 months of age than its co-twin (Mann, 1992). Perhaps because they evoke less nurturance, sick infants are at risk for abuse. Thus, proper prenatal care is important not only because of its direct health benefits but also because healthy infants tend to be rewarding and to elicit high-quality care. The diminished care of impaired offspring is a general mammalian trait; in fact, abnormal offspring are often abandoned. Selection would have favored parents that discriminated between healthy and sickly offspring.

The affinity between a mother and infant serves as a basis for the vast array of maternal behaviors that she confers on him. As in other primates, the human infant depends almost entirely on its mother for meeting all of its needs: food, fluid, warmth, transportation, protection, cleanliness, and teaching. To provide this constant, variegated care, the mother must be easily influenced by the infant. The infant must actively communicate its needs to the mother, who must be motivated to respond appropriately and without hesitation.

In all mammals and every human culture, the female provides more direct parental care than the male (Daly & Wilson, 1983). However, ours is one of the rare mammalian biparental species. In every human culture, men contribute substantially to the survival of their children. In fact, fathers in foraging societies such as the !Kung San of Botswana interact relatively frequently with their children, so this may have been typical of our prehistory (Katz & Konner, 1981). Fathers aid children in many ways besides nurturant care. In many cultures, they protect, provide for, and teach their children. These sorts of aid are of great value and often entail considerable effort and danger. If parental care is defined biologically as enhancing the survival of offspring, then these forms of parental care are quite substantial (Mackey, 1996).

Father-child interaction varies across cultures in accordance with certain factors. Where wealth can be accumulated, economic stratification typically ensues. This, is turn, often leads to polygyny because some men become rich enough to support more than one wife. The need to provide for multiple households, however, decreases the time a man has available for child care. Also, polygynous fathers tend to remain somewhat aloof from their children so as not to show favoritism for one brood. Paternal care is more frequent where the mother is highly active in subsistence activities, as among foragers and horticulturists (Friedl, 1975). This is especially true if other relatives live elsewhere, that is, in cultures with nuclear family households. Father-child contact is less frequent where men are drawn away from the settlement by other duties, such as warfare and the need to guard resources. Resources can only be accumulated effectively in agricultural, pastoral, and mercantile societies, and in these types of economy, father-child contact is less frequent. Western society, although monogamous, has busy mothers but absent fathers and other relatives, resulting in a relatively low rate of child care by kin; further, that rate has been steadily falling with the rise in maternal employment.

Interest

Play is particularly important in primates. As arboreal gymnasts, primates exhibit great behavioral flexibility. A primate is capable of making many more discrete movements than is, say, a rodent. This means that we primates need to learn which response to make to which situation and how to execute responses smoothly. Much of this learning occurs through motoric play. Primates at play expend great amounts of time and energy, and incur risks of falling and other injuries. Primate play also involves manipulation of objects and social games.

The importance of play in our species is revealed by its developmental course. For most mammals, play essentially ends by maturity; they need to have learned the basics by then. Analogously, the body, brain, and behavior do not undergo dramatic changes after maturity following adolescence. But most humans and to some extent chimpanzees continue to play in adulthood, as, for example, with their offspring. The Latin appellation *Homo ludens* ("playful man") is appropriate. We need to learn throughout life because of the extreme flexibility of our behavior.

Exploration in primates is inhibited by fear. An infant monkey that encounters a strange stimulus is afraid and retreats to its mother (Harlow & Harlow, 1962). Its courage bolstered, it is now ready to explore the object. The infant may retreat to the mother repeatedly for assurance. Mother-deprived rhesus monkeys are fearful and explore but little. Similarly, a punitive, fear-inducing pigtail macaque mother tends to have a clingy, nonplayful infant (Rosenblum, 1971).

In primates, contact with peers is also essential for the normal development of play and learning. Peer-deprived monkeys are overly aggressive, as though they have not learned how to avoid fights (Harlow & Harlow, 1962). Also, peer-deprived females tend to be poor mothers, at least initially. In peer-deprived monkeys, sexual behavior is inadequate because they have not been able to observe and practice mounting and being mounted. Similarly, Victor of Aveyron, the "wild child" studied around 1800 in France, was attracted to women when he reached adolescence but did not know how to approach them sexually and finally gave up trying (Itard, 1932).

Ethological research indicates that primate play is highly social— that is, much of learning is social. Children tend to be especially interested in, and to imitate, competent models, presumably so they can improve their skills: One observational study of adolescent boys playing volleyball revealed that the better players provided instruction, criticism, and praise to the poorer ones (G. E. Weisfeld & Weisfeld, 1984). Furthermore, in adolescence, peers may possess greater abilities than do adults in some domains of knowledge; accordingly, peers gain influence relative to parents (Berndt, 1979). In one study, U.S. youngsters appeared to be more readily influenced by peers than Soviet youngsters but less so than British adolescents (Devereux, 1970).

Children also tend to imitate nurturant individuals. Consequently, if their parents are nurturant, children are more likely to be influenced by them. This is true for fathers as well as mothers. If parents are punitive or incompetent, children often gravitate to other models, including peers. If parents spend little time with their children, they are less likely to be influential, which is often the case today in families in which both parents work away from home and the child likewise is drawn away from parental contact by school and other activities. Charles Crawford (personal communication, 1988) has compared what might be called the abdication from parenthood of modern parents to the plight of young elephants in herds that have lost most of their adult members to poaching. In both cases, the young drift toward maturity with little guidance from their elders.

To direct a child's play or learning, it is helpful to know what activities are interesting. An interesting stimulus is one that is moderately novel or complex. Extremely strange stimuli evoke fear, for it is better to be cautious in the face of the unknown. Extremely complex stimuli are aversive, too, because they overwhelm our cognitive powers; investigation would be fruitless. However, familiar or simple stimuli are boring and aversive, for there is nothing to learn there. U.S. high school students found classes most enjoyable if neither too easy nor too difficult for them (Csikszentmihalyi & Larson, 1984). Finally, the act of understanding something—reducing the complex to the simple—is inherently satisfying. Thus, nature steers us toward stimuli about which we stand to learn something, rewards us for succeeding in understanding it, and punishes us for persisting at an unsolvable task. Learning is driven and directed by emotion.

Primates are naturally curious and will explore and learn if given an opportunity. Curiosity and learning drive primates to seek out increasingly complex stimulation. If stimulus complexity does not continue to increase as they get older, monkeys reduce their exploratory activity, and their learning falls off (Baldwin & Baldwin, 1976). Monkeys raised in enriched environments seek out and can process more complex sensory input. They prolong their play to an older age than do monkeys raised in impoverished environments. Children who are provided with appropriate play experiences, such as fantasy play, have shown cognitive gains and reduced impulsiveness (Saltz et al., 1977). By contrast, offering material rewards for tasks completed tends to reduce the development of the intellectual rewards of learning (Hoyenga & Hoyenga, 1984).

The properties of an interesting stimulus refer to moderate novelty and complexity for the individual. Because people have different sets of experiences and different aptitudes, individualized instruction, as by a parent or child, is likely to be more interesting and effective than mass education. U.S. high school students found individual conversations with the teacher to be their most enjoyable form of classroom experience (Csikszentmihalyi & Larson, 1984). Individualized or small-group instruction is the rule in puberty rites in other cultures (see Chapter 7).

However, some stimuli are inherently interesting to everyone. We are drawn to stimuli that have been important for our fitness: disasters, movement, large objects, bright colors (e.g., of fruit), people, violence, sex, and animals. The same sort of "sensational" news and television programs as those that have been popular in the United States evoke interest around the world. (Most other countries, however, also provide more edifying, commercial-free fare.)

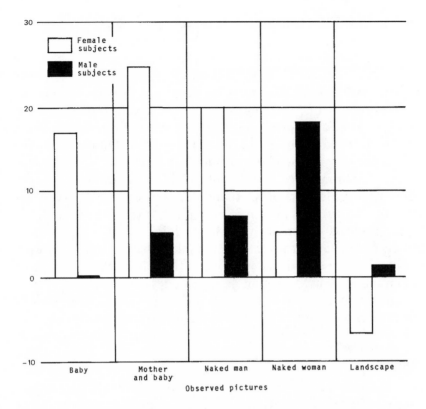

Figure 3.2   Changes in Pupil Size in Response to Various Visual Stimuli.
Source: Hess & Polt (1960). Reprinted by permission.

Hess (1977) gave a nice demonstration of the apparently biological basis for the appeal of some of these stimuli. The pupil of the eye is known to dilate in response to presentation of an interesting stimulus; this is an autonomic adjustment that accompanies the emotion. Hess used this unconditioned response as a measure of interest. Figure 3.2 shows some of his results.

Humor Appreciation

The function of humor is perplexing. A unitary explanation would have to account for the following diverse examples of humor, among others: plays on words, pratfalls, sexual jokes, irony, laughter accompanying social play in children and simians, jokes perpetrated by captive chimpanzees, and tickling in chimpanzees as well as in humans.

Many explanations of the function of humor rely on the discredited notion of group selection, or else they fail to suggest fitness advantages to both humorist and recipient. Another problem is that the presentation of humor is essentially a social act involving a distinctive emotional expression—laughter. One possibility is that our laughter reinforces others for providing us with enlightening and hence valuable stimulation or information. Laughter may convey appreciation for the humor and imply an obligation to repay the humorist in some way. Humor may provide information about important matters, such as danger (e.g., pratfalls and tickling that allows babies to practice defending vulnerable parts of the body), sex (lots of sexual jokes), language (word play), and human foibles (jokes with a butt or fool) (G. E. Weisfeld, 1990). Consistent with this informational explanation, children have shown a preference for jokes that are suited to their particular level of cognitive development (McGhee, 1979).

When humor is used to point out the foibles of another, it becomes aggressive or competitive. This may help to explain the notorious facetiousness of adolescents, who are highly competitive.

Anger

Anger seems to prompt retaliation for abuse. Abuse of an animal's prerogatives typically provokes an attack or threat of attack. These abuses include intruding into an animal's territory, usurping a dominant animal's prerogative, fighting too roughly in a dominance contest or at play, and usurping mating prerogatives. Thus, **moralistic aggression** is a punitive response to mistreatment, to having one's social rights violated (see Chapter 4). It is one of several forms of aggression, which can be distinguished on behavioral and neural grounds (Moyer, 1976). Each of these forms seems to be activated by a different emotional modality. Moralistic aggression arises out of anger, and it protects the individual from exploitation. **Defensive aggression** seems to derive from fear in animals that are attacked and cannot escape. **Maternal aggression** extends this protection to one's offspring and may arise vicariously. **Predatory aggression** is prompted by hunger and can be viewed as part of feeding behavior.

Intermale aggression occurs mainly but not exclusively between males. This tendency ensures that the male will seek either to establish a territory or to attain high dominance status, depending on the species's form of social organization. Without this tendency, a male in such a species would fail to win a female and would not breed. Because this behavior often occurs during a breeding season and has a hormonal basis, it seems to arise spontaneously out of a competitive urge. Humans are among those species that compete for dominance, or social status. Like other species, we may be said to have a dominance drive. The list of emotions in Chapter 2 refers instead to the affects of pride and shame, but the parallel with other primate species that strive for dominance might be better expressed by using "feelings of dominance and submission." This emotion will be discussed further in Chapter 4.

Summary

Certain emotional modalities are prominent in adolescence. The most obvious of these is sexual feelings. Sexual behavior has many evolved aspects, including stereotypic flirtation signals, autonomic and hormonal factors in libido and copulation, universal somatic elicitors of sexual interest, and universal incest avoidance. Loneliness is also an important emotion, particularly with respect to amorousness and the parent-adolescent bond. Amorousness and sexual feelings are intertwined but distinct emotions; they seem to depend on somewhat different hormonal mechanisms. Jealousy seems not to be a basic emotion but rather a combination of emotions that arise in response to the threat of mate loss. Nurturant behavior is also salient in adolescence, especially in girls. Primate nurturance, which depends heavily on the capacity for empathy, is primed by hormones but requires learning, too. Father-child contact is less extensive in modern industrial society than it was among our forager ancestors. The emotions of interest and humor seem to function to enhance the acquisition of knowledge that has adaptive value. The facetious humor of adolescent boys has a strong competitive element. Anger promotes retaliation for violations of social norms and is separate from other forms of aggression, such as dominance (pride and shame).

4   Pride and Shame

Because pride/shame is a very complicated and neglected emotion, I have devoted an entire chapter to it. Before describing this emotion in humans, it will be helpful to describe dominance hierarchies in animals, since our capacity for pride and shame probably evolved from dominance hierarchization in our primate relatives. The dominance hierarchy model will also be useful for explaining peer interactions, especially among boys, in Chapter 11.

Dominance Hierarchies

Many species, including many terrestrial primates, compete for dominance. The consequence of this dominance motive is that animals fight to establish their place in a "pecking order." Each animal usually takes precedence over its subordinates in disputes over resources and mates. High-ranking animals also seem to benefit from being less fearful of attack, and they may even sleep more soundly (Barchas & Barchas, 1975). If an animal did not compete, it would not gain the benefits of access to the material resources and mates necessary for fitness. Pacifists might live longer because they would avoid the costs of combat, but they would leave fewer progeny. This argument applies to our own species as much as to other social animals and therefore implies an evolved basis for the competition that occurs in every human culture.

On the affective level, animals in dominance hierarchies seem to enjoy high rank, in that they fight for it. For example, a male stickleback fish will perform work for an opportunity to attack another male (Sevenster, 1973). An animal that secures a high rank apparently is inclined to assume its attendant prerogatives. Low-ranking animals, by contrast, seem to be disheartened and readily cede prerogatives to their superiors. This arrangement would be adaptive in that animals would seek to be dominant and thereby gain the tangible prerogatives of high rank that translate into fitness benefits, and they would avoid low rank. Similarly, people seem to enjoy high status and readily accept its benefits, whereas low status is unpleasant. This feeling of triumph is referred to as pride in this book, and the feeling of failure is referred to as shame.

Each individual in a hierarchy defends its prerogatives of rank. This is the intense aggression that is referred to as angry aggression, or rage. For example, if a subordinate monkey presumes to precede a dominant one onto a branch, the latter typically reacts with apparent anger. Often, this reaction is out of proportion to the material value of the prerogative, which suggests that a principle is involved. Indeed, if a dominant animal allows a subordinate to usurp any such prerogative, the former has effectively yielded its rank to the latter. Thus, animals seem to recognize certain principles of conduct that define proper competitive behavior, just as humans do, and a violation of these expectations can bring retaliation.

In animals in dominance hierarchies, these expectations seem to include: not usurping a superior's prerogatives, not attacking an opponent that has submitted, and (in some but not all species) not fighting too roughly. One example of the latter rule is the fighting behavior of bighorn sheep. The rams line up to butt heads, making a fearsome noise, but they do each other little harm in the process of establishing the greater strength of the victor. Sideswiping the other's flank is evidently forbidden; such a violation would precipitate rage in the victim. Similarly, giraffes fight for dominance by swinging their necks against each other; they reserve the use of kicking—they can kill a lion with their legs—for fending off predators.

Dominant animals, especially primates, exhibit direct gaze and a relaxed, expansive demeanor. They carry the head erect and generally act as though they do not fear attack. These **dominance displays** effectively intimidate other animals. Subordinate animals, however, avert their eyes and lower their heads, make attenuated movements, and crouch. These postures constitute fragments of flight or concealment behavior, as though the animal is signaling its disinterest in fighting further. **Submission displays** convey a message of conditional surrender: If you leave me alone, you may take whatever you want, but if you continue to attack me, I shall retaliate. After submitting, a chimpanzee may receive a **reconciliation gesture,** which helps to reestablish friendly relations between the two former combatants (de Waal, 1996). Reconciliation displays have been observed in gorillas, bonobos, and a variety of Old World monkeys as well. Evidence indicates that reconciliation is more common when the animals have a cooperative relationship that, presumably, is worth maintaining.

Hierarchical animals do not fight very frequently because they recognize each other as individuals and they know each other's ability. To challenge a stronger animal would be foolish, and so fights tend to be confined to cases in which relative fighting ability is uncertain. Fights are indeed relatively frequent when a new group forms, when a new animal appears, or when two animals are close in ability. Among adolescent boy campers, one study showed, dominance competitions were frequent during the first few days of camp, but then dominance ranks stabilized and competition dropped off and remained low for the next several weeks (Savin-Williams, 1976). Also, dominance contests were most frequent between closely ranked boys.

Animals in a hierarchy "size each other up" in various ways. They seem literally to be intimidated by large size, formidable anatomical weapons, apparent vigor, and so forth. They also seem to remember each other and the outcome of previous fights, even those in which they were bystanders. They respond to the dominance and submission displays that a potential opponent exhibits, for these expressions reflect the opponent's fighting history and are usually reliable.

Why would a subordinate animal not try to bluff opponents by swaggering about? Researchers have observed that when an animal is given an artificial bodily sign of dominance, it is occasionally challenged by a subordinate anyway, as if to test for bluffing (Trivers, 1985). If the ruse is discovered, an angry attack may ensue. This may help to explain why we resent "arrogant" individuals who seem to have an exaggerated opinion of themselves. By bluffing us in this way, such individuals might claim more prerogatives than they deserve.

However, a certain degree of self-delusion about one's abilities may be advantageous, since it will result in some victories by bluffing and in perseverance that may allow the animal to outlast a more faint-hearted opponent. But persistence in the face of certain defeat is costly; one needs to live to fight another day. On balance, healthy self-confidence is necessary for moving up the hierarchy and challenging opponents that have been more successful in the past. If an animal acted perfectly objectively on the basis of past outcomes, it would never challenge a superior and would never rise in rank. This involves the notion of the overweening male ego, to be discussed in Chapter 9.

People sometimes wonder why a subordinate animal stays in the group. One reason is that there are advantages to group membership, especially in terms of protection from predators. Furthermore, a low-ranking animal may still secure some resources—that is, it will dominate even lower-ranking members and may also gain resources by outscrambling its competitors. Low-ranking males of various species sometimes gain "sneak fertilizations" of females. In addition, low-ranking primates are often juveniles or adolescents that will ascend the hierarchy in time. They gradually work their way up by growing and learning, and they would sacrifice fitness by leaving their group and starting over in a new one.

Another puzzle is why animals typically attack a subordinate, for they cannot hope to advance their standing by doing so. Such attacks probably discourage the subordinate from challenging them in the future, for a challenge is likeliest to come from those immediately below. Thus, bullying behavior, common in young boys, may reflect the "peck right": an evolved tendency to launch unprovoked attacks against easy opponents. Consistent with this, bullying is common at the beginning of secondary school, when older boys can victimize the newcomers (Ahmad & Smith, 1994).

In light of this sort of strategic thinking, dominance behavior makes good adaptive sense. These evolutionary explanations do not require the dubious notion of group benefit. Instead, dominance behavior generally can be seen to benefit the individual. Sometimes, the illusion of group benefit results, as when two combatants constrain their fighting within limits or when one animal peacefully yields a resource to another. However, in these cases, it is usually apparent that each animal benefits individually as well.

Evolved Basis of Status Striving in Humans

In humans, even in childhood, competition takes aggressive form only part of the time. Social standing rests predominantly on our ability and inclination to help others. Indeed, we can gain social status by helping others. When we receive credit for helping someone, we feel proud. When we fail to be helpful or otherwise to fulfill the values of our culture, we feel ashamed. That is, our striving for social success is the human version of dominance competition. Despite the fact that social status in our species can rest on criteria other than brute force, there is reason to believe that human status striving evolved from the primate capacity for dominance behavior. Many ethologists have made this argument (e.g., Barkow, 1975; Darwin, 1872/1965; Mazur, 1985; McDougall, 1921; Pugh, 1977; Rajecki & Flannery, 1981; G. E. Weisfeld & Linkey, 1985; G. E. Weisfeld, 1997a). They have demonstrated numerous behavioral parallels between success striving in humans and dominance hierarchization in other species. Some of these parallels, or demonstrations of phylogenetic continuity (see Chapter 1), will now be described.

In both human and animal hierarchies, privileges are allocated systematically in proportion to individual prowess. In various traditional cultures, men who are physically powerful, wealthy, or high in social status—that is, socially dominant—have the most children (Barkow, 1989). Equity in social competition is maintained partly by aggressive retaliation; animals as well as people seem to get angry if their prerogatives under the social system are infringed, as when a subordinate usurps a dominant individual's privilege (de Waal, 1996).

Perhaps most convincingly, some of the dominance and submission displays of primates resemble those of socially successful humans, suggesting a common evolutionary basis (Darwin, 1872/1965; Mazur, 1985). Dominant, successful humans stand erect, gesture expansively, command attention, are relaxed, and gaze directly. Similarly, dominant simians hold the head and tail erect; move with a relaxed, expansive gait; and draw attention. Dominant, successful animals and people also seek out others, presumably because social contacts have been rewarding for them. In contrast, subordinate humans and simians show the opposite, antithetical emotional expressions. Such primate dominance and submission displays seem to operate in humans, as do primate reconciliation gestures, for example, embracing and hand holding. Research on children has shown that crouching does indeed stop an attack (Ginsburg, 1980), and children who are defeated in a competitive encounter tend to break off eye contact with the opponent (Heckhausen, 1968). However, it should be noted that chimpanzees, for example, also employ additional dominance and submission signals, including mounting, charging, and making a submissive pant-grunt (de Waal, 1996).

Some research has involved the dominance display of erect posture. Boys who had been physically dominant ("tough") at ages 6 to 10 tend to exhibit erect posture at ages 14 to 16 (G. E. Weisfeld & Beresford, 1982). That is, erect posture in adolescent boys seems to reflect childhood dominance status, demonstrating the stability of the latter trait.

Erect posture also typifies individuals who excel at other, nonaggressive, short-term endeavors. In another study, university students were observed before and after they received an examination grade (G. E. Weisfeld & Beresford, 1982). Those who received a high grade tended to show an increase in erectness of posture upon learning of the outcome, whereas students who did poorly showed a decrease. Similarly, adolescent boys and girls who classmates believed exhibited erect posture, direct gaze, and a relaxed demeanor tended to possess attributes valued by the group, such as athletic ability and attractiveness (G. E. Weisfeld et al., 1983, 1984a).

Another example concerns eye gaze as an expression of dominance. Mazur and colleagues (1980) argued that direct gaze is physiologically arousing and affectively unpleasant, perhaps because being stared at constitutes a threat display in primates. The individual who breaks off eye contact first is very likely, they found, to be less influential—in other words, subordinate—in subsequent social interaction. Specifically, these subordinates did less speaking than those who had outstared them. Similarly, Zivin (1985) found that a "win face" predicted success in children's dominance contests.

The notion of homology, or phylogenetic continuity, between status striving in humans and dominance in simians is strengthened by their apparently having a common neural basis (G. E. Weisfeld & Linkey, 1985; G. E. Weisfeld, 1997a). Lesions to the orbitofrontal cortex in simians can yield a fall in rank (as though the animal strives less for social success), the issuing of inappropriate challenges (as if it does not "know its place"), or a loss of its former tendency to be angered when an earned reward is withheld. If the homologous brain area is damaged in humans, an indifference to social evaluation often occurs. A patient with this affliction typically loses his or her former social graces and acts boorishly or may show a disregard for performing a job conscientiously. Some authors refer specifically to a loss of the capacity for guilt.

One hormonal parallel involves the male hormone testosterone. A male monkey that rises in dominance rank typically experiences elevated testosterone levels (Rose et al., 1975). This effect occurs even if the monkey rises in rank because its superiors have been removed from the enclosure. A rise in testosterone has also been observed in men who won tennis or chess matches, or graduated from medical school (Mazur & Lamb, 1980). Interestingly, no such change occurred in men whose success was due to chance, as in winning a lottery.

The adaptive advantages of the rise in testosterone with a rise in rank may be to increase the male primate's competitive motivation further, given its "hot hand"; to increase muscle mass, again so it can take advantage of favorable social conditions; and to increase sperm production, since it can exploit its enhanced mating opportunities as a high-ranking male. Along related lines, the males of most species are more competitive than the females, and in both sexes, competitiveness can usually be increased by giving testosterone. This includes our species, thus strengthening the comparative interpretation of human competition.

Another physiological parallel concerns the neurotransmitter serotonin (Masters & McGuire, 1994). Like testosterone, this biochemical rises in successful men and male simians. Vervet monkeys that have been submitted to or have copulated register a rise in serotonin. Levels fall in those that have been defeated or have observed another male copulate. Analogously, men with high serotonin levels tend to be high ranking in their group, and low serotonin characterizes depression. Drugs that enhance the effect of serotonin (selective serotonin reuptake inhibitors, such as Prozac) are used to treat depression. Vervet and human males with low serotonin tend to be more aggressive, as measured in various ways.

In addition to this evidence of phylogenetic continuity and a specific neural mechanism for this behavior, the consistent developmental pattern of dominance behavior in children also implies an evolved basis. At about 2 years of age, children begin to blush and to respond to social evaluation, such as praise (G. E. Weisfeld & Linkey, 1985; G. E. Weisfeld, 1997a). By about age 3, their cognitive development seems to allow them to compete—to compare their performance with that of others (Stipek, 1995). Thus, they begin to exhibit rivalry, competitiveness, and dominance struggles (G. E. Weisfeld & Linkey, 1985; G. E. Weisfeld, 1997a). Mentally retarded adults exhibit achievement motivation only if they possess a mental age of 3 1/2 (Heckhausen, 1968). The fact that all of these terms—rivalry, social comparison, dominance striving, success motivation, and so forth—refer to conceptually similar behavior (namely, social competition) suggests that their common onset is not a coincidence. Rather, the terms probably refer to the same evolved system, featuring the emotion of pride/shame.

A final argument for the evolved basis of this system in humans is its universality. People everywhere strive for social status, or prestige (Barkow, 1975, 1989). This fact is often ignored because the criteria for social success vary from culture to culture. Despite these behavioral variations, the same emotion of pride/shame occurs worldwide. Just as people satisfy their hunger by ingesting different foods around the world, so they seek social recognition according to different behavioral means.

Initially, however, children in all cultures compete aggressively, just as many animals do (G. E. Weisfeld & Linkey, 1985). A group of children typically establishes a clear, linear rank order based mainly on physical prowess (Strayer & Strayer, 1976). Thus, despite the diversity of criteria for social status in adulthood, the primordial criterion of aggression seems to operate in childhood. Even in adolescence, competition retains some aggressive elements, such as threats of attack and physical displacement (Savin-Williams, 1987).

The power of the dominance hierarchy model is illustrated by an observational and questionnaire study of adolescents (Savin-Williams & Demo, 1984). High self-esteem (i.e., high social status, or dominance) was characterized by the dominance expressions of maintaining eye contact and facing others, and by seeking out others. Adolescents with low self-esteem stood submissively, glanced around to monitor others, and showed signs of dissatisfaction with their dominance status: excessive bragging or self-deprecation, giving excuses for failures, and belittling others. These individuals were socially withdrawn in that they seldom expressed their opinions, especially when asked.

Emotions Underlying Reciprocal Altruism

The dominance hierarchy model is useful for explaining certain aspects of human status striving, especially the affects and emotional expressions of success and failure, the development of competitiveness, the roles of testosterone and serotonin, and the distribution of prerogatives. Another evolutionary model, the idea of **reciprocal altruism**, is useful in further explaining how cooperative behavior can involve human status striving.

Trivers's (1971) model of reciprocal altruism explains how altruistic behavior can evolve, that is, how it can enhance the fitness of the individual. **Altruism** is defined by sociobiologists as the performance of an act that benefits another individual at one's own fitness expense, at least in the short run. The term refers to observable behavior, not to motivation or ethics. Trivers's theory provided a cogent explanation for one of evolutionary biology's troublesome observations: the fact that, in apparent violation of its biological interests, an animal sometimes aids nonrelatives or even members of other species. Trivers showed that these apparent sacrifices are probably reciprocated by the beneficiary, so that both parties realize a net increase in fitness. For example, in cleaning symbioses, the cleaner fish can forage with impunity in the mouth of the host, and the host receives low-cost dental care.

In the same publication, Trivers proceeded to describe the emotional mechanisms that support the equitable exchange of favors in our species, which exhibits extensive reciprocal altruism. He envisioned an exchange of favors between two individuals of approximately equal status (e.g., friends). However, the model can also be applied to a relationship between two people of unequal status, that is, in a dominance relationship.

According to Trivers, the affects of moralistic anger and gratitude serve, respectively, to punish selfish individuals and to reward altruists for their actions. He supported his model by citing evidence from social psychological research indicating that people do react with anger and aggression toward those who have harmed them and with assistance toward those who have helped them. This tit-for-tat "strategy" generally ensures that fairness reigns. It rewards altruism, thereby helping to establish relationships of reciprocal exchange of favors. Both parties gain from such an exchange, and it is presumably adaptive to enter into certain of these relationships. If we conferred favors on others indiscriminately, however, we would be taken advantage of by nonreciprocators, so we need to detect and punish "cheaters" (or at least to cease helping them).

Thus, if we wrong others, we risk incurring their wrath, or moralistic anger. According to Trivers, we are protected against this unwise course by our capacity for guilt, or shame. This unpleasant state impels us to redress the misdeed and thus avoid being punished or punished further. As laboratory studies have shown, guilty individuals tend to give up resources, thus restoring equity. The capacity for guilt also deters us from misbehaving in the first place. Misbehavior results in "losing face," that is, the concealment of one's face from the gaze of others; compare this with Mazur's (1985) observations on the aversiveness of prolonged eye contact in staring contests.

Having offered plausible functional explanations for our emotions of anger, guilt, and gratitude, Trivers concluded by discussing sympathy. According to Trivers, reciprocal exchanges are initiated by feelings of sympathy for the beneficiary of the initial act of help. Sympathy (or the capacity for vicarious identification) inclines us to enter into social exchanges that will ultimately benefit us. But our sympathy is not indiscriminate. We are more sympathetic toward those who have earned our trust, which is only sensible. We are also more sympathetic toward those who are in greater need. These biases make the recipient more grateful toward us and more generous in return, as confirmed by research.

The pleasant emotion of pride, the opposite of shame, may also be part of this emotional system for promoting reciprocal altruism (G. E. Weisfeld, 1980, 1997a). Pride inclines us to perform favors for which others will give us credit. Accordingly, subjects reported feeling happy after helping someone (Yinon & Laudau, 1987). Pride also inclines us to expect and accept rewards for our good deeds; it is adaptive to claim prerogatives that others yield. Success inclines subjects to claim more rewards; for example, attractive men took more candies as compensation for participating in a study than did less attractive ones (G. E. Weisfeld & Laehn, 1986).

In sum, these emotions guide us along behavioral channels that will result in our obtaining social recognition and its attendant tangible benefits. Pride is the carrot that entices us to perform deeds that society values and rewards, and shame is the stick that discourages us from violating societal standards. Gratitude may be affectively identical to shame; both of these unpleasant affects impel the individual to cede resources.

Although many species exhibit dominance hierarchization, only a few seem capable of reciprocal altruism. Reciprocal altruism requires some ability to aid **conspecifics** (members of the same species) and to recognize other individuals and remember their past actions. For example, chimpanzees aid each other by forming fighting coalitions (de Waal, 1982), and chimpanzees and other primates sometimes share meat. But we Old World primates are not the only mammals to have evolved a capacity for reciprocal altruism. The vampire bat—an improbable altruist—regurgitates blood to hungry nonrelatives on a basis of reciprocity and need, as well as to "blood relatives" (Wilkinson, 1984). Thus, the bat sometimes shares blood even when it doesn't!

In humans, the opportunity for reciprocal altruism is enhanced by several factors. Language and foresight allow us to arrange to defer the restoration of equity to a later time by means of thanks, apologies, threats, and demands. Also, specialization of labor permits us to exchange a great variety of services. The exchange of meat for plant food may have formed the original basis for the human family (see Chapter 6). It has also been suggested that a successful Pleistocene hunter may have given away his excess but perishable meat and received credit in the form of prestige, or status. This credit could then have been exchanged for some form of assistance at a later time.

The existence of this system for reciprocal altruism does not mean that people are consciously aware of its benefits or that they are Machiavellian when they strive for social recognition or behave altruistically. In fact, it has been observed that Machiavellian behavior would raise suspicions in others, so it would be trusted less than spontaneous altruism. Consequently Machiavellianism is probably less adaptive and therefore less common than is altruism based largely on sympathy and an adherence to altruistic values (Trivers, 1971). Thus, although altruistic behavior tends to be reciprocated and to benefit us eventually, our motives are usually noble.

At the same time, people cannot afford to have their altruism go unreturned indefinitely. Everyone has his price; there is a limit to his unreciprocated altruism and the credit he will allow to accumulate. And every society endorses some version of the reciprocity norm— the tit-for-tat strategy (Gouldner, 1960).

Given the evolutionary importance of these behaviors in our species, it is small wonder that we spend so much time trying to understand each other's motives, values, and behavioral tendencies. The huge increase in hominid brain size may have been due mainly to the need to optimize one's social behavior rather than to do higher math or other abstract tasks (Humphrey, 1976; Dunbar, 1991).

Integrating Various Models of Social Behavior

The notion that humans have a capacity for reciprocal altruism provides a useful model for integrating various aspects of social behavior that have been recognized by social scientists. Trivers envisioned a dyadic relationship in which skills or resources were traded. But his model can be extended to characterize the social contract between the individual and society. According to this notion, the individual performs certain socially desirable deeds and is rewarded by the collectivity; misdeeds are punished by society. In other words, the individual strives for social success by adhering to societal values. She participates in an exchange relationship with society.

On a smaller scale, the model is also consistent with **exchange theories** of how equity is maintained in a small group performing a task. The most competent person typically becomes the leader and receives various privileges in exchange for her extraordinary contributions to the group. These privileges may include attention, influence, or material rewards. Other members receive less because they contribute less. Again, a meritocratic system can be said to operate. Inequalities in the distribution of resources result, but the allocation process is orderly and reflects accomplishments. In this respect, group processes resemble the operation of a dominance hierarchy.

Thus, group behavior can be explained in terms of any of several models, including reciprocal altruism, the dominance hierarchy, and exchange theory. So can other social behaviors referred to by various terms, including prosocial behavior, moralistic behavior, social comparison, self-esteem, the power motive, and approval motivation. Surely, these are not all separate behavioral phenomena that evolved independently from each other. What is the defining property of these behaviors? Lo and behold, all of them refer to social behavior in which pride and shame are prominent. Pride and shame induce the individual to seek higher status (dominance, in comparative terms) and its attendant tangible rewards.

The dominance hierarchy model of human social interactions can also be applied to the concept of **achievement motivation** (McClelland, 1961; Atkinson, 1958). Individuals are said to differ in the extent of their motivation to succeed at school, work, and other aspects of life. Achievement motivation is measured in terms of the extent to which subjects read themes of success into neutral scenarios. Those who imagine successful outcomes are said to rank high in "need for achievement" and low in "fear of failure." The theory has led to some interesting research on individual differences in competitive behavior. But these results can be understood by liberal use of everyday terms and the dominance model, thus avoiding the rather arcane terminology of achievement motivation theory.

Individuals high in achievement motivation seem to anticipate being successful. Those low in achievement motivation (or high in fear of failure) expect to fail. In layman's terms, these subjects differ in self-esteem and self-confidence. Both groups may wish to succeed, but they differ in their expectations of success. One troublesome term from achievement motivation theory is *need for achievement.* This refers to individual differences in expectation of success, not to differences in the desire to succeed. Some people expect success and fantasize a good deal about success, whereas others expect to fail and, on projective psychological tests, fantasize about failure. Instead of using confusing terms such as *need for achievement, motive to seek success,* and *fear of failure,* it may be better to refer simply to *self-confidence.*

Research results on achievement motivation make sense if interpreted in terms of self-confidence. High achievement motivation (self-confidence) is associated with both previous success and subsequent success. Logically, people who have been successful expect their success to continue; in other words, they are self-confident. Their self-confidence inclines them to seek out moderately difficult challenges, persist at tasks, and remain calm and effective—so they continue to succeed. Even animals seem to show self-confidence, in that success makes them more aggressive in fights (G. E. Weisfeld, 1980). People who habitually fail and hence have low self-confidence select tasks that are either very easy or very hard—tasks that prove little. They may even try to avoid the challenge entirely in order to avoid risking their self-esteem, or pride. Lastly, individuals high in achievement motivation tend to attribute successes to their own ability (Powers & Wagner, 1984) and failure to mere lack of effort because this is consistent with their image of themselves as successful. Individuals low in achievement motivation, that is, those lacking in self-esteem, tend to attribute their successes to luck and their failures to lack of ability.

These individual differences have been demonstrated in some important practical situations. U.S. college students who have high achievement motivation (who are self-confident) tend to choose moderately challenging, realistic major subjects (Isaacson, 1964). Students low in self-confidence tend to select either very ambitious or excessively modest career goals. People with high need for achievement prefer personal responsibility for their job, seek out and use feedback on their performance, and make adjustments in order to improve (McClelland, 1971). Men with high achievement motivation are more likely to choose entrepreneurial positions, to perform better at these occupations, and to be upwardly mobile (Munroe & Munroe, 1975). A parental style that enhances the adolescent's self-confidence but insists on rather high standards is associated with high achievement motivation and actual academic success (Santrock, 1996; see Chapter 14).

Most people tend to be moderately self-confident and to overrate themselves, as shown in research on Chinese adolescents (Dong et al., 1996). That is, people's opinion of themselves is generally somewhat higher than that which their associates hold of them. Overrating of self may be a perceptual bias that gives us the courage to seek out challenges. Analogously, an animal that did not believe it could defeat a superior would never rise in rank.

Research indicates that it is especially important to foster self-confidence in poor students, for they are prone to try to escape from school tasks if the outcome is always aversive, and to have their concentration disrupted by fear of failure. For this reason, praise and encouragement are essential for such students. Superior students, by contrast, usually maintain effort best if they receive occasional criticism; if they habitually receive praise, they may become complacent. Thus, all children need appropriate challenges—challenges that are neither too discouraging nor too easy for them. They need to be evaluated according to their individual aptitude. At the same time, if praise is undeserved but is given gratuitously to enhance self-esteem, it will not reinforce effort.

Summary

A raft of psychological terms has been used to refer to various competitive social behaviors, but these behaviors all entail the emotion of pride/shame. For most purposes, we can reduce the profusion of terminology to this single emotional construct. Additional insights can be gained by recognizing that this human emotion evolved from dominance behavior in other primates.

The dominance hierarchy model clearly shows that our competitive behavior is governed by conventions and hence is cooperative in a sense. Just as animals fight for dominance within "rules" that are enforced by violent retaliation, humans compete for social status according to social expectations. One can feel proud of success but also of competing within the rules; one can feel ashamed of failure but also of breaking the rules of competition, that is, of acting immorally. Violations of the rules of competition are punished by angry retaliation in humans and other species.

A simple dominance model of human social competition breaks down with respect to the means of competition. In most hierarchically organized species, aggression mainly determines success. In adult humans, competition takes various forms, including competition to be altruistic, to be cooperative, and to contribute to others or the group. But this difference should not obscure the many similarities between human and animal social competition. These similarities constitute evidence for a common evolutionary origin and include enforcement of social norms governing competition, the orderly distribution of prerogatives, the forms of expression of social status, neural bases, and hormonal effects.

Another evolutionary model—reciprocal altruism—sheds further light on the operation of this complex behavioral system. This model explains how the equitable exchange of prerogatives or resources is promoted and enforced by the same emotions: anger, pride, shame, and gratitude (possibly identical to shame), plus the vicarious state of sympathy. The dominance hierarchy model seems to cover more social contexts than reciprocal altruism and to provide a phylogenetic basis for the behaviors it describes. The dominance model is also useful for interpreting data arising from various psychological models of social behavior, such as small-group processes and achievement motivation. This illustrates the fact that human social behavior can be studied comparatively, just like other behavioral phenomena such as sensation, perception, cognition, and learning

Thus, adhering to one's social values—often described as purely learned, rational, or cultural behavior—actually has an emotional, evolved basis. Conscience has a specific affective component: pride and shame. Resisting the pull of emotions such as anger and sex does not constitute a triumph of reason over passion, but rather a temporary supremacy of pride/shame over these other adaptive emotions. In such cases, pride/shame allows us to defer fulfillment of other emotions to a more suitable occasion, i.e., to fulfill our needs without losing social status.

5 Sex Differences in Reproductive Behavior

The last three chapters have provided a vocabulary for discussing the basic human motives, or emotions. Although these particular emotional categories and distinctions are somewhat arbitrary and idiosyncratic, the emotions are explained in functional terms that make their existence plausible. Now we can begin to consider these motives, especially the reproductive ones, as they emerge in adolescence.

Adolescence means becoming adult. The adolescent changes from an immature, dependent organism to a fully functioning adult with the potential to have dependent young of its own. This constitutes a radical transformation, as indicated by the major bodily changes that occur at puberty. Perhaps only at birth, weaning, and parturition does a metamorphosis of this magnitude occur. Likewise, in other species, the attainment of reproductive maturity is a monumental transition.

Before reproductive maturation in most species, the sexes resemble each other quite closely. They follow similar ways of life and consequently have evolved similar adaptations. At maturity, however, sex differences are often profound, reflecting sharp differentiation of reproductive roles. This is true of our species, too. The morphology, physiology, and behavior of boys and girls diverge markedly at puberty. Behavioral sex differentiation is perhaps greatest during adolescence, and we can scarcely say anything about adolescents unless we specify their sex. One of the main reasons the study of adolescence has been so barren of theory may be a reluctance to acknowledge the central importance of sex and sex differences that occur as reproductive capacity is attained.

The main motivational changes of adolescence, then, are probably reproductive. Pubescence is sexual maturation. The organism must develop appropriate sexual, pair-bonding, and parental motives, including competition for and selection of mates. In terms of our model of human motives, this means sexual feelings, including the aesthetics of mate choice; empathic parental behavior; amorousness (a form of loneliness); pride and shame, especially in connection with competition for mates; and anger, especially with respect to mate competition and jealousy.

Trivers's Theory of Parental Investment and Sexual Selection

The study of behavioral sex differences was advanced profoundly by Trivers (1972), a giant of sociobiology whose theory of reciprocal altruism was described in Chapter 4. His theory of **parental investment and sexual selection** is essential for a modern understanding of sex differences and hence of adolescence. The theory is very broad. It accounts for sex differences in sexually reproducing species throughout the animal kingdom. Thus, it constitutes a theory of sexual selection—an explanation of the selection forces that have favored different traits in males and females across species lines. That is, the theory accounts for the broad trends in how males and females characteristically behave in the animal kingdom. Sex differences are not just species-specific ways for the male and female to court, copulate, and rear their young. Sex differentiation is much more fundamental and more consistent than that.

Trivers's theory begins with the fundamental difference between the sexes. Biologists define the sexes as follows. The female of any species is the form that produces the larger gamete—the ovum. The male produces the smaller spermatozoon. This differentiation constitutes a primordial specialization of function. The ovum is a gamete specialized to store food for the developing zygote. The sperm is specialized for mobility to reach the ovum; it often has a flagellum for propulsion. Apparently, separate sexes evolved because reproduction was more efficient with this sort of gametic differentiation than when two identical gametes merged (Trivers, 1985).

From this elemental specialization, others followed, their precise form depending on preexisting features of the particular species and on its habitat. In most species, since the ovum is fertilized near or within the female, she is likelier than the more distant male to gain in reproductive success by caring for the developing offspring. That is, she may increase the chances of her young's survival by providing some parental care, but this is less practical for the male. He is more likely than she to gain in reproductive fitness by pursuing additional mates instead.

Although the theory accounts for behavioral sex differences very widely, the mammalian case is naturally of greatest interest to us. In most mammals, the fetus develops within the female's body. The male cannot gain access to it, but the female nourishes it and protects it via the placenta throughout gestation. After birth, the mother again provides the bulk of care for the offspring through nursing and other behaviors. In Trivers's terms, the female makes a greater *parental investment* than the male. This is true in all mammals and in most other animals as well.

Even though the female bears more of the cost of raising the offspring than does the male, the sexes benefit equally in fitness terms. If the offspring survives, it will carry approximately half of the genes of the father and half of the genes of the mother. Therefore, the female's prodigious parental investment is biologically valuable to the male. Her effort allows him to pass on his genes with a minimum of effort on his own part, namely, the metabolic costs of insemination.

When something is valuable to an animal, that animal will work hard to get it. Not surprisingly, male mammals exert great effort to find and fight for females. Often, the male risks life and limb in competing with other males for mating opportunities. Here is where the male pays his price. In all mammals, the males do more of the *competing for mates* than do the females. Males are the courting, competing sex in most other species, too.

Because the mammalian female works so hard in raising offspring, she must be careful about which male inseminates her. She must try to choose a male of high genetic quality, so that her efforts will not result in an unfit offspring. Another reason a mammalian female benefits little from promiscuity is related to internal gestation. Once she has been fertilized, she will not gain directly by copulating with additional males; except in rare cases, she cannot get any more pregnant.

On what basis should the female select the male? Since she cannot observe males' genes directly, she must evaluate males on the basis of their appearance, their **phenotypes**. Accordingly, in many species, the female will prefer a male that is a good fighter, that is, dominant over others. These males will tend to be large, strong, and vigorous—traits that are good indicators of genetic quality. In species with dominance hierarchies, these males will be the high-ranking ones. Dominant males are preferred by females in many mammals (H. D. Ellis, 1995).

The male, by contrast, benefits from not being too choosy. He should seek females of high genetic quality, too, but he should not turn down chances to inseminate even poor-quality females. If he inseminates a weak female and the offspring dies, he will not have expended much effort, but if the offspring happens to survive, the male will have succeeded in passing on half of his genes. Moreover, his fitness will increase as he fertilizes more females. Thus, Trivers's theory explains another widespread sex difference: *Females are selective* in their mating, and *males are more promiscuous*. This holds for all mammals and most other animals, as well.

Trivers's theory elegantly accounts for some very widespread behavioral sex differences in the animal kingdom. The more nurturant female is sought by males and is more discriminating in choosing sex partners. Males compete for mating opportunities, but because of male eagerness, females usually have little difficulty attracting sex partners.

In some species, including some fish, amphibians, and birds (but no mammals), the male provides the greater parental investment. One example is the male midwife toad, which carries the fertilized eggs around on his body while they develop. Consistent with Trivers's theory, greater parental investment by the male constitutes a biological resource for which females compete. In this case, roles are reversed. The male is less selective than the female, and the female is often larger and more brightly colored, in order to fight effectively and to attract mates. Rather than constituting exceptions that undermine the theory, these examples actually support it.

Trivers's theory is complicated somewhat by the case of species in which the male provides some parental investment beyond the sperm itself. In many birds, this takes the form of access to the male's territory. In many insects, the male must provide the female with a morsel of food in order to copulate with her. Male chimpanzees sometimes offer meat to an estrous female. Male olive baboons that defend a female and her young gain copulations with her (Smuts, 1985). In the black widow spider, tragically, the male must himself be the food, and he is eaten even as he copulates. In these species, the female may evaluate the male's apparent genetic quality and also his nuptial gift. The male must be somewhat discriminating, too; he does not want to waste his parental investment on a low-quality female—especially if his first, fatal copulation will also be his last!

In some animals, the male's parental investment is prolonged and extensive. Some male mammals may stay with the female through part or all of gestation or even longer. He may feed or protect the offspring either directly or indirectly by aiding the mother before or after she gives birth. These are the pair-bonding, biparental species, with highly dependent young that need the care of both parents.

Incidentally, a pair bond need not be **monogamous**. **Polygamous** breeders are those that form more than one pair bond simultaneously. If a male has multiple mates simultaneously, the condition is called **polygyny**. If a female has multiple mates, it is called **polyandry**. Species that do not form pair bonds are said to be **promiscuous** breeders.

In a pair-bonding species, the female will benefit from choosing a male that will stay with her during pregnancy or even thereafter to provide parental help. Thus, in pair-bonding species, females are highly selective, choosing males for their ability and willingness to provide parental investment, as well as apparent genetic quality.

For a female mammal, the choice of a male should always be made judiciously. If no pair bond is formed, she needs to choose a male with high genetic quality so that she does not waste her substantial parental effort on weak offspring. If a pair bond is formed, she needs to choose a male that is strongly bonded to her, as well as one of high genetic quality. In bird species, most of which are biparental, the female often coyly tests the male for signs that he is already mated before she copulates with him.

In animals that form pair bonds that last indefinitely rather than just for one litter or brood, both sexes need to take a long view in selecting a mate. Males of these species will benefit from choosing a female of high **reproductive value**: expected future number of offspring. An animal that is just entering its reproductive years theoretically has the highest reproductive value. As it gets older, its reproductive value declines. An immature animal has lower reproductive value than one just entering its reproductive years because it may die before maturing and thus have no future offspring (Figure 5.1). Thus, a male should choose a female that is just becoming fertile, in order to have all of her reproductive span ahead of him. If he selects an older female, he will have to spend **mate search time** replacing her when she ages.

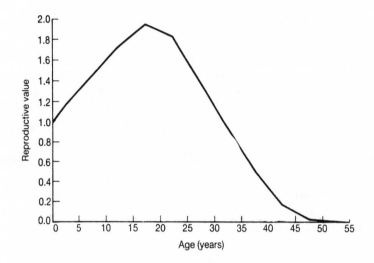

Figure 5.1 Characteristic Variation of Reproductive Value with Age. Data from Mexico, 1966. Adapted by permission from Crawford (1989).

Unlike females, a male need not be too choosy about casual sexual partners. If he inseminates a weak or old female, he will lose little in terms of time and effort if she does not give birth. Only if he forms a pair bond with her does it pay for him to be highly selective because he will incur a considerable commitment of time and effort.

A pair-bonding male should also guard against being **cuckolded**, that is, deceived into caring for the offspring of a rival. If cuckolded, he will wind up expending time and effort in helping a rival male to reproduce—which is about the worst thing he can do in terms of his fitness. Consequently, males in pair-bonding species will be selected for guarding their mate against interloping males and for other **anti-cuckoldry tactics.** For example, a male hamadryas baboon will repel an intruding adult male and will punish his mates if they stray from him (Kummer, 1971). This is similar to sexual jealousy in men, which occurs universally and may be functional in maintaining the pair bond. In a longitudinal study, couples with low jealousy scores were subsequently more likely to break up (Mathes, 1986).

Males in a pair bond, then, must guard against (be made jealous by) even a single sexual encounter between his female and another male. If a conception occurs, he may wind up cuckolded. If, however, his mate leaves him permanently, he at least will not waste any parental effort on another male's offspring.

A female in a pair bond will, in theory, experience jealousy under somewhat different conditions from a male. If her mate deserts her, she loses his continuing parental efforts. But if he strays only temporarily and does not become committed to another female, she loses little. In other words, her biological fitness is threatened more by a "homewrecker" who takes away her male's parental services than by her husband's one-time lover.

In summary, sexual reproduction has resulted in a general differentiation of males and females that extends to behavior. Trivers's theory accurately accounts for sex differences in reproductive behavior and anatomy in all species that have been studied. For example, in all mammalian species, the female provides the greater parental investment and is more selective sexually than the male. The male mammal is usually larger and more muscular than the female, and he takes longer to mature into that larger size (see Chapter 8). Males are also at special risk for injury and premature death in competing for females (see Chapter 9).

Thus, the male pays a price for the female's nurturance of their common offspring. The female reproductive strategy maximizes **parental effort;** the male strategy maximizes **mating effort** or competition for females. It is indeed true that men want only one thing. But so do women. And it is the same thing: Both want reproductive success. The sexes partition their **reproductive effort** differently, but they are equally interested in reproducing. The female's parental effort happens to benefit the male, and the male's mating effort benefits the female by revealing his value as a mate. Ultimately, however, each sex behaves as it does solely in the interests of its own reproductive fitness. These behaviors have resulted from sexual selection, that is, natural selection operating on the sexes differently.

Trivers's Theory Applied to Humans

A review of behavioral sex differences in our species reveals a number of findings consistent with Trivers's theory. With regard to *parental behavior,* women perform more child care than men in every culture (Daly & Wilson, 1983; Friedl, 1975; G. Mitchell, 1981; van den Berghe, 1980). Worldwide, other caregivers are also more likely to be female. In nonhuman primates, too, juvenile as well as adult females tend to exhibit more nurturant behaviors and fewer hostile behaviors toward infants than do males (Munroe & Munroe, 1975; G. Mitchell,

1981). Women spend more time in and around the home than do men and hence are in the better position to provide child care and other domestic labor. In prehistoric times, women were constantly pregnant or lactating, and so were less able to travel far from the settlement. Thus, the sex differentiation of labor in the human family parallels the primordial sex differentiation of the gametes—one for nurturance, the other for mobility.

Other motivational sex differences in humans are also consistent with Trivers's theory. Much evidence exists for greater *male promiscuity and interest in sexual variety*. Pornography and prostitution cater overwhelmingly to males' interest in sexual variety cross-culturally (Symons, 1979). In a large survey of U.S. adolescents, 80 percent of the respondents who were in the "promiscuous" category (several different sex partners in the past month) were boys (Sorensen, 1973). Desire for extramarital affairs seems to be very common in men (Frank & Anderson, 1979), with 48 percent of U.S. men saying they would like to engage in extramarital sex if they could do so with impunity, but only 5 percent of women saying so (Daly & Wilson, 1983). Similar results were reported in Germany. The human tendency toward polygyny also attests to greater male promiscuity. Polygyny is allowed in about 80 percent of cultures, whereas polyandry is very rare (Murdock, 1967). The less-discriminating sex drive of the male is also indicated by the far higher incidence of **paraphilias** (atypical sexual attraction) in males. Still, in all cultures, almost all men seek to marry, and do marry if they can afford to. Men tend to follow a mixed strategy of marrying but also seeking—or at least not declining—extramarital sexual opportunities.

Also consistent with the theory are data on sex differences in *sexual assertiveness*. In no culture are the women more forward sexually than the men (Stephens, 1963). Despite this, women are actually more selective than men, as the theory holds. Men may be the initiators, but women are usually the deciders (cf. Kummer, 1971). Men typically make many sexual approaches, of which but few are accepted. Accordingly, women often initiate romantic encounters—but they do so covertly, perhaps so they will not appear promiscuous. Observational research in U.S. bars has shown that women typically made the initial approach by means of nonverbal signals (Moore, 1985). As noted previously, female flirtation behavior is similar in different cultures, suggesting an evolved basis (Eibl-Eibesfeldt, 1989). Flirtation seems to involve alternating threat and submission (or intimacy) signals, perhaps allowing the woman to keep the man interested—but not too assertive—while she evaluates him as a potential mate. A woman encourages a man by eye contact and smiling (intimacy and submission) and raised eyebrows (interest and nonanger), and she coyly keeps him at a respectable distance by looking away (rejection). Lastly, sexual modesty is primarily a female trait; females very seldom go nude in cultures where males cover the genitals (Munroe & Munroe, 1975). At about 9 years of age, Israeli kibbutz girls insisted on sex-segregated showers despite a very liberal cultural attitude toward sex (Spiro, 1979).

The *competitiveness* of males and females differs as expected, with males more competitive and aggressive than females (see Chapter 9). Even as young children, boys tend to be more competitive than girls in the sense of wishing to "be the best" (Freedman, 1979). Men often compete for social rank and advertise their status, and gain mating opportunities thereby. Around the world, a man's social rank is a more important factor affecting his marriageability than is a woman's (Buss, 1994). Cross-culturally, men's dress and ornamentation typically express their social rank, whereas women's dress usually communicates their marital status (Low, 1979). The relation of male ornamentation to gaining mates is suggested by the fact that men's clothing is more ostentatious in polygynous societies (in which mate competition logically is more severe) than in traditionally monogamous ones.

Sexual jealousy in men and women follows expectations from Trivers's theory. Cross-culturally, infidelity in a wife is typically grounds for severe punishment of both the wife and the intruder (Hobhouse, 1924). An unfaithful husband, by contrast, is seldom punished or criticized, as long as his paramour is not married. In most cultures, a cuckold is ridiculed (Freedman, 1967), another indication perhaps of the fundamental undesirability of being cuckolded. Sexual jealousy is a frequent cause of murder worldwide, and the vast majority of perpetrators are men (Daly & Wilson, 1988). The great distress that his wife's infidelity causes a husband probably helps explain the rarity of polyandry. Only a few such cases occur, and those that do always happen under extraordinary circumstances, such as brothers sharing a wife (Daly & Wilson, 1983).

Again consistent with Trivers's theory, the releasing stimuli for jealousy differ somewhat between men and women. When U.S. college couples were asked to role-play a situation that would make them jealous, men were more likely to depict a sexual encounter between their girlfriend and a rival. The women tended to refer to losing their boyfriend's attention (Teismann, 1975). Similarly, men reported that they would feel the most jealousy if their girlfriend had sex with another man, whereas the most potent releaser of jealousy for women was their boyfriend's showing romantic interest in another woman (Buss, 1994; Wilson & Daly, 1992).

The theory also accounts for other universal criteria for mate choice in humans (see Chapter 13 for details). For example, it explains *men's preference for youthful mates.* In seeking a wife, men tend to prefer a young woman because youth in a female is a better predictor of her reproductive value than it is in a male. A young bride is likely to bear more children than an old one, but an old man will be almost as fertile as a young one. Around the world, youth is more highly valued in brides than in grooms (Daly & Wilson, 1983; Buss, 1994). In fact, the bride is usually around the peak of her reproductive value (in her late teens) in traditional societies (see Chapter 7).

In Buss's (1994) cross-cultural research, however, men's preference for a young bride was actually weaker than women's desire for an older groom. Women preferred a husband who was 3.5 years older than they, whereas men desired a wife who was only 2.5 years younger. Women may prefer a husband older than they because men need time before they can compete effectively for social and economic status. As stated earlier, around the world, men tend to marry when they can afford to do so.

Women in all cultures prefer to marry a wealthy man (Buss, 1994). In polygynous cultures, those men with more than one wife tend to be wealthy (Daly & Wilson, 1983). In monogamous societies such as the United States and Germany, a wealthy man tends to get an attractive wife. In most cultures, the bride's family expects the husband to pay a bride price, in the form of goods or economic services; the payment of a dowry is a rare phenomenon. Nuptial gifts from courting males are common across cultures, in courtship and marriage, or in the form of prostitution, which is virtually universal and is legal in about 100 countries.

Evidence abounds for the importance of *physical attractiveness* in mate selection in both sexes. For example, strong, dominant men who would be good fighters tend to be preferred as mates around the world (Buss, 1994). Standards of attractiveness show some cross-cultural consistency, suggesting an evolved basis (Jackson, 1992). If attractiveness is important in mate selection, it is not surprising that appearance is very closely related to self-esteem in adolescence (Harter, 1989; Lord & Eccles, 1994).

Motivational Changes at Adolescence

Trivers's theory helps to explain the profound motivational changes of adolescence. As young people move into reproductive maturity, they increasingly exhibit the sexual and amorous emotions. Sex and love become obsessions. For girls, interest in babies increases (see Chapter 10). For both sexes, too, concern with social standing increases, as though the modality of pride and shame is intensified. Both sexes cultivate and show off their desirable attributes (Buss, 1994). In particular, boys and girls become preoccupied with their appeal to the opposite sex.

The ultimate reason for this increasing competitiveness seems to be that a new biological resource is now at stake. This would explain why *competition intensifies at reproductive maturity, especially among males.* This occurs in many species, from bullfrogs to horses. The young males begin to compete with the older males, as well as among themselves.

Although difficult to document, this same phenomenon seems to occur in humans (see Chapter 2). As in other primates, male youths in all cultures rise in status. To accomplish this, they may very well undergo an increase in competitive motivation—in sensitivity to pride and shame. Neill (1985) concluded from a review of observational research on boys that "roughness peaks in adolescence" (p. 1381). Boulton's (1992) 13- to 16-year-old British subjects reported that rough-and-tumble play had become rougher as they had become older.

Pride/shame seems to play several additional roles in the maturing individual's emotional life. An individual's *pride, or self-esteem, largely reflects success in exhibiting high mate value* (see Chapters 11 and 12). For males, pride seems to reflect physical attractiveness, sexual conquests, economic success, and general social dominance. For females, pride appears to result from physical attractiveness, success as a parent, and having a devoted, high-status husband. A man is shamed by being cuckolded or humiliated by his wife, and a woman is shamed by being deserted or being viewed as promiscuous.

Thus, adolescents do seem to undergo the motivational changes that are expected on theoretical grounds. Aristotle's characterization of youth as sexually unrestrained, passionate, irascible, facetious, and fond of victory begins to make some sense.

Summary

Men seem to exhibit the mating strategy typical of pair-bonding mammals. They are more promiscuous and sexually jealous than women. They prefer a young, attractive, sexually faithful mate but also seek casual, low-cost sexual variety. In this way, the male maximizes the advantages of both the *dad* (parental effort) and the *cad* (mating effort) ploys. Of course, the situation that the individual finds himself in may render one of these pure strategies preferable to a mixed strategy. As in many other species, competitiveness increases at maturity, especially in males.

Women are more parental, sexually selective, and wary of desertion than men. The ideal female strategy seems to be to choose an attractive, dominant, amorously faithful male who is a good provider. However, conditions may dictate an alternative strategy (see Chapter 13).

The foregoing passages emphasize sex differences, not similarities. But the sexes are similar in many ways. For example, both seek kindness in a mate, and in both sexes, pride, or self-esteem, seems largely to reflect mate value. However, specieswide sex differences do exist, and they must be explained. Trivers's theory provides a powerful explanation for them. It is particularly relevant to the study of adolescence, when sex differences in behavior intensify in all cultures (Whiting & Edwards, 1988).

Even so, human sex differences within a population are seldom absolute. They are only average differences. Usually, there is a great deal of overlap between the male and the female distributions for a given trait, since ours is only a mildly dimorphic species. Moreover, individuals who are less sex differentiated are no less normal than are individuals who are more sex differentiated. If more sex differentiation had been adaptive, we would have it. Although individuals who are somewhat more sex differentiated than average may enjoy some benefit in mate competition, this presumably was offset in evolution by some disadvantage in nonsexual pursuits, such as parental competence or physiological efficiency.

It should be emphasized that no value judgment is being placed on these examples of evolved sex differences. They simply exist around the world. They are not "stereotypes," if that term is used to mean inaccurate characterizations. They are also not "roles," if that term is meant to suggest that they are scripted solely by culture. Moreover, because evolution takes a very long time, there is no point in waiting for things to be different or pretending that the sexes are more similar than they are. We are stuck with our human nature, and this includes some significant sex differences in behavior. Evolution takes too much time to adjust to the comparatively fleeting cultural norms and practices. It is culture that has to do all the adjusting to biology, if the two are to be compatible.

In a sense, each sex has only itself to blame for the attributes of the opposite sex. Our same-sex ancestors chose the sort of mates they liked and hence the opposite sex we now have. These choices tended to be advantageous, often in subtle ways, to the individuals making them.

Evolved sex differences may, in theory, be overridden by socialization, but the best attempt to do so was a failure. Early in the twentieth century, Israeli kibbutzniks began trying to abolish sex roles. They attempted this out of their own ideological convictions, not because of outside coercion. Yet every generation of kibbutzniks became more traditional than the previous one, and the attitudes of kibbutzniks eventually became more traditional than those of Israelis in the surrounding society (Tiger & Shepher, 1975). Moreover, individual kibbutzniks became increasingly traditional as they grew older; their own experience led them toward the old sex roles. Many women, some of whom had experienced miscarriages, voluntarily abandoned hard labor in the fields in favor of jobs in the nursery. Surveys showed that women played as large a role in the drift toward traditionalism as men; no male plot was perceived (Spiro, 1979). The outcome of this social experiment emphatically does not mean that abolishing traditional sex roles would be impossible. But it does suggest that strong external incentives would have to be applied and that many people would resist.

Given the power of this theory, evolved sex differences in human reproductive behavior need to be recognized by social scientists. It is unreasonable to view sexual jealousy as solely a cultural artifact when it also occurs in other pair-bonding species and when it makes good adaptive sense. Likewise, notions of equal male and female potential for nurturance are cast into doubt by the ubiquity of female predominance in parental care in our species and all other mammals. Mammalian motherhood has had 50 million years to be refined by natural selection.

These are questions of motivation, not of motoric ability. A man may be able to feed or bathe a child, but he may have little motivation to do so. Consequently, he may perform these tasks badly. Socialization can indeed change this to some extent. In some cultures, fathers interact often with children, and in others they hardly do so at all (Stephens, 1963). Also, there are individual differences within any culture, with some fathers being more nurturant than some mothers. The great variety that exists in human cultures testifies to the fact that many social arrangements are consistent with our human nature and have stood the test of time. However, there are biological limits to motivation, just as there are to sensation, perception, and cognition. And the sexes are not identical in motivation, any more than they are in sensory and cognitive properties (see Chapters 9 and 10).

6 The Social Context of Human Adolescence

The study of function is the analysis of how the environment has applied selection pressure to the members of a species. "Environment" includes an animal's social circumstances as well as its habitat. To understand the evolved basis of adolescent behavior, we need to know about the hominid social environment. These social features will be described in this chapter, with particular emphasis on how they affect adolescents.

The hominid line diverged from the great apes several million years ago. Hominids characteristically subsisted by hunting and gathering: In fact, about 99 percent of our evolution as hominids occurred when we were hunter-gatherers in East Africa (Stoddart, 1990). Our ancestors were seminomadic foragers living in small communities. Technology was very simple. It was these conditions that shaped human nature. Because evolution occurs so slowly, it is thought that no major changes in our genome have occurred since then. Our motives are basically those of the hunter-gatherers, or foragers. Even though our species has multiplied and migrated to cover the earth, we have retained many basic social features that derive from forager times.

Ethologists and others interested in the basics of human nature, therefore, have paid close attention to what we know of surviving hunter-gatherer peoples. By studying the behavior of contemporary hunter-gatherers, it should be possible to learn a great deal about our evolved behaviors and their functions. The behavior of foragers is prototypical of the behavior of our species, and therefore should provide clues to the evolved basis of human behavior—human nature, or the human ethogram. However, many characteristics of forager life vary from one hunting people to another; this way of life is found from the Arctic to the Tropics, so local differences are inevitable

(Bicchieri, 1972). These variations are of less interest to us here than are the typical traits of foragers.

In addition, clues about prototypical human social structure can be gained by identifying human universals in traditional societies, including foragers, pastoralists, and horticulturists. Specieswide behaviors, like specieswide anatomical traits, are likely to have an evolved basis, to be adaptive, and to be hard to alter (van den Berghe, 1980; see Chapter 1). Therefore, they provide a view of the prehistorical context for human adolescence. Accordingly, the first part of this chapter will describe various aspects of forager and/or universal human social life. This will be followed by a description of some aspects of modern adolescence that diverge from the prototypical model.

Human Social Adaptations

Group Living

One of the oldest social adaptations of our species is group living, or sociality (see Chapter 3). Arboreal primates tend to be solitary, and terrestrial ones, such as humans, tend to be social. The likeliest explanation is that terrestrial primates band together for collective defense, whereas escape in the trees suffices for arboreal species. Defense against predators and combat against enemies were doubtless collective efforts in hominids, as they are in chimpanzees (Ghiglieri, 1987).

Groups of foragers typically include from 20 to 60 members, as do other terrestrial primates (van den Berghe, 1980). Each forager band occupies a territory of between 30 and several hundred square miles (Coon, 1971), with seasonal migrations often occurring to pursue game or seek milder weather. These bands usually belong to a tribe of more distantly related individuals who share a language and culture, and who intermarry.

One of the best-studied forager cultures is the !Kung of southern Africa, who inhabit savanna grassland similar to that of our hominid ancestors. The !Kung live in bands of about 30 (mostly related) individuals, and they move occasionally in search of food or for other reasons (M. S. Smith, 1987). The !Kung, a rather short people, live in grass huts in semipermanent villages; they sing and play music, tell stories, settle disputes by consensus, exchange gifts rather formally and keep track of obligations, and are intimately familiar with the plants and animals of their environment (Shostak, 1981). At the core of each village are the huts of a group of closely related older people who share food and other goods, travel together, and maintain the traditions of the group. !Kung women gather plant food for about two days per week and spend about four hours per day at child tending and domestic tasks. The men hunt about three days a week but are successful only about one day in four. They spend about three hours a day working around the village.

Age Structure

Because of the long period of immaturity in our species, child rearing lasts a long time. Even in the chimpanzee, a daughter remains with its mother until transferring to another troop before its first offspring is born, which occurs at about age 13. Chimpanzee daughters sometimes return to stay with the mother between estrous periods for life (G. Mitchell, 1981), and in some troops, few females transfer troops (Nishida & Hiraiwa-Hasegawa, 1987). A chimpanzee son begins to travel away from its mother for a few days at a time at age 7 or 8 but not longer until age 10; social maturity in male chimpanzees is reached at about age 15. Despite this prolonged association with the mother, chimpanzees must forage independently once they are weaned and build their own nests at night.

Parental care is even more extensive in our own species. Humans continue to rear their offspring actively for 10 to 12 years after weaning (H. Fisher, 1992). Moreover, maturity comes later in humans than in chimpanzees; women in forager societies typically marry around menarche (first menstrual period), at about age 16, and men marry in their early twenties. However, even adults with children continue to associate closely with both their parents. Humans in traditional, technologically simple cultures raise about half of their offspring to adulthood (Lancaster & Lancaster, 1983). This survival rate is relatively high for a primate and is due mainly to our extensive parental behavior.

Humans have evolved several unusual means of providing for and protecting the young. Food sharing is rare in primates, even between mother and infant; juveniles are especially prone to starvation because older individuals crowd them out in food competition (Lancaster, 1984). Adult humans, however, share food with juveniles, a behavior that may have contributed to humans having shorter interbirth intervals (3 to 4 years) than the great apes (Lancaster, 1984). In addition, human neonates have unusually abundant body fat, which provides a reservoir of calories (Worthman, 1993).

In the absence of modern medicine and sanitation, few people live past their forties. This life expectancy is similar to that of the great apes. Death in childbirth is a common source of mortality for women in traditional cultures; men are prone to death by accident or homicide (Chagnon, 1977). Even if hominid longevity averaged no more than 40, archeological evidence indicates that a few individuals lived to their seventies.

Food Acquisition

Subsistence patterns are important in shaping the anatomy and behavior of a species. In our closest living relative, the partially bipedal chimpanzee, the males exhibit a little cooperative hunting. However, our species regularly engaged in cooperative hunting and scavenging. In foraging peoples, anywhere from 12 to 86 percent of the diet is meat (K. Hill, 1982); among the !Kung the figure was reported as about 30 percent (Shostak, 1981). Acting cooperatively, several men could kill even large animals. Meat provides all essential amino acids, is calorically dense, and is well suited to our digestive system. But plant food, which was provided mainly by the women, is a more plentiful and reliable source of calories than meat. Thus, the sexual division of labor among hunter-gatherers allowed families access to both types of food (Friedl, 1975).

An early scenario to explain how collective hunting came about emphasized bipedalism, which supposedly freed the hands for hunting and weapon making. However, this does not account for bipedalism in females (Barkow, 1989). Moreover, stone tools appeared much later than bipedalism, and chimpanzees use tools, although not in hunting. The tool kits of Tanzanian chimpanzees and those of Tasmanian aborigines (thought to have the simplest human technology) are actually quite similar (McGrew & Feistner, 1992). However, once bipedalism freed the hands from use in locomotion, grasping ability eventually became serviceable for making and using tools, including weapons. But the first tools may have been not weapons for the hunt but rather stones for grinding plant food, slings for carrying infants, or sacks for transporting food (Fedigan, 1992).

More recent scenarios have stressed the freeing of the hands for carrying (M. S. Smith, 1987; S. Jones et al., 1992). About 8 million years ago, the woodlands of East Africa had become savanna grasslands. Our hominid ancestors, the Australopithecines, became fully bipedal about 5 million years ago, as evidenced by skeletal remains. Bipedalism may have evolved in order to allow hominids to carry food, including meat, back to the protective group. Chimpanzees show rudiments of manual carrying; they sometimes carry nuts or tools while traveling tripedally (McGrew & Feistner, 1992).

Bipedalism may also have been a more efficient form of locomotion for traveling between scattered food sites, such as fruit trees, on the savanna (Barkow, 1989). Improved grasping ability may then have arisen to facilitate the gathering of seeds, which became plentiful during the prolonged drought in the Miocene Age that expanded the African savanna (C. Jolly, 1970).

Another possible explanation for bipedalism is that upright posture exposed less of the body surface to the intense sunlight of midday, thereby facilitating cooling of the body and especially the burgeoning hominid brain (Campbell, 1966). According to this theory, hair was retained on the head to shield it from sunlight but was lost elsewhere in order to promote heat loss through sweating and radiation. Fisher (1992) suggested that sweating was necessitated by the energetic pursuit of game, but of course this does not explain the even greater hairlessness of women, so the brain-cooling theory may be better.

Upright posture and especially running are facilitated by a narrow pelvis. But a narrow pelvis restricts the birth canal, which may have led to hominid infants being born rather prematurely by simian standards. These premature infants, unlike simian infants that grasp their mother's fur with hands and feet, had to be carried for many months by the mother—another possible factor in the evolution of bipedalism. Hominid mothers therefore were impeded when they foraged for food; simian mothers can forage even in trees in relative freedom. Hominid women's difficulty in foraging may have increased the advantage of establishing pair bonds with males who furnished meat and protection.

Evolutionary scenarios such as this are highly speculative; it is difficult to determine the sequence of events. But the main point may not be to determine whether helpless infants led to pair bonding or vice versa. It is more instructive to note the adaptive interaction among the features of a species, however that behavioral and anatomical system evolved. Regardless of the precise sequence of events, a given trait, such as bipedalism, may have come to be adaptive in multiple ways.

Large-game hunting provided an opportunity to share food. If some hunters were left with a surplus of meat, they could share it with other hunters or family members. Similarly, many social carnivores (e.g., wolves, lions, African hunting dogs, and hyenas) hunt large game cooperatively and share the kill with mates and young (McGrew & Feistner, 1992). Some of this sharing among social carnivores occurs reciprocally. Likewise, human hunters shared meat with other hunters, as well as with kin. Further, they traded meat for plant food and other goods that women possessed. "Food sharing and the division of labor provided a kind of insurance policy that compensates for fluctuations in individual success in the food quest at the same time that it permits regular feeding at two major levels of the food chain" (Lancaster, 1984, p. 11). In most hunting peoples, meat is divided according to social status, role in the hunt, and/or personal favoritism, which may reflect past obligations (Coon, 1971). A man then parcels out his share to his kin. Women distribute plant food to their families, but, because of its slow rate of spoiling, plant food can be preserved rather than being shared with other families.

Pair Bonding

Marriage may have begun as an exchange of meat for sexual access. In chimpanzees, temporary **consortships** sometimes occur between a male and female (Goodall, 1986). The female typically receives grooming, meat, and other favors from the male, and sex occurs at a high rate, even when she is not ovulating and cannot conceive. Although chimpanzees engage in much promiscuous mating, most conceptions occur during consortships (McGrew & Feistner, 1992). Chimpanzee consortships do not persist past conception, so the female does not receive any parental investment from her mate. However, consortship may have increased in frequency and duration in hominid evolution, until the full pair bond was **evolutionarily stable,** that is, a successful genetic variant.

Men may also have provided protection to their mates and offspring; male olive baboons receive sex in exchange for protection (Smuts, 1985). In almost all primates, males surpass females in protection, vigilance, and territorial defense (G. Mitchell, 1981), but in most species, this protection is provided on a collective (troop) basis.

Regardless of just how pair bonding came about, it eventually attained stability. Presumably, men and women who formed pair bonds reproduced more successfully than promiscuous breeders. They and their highly dependent children had the advantage of an efficient system of division of labor. The man performed most of the hunting and protection, and the woman did most of the gathering and nurturing. In species in which the male and female differ in size, there is often some specialization of foraging behavior. For example, the male orangutan usually forages on the ground, whereas the smaller female stays in the trees (Galdikas, 1979). This arrangement reduces food competition between mates. In chimpanzees, the males hunt mammals, whereas the females gather insects (McGrew & Feistner, 1992). In humans, too, men prefer more protein than women, and women want more carbohydrates than men.

Exchange of meat and plant food between men and women may have been abetted by the innovation of the home base, something that is absent from other primates. This would have provided a rendezvous point and perhaps a protected area for preparation and consumption of food and care of children. In contrast, chimpanzees usually consume their food where they find it, and they have no home base except for temporary nests shared by mother and infant (McGrew & Feistner, 1992).

The importance of the opportunity for sex in maintaining the pair bond is a subject of debate. Humans are unique among the primates in that women exhibit sexual receptivity throughout the menstrual cycle, which means that sex can occur at any time rather than just at **estrus** (heat, or heightened libido around the time of fertility). The availability of a regular sex partner does seem to solidify pair bonds in our species (van den Berghe, 1980). Couples with poorer sexual adjustment tend to be less happy (G. E. Weisfeld et al., 1992). Moreover, women sometimes experience increases in sex drive during pregnancy (Masters & Johnson, 1966); in other words, sex provides a powerful marital adhesive just when a strong bond is most needed. Many birds and mammals, by contrast, maintain lasting pair bonds without engaging in frequent sex (Kleiman, 1977). Moreover, non-pair-bonding apes and the rhesus monkey sometimes copulate before and after estrus (G. Mitchell, 1981).

Another possible reason for the male to stay close to the female was the necessity for constant mate guarding. Whereas other female mammals signal their fertility by becoming sexually receptive, this clue was obscured by the hominid phenomenon of **concealed ovulation.** A man would need to guard his mate constantly against interlopers because he would not know when she was fertile (Alexander & Noonan, 1979). Thus, concealed ovulation would promote monogamy and its benefits to the female in terms of gaining paternal care. However, females in other primate species also sometimes are sexually receptive outside of their fertile period, and some of these species are not pair bonding (Hrdy, 1981). Moreover, the hominid male's need for constant mate guarding may have been too great a price to pay for forgoing a promiscuous strategy.

Hrdy (1981) pointed out a possible advantage of concealed ovulation for promiscuous-breeding female primates. By copulating with all of the males, a female primate would make each a possible father of her offspring. Therefore, no male would harm her subsequent offspring. In langurs and other pair-bonding mammals, by contrast, the male that supplants another male often kills his rival's offspring. Concealed ovulation is more characteristic of promiscuous than monogamous primates, thereby supporting the defense-against-infanticide explanation advanced by Hrdy (Sullen-Tullberg & Moller, 1993). However, since humans are a pair-bonding species, this is probably not the explanation for us.

We humans are very unusual, and perhaps unique among the primates, in that our single-male units live near each other (Daly & Wilson, 1983; Stoddart, 1990). Most pair-bonding species, such as the gorilla, arrange themselves in isolated single-male units; the male and his mates and offspring seldom interact with other units. This arrangement probably results from sexual competition among the males, as each male defends his harem and personal space from intruding males. In humans, the advantages of cooperative group living must have outweighed the increased risk of sexual rivalry; among foragers, cooperation extends to food gathering, food exchange, defense, and child rearing. Human family dwelling places may, like animal territories, serve to insulate, if not isolate, single-male units from each other. Human homes are considered private, in that permission is required by outsiders to enter them (Eibl-Eibesfeldt, 1989). The woman's constant sexual receptivity may also have helped to keep her man safe at home.

Among hunting peoples, wives are obtained mainly by exchange between bands but also by capture, usually across tribes (Coon, 1971). Women have been obtained by purchase where differences in wealth occurred, as among Northwest Coast Indian tribes. Outbreeding, or **exogamy**, serves to establish cooperative ties between groups that exchange wives, as well as to reduce inbreeding (van den Berghe, 1980). Other cross-cultural generalizations about marriage, such as the universality of the double standard (Daly & Wilson,

1983), are readily explained by Trivers's model of sexual selection (see Chapter 5).

Child Rearing

Women everywhere provide most of the active socializing of children (Tanner & Zihlman, 1976). Hunting requires men to travel away from the settlement and to encounter danger, but women can tend the children while foraging for plant food. Women collect plant food together. This allows them to supervise the children cooperatively, as well as to exchange information about the location of food and other matters. Elderly men also provide child supervision, as did the other men when not hunting.

In traditional societies, children experience extensive physical contact with the mother. In the great majority of cultures, infants sleep in the same bed as their mothers while they are nursing, that is, for the first 2 or 3 years (J.W.M. Whiting et al., 1968). These authors reported that in fewer than 10 percent of societies did infants sleep in a crib or cradle, and when they did, the mother was invariably in a bed within easy reach. In slightly fewer than half of cultures, the father also shared a bed with mother and infant. Only in Western societies, notably in middle-class U.S. families, do infants have a bed of their own. In a Japanese study, a child had a 50 percent chance of sleeping with one or both parents until age 15 (Caudill & Plath, 1966); from 16 to 26, sleeping with a sibling was more common, but in the absence of a sibling, the adolescent often slept with a parent.

!Kung youngsters are highly indulged by their parents. Physical punishment of any degree is rare, and children are not even scolded very often. They are in continuous contact with their mothers, being carried about in a sling during the day and sleeping with them at night. Infants feed on demand, and breast-feed for about 4 years. Mothers are very sensitive and responsive to their other needs as well; consequently, infants rarely cry for long, and thumb sucking is minimal. Fathers, older siblings, and other kin assist the mother in child care. The father furnishes meat, protection, and instruction.

Child Labor

In most traditional cultures, demands for work are placed on children. Typically, children begin performing useful labor between 3 and 6 years of age. In a study of four cultures, children spent 23 percent of their time working, including 16 percent in child care (Munroe et al.,

1984). Since all children are expected to engage in these activities, they do not feel oppressed. The children may, in fact, view this work as play, but utilitarian results obtain. This work is often performed in the company of mothers or other children who act as supervisors. Besides child care, children frequently run errands, gather and prepare food, and tend livestock (Bogin, 1988; Zeller, 1987). Because of their usefulness, as well as for companionship reasons, children are often adopted by grandparents and others without youngsters.

Zeller argued that children's ability to gather food and provide other labor contributed to the short birth intervals of humans and hence to our success as a species. Tending younger siblings is especially important in traditional cultures, and siblings are expected to cooperate even as adults (Cicirelli, 1994). Children's ability to learn childcare tasks would have been abetted by the evolution of language. Also, mothers would have been freed to leave unweaned children behind in the care of older children and a few adults, and thus to forage unencumbered. This arrangement would have reduced stress on the mother and thereby improved her milk supply, thus speeding weaning and reducing interbirth intervals.

The degree of responsibility that these tasks entail usually increases with the child's age. In a study of Nepalese and Javanese children 6 to 8 years old, about four hours a day were spent working. This figure rose to almost five hours for children 9 to 11, and it continued to rise up to adulthood (Nag et al., 1978). In traditional cultures, children typically begin to work full-time at 10 to 12 and take on a full adult workload at 14 to 16 (Neill, 1983). By age 12, Tiwi (Northern Australia) and Cree (Ontario) children are already self-supporting in the subsistence sense. Some tasks are not begun until the early teen years, such as cooking, hunting fairly dangerous animals, and heavy gardening chores. Among the Bakgalagadi of the Kalahari Desert, 12-year-old girls can run a household, not just put in a full day's work. Note, too, that children in less well nourished societies mature years later than modern youth, so to perform heavy or dangerous work at 15 or so is indeed challenging.

In foraging societies, older children help in raising younger ones. At about age 8, girls begin tending their younger siblings. In these small communities, there are few children close in age, so older ones must interact with younger ones. This is especially true of siblings because of protracted breast-feeding and the resulting birth spacing. Perhaps because it is boring to compete with a younger child, older children often relate to younger ones in more cooperative ways. Multiage groups tend to facilitate cooperative play that emphasizes complementarity of roles (Draper, 1976). In particular, older children in traditional societies often teach younger ones. Younger children, in turn, imitate older ones and aspire to acquire the skills that will allow them eventually to be the teachers themselves. The difficulty level of skills increases with age, so that tasks are appropriate for the child's abilities and so are not too boring.

Contact with Kin

Thus, children were tended by many individuals of both sexes and various ages. Most child rearing was provided by kin, who had a direct biological interest in their welfare.

In fact, all people in traditional cultures interact frequently with relatives. In virtually all of them, the extended family lives together—usually in the same dwelling (Stephens, 1963). Only about one-quarter of cultures have monogamous nuclear family households (J.W.M. Whiting & Whiting, 1960), and in these, other relatives almost always live nearby. With the exception of the Copper Eskimo, industrialized society may be the only case in which people usually do not live within residential kin groups, that is, within extended family compounds (Stephens, 1963).

In some cultures, the husband sleeps not in the house but in the men's lodge. If polygynous, he will rotate among the dwellings of his wives or else sleep in the men's lodge, which is a common feature in our species. The men's lodge is also used for communal ceremonies.

Sexual Division of Labor

The division of labor by sex is universal. The advantage of assigning some tasks to one sex and the rest to the other, rather than expecting everyone to perfect every skill, is obvious. Every culture has definite expectations about which sex is to perform most tasks (Table 6.1).

A few tasks are performed mainly by men in some cultures and by women in about as many other cultures. The manufacture of ornaments and leather products, erecting of shelters, and tending of domestic animals are as likely to be done by men as by women cross-culturally (Murdock, 1965). However, the great majority of tasks are performed significantly more often by one sex or by the other cross-culturally. Of the 46 tasks listed by Murdock (1965) in terms of how many cultures assigned the task to women, how many to men, and

TABLE 6.1   Division of Labor in Human Societies

	Number of Societies in Which Task Is Done by				
Task	Men Only	Men Usually	Either Sex	Women Usually	Women Only
Metal working	78	0	0	0	0
Weapon making	121	1	0	0	0
Pursuit of sea mammals	34	1	0	0	0
Hunting	166	13	0	0	0
Manufacture of musical instruments	45	2	0	0	1
Boat building	91	4	4	0	1
Mining and quarrying	35	1	1	0	1
Work in wood and bark	113	9	5	1	1
Work in stone	68	3	2	0	2
Trapping small animals	128	13	4	1	2
Lumbering	104	4	3	1	6
Work in bone, horn, shell	67	4	3	0	3
Fishing	98	34	19	3	4
Manufacture of ceremonial objects	37	1	13	0	1
Herding	38	8	4	0	5
House building	86	32	25	3	14
Clearing land for farming	73	22	17	5	13
Net making	44	6	4	2	11
Trade	51	28	20	8	7
Dairy operations	17	4	3	1	13
Manufacture of ornaments	24	3	40	6	18
Soil preparation and planting	31	23	33	20	37
Manufacture of leather products	29	3	9	3	32
Body mutilations (e.g., tattoos)	16	14	44	22	20
Erecting, dismantling shelter	14	2	5	6	22
Hide preparation	31	2	4	4	49
Tending small animals	21	4	8	1	39
Crop tending, harvesting	10	15	35	39	44
Gathering shellfish	9	4	8	7	25

(continues)

how many were indifferent, 36 tasks were predominantly (at $p < .001$) performed by one sex or the other (G. E. Weisfeld, 1986). In a few cultures, the usual trend was overridden. For example, in 91 cultures, boat building is done by the men, but in 8 cultures, it is done by both sexes and in 1, it is done by the women only. Obviously, however, boat building is usually done by men in our species, possibly because

TABLE 6.1 (continued)

| Task | Number of Societies in Which Task Is Done by | | | | |
	Men Only	Men Usually	Either Sex	Women Usually	Women Only
Manufacturing nontextile fabrics	14	0	9	2	32
Fire making	18	6	25	22	62
Burden bearing	12	6	35	20	57
Preparation of drinks, narcotics	20	1	13	8	57
Manufacture of thread, cord	23	2	11	10	73
Basket making	25	3	10	6	82
Mat making	16	2	6	4	61
Weaving	19	2	2	6	67
Gathering of fruits, berries, nuts	12	3	15	13	63
Fuel gathering	22	1	10	19	89
Pottery making	13	2	6	8	77
Preservation of meat, fish	8	2	10	14	74
Manufacture, repair of clothes	12	3	8	9	95
Gathering of herbs, roots, seeds	8	1	11	7	74
Cooking	5	1	9	28	158
Water carrying	7	0	5	7	119
Grain grinding	2	4	5	13	114

Adapted from G. P. Murdock. 1937. Comparative data on division of labor by sex. *Social Forces, 15,* 551–553. Reprinted by permission.

Note: In addition to these tasks, Stephens (1963) noted that in all societies, house-keeping and care of young children are primarily women's work.

men used boats for fishing and hunting sea mammals and therefore knew how they had to be constructed (Friedl, 1975).

These data suggest that there is an evolved basis to the particular details of division of labor by sex, that it is not merely a cultural artifact. Men and women probably found their assigned work congenial to their aptitudes and interests (see the description of Israeli kibbutzim, Chapter 5). Cultures that assigned work according to the aptitudes and interests of men and women presumably had an advantage over those that ignored them. For example, women may forage for plant food partly because of their aptitude for recalling the location of objects (see Chapter 9).

Why are tasks assigned to the sexes in the patterns in which we find them? Around the world, women perform tasks near the home, including washing, cooking, water carrying, and sewing (van den

Berghe, 1980). Men hunt, make war, herd livestock, occupy leadership positions, and work with heavy, hard materials. This arrangement is compatible with the greater parental investment of women. A hunter-gatherer woman spent about 15 years lactating, 4 years being pregnant, and only 4 years doing neither (Lancaster, 1984), so she was perennially burdened with either pregnancy or an infant. Women can tend children if they are performing repetitive, interruptible, safe tasks but not if they are to hunt or herd (J. K. Brown, 1979). Moreover, they can gather plant food if accompanied by children, but they could not have hunted if pregnant (Friedl, 1975). Murdock and Provost (1973) concluded from their factor analysis that much of the division of labor between the sexes can be accounted for by the need for childbearing women to remain near the settlement and by the need for masculine strength and endurance for hunting and related tasks.

Exercise of Authority

In all traditional cultures, older individuals dominate younger ones, and males have authority over females (van den Berghe, 1980). Tribal leaders tend to be men in late middle age. Even married men with children are under the authority of their fathers. Women in traditional cultures defer publicly to their husbands; the West, with its tradition of chivalry, is the only exception in this regard besides the Berbers of North Africa (Stephens, 1963). This may be related to the fact that in all cultures, men tend to be older than their wives (van den Berghe, 1980). However, women usually exercise authority in domestic and child-rearing matters, and they are often quite influential over their husbands in the privacy of the home (Friedl, 1975; G. E. Weisfeld, 1990).

Among foragers, individual differences in status and authority are relatively minor. Since most foragers are seminomadic and can preserve and transport food only with difficulty, wealth is hard to accumulate. Some hunters obviously are more successful than others and can give away surplus meat in exchange for social prestige or a desirable bride. But among foragers, few men can afford more than one wife. Polygyny only became common with the advent of agriculture, which allowed some men to store surplus food and hence accumulate wealth.

Foraging societies are relatively egalitarian. In most hunting societies, a chief emerges informally because of his hunting prowess, generosity, wisdom, and other such traits. He exercises authority subtly rather than bluntly. Decisions are typically confirmed by consensus.

Ensuring Good Conduct

In hunting cultures, relatively few disputes arise either within or between families (Coon, 1971). Theft is rare because everyone knows who owns what—and because there is little to steal. Alimony disputes do not arise because wives retain their own possessions when they marry and if they divorce. When trouble does arise, the most common issues concern the distribution of food, adultery, and violation of a tribe's territory. Cross-culturally as well as in foragers, disputes over women are the most frequent cause of within-group murder (Freedman, 1967; Coon, 1971).

In most traditional cultures, young people are under the close supervision of older children and adults, including nonparents. Order is maintained by respect for and observation of elders, by moral tales, and by instructive rites (Coon, 1971). Merely pointing the way or a mild rebuke usually suffices to bring about good conduct. This is probably because, in a cooperative society, an uncooperative individual is severely disadvantaged. No such institution as police or prison exists or is needed in most traditional cultures.

In extreme cases, a miscreant is ostracized from the tribe, as happens among the G/wi Bushmen of Botswana (Coon, 1971). This fate is usually tantamount to a death sentence because of the difficulty of surviving on one's own. Alternatively, the group decides to allow the kinsmen of the victim of the misdeed to kill the perpetrator. If a dispute cannot be resolved by negotiation of a settlement by the principals or the group, fights sometimes arise and escalate as kin become involved. Sometimes, a tribal chief is selected to rule over several bands in order to keep the peace.

In larger traditional societies, disputes may be avoided because they can escalate to involve the partisans of each disputant (Friedl, 1975). There would seem to be an incentive for the original disputants to settle their differences rather than have to call in their kin for support, thus leading to a wider and more costly confrontation and to obligations to one's supporters. But feuds of this sort are fairly common, as in pastoral cultures in which livestock can be stolen (Nisbett, 1996).

Another factor of forager social life that may promote good conduct is the dearth of privacy. Homes with private rooms are a fairly recent Western invention. Certainly, it is restful to be able to retreat to one's own personal space occasionally, but closed doors can also provide a barrier to the detection of misdeeds such as child abuse and adultery. Smith (1987) cited lack of privacy as one explanation for the rarity of child abuse among the !Kung. He also noted that the small, closed group of the !Kung makes it necessary to resolve many disputes that might otherwise fester in a larger society. Again, the social structure forces !Kung people to learn how to cooperate.

Cooperation may also be enhanced by the dearth of strangers, with whom reciprocal altruism is risky. Among the !Kung, children virtually never met a stranger (M. S. Smith, 1987). Since they were always among friends and kin, altruism must have been the prevailing norm. Accordingly, a high degree of cooperation is observed in traditional cultures compared with industrialized countries. In a game requiring dyadic cooperation for individual success, children from rural or traditional societies easily surpassed urban U.S., Mexican, and Israeli children (Munroe & Munroe, 1975). The relative social and kin isolation of industrialized society may also help explain the extraordinary devotion to pets and the extreme grief experienced upon loss of a loved one (G. Mitchell, 1981).

Patrilocalism

As mentioned previously, in most cultures, three generations dwell together. Usually, the house or compound includes the husband's parents rather than the wife's. Patrilocalism characterized 62 percent of 167 foraging societies; matrilocalism characterized only 16 percent (Ember, 1978). Patrilocalism, maintained by the practice of the bride moving in with her husband's family, ensures that the adult men in the community are related by blood but that the women are less so. This arrangement enables men to depend on their kinsmen for support in hunting and warfare. It also conserves the family land or herd within the male line of descent.

In most mammals, one sex or the other leaves its natal community before reproductive maturity occurs. This reduces inbreeding. But in many primates, the young remain with the parents until reproductive maturity, at which point one sex or the other usually transfers troops.

As a general rule, patrilocal primates form strong male-solidarity units just as humans do (Wrangham, 1980). For example, male chimpanzees stay in their natal troops and cooperate with their male kin in various ways. They inform each other of the location of food sources. (Female chimpanzees do not do this.) Male chimpanzees defend their territory collectively. They raid other troops, sometimes killing foreign males and infants. Another close relative of humans, the gorilla, also practices female transfer.

In matrilocal primate species, the vast majority, the adolescent males leave the natal troop to seek mates. The females tend to form kin-solidarity units. For example, in rhesus macaques, mothers support daughters in dominance interactions. Kin altruism would explain why the females cooperate in matrilocal species and the males in patrilocal ones.

Sexual Behavior

Human sexual behavior is very different from that of the chimpanzee. An estrous female chimpanzee attracts males by means of her red, swollen vulva, or **sex skin**, which is typical of promiscuous primate species (Harvey & Bennett, 1983). Chimpanzee males sometimes literally line up to copulate with a female at the beginning of estrus—an unusual "state of affairs." This cooperation is thought to be due to the genetic relatedness of males in a troop. However, once a female chimpanzee nears ovulation, competition for her is often quite violent (Goodall, 1986). But during the period of promiscuous breeding, sperm competition predominates (see Chapter 1). Accordingly, chimpanzees have large testes. By contrast, humans are a pair-bonding species; accordingly, men's testes are almost embarrassingly diminutive. However, some sperm competition does occur in humans (see Chapter 13).

Furthermore, as described earlier, often a high-ranking male chimpanzee establishes a consortship with a female, monopolizing her sexual services. The male and female stay together for several days around her fertile period, with the male often sharing meat with her. If the female is frightened, she may run to the male and embrace and kiss him (Goodall, 1986). In turn, the female usually provides more grooming to the male than vice versa.

Unlike the chimpanzee, we humans form pair bonds. Most human marriages are monogamous, even though polygyny is allowed by most cultures. And even where polygyny is permitted, usually only a few men can afford more than one wife at a time (although serial monogamy is rather common).

Even before puberty, sex play is ignored or tolerated by parents in most traditional societies. Among the !Kung, for instance, older children "play house." They set up a small "grown-up" village and play at food gathering, dining, and sex (Shostak, 1981). Later on, pairs of girls play at mother and baby, and boys and girls play as married couples, including polygynous arrangements. !Kung parents make some attempt to conceal their sexual activity from their children, but much of the time, it is impossible to do so.

Little effective restriction is placed on adolescent sexual activity in about two-thirds of cultures (Broude & Greene, 1976). Similarly, Murdock (1949) reported that premarital license prevailed in 70 percent of his sample of 158 cultures. This permissive pattern is especially typical of foraging peoples, and therefore, it presumably characterized adolescent sexuality in prehistory. Adolescent sexuality tends to be permitted where the wealth needed for bride prices is difficult to accumulate, as in forager cultures (Friedl, 1975). Nevertheless, premarital pregnancy is rare in traditional societies because girls are usually married around menarche when they are still infertile (Schlegel, 1995). Adolescent boys may be allowed to visit prostitutes if they can afford to do so, and homosexual experimentation may be permitted among adolescent boys even if it is not allowed for adult men.

Sexuality is more often restricted in pastoral and agricultural societies, which can accumulate wealth—especially in the upper social classes of these societies (Goethals, 1971). Arranged marriages and public weddings are usual in traditional cultures, especially in economically stratified societies (Daly & Wilson, 1983; Rosenblatt & Unangst, 1979). Parents in these cultures employ various means to prevent love matches with someone deemed unsuitable to the family's material goals (Lee, 1982). They may arrange a marriage early, even in childhood. Alternatively or in addition, they may sex segregate nubile youths, as is done by secluding girls on the Arab model (G. E. Weisfeld, 1990). They may have their daughter's genitals mutilated to control her sexuality (see Chapter 7). Or they may strongly disapprove of premarital sex; thus, promiscuity or even speaking publicly of sexual matters is considered "low-class," or vulgar (L. *vulgus,* "common people"). And parents may employ indirect methods of matchmaking. The main function of U.S. university sororities has been interpreted as regulation of sexual contacts (Scott, 1971).

Establishing an Identity

In traditional societies, personal options for adolescents were limited. For example, among hunter-gatherers, there might be no choice of occupation for boys except hunter or sorcerer (Friedl, 1975). Other decisions, such as whom to marry, were largely subjugated to the interests of family and tribe in many cultures, although not so much among foragers. The number of same-age acquaintances was small, thus further limiting one's choices of friends and lovers. The language barrier made communication beyond the borders of the tribe difficult, so that new ideas diffused only slowly. As a result of these realities, the notion of an identity crisis would have been untranslatable in, say, a forager society. Therefore, this Eriksonian notion (Erikson, 1968) provides us with little help in understanding adolescence in a fundamental, specieswide sense.

Still, adolescents in traditional cultures do undergo a number of important role changes (Schlegel & Barry, 1991). Adolescents tend to perform adult work and to dress like adults; however, they usually pursue different leisure activities. Adolescents often take on religious responsibilities but seldom political ones. Occupational choices are made by at least some boys in 65 percent of traditional cultures and by girls in 43 percent. An adolescent may have to decide whether to become a shaman, a midwife, or a master carver, all of which require prolonged training. Adolescents are judged largely as workers; boys' physical skill and girls' sexual attributes are also valued. Then, too, sexual behavior begins in most cultures during adolescence. In about half of cultures, the adolescent is expected to select a spouse, even if the choice must be confirmed by others. Furthermore, adolescents are less likely to be forgiven their transgressions than children, so the consequences for their reputations are now more momentous. The fact that adolescence lasts only a few years in traditional cultures means that they must prepare for adulthood in a hurry.

The Adolescent in Modern Society

If people in foraging and other traditional societies can be said to pursue a time-honored form of life that suits our human nature, then perhaps the unusual features of modern life impose difficulties on us. These species-atypical characteristics may be the source of some of our social problems. In other words, social problems may occur when institutions and social norms do not suit human nature (Benedict, 1934). Since adolescents seem to have more than their share of problems, it may be helpful to identify some of the experiences of modern adolescents that differ from those of adolescents in traditional societies.

The rest of this chapter highlights some of these differences. Many of the contrasts between modern and traditional society, such as those related to technology, are obvious and are readily recognizable from the preceding description of the latter. Therefore, emphasis will be placed on some less obvious idiosyncrasies of modern adolescent life. The following characteristics of modern adolescence, like those of traditional society described earlier, are simplifications. For example, the statements that follow apply only weakly to "ethnic" immigrant families in North America, which exhibit many traditional features, such as performing useful labor starting in early adolescence and having close identification with the family (Queen et al., 1985). Nevertheless, these generalizations may at least help us to consider the situation of the modern adolescent in comparative perspective.

Less Useful Labor Performed

The adolescent in modern society contributes little useful labor to the family, apparently because of the economic complexity of modern societies. The Six Cultures Study suggested that a low chore load for children is associated with economic complexity as exhibited by the United States and, to a lesser extent, India and Okinawa. Cultural complexity breeds an efficiency that reduces the need for child labor (J.W. M. Whiting & Whiting, 1973; B. B. Whiting and Whiting, 1975b). At the same time, formal schooling to provide training for these complex jobs occupies much of children's and adolescents' time.

This economic explanation is supported by historical data. Induction into adult work at a young age still occurred in Europe before the Industrial Revolution. Although the age at which children were sent away to work as servants began to rise in wealthier families from the seventeenth century on, it remained low until the middle of the nineteenth century in families working in agriculture and rural industry (Neill, 1983). For example, in Colonial America, young men who were fully grown were capable of performing a man's labor in the fields and so were regarded as adults. They could afford to marry and were assigned adult privileges and responsibilities, such as military service and jury duty.

Nowadays, however, children remain isolated from most forms of adult work until after puberty and are not granted adult status no matter how big they are. The modern strategy seems to be to sacrifice fertility for parental investment. Parents' investment in the form of

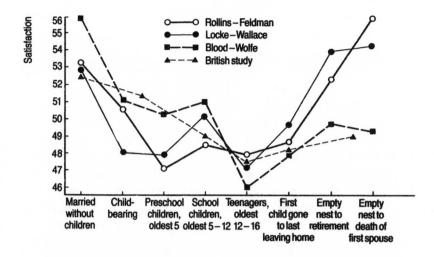

Figure 6.1   Developmental Course of Marital Satisfaction. Source: Argyle &
Henderson (1985). Reprinted by permission.

education of children mainly serves to increase the children's reproductive success, rather than that of the parents.

The exclusion of children and adolescents from performing much
useful labor may be developmentally disadvantageous for them. In
traditional cultures, adolescents are valued and respected because of
the adult-type labor they contribute. Families tend to have more children where child labor is valuable, as it is among farming peoples
(Mackey, 1996). In industrialized societies, by contrast, family size is
small. Adolescents are usually economic liabilities, consuming large
quantities of food and perhaps struggling over their textbooks but
not performing much tangibly useful labor. In the United States, the
situation may be especially bad because the parents of many adolescents must save money for expensive college tuition. As a result of
this economic dependency, adolescents may feel vaguely worthless,
and they may be resented by parents and other adults. In the United
States, Sweden, and Britain, marital satisfaction is lowest when the
children are adolescents (Argyle & Henderson, 1985; Stattin &
Klackenberg, 1992). (See Figure 6.1.)

The menial, boring jobs that U.S. high school students typically
perform do not seem to be advantageous to adolescent development.
They are associated with poorer school achievement, less parental
contact, lower ethical standards toward work, and more drug use

(Steinberg, 1996). Things may be somewhat better in other industrialized countries, such as Norway and Japan, where adolescents typically perform one or two hours of domestic work a day.

Adolescents might be given more fulfilling labor. Many do work as volunteers in social institutions. Greenfield (1974) recommended that day-care centers involve older children in child care. This would enhance parental skills, which young people in traditional societies practice extensively. Another suggestion is peer tutoring. Research has shown that peer teaching has benefits for tutor and student alike (Hartup, 1984). The tutor may or may not learn by teaching, but tends to exhibit more prosocial behavior and an improved attitude toward school. Students tend to learn in this setting, perhaps mainly by receiving individual instruction. Given a chance to do so, children spontaneously instruct each other, and they seem to enjoy such opportunities. They prefer that the tutor be an older child and of the same sex. In U.S. history, age-integrated schoolrooms in small towns compelled teachers to recruit older children to help younger ones, with generally good results. Similarly, Chinese middle schools are organized into study teams whose members help each other learn (Kessen, 1975).

However, it should be noted that traditional cultures differ greatly in the degree to which children work. Blurton Jones and colleagues (Blurton Jones et al., 1993, 1997) have observed that different cultures practice different reproductive "strategies" that affect the extent to which children perform labor. The !Kung indulge their children and expect little work from them—in fact, they discourage their children from foraging. Prolonged breast-feeding results in long interbirth intervals and a low rate of fertility but a high rate of child survival, a pattern also identified by Zeller (1987). Nevertheless, !Kung girls and boys begin to work seriously at about age 15.

By contrast, the Hadza of Tanzania are more punitive and demanding. Since food is more abundant for this group, their strategy is to produce more offspring but provide them with less parental investment and maintain higher expectations for labor.

But just how do Hadza adolescents benefit from foraging? As everyone knows, children and adolescents do not just passively obey their parents. In evolutionary terms, individuals who do not engage in adaptive behaviors will be selected out—whether they are obedient or not. That is, the genetic interests of parent and offspring, although closer than those of nonkin, are not identical; selection will have favored self-interested offspring over those that merely tried to fulfill their parents' genetic interests. Therefore, some **parent-offspring conflict** is to be expected in terms of goals (see Chapter 14).

To learn how adolescents' fitness is raised by foraging, Blurton Jones et al. (1997) gathered and analyzed observational data on foraging time and food gathered. They considered several hypotheses that might explain this behavior. They found that Hadza adolescents do not benefit from *practicing foraging techniques*, since these are already largely perfected by the end of childhood. Boys are good shots with arrows even before their teenage years. Nor do adolescents forage in response to *family size*, for time spent foraging was not correlated with number of siblings. Young Hadza children forage to enhance their *individual health*, since those who forage more tend to be heavier and since children's foraging is quite efficient (e.g., the most nutritious foods are targeted). However, many Hadza adolescents (older than age 10) are rather inefficient foragers. Some of the adolescent girls bring home much more than they can possibly eat, and the boys target unrewarding foods—honey and birds. Therefore, health is not a goal of adolescent foraging.

Adolescents do benefit from helping their kin to survive, since giving was biased toward close kin and toward young recipients, who are more needy. That is, Hadza adolescents gain from *kin altruism*. And they gain from helping their kin to survive because adolescents with more siblings subsequently have more live children. Younger siblings act as allies later in life, so, by helping them, adolescents gain via *reciprocal altruism*. But Hadza adolescent boys engage in less kin altruism than do girls. Why is this so? The boys must have an additional goal.

It turns out that Hadza adolescent boys also benefit by cultivating *reputations* as successful hunters, thereby enhancing their later reproductive success. The boys focus on gathering honey and hunting birds because these pursuits, though inefficient for foraging, enhance one's reputation as a hunter. Reputation is important for Hadza adolescent girls, too, since those with reputations as good foragers tend to marry successful hunters. The benefits of a reputation as a good forager may account for the fact that girls bring home more than is consumed. However, competition may be more intense among the boys, consistent with the general trend in animals (see Chapter 5).

Thus, Hadza adolescents compete for reputation, or social dominance, by the criteria of their particular culture. Likewise, among the

Bemba of East Africa, adolescent boys and young men try to prove themselves by feats of valor—making war, climbing trees to prune them, and hunting (Friedl, 1975).

This sort of functional analysis also offers a way to propose and test hypotheses about individual differences within a culture (Blurton Jones et al., 1997). Perhaps Hadza adolescent boys with needy kin eschew the goal of reputation in favor of that of kin altruism. This would explain why some boys act more "responsibly" than others. And adolescent girls with infant siblings may dig for roots with the women (an inefficient foraging technique) in order to help entertain the infant while the mother digs.

Blurton Jones and colleagues suggested that this sort of functional model may also help to explain divergences in goals between adults and adolescents in a given culture. For example, they proposed that in cultures with arranged marriage, such divergences may be minor: Adolescents may be eager to adopt adult values in order to exhibit behaviors that qualify one for a desirable spouse. In these cultures, adolescents may likewise embrace their parents' judgments about potential spouses. In the Hadza case, adolescent girls did not seem to know much about the boys' reputations as hunters and so may have readily heeded the wisdom of their parents in choosing a husband.

What motivates Hadza adolescents to behave as they do? Blurton Jones et al. say nothing about this, but there are several possibilities. Parents provide guidance, of course, being biologically interested in their children's mating success. Adolescents may also learn by observing their peers and elders. It seems highly probable that adolescents would admire and imitate older individuals who seemed successful with the opposite sex. Trial-and-error learning is another possibility, although it would not account for the selection of a long-term behavioral strategy such as investing in siblings who may return dividends. In any case, to attribute this behavior merely to "cultural values" is a bit vague and begs the question of why these values operate in just these classes of individuals within the culture.

Less Contact with Kin

If adolescents benefit from frequent contact with their parents, as they do in traditional cultures, then the modern trend in the opposite direction is cause for concern. In traditional societies, children begin to learn practical skills and values from their parents. In modern society, children and adolescents have relatively few opportunities to observe their parents at work, to be taught by them, or even to talk with them.

Fragmentation of the family seems to have occurred with industrialization (Lasch, 1977). First, fathers were drawn away from the family farm and to jobs in the city. Resulting wage differentials undermined extended family ties by discouraging sharing because wealthier individuals kept their earnings for themselves and their nuclear families. In a U.S. study, 60 percent of women had no relatives living nearby (Fischer, 1977). A study of the elderly and their families in the United States, England, Denmark, Yugoslavia, Poland, and Israel found that most lived within ten minutes of one of their adult children, and 70 percent saw at least one child each week (Shanas, 1973). But this is a far cry from traditional cultures, in which virtually all of the elderly live with or near their children and see them every day.

Second, wives have gravitated away from home and children. Early in the Industrial Revolution, wives stayed at home when men took factory jobs. Women who had worked as adolescents usually quit their jobs upon marriage or the birth of the first child (Hareven, 1984). However, women were eventually drawn to work outside the home. By the middle of the twentieth century, U.S. wives typically worked part-time and were at home when their children returned from school (Steinberg, 1996). But by 1990, over half of U.S. married women with children (including those with children under 6) worked outside the home (Popenoe, 1993). One U.S. study found that mothers who worked more than 20 hours away from home spent significantly less time with their children and adolescents than did women who worked fewer hours (Hill & Stafford, 1978).

Third, formal schooling was increasingly undertaken to gain training to be a factory worker, thereby reducing children's time at home and their contact with parents. With the spread of high school education, contact between adolescents and their kin was reduced further (Steinberg, 1996).

The trend continues, with families becoming ever smaller and more isolated from their kin. As women's full-time employment has increased steadily since the Industrial Revolution, so has the divorce rate (Goode, 1993; see Chapter 13). Also contributing to the low marriage rate in the United States is the large number of men who are too impoverished to marry (W. J. Wilson, 1987). By 1990, the proportion of single-parent children was 24 percent (Popenoe, 1993). Thus, even the nuclear family has become less common.

Even in intact families (those with both biological parents in the home), as mothers (and, to a lesser extent, fathers) increase their hours worked outside the home, parent-child contact is reduced. Over the last 25 years, the number of contact hours between U.S. parents and children has gone from 30 to 17; for foragers, the comparable figure is about 35 (Hewlett, 1991; Louv, 1990).

In particular, there seems to have been a decline in social contact between boys and men. In a representative sample of ten traditional societies, the combination of an older boy with a man was the most frequent form of adult-child association (Mackey, 1983). These contacts were found to be much less common in the United States than among the !Kung (Katz & Konner, 1981). It seems likely that these boy-man contacts are especially rare in the United States because most teachers are women and because of a dearth of all-male groups, especially in the middle class (Rubin, 1986).

Thus, adults' work takes place mainly away from home and in isolation from children. Fewer opportunities exist for children to observe their parents at work and in social contexts, and to interact with kin who have a shared genetic interest in them. Instead, children spend more time with nonkin in highly structured educational settings in which they receive little practice in social skills.

Is there evidence that contact with the extended family has developmental advantages? Child maltreatment seems to be less frequent where an extended kinship network is present (Giovannoni & Billingsley, 1970). In cultures where one or both grandparents serve as significant child rearers, the children tend to receive a lot of warmth (Rohner, 1975). In a Hawaiian longitudinal study, at-risk adolescents and youth who nevertheless developed into successful adults tended to have a multigenerational network of kin (Werner & Smith, 1982).

Sociobiologists have explained grandparents' indulgence of their grandchildren by noting that once the end of reproduction has been reached, one's fitness benefits come entirely from aiding kin. Kin may exert beneficial effects in a number of ways. One of the less obvious is that grandparents can continue to socialize parents, who then behave better toward their own children. Another, more direct possibility is that young people benefit from exposure to a multitude of adult models. According to one German study, the child's social development was a function of his or her involvement in the parents' adult social networks (Bronfenbrenner et al., 1984).

There are clear advantages to the intact family compared with step-families and single parenthood, as one would predict from sociobiological principles. Child abuse and homicide, sexual abuse, adolescent pregnancy, drug use, delinquency, school difficulties, and other developmental problems are far less likely in intact families than in others (e.g., Daly & Wilson, 1988; see Chapter 14). There is also some evidence of problems arising from the mother's working away from the home and turning a substantial share of child care over to hired workers (see Chapter 14). Not all types of family are equally likely to produce well-adjusted children.

Decline in Community

Other factors of modern life hamper the development of community. Large, "impersonal" cities with a high turnover of neighborhood residents allow people to remain anonymous and hence to misbehave without being detected. By the same token, community benefactors probably seldom become widely recognized. In terms of reciprocal altruism, unstable groups are prone to cheating. Studies in the United States and Finland (Pulkkinen, 1982) have shown that geographic mobility during childhood is a predictor of aggressiveness and dependency in adolescence and early adulthood.

Urbanization alone does not seem to explain this social breakdown. Some Chinese cities are huge and yet are divided into manageable, self-governing neighborhoods. Similarly, in some very large Dutch cities, neighborhood turnover is slow and neighbors are well known and hence subject to effective social pressure. Japanese cities likewise can be very large, but strong family ties help to minimize antisocial behavior.

Around 1980, about half of the U.S. population changed residence each five years (Steinberg, 1996). Although this figure is lower today, geographic mobility remains relatively high in the United States, with many Americans changing residence in pursuit of better jobs. Economic success seems to be more important to many Americans than social ties. In Sweden, by contrast, a philosophy of "normalization" is pursued. It is not considered normal to have to move to find a job. Previously, the Swedish government provided subsidies to enable unemployed workers to move to a city where they could find work. Presently, however, the policy is to provide incentives to businesses to open plants in areas of high unemployment, thereby bringing jobs to the people.

A sense of community is fostered, in theory, by similarity (see Chapter 11), and so economic disparities probably undermine that sense of community. The United States, being extremely stratified economically and with low and regressive taxes, provides relatively little support for the common good. The United States consistently scores among the worst of the industrialized nations in terms of drug abuse, births to unwed adolescent mothers, divorce rate, infant health, criminal violence including homicide and rape, sexually transmitted disease, educational achievement in all subjects, and literacy itself. Many of these problems directly or indirectly affect adolescents and young adults. Perhaps drawing comparisons among modern nations, not just between modern and traditional society, can provide examples of policies to be pursued in one's own country. For example, Sweden gives tax incentives to businesses that hire the young. Hungary provides subsidies to expectant mothers if they report for prenatal visits. Almost all industrialized countries guarantee paid parental leave and universal health care. The Netherlands allows mothers to work part-time while receiving full fringe benefits.

The automobile is another factor often cited as fragmenting U.S. neighborhoods and undermining socialization of children (Kay, 1997). With cars so widely used in the United States, few destinations are reached on foot. Suburban Americans seldom meet their neighbors, preferring the isolation of the auto-accessed shopping mall, dispersed houses, and even gated communities to the city square, park, front porch, tram, and pedestrian shopping street of earlier neighborhoods. As the auto industry promoted the building of expressways and the destruction of urban light-rail systems, U.S. cities were impoverished by the flight of affluent residents and jobs.

Another likely factor in the decline of community in the United States is television. Putnam (1996) argued that participation in civic organizations fell with the rise of television watching. Likewise, a Canadian study showed that the introduction of television was followed by a reduction in participation in social, recreational, and community activities. Heavy television viewers tend to be homebodies and suspicious of others, and therefore, perhaps they are disinclined to join with others for community improvement. Newspaper readership in the United States fell as television viewing rose, and it is lower than that among Europeans and the Japanese. This is probably a factor in Americans' relative ignorance of current events and lower voter turnout, and it likely detracts from citizens' political power. Television viewing is especially high among children and adolescents. It is associated with lower school achievement, and adolescents report it to be rather numbing rather than distinctly pleasurable (Csikszentmihalyi & Larson, 1984).

Pronounced Age Segregation

In most cultures, same-sex adolescent peer groups engage in leisure activities or work together (Schlegel & Barry, 1991). However, adolescents are well integrated into the social order and are typically constructive members of the community (Neill, 1983). This seems to be due mainly to the small number of adolescents and to a dearth of opportunities to operate independently of adults.

Modern society is relatively age segregated (Steinberg, 1996). Adolescents as well as children experience infrequent contacts with older or younger individuals, such as cousins. Large cities contain many children, who can be conveniently educated together with their age mates. U.S. teenagers spend more time talking with peers than in any other activity (Csikszentmihalyi & Larson, 1984). This is partly a matter of preference, but adolescents report that talking with adults is also pleasurable; however, adolescents seem to receive fewer opportunities to do so. Even when they work at part-time jobs, adolescents tend to work with people their own age (Greenberger & Steinberg, 1986). Suburban youngsters have even fewer adult associates than do their urban and rural counterparts (Garbarino et al., 1978).

Age segregation limits adolescents' opportunities for instructing others, as well as for being instructed. In traditional societies, older children are admired by younger ones for their abilities and the labor they perform. As children get older, they take on harder and harder tasks and gain in status accordingly. In our age-segregated society, there is little incentive for working one's way up this status hierarchy.

Siblings provide one form of cross-age contact, but there has been little research conducted on this relationship. In theory, siblings should have a strong tendency to help each other because they share half their genes on average (one-fourth if half sibs). In simians, siblings tend to be preferred as play partners over others of the same age and sex (Walters, 1987). However, this affinity is tempered by the fact that siblings often compete for the same parental resources. The resolution of these considerations seems to be that siblings behave like very close friends. Adolescent siblings report feeling about as close to each other as to best friends (Greenberger et al., 1980). Help between adult siblings tends to be reciprocal rather than unilateral as in other kin relationships (Essock-Vitale & McGuire, 1985). However, as expected, monozygotic twins are extremely close and cooperative (Segal, 1988).

One consequence of adolescent age segregation seems to have been the emergence of a youth subculture in the latter half of the nineteenth century in the United States (Hareven, 1984). During this period, various institutions arose that segregated adolescents from other age groups (Kett, 1977). These institutions included high school, juvenile reformatories, Sunday school, scouting organizations, and vocational schools. Ironically, these institutions emerged in order to socialize wayward youth, who were becoming less closely controlled by their families as industrialization proceeded. These institutions, especially high school, provided a setting for development of a distinct youth culture.

Out of the range of parental authority, adolescents often revel in their independence, cultivating in-group norms, slang expressions, distinctive clothing styles, and so forth to further separate themselves from adults (Barkow, 1989). If they have some disposable income, they can further isolate themselves in cars and other settings. A favorite ploy is to retreat behind a sound barrier of "music" that is insufferable to adults. The same adolescents often engage in a variety of delinquent behaviors, as though they have adopted the adolescent culture in favor of the adult one (Jessor & Jessor, 1977). For example, a study of 12- to 14-year-olds in the United States found that as more time was spent listing to youth-culture music, the adolescent's grades declined, as did the amount of time spent in study and academic aspirations (Burke & Grinder, 1966).

Any antisocial tendencies of adolescents may be aggravated by a possible sociobiological tendency for adolescents to be selfish family members. As humans reach the end of their reproductive years, they can only contribute to their fitness by aiding relatives, including their children and grandchildren. Hence, they tend to become highly altruistic toward their kin, as mentioned earlier. Adolescents are in the opposite situation. They are making the difficult transition to maturity and therefore greatly benefit from receiving altruism. Any aid that they receive may pay large dividends in terms of increasing their reproductive success, since all their reproductive years lie ahead of them. This may incline adolescents to be selfish or "obnoxious."

Summary

Humans succeed in raising a relatively large fraction of their young to maturity, yet our interbirth interval is rather short for a primate. Several adaptations have been credited with increasing our reproductive efficiency, including the protected home base, provisioning of juveniles by parents, and labor provided by juveniles starting around middle childhood. In traditional cultures, full-time work begins at about 10 to 12 years of age, and an adult workload is assumed at 14 to 16. Humans are highly cooperative in other ways—in foraging collectively and in the division of labor (including hunting and gathering) between husbands and wives. Child rearing takes place within a close-knit, stable kin and community network. Married couples live in clusters despite the risk of infidelity. Most cultures are sexually permissive toward their adolescents, but young people's sexual behavior tends to be restricted in societies in which major property transactions occur at marriage.

Research on the Hadza illustrates that traditional cultures vary considerably in the amount of work performed by adolescents. Many Hadza adolescents seem to be less dedicated to efficient foraging and more intent on cultivating a favorable reputation, or dominance status, which leads eventually to reproductive dividends. Other adolescents seem to follow the strategy of foraging efficiently so as to sustain younger siblings, who may later aid their reproductive success by acting as allies. Individual differences such as these may reflect family circumstances (e.g., age and number of siblings, arranged marriage versus love matches) and not just parental exhortations. The fitness interests of parents and their offspring are not identical. In particular, adolescents, who are embarking on the difficult transition to reproductive life, may tend to be demanding.

In modern society, kin ties are weaker and individualism is more prominent. The family was weakened by industrialization, which displaced labor from the farm and home. The extended family dispersed, giving way to the nuclear family, which is an aberration for our species. Family fragmentation has continued into the present, especially in the United States, where divorce and single motherhood are particularly common and where parents spend increasing hours at work and fewer in socializing their children. Developmental problems are less likely when children are raised by both biological parents (see Chapter 14).

Urbanization further undermined the sense of community by grouping adolescents into large, age-segregated high schools and other institutions, precipitating the emergence of a youth subculture. Age segregation reduces opportunities for socialization across age levels. Partly because of technological complexity and formal schooling, children and adolescents perform little labor for the family, and they experience few opportunities to be of service. Due to the lengthy training required to perform adult labor, adult status comes late.

7   Puberty Rites

In order to develop a further understanding of the basic characteristics of human adolescence, it may be helpful to describe one of its widespread features: puberty rites. That is, the specific functions that puberty rites serve may shed light on the functions of adolescence itself (cf. Schlegel, 1995). If the individual's biological and cultural programs tend generally to address similar functions, then a functional analysis of a major cultural institution such as puberty rites may elucidate the main features of the biological program.

Puberty rites are a widespread cultural *training or testing period and ceremony for inducting adolescents into adulthood.* They last anywhere from a day to a year. Puberty rites are common in traditional cultures, especially for girls. Even limiting their definition to the initiation ceremony alone, Schlegel and Barry (1980a) found them in one or both sexes in 56 percent of traditional societies around the world. Therefore, they may offer some general utility to members of our species.

The main utility of puberty rites may be that they help prepare the adolescent for social maturity. If so, then puberty rites constitute the cultural analogue of biological puberty, which likewise provides an intense, final preparation for mature functioning (G. E. Weisfeld & Berger, 1983). More specifically, puberty, and perhaps puberty rites as well, usher a child who is dependent on her parents into maturity when she will bear and help raise children of her own. As Charlesworth (1988) put it, the human life history can be partitioned into a prereproductive and a reproductive phase.

The young adult must be prepared to perform a number of social roles. She or he must establish a family and also participate in the adult community at large. Perhaps some of the universal tasks in attaining adulthood—mastering adult subsistence roles, finding and keeping a mate, caring for children, developing an allegiance to the community—are facilitated by puberty rites.

Ethologists typically analyze the function of a given trait by first specifying its phylogenetic distribution (see Chapter 1). Puberty rites, of course, are a uniquely human phenomenon and hence do not avail themselves of direct comparative functional analysis. However, puberty rites may enhance certain behaviors that we do share with other species in ways that can be understood functionally. For example, in various animals, pair bonds first form at reproductive maturity; analogously, when humans reach maturity, puberty rites usually entitle the initiate to marry. Pair-bond formation tendencies and cultural permission to marry share the same function of fixing the onset of nuclear family formation at the time of reproductive maturity.

As this example illustrates, parallels may exist between features of puberty rites and pubertal changes observed in humans and other primates. These parallels may not be merely surface resemblances but may also have functional significance. That is, the practices of puberty rites may interact adaptively with our ancestral behavioral and anatomical changes of puberty. They may form an adaptive complex that can be understood by considering all three domains. If a particular pubertal change in body or behavior evolved to accomplish some function, then it is likely that some cultural practice, such as an aspect of puberty rites, also arose to help fulfill this function.

In this chapter, functional explanations for some of the widespread features of puberty rites will be proposed. Sometimes, the function of a particular feature will be suggested by a parallel in primate adolescent behavior or anatomy. Because this is only a preliminary effort, some of these proposed functional explanations are speculative.

Puberty Rites in Overview

An overview of puberty rites may be helpful at this point, with emphasis on the general functions of this institution. It is necessary to focus on the modal, species-typical form of puberty rites in order to make adaptive sense of them and also to avoid entanglement in details of cultural variability. This is not to deny the importance and local adaptive value of cultural variations in puberty rites, but only to simplify the phenomenon for purposes of initial analysis.

Many scholars contend that one of the main functions of puberty rites is to help prepare the initiate to perform adult tasks. Puberty rites may be regarded as a crash course in adulthood, following the more leisurely training of childhood. To take one example, a !Ko

Bushmen girl at her puberty rites is taught to respect older people, to avoid sitting down at a stranger's fireside, not to shame her husband, and not to touch his hunting gear (Eibl-Eibesfeldt, 1989). She learns about birth and infant care. These lessons have already been imparted, but they are reviewed and stressed on this occasion, which lasts six days. For this instruction, the girl moves to a hut near the village, where she is attended by her grandmother or another older woman. Each day, the antelope dance symbolizing fertility is performed outside her hut by some of the women.

This example shows that puberty rites can supplement and underscore instruction that has occurred previously in adolescence. In societies where little learning occurs during the rites themselves, the reason is often the brevity of the rites (G. E. Weisfeld, 1997c). From a functional point of view, it seems rather unimportant when learning occurs—whether solely before or also during or after puberty rites. For this reason, the term *puberty rites* as used here will include intense adolescent socialization before as well as during or after the ceremony itself. This expanded definition also means that a larger fraction of societies have puberty rites. Probably all cultures provide accelerated socialization of their adolescents, even if this occurs and terminates informally. Thus, puberty rites as defined narrowly are nowhere near being universal, but their functional essentials may very well be.

What is taught during puberty rites? In traditional cultures, different skills are required of men and women. Therefore, the training that boys and girls receive during puberty rites is usually sex segregated, contact with the opposite sex being limited or completely taboo. Instruction typically is provided by a same-sex elder. Thus, one widespread function of puberty rites is probably *instruction in adult sex roles.* The adolescent not only is taught economic skills, which have been practiced already and may (especially among boys) continue beyond the initiation ceremony, but also receives guidance about being a husband and father, or wife and mother.

Puberty rites also seem to foster identification with the culture as a whole: *ethnocentrism.* The customs, ceremonial duties, legends, secrets, and values of the culture are imparted, resulting in allegiance to the culture (e.g., R. M. Berndt, 1972). Ethnocentrism may be viewed as a practice selected for on the cultural, rather than genetic, level. Cultures lacking ethnocentrism may have suffered from greater attrition by exogamy or military defeat than did chauvinistic societies. Likewise, group-living primates must possess some tendency (generally confined to one sex) to stay with the troop even after they have become independent of their parents. Furthermore, resident male chimpanzees join forces to attack or defend themselves against other troops.

Another function of puberty rites, many scholars claim, is to signal to the community the mature status and *marriage eligibility* of the initiate. As mentioned earlier, this aspect of puberty rites is analogous to the bodily changes of pubertal maturation, in that both communicate the attainment of maturity. Puberty rites for girls typically commence at menarche. Doubtless, marriage is also promoted by the emergence of the potential for romantic/sexual love at puberty (see Chapter 3). Thus, cultural, anatomical, and behavioral factors seem to conspire to incline the adolescent to marry; they serve a common function.

Features of Puberty Rites
Analyzed Functionally

Some of the common characteristics of puberty rites will now be analyzed functionally. The focus will be on widespread but not necessarily strictly universal features of puberty rites. If a trait is widespread but not universal, it may still have an evolved basis (see Chapter 1).

In his classic work, van Gennep (1909/1960) described all ceremonial rites—including those at birth, marriage, parenthood, and death, as well as puberty—as encompassing three steps: **separation, transition,** and **incorporation**. These steps provide a useful organizational framework for describing pubertal initiation ceremonies chronologically, even though all three actually occurred in only 17 of the 37 societies studied by Precourt (1975).

1. *Separation* from parents and the opposite sex commonly occurs at the start of the process. This practice may ease attainment of independence from parents and assimilation of adult sex roles. Typically, adolescents of both sexes continue to be trained in instrumental tasks by their same-sex parent during much of the day. But they often sleep with family, friends, or relatives, or in a special residence for initiates (Cohen, 1964); this is more common for boys (Schlegel & Barry, 1991). Here, the youth is tutored in social matters, away from parents, siblings, and the opposite sex. However, the bachelor hut sometimes provides a place for boys to practice sex, as well as to be instructed in it by elders (Bancroft, 1990; Schlegel, 1995).

Physical separation lends an air of significance to the process. One theory holds that prehistoric caves were sometimes used for pubertal instruction (Pfeiffer, 1982). The solemnity of the training period usually is underscored by the observance of food taboos or other restrictions; adoption of special garb, hairstyle, or bodily markings; or subjection to an ordeal. These markers also notify others of the initiate's special status.

In some societies, seclusion from the entire settlement takes place, especially for girls (Schlegel & Barry, 1980a). Upon reaching menarche, a girl of the Tukuna Indians of the upper Amazon hid from men for three months in a "seclusion hut" (Schultz, 1959). Among some Amerindians, boys undertook a pilgrimage to seek their vision, and Australian aborigines set out on a long "walkabout." In the nineteenth-century United States, some adolescents and young adults left home periodically to serve as an apprentice or domestic servant (Kett, 1977). Nowadays, young people may be sent away to boarding school or summer camp.

Separation from the family is exemplified dramatically by the Tiwi of northern Australia (Spindler, 1970). When a boy is about 14, a group of armed strangers appears at mealtime to demand the boy. The father, who has arranged for this visitation, feigns alarm and rushes for his spears; the mother begins to wail. The father is "subdued" by other villagers so that the strangers can carry out their duty, and the boy is borne off into the night. Subsequently, he is expected abruptly to shed the frivolous ways of childhood and exhibit solemnity and self-restraint as he undergoes his period of instruction.

The *sex segregation* of puberty rites doubtless facilitates mastery of sex-specific tasks. This cultural practice reinforces a universal sex-segregation tendency in early adolescence. Children everywhere show a marked increase in spontaneous sex segregation at about age 9. First the girls and then the boys show a decided preference for same-sex playmates during this "gang stage" (Nash, 1978; Vernon, 1969). These adolescent peer groups pursue leisure activities but may also perform work collectively (Schlegel & Barry, 1991). Also, cross-cultural research reveals that adolescent boys frequently follow around and observe older men (Mackey, 1983, 1996). Similarly, juvenile terrestrial primates typically play in sex-segregated groups, and adolescent male chimpanzees shadow older males (Goodall, 1986). Thus, puberty rites tend to institutionalize what may be a general primate tendency toward sex segregation (cf. Schlegel, 1995).

A *same-sex nonparent* typically provides the instruction in social matters (Hotvedt, 1990). The same-sex parent still furnishes adolescents with most of their training in subsistence tasks (Schlegel, 1995). Schlegel and Barry (1991) found that the mother was the girl's single most important socializing agent in 85 percent of cultures sampled, just as the father was the boy's in 79 percent. However, other elders, who may or may not be relatives, take over the responsibility of instructing the adolescent in social matters.

Why does the same-sex parent not continue to socialize the child during puberty rites? Spindler (1970) suggested that the adolescent, particularly the adolescent boy, gains in power and ability so dramatically that his parents cannot deal with him effectively. The problem is resolved by distancing the youth from the family and subjugating him to the authority of an outside sponsor whom he has not known in more nurturant contexts. !Ko Bushmen explained this practice by saying that young people do not listen to their parents (Eibl-Eibesfeldt, 1989).

Some observational data are consistent with this explanation. Steinberg and Hill (1978) and others have found that as U.S. adolescents proceed through puberty, they interact more acrimoniously with their parents (see Chapter 14). Assertiveness increases on both sides, and fewer reasons are offered for statements made. Acrimony declines after the peak of the growth spurt, suggesting that there is a hormonal basis to this acrimony. Thus, adolescents may need to be supervised by older, higher-status adults who can intimidate them.

Some additional aspects of the social organization of puberty rites may dovetail with primate behavioral tendencies. Boys are somewhat more likely to be initiated in a large group than singly (Schlegel & Barry, 1980a). This male age cohort parallels the common tendency for terrestrial primates to form all-male groups on the periphery of the troop (G. Mitchell, 1981; Schlegel, 1995). Cross-culturally, boys gravitate toward the periphery of the group more than girls do (G. Mitchell, 1981), and they form larger play groups (Schlegel & Barry, 1991). Adolescent boys associate with their fathers when working, but at other times, they join the male peer group (Schlegel, 1995). For example, Chicanos typically join an informal youth group called a *palomilla*, in which they compete for masculine status (Queen et al., 1985). Groups of same-age young males are a common feature of human society, possibly because of the value of cooperation in warfare and hunting.

For girls, the peer group is less important cross-culturally. Girls usually stay closer to home, spending time with their mothers and other adult female kin. Even when they assemble with age mates, they socialize in smaller groups than do boys (Schlegel, 1995). Likewise, primate juvenile and adolescent females tend to stay with their mothers and other adult females and young (G. Mitchell, 1981). For girls, the family is generally more important than the peer group, whereas they are about equally important for boys (Schlegel & Barry, 1991). Consistent with this pattern, girls are usually (in 73 of 84 cases) initiated singly rather than within an age cohort (Schlegel & Barry, 1980b).

2. Van Gennep referred to the instructional period of puberty rites as the *transition* (Fr. *marge,* "border"). Instruction received earlier is supplemented by information on ceremonial and religious matters, and on social issues such as cultural values and practices, personal conduct, courtship, and duties to one's spouse and in-laws.

The mass of knowledge conveyed during the transition period is directed to a youth who is biologically prepared to receive it. Some of the cognitive maturational changes of late childhood and early adolescence appear to facilitate the rapid and uncritical absorption of cultural information during puberty rites. **Latent,** or **incidental, learning** (remembering details without having been told to notice them) peaks at about 11 years of age (McGraw, 1987). Conformity is also maximal at this age (Steinberg, 1996), perhaps making for a receptive, malleable attitude. Questioning of authority is more likely to appear later, when the potential for formal operations is attained.

Instruction during adolescence is usually more elaborate for boys than girls (Muuss, 1970). Following the ceremony, boys' intensive adolescence training may continue for several years, whereas that for girls usually concludes with the ceremony: "By puberty almost everywhere most girls have mastered the skills they will require as wives and mothers" (Schlegel, 1995, pp. 15f). In some cultures, there is no intensive instructional period at all for girls, but just an initiation ceremony. For example, in Central Africa, no activities were provided for the girl, but she was instead fed a rich diet for several years so that she could attain the corpulent ideal of beauty (Benedict, 1934).

Coon (1971) suggested that boys may need more formal, intensive training because of the difficulty of mastering hunting and warfare skills, but this view may reflect an underestimation of the complexity of female tasks. Nevertheless, in cultures in which women participate heavily in subsistence activities, the girls' instruction does tend to be lengthy (Friedl, 1975) and the ceremony elaborate (J. K. Brown, 1969). Elaborateness of the ceremony may serve to justify or celebrate completion of the long transition period.

Primate maturation shows a similar sex difference: Males take longer to mature than females. Male simians devote the extra time to play fighting and growth (see Chapter 8). They apparently require more time to compete successfully for mates, as do young men.

3. The initiation ceremony is the culmination of the training period. The novices are *incorporated* into adult society (Fr. *agrégation*). Thereafter, they will be regarded as marriageable and as responsible adults, in an abrupt departure from past treatment. Frequently, this ceremony bestows upon the initiate permission to engage in sex (Schlegel & Barry, 1980a). Heterosexual intercourse occurs during 36 percent of girls' ceremonies and 21 percent of boys'. For both sexes, relations with the family may change—taking the form of greater independence from the family or more responsibilities within it.

A formal ceremony often occurs for boys (in 36 percent of all cultures) and girls (in 46 percent) (Schlegel & Barry, 1980a). The celebration may occupy only a day or may entail a series of events lasting up to a year. Girls' ceremonies commonly are restricted to the immediate family or local group, whereas boys' ceremonies often involve the entire group. Boys and girls are initiated separately (this was true in all of Schlegel & Barry's [1980b] cases), but frequently, members of the opposite sex attend as observers. In the absence of a formal ceremony, a period of intense instruction still occurs, but it is terminated in other ways. For example, the appearance of secondary sex characteristics may be noted as evidence of maturity.

At the ceremony, the adolescents typically break a food taboo that they have been observing, don adult clothing for the first time or otherwise change their appearance, or take new names. Secrets may be revealed to the initiates. Among the !Ko Bushmen, a girl is given gifts and is symbolically accepted by each individual in attendance (Eibl-Eibesfeldt, 1989). In most societies, feasting, dancing, music, drug taking, speeches, costumes, or various pyrotechnics (e.g., use of incense) mark the event as special and render it memorable (Ottenberg, 1994). Emotionally tinged stimuli tend to be remembered better than neutral ones (Bower, 1994).

A theme usually characterizes the event. For boys, a theme of rebirth or door opening is sometimes developed; the initiate is welcomed back into society after having been separated from it. Similarly, group cohesion is frequently stressed (Hotvedt, 1990). Both these notions are exemplified by the ceremony of the Arunta. The boy was literally snatched away from his mother and then emerged from the men's ceremonial "baby pouch," reborn as a man; his blood was then mixed with that of the men, symbolizing male solidarity (Benedict, 1938). The boy's individual achievement, such as successfully undergoing his ordeal, often is celebrated, too (Hotvedt, 1990). The assumption of adult responsibilities is the main theme for boys in 42 percent of cultures with puberty rites (Schlegel & Barry, 1980a). Thus, the theme for boys usually reflects one of the main functions of puberty rites: *successful attainment of adult status.*

For girls, the theme often concerns *reproduction*—fertility, beauty (Sommer, 1978), or the responsibilities of being a wife and mother (La Fontaine, 1985). Schlegel and Barry (1980a) found that a theme of fertility or sexuality, the latter "referring to the acquisition of sexual capacity or attractiveness" (p. 702), occurred in 60 percent of cases. Thus, themes of puberty rites reflect the ubiquitous importance of fertility for women and of status for men. Around the world, a man's social status and a woman's youth and beauty (i.e., her apparent reproductive value) are important contributors to their mate value (Buss, 1994).

At an initiation ceremony or leading up to it, an ordeal or a test often must be endured. Ordeals occur in about two-thirds of cultures for boys and one-third of cultures for girls (Schlegel & Barry, 1980; Sommer, 1978). The boy may need to kill game or count coup on an enemy (van Gennep, 1909/1960). Frequently, some form of abstinence is imposed (Eibl-Eibesfeldt, 1989). !Ko boys had to endure cold and hunger, and were deliberately frightened at night (Eibl-Eibesfeldt, 1989). They were not permitted to look up, or to touch anything manually. At the initiation ceremony, they received a painful scar. Apache boys were forced to bathe in icy water and were humiliated on their trial war parties and generally bullied (Benedict, 1934).

Ordeals are usually less dangerous and severe for girls (Muuss, 1970). A girl may grind grain, for example, or remain secluded for a couple of days (Schlegel & Barry, 1980a). Bemba girls (in Zambia) had to learn a series of words and emblems (Vizedom, 1976). However, among the Tukuna Indians, girls had their hair plucked out and occasionally fainted (Schultz, 1959). The main function of ordeals for girls seems to be to guide them further along domestic and reproductive lines (J. K. Brown, 1963).

The close supervision and harsh ordeals of puberty rites may also provide a means of *subduing recalcitrant youths* (Spindler, 1970). The initiate is ushered into adult society only on condition that he subjugate himself to the tribal elders (Vizedom, 1976). The higher incidence of harsh ordeals for boys can be explained by the fact that they commit more antisocial behavior cross-culturally. "Patterned" antisocial behavior by adolescent boys was found to occur in 44 percent of cultures, by girls in 18 percent (Schlegel & Barry, 1991). Males' antisocial behavior may reflect their greater competitiveness (Schlegel, 1995). That is, males' competitiveness may tempt them to break social norms in their quest for social status and its benefits (L. Ellis, 1993). One of the offshoots of this excessive competitiveness at adolescence may be that adolescents perform the adults' "dirty work" of ridiculing and harassing the community's social deviants (Schlegel, 1995).

Consistent with the notion that ordeals subdue the adolescent, the severity of ordeals sometimes varies with the individual involved. The parents of a troublesome Hopi boy, for instance, have the option of selecting, as his godfather and sponsor in his ceremonial career, a man who belongs to a certain Whipper Kachina society that is notorious for the harshness of its sponsors; this individual will then whip the boy publicly (Thompson & Joseph, 1944). "Whipper Kachinas" are feared because they are known to whip troublemaking boys especially harshly at the initiation ceremony. A 7-year-old Hopi boy told me quite earnestly of fearing being assigned such a sponsor. In a longitudinal study, Granzberg (1972) found that Hopi boys who underwent initiation showed a decrease in aggressiveness that was not seen in those who did not. Societies with a child-rearing pattern of early indulgence followed by compliance training, such as Hopi society, were more likely to have harsh initiation rites than other societies (Granzberg, 1973).

Harsh ordeals may also *enhance male solidarity,* for a common danger strengthens group cohesion. Solidarity may be advantageous because, in some cultures, the male initiates proceed to join a formal **male solidarity unit** (or **fraternity**, or **warrior society**), which hunts or wages war together (Young, 1965). Same-sex bonding characterizes boys' rituals more often than girls' (in 37 percent versus 7 percent of the groups studied by Schlegel & Barry [1980b]). Bonding in puberty rites is common where same-sex coalitions are a prominent adult societal feature: for boys where extensive agriculture is practiced, and for girls in African societies, where women often form social groups based on occupational or religious interests (Schlegel & Barry, 1980b).

Schlegel and Barry explained the absence of puberty rites in industrial societies as due to the fulfillment of this bonding function by means of induction into specific civil, religious, military, or educational institutions. Other functions of puberty rites, such as intensive instruction, testing, and graduation, are fulfilled by specialized institutions in industrial societies.

Cohesion may also result from undergoing puberty rites together (Eibl-Eibesfeldt, 1989), since a common goal enhances group solidarity. So, too, does similarity. Boys undergoing puberty rites share many experiences and secrets, and they are made to look alike. They may also be disposed to imitate each other by the peaking of conformity in early adolescence; this, too, would increase similarity and hence solidarity. Evolutionists have suggested that our affinity for similar others may reflect the general tendency to aid kin, who are recognized partly on the basis of phenotypic similarity (Nielsen, 1994).

One issue concerning male ordeals is the extent to which they entail circumcision. Genital operations (circumcision, subincision, or superincision) are performed on adolescent boys in 32 percent of cultures with pubertal rites (Schlegel & Barry, 1980a). It is possible that the male genitals are mutilated in order to celebrate the boy's masculinity; recall that all cultures ascribe higher status to males than females (Stephens, 1963).

Another possibility is that undergoing a harsh ordeal, whether in the form of circumcision or not, *toughens the individual* by inuring him to pain and privation. If a boy can endure conditions of cold, for example, he may bear up under similar hardship if required to do so later. Males are more likely to endure such privations because of the dangers entailed in warfare and in traveling farther from the comforts of the settlement.

Perhaps the main function of male ordeals is that they serve as a form of *sexual competition.* In most species, the males are more competitive than the females (see Chapter 5). Male animals compete strenuously to acquire nuptial gifts, territory, or high dominance rank. Similarly, in none of 240 cultures studied were the adolescent girls more competitive than the boys (Schlegel, 1995). As noted earlier, a boy who fails to endure the ordeal or elects not to undergo it is denied adult status and is considered unmarriageable. Thus, males typically must pass two tests in order to reproduce: They must demonstrate valor during their puberty rites ordeal, and they subsequently must succeed economically. The intensity of boys' puberty rites in agricultural societies may reflect the intense male competition in these highly stratified societies. In agricultural societies, boys' rites tend to be more common and more lengthy, and to involve more participants and observers, than in other societies (Schlegel & Barry, 1980b).

Sometimes, the members of a culture are quite aware of this culling process and see societal benefits to it. The Carolina Siouans explained the starvation, purgation, and near poisoning to which boys and girls were subjected as necessary to subjugate youths; to harden them for war, hunting, and other privations; and to carry off "those infirm weak bodies that would have been only a burden and disgrace to their nation," saving "victuals and clothing for better people" (Driver, 1969, p. 356).

Girls likewise undergo sexual selection. Although a girl's skill and industry, like a boy's, are valued, her putative fertility is a more important determinant of eligibility for marriage and hence of the timing of initiation rites. As mentioned earlier, beauty and fertility are common themes for girls' rites.

In many but less than half of cultures, a girl's virginity is a major concern. Chastity-certifying practices such as genital mutilation and virginity tests tend to occur where large bride prices are paid (Daly & Wilson, 1983; Paige, 1983). Guarding against being cuckolded makes particular adaptive sense in cultures in which paternal investment is extensive. These operations are often viewed as enhancing the girl's chastity and hence her value as a bride, rather than as ordeals (Daly & Wilson, 1983), and they are arranged by the girl's parents rather than by the community at large. Incidentally, genital mutilation occurs more often before puberty than at it (Hotvedt, 1990); it accompanies initiation rites in just 8 percent of societies that conduct such rites (Schlegel & Barry, 1980a).

The usual timing of puberty rites at menarche can be understood as maximizing the girl's mate value. Menarche occurs about 2 years before the onset of fertility (when reproductive value peaks). A bride at the peak of her reproductive value will be most valuable to a husband for maximizing his reproductive success. And, since she is just beginning to ovulate, she will not yet be pregnant by another man. Thus, the girl's mate value nears its peak at the time of puberty rites, and her virtues as a potential wife are widely discussed (Daly & Wilson, 1983). Her father is often quick to publicize her industry, beauty, and character. At the ceremony or shortly thereafter, he may negotiate or finalize her marriage.

Schlegel and Barry (1980b) offered another explanation for girls' puberty rites and their occurrence at menarche. They suggested that this ceremony notifies the society that the girl must now observe the menstrual taboo, which requires menstruating women to avoid men. This would aid hunters, since the scent of blood drives off prey. Consistent with this hypothesis, Schlegel and Barry confirmed that rites for girls are particularly common in forager societies. In societies that later abandoned foraging, puberty rites and the menstrual taboo were usually retained, perhaps because blood attracts predators and might endanger men away from the protective settlement.

The Timing of Puberty Rites and Adolescence

It may be useful to explain the sex differences in the attainment of maturity. Although puberty rites may occur at any time between about ages 8 and 18 (van Gennep, 1909/1960), they usually take place when the adolescent shows signs of puberty. For girls, menarche is almost always the signal for the instructional process to begin (Schlegel & Barry, 1991). Because girls reach menarche at different ages, they usually undergo instruction and ceremonial initiation individually— although there may be an additional, collective ceremony (Schlegel & Barry, 1980a; Young, 1965). Girls may be initiated individually so that each can marry just at the time of peak reproductive value, when she is most marriageable.

Menarche is a rather late pubertal event, occurring when the body is almost fully grown, at about age 14 in traditional cultures (Eveleth & Tanner, 1976) and perhaps at 16 or 17 in prehistoric forager times, as indicated by the present-day !Kung (Shostak, 1981). Therefore, since puberty rites start at menarche and end shortly thereafter, *puberty rites occur toward the end of pubertal maturity for girls.* (See Figure 7.1.)

For boys, there is no distinct sign of puberty analogous to menarche. Accordingly, boys are usually instructed and initiated as a group every few years. The boys' group, called an age cohort, actually spans several years in age. Among the Arapesh, boys' rites were held only

	Age 12	*Age 14*	*Age 16*	*Age 17*
GIRLS	Puberty Begins	Menarche—Rites Begin Puberty Ends	Fertility Begins	
BOYS		Pubic Hair—Rites Begin Puberty Begins	Fertility Begins	Puberty Ends

Figure 7.1   Onset of Puberty Rites in Traditional Cultures

every 6 or 7 years (Mead, 1935). There seems to be no reproductive disadvantage for a boy to be relatively old when he is initiated, even if this occurs several years after he reaches fertility. He is unlikely to marry until years later, when he can afford a wife. For male mammals, reproductive success is less tied to length of the reproductive span than for females, and is more tied to dominance rank or territory.

For boys, puberty rites typically take place when the bodily changes of puberty begin, at about age 14 in traditional cultures, and they probably occurred a few years later prehistorically. Often, the appearance of pubic hair in the boys is the signal for the event (Schlegel & Barry, 1980a). Thus, whereas puberty rites for girls occur at the end of puberty, *puberty rites for boys usually precede pubertal maturity.*

Why does this sex difference in regard to the timing of puberty rites exist? One possibility is that, for both sexes, puberty rites mark the onset of fertility in traditional cultures. Girls reach fertility 1 or 2 years after menarche, at about age 16; boys become fully fertile 1 or 2 years after the appearance of pubic hair, also at about age 16. Thus, *for both sexes, initiation occurs shortly before the onset of fertility,* at roughly age 16. It just so happens that at this point, the boys' growth spurt has barely begun, whereas the girls' growth spurt is terminating.

Evolutionists explain the sex difference in the temporal order of fertility onset and growth spurt by pointing out that a female's body has to be grown before she can bear offspring safely, whereas males can reproduce if they become fertile even while they are still small (Pereira & Altmann, 1985; G. E. Weisfeld & Billings, 1988). The later bodily maturation of boys as compared with girls reflects males' greater need for large body size, which takes time to attain. Large male size relative to female size (**sexual size dimorphism**) is observed in animals with a high degree of male sexual competition, for example, in polygynous species (Daly & Wilson, 1983). Males need large size in order to fight well for mates. Consistent with this explanation, men are somewhat larger than women and mature somewhat later (**sexual bimaturism**), and ours is a moderately polygynous species.

It makes adaptive sense for puberty rites to conclude at the onset of fertility for both sexes. Puberty rites prepare the adolescent for reproductive life. This interpretation also conforms with Schlegel's (1995) statement that "adolescence as a social stage is a response to the growth of reproductive capacity" (p. 16).

The later pubertal maturation of boys is mirrored by their later socioeconomic maturation. Even though a boy is allowed to marry once he completes his puberty rites, he seldom can afford a wife until his late teens or early twenties. In some societies with complex economies that require lengthy training, boys do not even conclude their puberty rites and enter adulthood until their late teens or twenties. Among the Hottentots of South Africa, for example, separation from the mother did not occur until about age 18 (van Gennep, 1909/1960). More commonly, training or wealth accumulation continues after the initiation ceremony.

This longer social and physical maturation for boys is recognized by most cultures, in that boys are perceived as taking longer than girls to pass through adolescence. Contrary to what is sometimes claimed (e.g., by Cobb, 1995), adolescence is not a Western invention of the Industrial Age. All cultures recognize adolescence as a distinct stage of life, even if there is no specific term for it (I. C. Brown, 1963; Muuss, 1970; Schlegel & Barry, 1991). Adolescence is a time for assuming new religious responsibilities and more challenging economic tasks (Schlegel & Barry, 1991). It is usually delimited by observable pubertal changes. Adolescence is perceived as lasting for roughly 2 years in girls and 3 years in boys and as occurring earlier for girls. Thus, boys mature later biologically, economically, and culturally— these "programs" are compatible. For girls, puberty rites and the completion of puberty signal the end of adolescence and the advent of adult status. For boys, puberty rites actually usher the initiate into adolescence, not adulthood (Schlegel & Barry, 1980a).

In about 25 percent of cultures, especially those with either a warrior fraternity or late marriage, a boy passes through a period of **youth** after his puberty rites before becoming a full-fledged adult (Schlegel & Barry, 1991). For example, among horticulturists, a common pattern is for boys around ages 12 to 30 to serve as warriors.

These youths practice athletic skills such as wrestling and spear throwing, and they have sex with unmarried girls (Friedl, 1975). Analogously, in some terrestrial primates, the subadult males occupy the periphery of the troop, where they serve as sentinels and as the first line of defense against predators (Kaufmann, 1967; Chance & Jolly, 1979).

Even for girls, a period of youth is recognized in 20 percent of cultures, especially those with late marriage. In many traditional cultures, the postmenarcheal girls live in a special house and spend much of their time primping, dancing, and visiting. They are exempted from their usual chores for up to 1 or 2 years, and are courted by the boys (Friedl, 1975). Youths tend to enjoy more privileges than adolescents but fewer than married adults (Schlegel, 1995).

The final practical attainment of adulthood usually comes when the person actually marries (Stephens, 1963; van den Berghe, 1980). Formal or informal elevations in status also accompany having children, especially for women, and gaining in economic or ceremonial competence, especially for men. Lastly, the death of either parent raises a woman's status, and the death of the father raises a man's, who is already ascendant over his mother.

Summary

The typical features of puberty rites can sometimes be analyzed functionally by regarding them as analogous to biologically based changes of puberty in humans and other primates (cf. Schlegel, 1995). Puberty rites seem to conspire with the evolved bodily and behavioral changes of adolescence to prepare the individual for reproduction. For example, the training of puberty rites provides a period of intense preparation for adulthood—a sociocultural growth spurt analogous to the physical one. Because many aspects of puberty rites appear to serve the same functions as various pubertal changes, a functional appreciation of puberty rites may shed light on the general adaptive features of adolescence itself.

Although highly variable in form and duration across cultures, puberty rites have been described as having three typical steps. The initiate is partially **separated** from the family and the opposite sex. This doubtless promotes independence and the acquisition of sex-specific behaviors and skills. Sex segregation also seems to occur spontaneously in early adolescent children and simians. Analogously, the body becomes more sharply sex differentiated at puberty, just as behavior does (see G. Mitchell, 1981, on the emergence of sex differences in cognitive abilities). This sex differentiation of body and behavior is functionally consistent with the onset of reproductive maturity.

Some of the sex differences in the separation process also have parallels in nonhuman primates. Boys are usually initiated in groups rather than singly, as girls are, and sometimes they proceed to join a warrior fraternity. Similarly, male primates, including boys, tend to form large peer groups, partly for troop defense, whereas females remain closer to their mothers.

Some features of puberty rites possess no obvious primate homologue but do have possible functional significance. For instance, the observance of taboos and other special practices add salience to the initiation process.

The instruction provided during the **transition** period is typically tendered by a same-sex elder. This probably facilitates the assimilation of sex roles. The fact that this elder is not the parent may reflect the necessity of breaking the filial bond and imposing outside authority. Initiates receive instruction in marital, parental, and societal responsibilities. Young adolescents are receptive to this intensive training because of their capacity for latent learning and conformity. Boys may be drawn to the company of men who serve as models. Concentrated instruction may also precede and follow puberty rites, especially if they are brief.

The transition period culminates in the **incorporation** into adult society and the acceptance of allegiance to the culture and its mores. Various ceremonial pyrotechnics render the occasion memorable and significant. For boys, a theme of graduation into the larger society is common. For girls, attractiveness and fertility are often emphasized. The initiation ceremony sometimes provides an occasion for showing off one's daughter and advertising her marriageability. Sexual relations are a common feature, thus confirming the reproductive significance of puberty rites.

Ordeals are prominent in many cultures, especially for boys. They may function as a form of sexual competition and selection, which are sharper among males than females in most species. Ordeals may also be more important for boys in order to subjugate them. Girls' ordeals, before or at puberty, sometimes involve genital mutilation. Rather than being seen as a test, genital mutilation for girls is regarded as enhancing their chastity and hence their mate value.

For both sexes, incorporation and hence eligibility to marry typically occur before the onset of fertility. This ensures that the individual is formally prepared for the responsibilities of parenthood. Girls are usually initiated at menarche, which makes them eligible to marry just as they approach the onset of fertility, when reproductive value peaks. Marriages tend to occur as fertility approaches.

Although eligible to marry after incorporation into adult society, men usually need more time before they can afford to marry. Analogously, boys take longer than girls to become fully grown. Thus, males undergo rather intense economic competition, as well as difficult ordeals, to enter the marriage pool. This is analogous to the greater sexual competition among male mammals. Unmarried male youths may serve as warriors while accumulating the skills, herds, or goods that will qualify them to marry. Ability to survive and excel as a warrior constitutes an additional form of male competition.

8 Pubertal Changes
in Primates

Most of the bodily differentiation of males and females in our species occurs at puberty. This parallels the profound sex differentiation in behavior that occurs concomitantly (G. Mitchell, 1981). In any organism, behavior, anatomy, and physiology must fit together. Therefore each helps explain the other.

Growth and Maturation in Primates

The higher primates differ from other mammals in undergoing a growth spurt at puberty (Worthman, 1993). In most other mammals, growth rapidly accelerates after birth and decelerates later (Figure 8.1). In primates, this smooth mathematical function is interrupted by a period of rapid growth as maturity is approached—the adolescent growth spurt (see also Bogin, 1988, 1994).

The growth spurt is preceded by a slowing of growth during the juvenile period, which is defined as the time after infancy and before puberty. It has been argued that the true primate anomaly is this slowing of growth before adolescence, with the adolescent growth spurt simply compensating for it, at least partially (Tanner, 1955). After the growth spurt, the early-childhood growth trajectory resumes. Therefore, it is *slow juvenile growth* that requires a functional explanation in terms of unique features of primate evolution.

The juvenile growth pattern has two components: *slow growth* and *delayed sexual maturity*. The primate body grows slowly during this period. In addition, given their final body size, primates take a relatively long time to reach sexual maturity. Both components need to be explained.

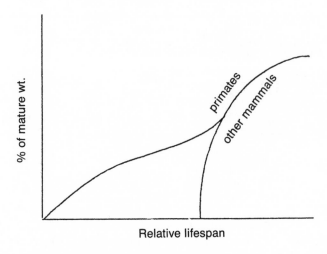

*Figure 8.1 Weight Growth over the Life Span. Source: G. E. Weisfeld &
Billings. (1988). Reprinted by permission.*

Let us begin with slow growth. Most of the bodily systems indeed
grow slowly in primates, including the body as a whole. The reproductive system grows the most slowly of all because it is not needed yet
and because the body would waste calories to maintain it prematurely.

However, the brain grows rapidly; it does not undergo a growth
plateau (Figure 8.2). One can say that the rest of the body, especially
the reproductive system, defers to the brain during the juvenile period. This exception to the rule of slow juvenile growth may help to
explain the overall pattern.

Why is the primate brain so large? Primates seem to require large
brains to mediate their highly flexible behavior. Locomoting in trees
demands acrobatic flexibility. Primates also evolved extensive flexibility in other behavioral domains. For example, they are flexible in
their foraging behavior, many of them being omnivores. Many primate species are also highly social and respond differently to different
individuals (Cheney & Seyfarth, 1990). This flexibility—the capacity
to do different things in different situations—is developed through
exploration, observation, and play—through the motive of interest
(see Chapter 3). Primates' extensive play during the juvenile period
presumably evolved to motivate them to practice various behaviors.

The young primate needs a long period of immaturity in which to
learn and practice its behavioral options (Janson & van Schalk, 1993),

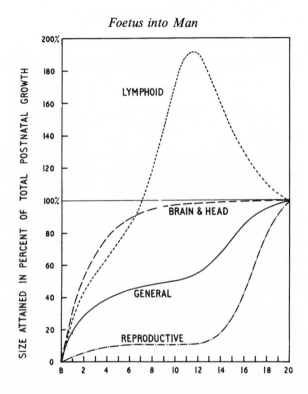

*Figure 8.2   Growth of Various Tissues as Percentage of Size at Age 20.
Source: Ganong (1987). Reprinted by permission.*

hence, their maturation is delayed. A long period of maturity does not seem to be necessary for the brain to grow large. The primate brain grows rapidly at first and only slowly as adulthood approaches (Janson & van Schalk, 1993). However, the differentiation of this large brain as new cognitions and behaviors are acquired takes time. The increase in brain size is due largely to an increase in synaptic connections, which reflect learning.

These learned skills enhance survival, and they repay the organism for the delay in reaching its reproductive period. The overall primate life-history strategy is to produce a limited number of offspring but to raise many of them successfully—the **K-selection** strategy, as contrasted with the **r-selection** gambit of producing many offspring but providing little or no parental care. By maturing slowly, primates apparently use the time to learn how to survive. This interpretation is supported by the fact that species that take a long time to mature enjoy a long life span thereafter. Age at death is correlated by more than 0.90 with the onset of reproduction in mammals (Harvey & Zammuto, 1985). Slow-growing, long-lived animals tend to produce relatively few offspring but rear many of them successfully. During their long apprenticeships, the large-brained primates learn how to select food, locomote through the trees, identify predators (Janson & van Schalk, 1993), care for their young, fight, relate to particular individuals, and so forth.

Which is more important—learning to survive as a juvenile or learning to produce more offspring as an adult? Rubenstein (1993) suggested that juvenile learning may be more important to juvenile survival than to adult fitness in primates. For example, motor skills are acquired at an early stage. Learning what foods to eat and which predators to avoid would be serviceable for juveniles as well as adults. Juvenile squirrel monkeys master adult foraging techniques well before they reach adult size. Other skills, such as how to care for an infant, would be more important in adulthood. The point is that the organism must survive *before* it reaches maturity, as well as after. Contrary to the implications of most psychological stage theories of development, a child is more than an incomplete adult.

We have now accounted for the rapid growth of the primate brain and the lengthy period of immaturity. But we still have not explained the distinctive primate feature of slow juvenile bodily growth. Primates reach maturity late so they have time to acquire behavioral flexibility. But why do they remain small for so long a period? A rapidly growing animal with a high metabolic rate is vulnerable to starvation (Janson & van Schalk, 1993). By growing slowly, an animal can reduce this risk. But why, among the mammals, do only the primates remain rather small during the juvenile period? Juvenile primates are especially vulnerable to starvation because they burn up calories rapidly due to their high activity rates as playful, arboreal animals. Juvenile primates also must compete with larger, more experienced adults for food, since they must stay close to the adults for fear of predators.

Juvenile primates may also have a limited need for large body size. One advantage of large body size is greater conservation of heat. Primates do not suffer much from the cold because most of them live in warm climates, and young primates typically sleep with their mothers at night (Altmann, 1986). Also, their large brains and active play generate a lot of heat.

But the main advantage to an animal of large body size is likely defense against predators. Predator pressure on arboreal primates is probably comparatively minor because tree-dwellers seldom need to fight off predators. And juveniles in terrestrial species can usually count on adults for protection.

There are multiple advantages to small size. Small animals need less food, can be more selective in choosing food, and do not need to roam as far (Hrdy, 1981). But here again, special factors pertain to primates. Small juvenile primates can forage on thin branches that would not support the weight of heavier animals. For example, Barbary macaque juveniles spend more time in trees than do adults and eat different things as a result (Janson & von Schalk, 1993). Small size also allows escape onto thin branches that would not support a larger predator.

Perhaps most important, less time spent feeding would leave juvenile primates more time and energy for play. Juveniles play more than do primates at any other stage (Walters, 1987). Adolescent primates grow faster than juveniles, and they play less (Pereira & Altmann, 1985). Presumably, the increased foraging efficiency that is required during the growth spurt is enhanced by a reduction in play and an increase in fighting ability and aggressiveness, especially in males. As large size is attained, the risks of predation decline, and the adolescent is able to forage farther afield with less danger.

The advantages of this primate pattern of slow growth and delayed maturation are illustrated by the chimpanzee (Hrdy, 1981). A newborn is transported and groomed by the mother for about six months, so small neonatal size will be a distinct advantage. Slow growth also means less of a lactational burden for the mother. Through play, the infant learns motoric and social skills. The basic adult feeding repertoire is acquired by the end of infancy (Watts & Pusey, 1993). For the next six years, the offspring will accompany its mother daily and nightly; the smaller the offspring, the less competition it has with its mother for food. The offspring need not be large because its mother and other troop members can protect it.

This protracted bond also allows the offspring to learn from its mother. The young chimpanzee learns what routes to follow through the forest, how to build a nest, which foods to eat and which to avoid, how to fish for termites, how to detect and avoid predators, and how to care for an infant. The chimpanzee brain grows to be particularly large, in part because chimpanzees are mainly frugivores (fruit-eaters). Folivorous primates (leaf-eaters) such as the gorilla tend to have smaller brains than frugivores (Watts & Pusey, 1993). As indicated by the anatomy of our intestines, humans are mainly carnivore-frugivores (S. Jones et al., 1992).

Being highly social, chimpanzees face stiff competition for food. But the adult males protect the younger troop members from invaders. Females usually transfer to a new troop at maturity, around age 13, but before this, they forage mainly with the mother alone and so do not sustain very great foraging competition and can imitate her food selections.

Sexual maturation is even slower in humans than in chimpanzees. Early humans had to master complex foraging skills in order to exploit the seasonally variable supply of encased, embedded, and hidden plant foods (Lancaster, 1984). With the evolution of the capacity for language, tool use, and other aspects of hominid culture, even more time would have been necessary to learn and practice the various economic and social behaviors necessary for successful reproduction. Accordingly, sexual maturation became delayed even longer. Wild chimpanzees reach menarche at 10 or 11 (Goodall, 1986), whereas in nonindustrialized human cultures, the figure is about 16 (Friedl, 1975). In captivity, chimpanzees reach menarche at about 9, and members of well-nourished human populations reach it at about 12.5. Male chimpanzees first ejaculate at age 9 or 10; in boys, this occurs at about age 13 in the West (Katchadourian, 1977).

This further delay in hominid maturation would have necessitated a compensatory increase in survival, which did indeed occur in hominids (see Chapter 6). Specifically, hominids seem to surpass other primates in feeding success. Tool-using humans have been calculated to extract about twice the calories from a savannah environment as nonhuman primates (Bogin, 1988).

Other advantages stemmed from hominid social organization. In hominids, a long time passes before maturation, but offspring survival is enhanced by extensive care by parents and other kin. Complex social and kinship organization would have required still more time to learn roles and skills. Greater foraging efficiency would have lengthened the life span, which, in turn, would have permitted a still longer juvenile phase. Consistent with the social and technical complexity of hominid life, the human brain is about three times as large as the chimpanzee's (S. Jones et al., 1992).

Sexual Dimorphism

In most mammals, the male grows to be larger than the female. Sexual size dimorphism (Gr., "two forms") mainly reflects selection pressure on males to grow larger in order to compete successfully for females. The evidence for this belief is that the male is relatively large in polygynous birds and mammals (including primates) in which competition for females is vigorous, as compared with monogamous species (E. O. Wilson, 1975; Leutenneger & Cherverud, 1982). In monogamous mammals such as the primates, in fact, size dimorphism is rare (S. Jones et al., 1992). Another indication that size dimorphism is related to selection for fighting ability in males is that canine tooth dimorphism increases with polygyny in primates (S. Jones et al., 1992); primates fight mainly with the canine teeth. Size dimorphism in the terrestrial primates probably also reflects specialization of the male for defense (S. Jones et al., 1992), as occurs in chimpanzees.

Male primates' defense of females may have allowed the latter to become still smaller (Willner & Martin, 1985). Small size may have meant earlier breeding, more energy for juvenile learning, and more food left for offspring. Also, size dimorphism allows specialization in feeding (see Chapter 6). Note that some of these possible advantages of small size for female primates have been cited to explain slow growth in juveniles.

However, female size may have been increased by the great degree of lactation necessary for the rapid growth of the primate infant (Harvey & Clutton-Brock, 1985). In primates, lactation is an important factor contributing to adult female body size (Lancaster, 1984).

In our species, moderate size dimorphism exists, consistent with our moderately polygynous breeding system. Men are about 20 percent heavier than women (Harvey & Clutton-Brock, 1985). Dimorphism is essentially an adult phenomenon, since the sexes are similar in size until about age 15 in the West. Girls are actually somewhat taller than boys from 12 to 14, due to their earlier growth spurt (Tanner, 1978).

The fact that sexual dimorphism is an adult phenomenon suggests that its function pertains to reproduction. *Specieswide traits that begin in adolescence, as reproductive maturity approaches, usually have some reproductive function.* This underscores the sexual significance of adolescence.

Of all the bodily systems, the reproductive system shows the greatest degree of sexual dimorphism. But probably all other bodily systems show sex differentiation because they, too, play a role in reproduction, as explained in Chapters 9 and 10.

Sexual Bimaturism

In general, animals will be selected to mature early so as to maximize their reproductive span. However, if a newly mature male animal cannot compete effectively for mates, it may be better off delaying maturity until it is larger and more experienced. In this way, it avoids the metabolic costs of growing and maintaining a large nonbreeding body, the injuries of fights for mates, and the intimidation cost of defeats.

Slower maturation in one sex is called sexual bimaturism. It occurs in long-lived species in which mating competition is intense, for example, in polygynous rather than monogamous mammals. As expected, the sex that does more of the courting tends to be larger and slower to mature than the other sex. A few exceptions occur among the mammals. Some smaller mammals exhibit reverse dimorphism: The female is larger than the male, evidently because she needs to be large enough to bear offspring of sufficient size for that species (Willner & Martin, 1985). The monogamous white-handed gibbon exhibits reverse bimaturism. The male is 8 percent larger than the female, but he reaches sexual maturity at about 6.5 years whereas she does at 9 years.

Some male songbirds seem to compromise between the strategies of early and late maturation (Daly & Wilson, 1983). They reach reproductive maturity in the first year and try to nest, but they retain the immature, dull coloration. They are relatively unsuccessful at mating because they are less attractive to females and less intimidating to males. As a general rule, *mature male features attract females and repel males* of the same species (see Chapter 9). Yet these songbirds obtain some breeding success, and they avoid the cost of conspicuous coloration, namely, attracting predators and provoking adult males to fight. In the second year, they assume the adult male plumage that typifies polygynous birds, and are more successful at territorial defense and breeding. Similarly, subadult (adolescent) Barbary macaques are sneak copulators that steal inseminations when dominant males are absent or distracted (Kuester & Paul, 1989).

In some species, sneak copulation represents a permanent optional developmental "strategy"; the male will never become large. In these species, it is thought that all males have two genetic programs for reproductive maturation. If, at the crucial time, there are many large males present, the young male will opt for the sneak developmental course. Some evolutionists believe that humans possess numerous genetically based behavioral options, called **facultative** (or contingent or conditional) strategies, as contrasted with a single, **obligate** developmental pathway.

A third possibility is that a given animal population has a stable ratio of genetically directed sneakers and regular males. When one strategy becomes too common, natural selection favors the other. This results in a **balanced polymorphism,** indicating the existence of multiple genotypes in a stable ratio.

The apes for which data are available show that bimaturism is roughly proportional to dimorphism (Harvey & Clutton-Brock, 1985). Bimaturism probably reflects the males' need for extra time not only to grow larger but also to practice combat. Much of juvenile males' play consists of play fighting, which mainly accounts for the greater playfulness of male primates (Walters, 1987). Play fighting also helps explain the more prolonged juvenile plateau of male primates compared with females. Juvenile males begin play at an earlier age, and continue it longer, than females. This includes humans, since boys undergo the growth spurt later than girls and thus have a longer period for play. Male primates probably undergo a longer juvenile plateau than females primarily in order to practice fighting rather than to gain size, since growth is slow during this period.

In humans, this long juvenile period with its slow but steady growth leaves the male large enough to not need a much greater growth spurt than the female to reach his ideal adult size. In fact, more of the size difference between men and women is due to boys' longer juvenile growth period than to their greater growth during adolescence (Bogin, 1988; Tanner, 1978).

This is not the case with rhesus monkeys, baboons, or chimpanzees, however. In these primates, the male growth spurt is profound, and the female has only a very small growth spurt, especially as measured by weight (Watts, 1985). It must be that slow juvenile growth almost suffices to bring the female of these species to a size large enough to bear offspring.

This leaves us with the problem of explaining the prominence of the growth spurt in women. Human newborns are much larger than those of chimpanzees, so perhaps the human mother must grow quickly to be large enough to bear them. Evidently, her long juvenile phase relative to the chimpanzee's does not suffice to bring her to the requisite size fast enough. Hence, she undergoes a growth spurt that is similar in magnitude and duration to the male's. This results in her breeding only 68 percent later than the chimpanzee, despite the fact that her newborn is 88 percent larger (Harvey & Clutton-Brock, 1985). One factor in the extraordinary size of the human newborn may be the unusual hemochorial placenta, which allows an exchange of nutrients and waste between the fetal and maternal circulations across a broad but thin surface area; ours is the most efficient placenta of any primate (Bogin, 1988). The human newborn has an especially large brain, which permits the extensive learning and cognition of our species.

The slower maturation of males occurs throughout development. At birth, girls are about five weeks ahead of boys in maturity even though boys weigh slightly more (Tanner, 1978). Girls begin puberty about 2 years ahead of boys, and most corresponding pubertal changes occur about 2 years earlier in girls than boys. Boys reach fertility comparatively early in puberty, however, at about 13 or 14 (Tanner, 1978; Bogin, 1988). Girls reach fertility late in puberty, at about 14 or 15 in well-nourished populations (see Chapter 7).

Individual Differences in Maturation

Obviously, each species has evolved the best size and shape for its habitat. But in any animal, growth and development, including pubertal maturation, can only proceed as fast as environmental conditions allow. The organism exhibits great flexibility in accommodating to its circumstances. Our evolved maturational program takes into account existing environmental conditions, and makes appropriate adjustments that help explain individual variation in maturation. Some of these conditional adjustments will now be described.

One manifestation of this notion of ideal body size is **catch-up growth** (Worthman, 1993). If pubertal growth is slowed by some stressor, once the stressor is removed, catch-up ensues (Tanner, 1978). This compensates for the earlier period of slow growth for the corresponding developmental period. Even newborns show catch-up growth if development was slowed in utero, as occurs if the mother has a narrow pelvis. If stress is prolonged and severe enough, however, compensation may be incomplete, resulting in permanently short stature.

Human variation in adult size is partly due to genetic factors. The Chinese seem to be genetically predisposed to early puberty (R. E. Jones, 1991). However, members of the Caucasian and Negroid races reach puberty at a similar age if raised under comparable conditions, in the United States (S. Jones et al., 1992).

Female mammals are less vulnerable than males to environmental stressors (Tanner, 1978). For example, girls' growth is usually slowed less than boys' by malnutrition (but see Worthman, 1993). The functional explanation for this may be that females' reproductive success depends even more than that of males on attaining full body size. A small male may still manage some inseminations, but a small female will not be able to carry offspring. Also, if a female delays maturity too long because of adverse environmental conditions, she will lose valuable reproductive years. A male, by contrast, may delay growth and then grow to full size and make up for lost time by inseminating numerous females.

Because of the relative vulnerability of male fetuses, harsh environmental conditions result in a lower **sex ratio** (of males to females) in various mammals. Likewise, low-income couples and single mothers tend to have daughters, and high-income couples tend to have sons (R. R. Baker & Bellis, 1995). Shifting the sex ratio of offspring in response to environmental conditions is adaptive for animals (Trivers & Willard, 1973). Under favorable conditions, it is better to have sons that may reap a reproductive bonanza. Under harsh conditions, daughters usually outreproduce sons, so it is better to have daughters.

Nutrition

Growth can be retarded by malnutrition. Even in affluent countries such as the United States, children of high socioeconomic status (SES) grow larger than children of low SES, partly because of better nutrition. Low-SES children in these countries usually take in ample calories but lack particular nutrients. In poorer countries, the problem often is low caloric intake, as well. In these countries, menarche tends to occur late; for example, in a New Guinea study, menarche came at about 17 years (Eveleth & Tanner, 1976).

Improved nutrition is regarded as the main reason for the **secular** (long-term historical) **trend** in pubertal maturation. From the middle of the nineteenth to middle of the twentieth century, age at menarche fell by several years in Europe, Canada, Australia, and the United States (Tanner, 1978). The same effect has been observed in Japan (Bogin, 1988), China, and New Guinea (Worthman, 1993). The trend has been documented in boys as well as girls. Final adult height has also increased by about 2 inches in the West since 1850. Other factors besides nutrition may be at work, such as reduced child labor and improved sanitation.

The **critical fat hypothesis** has been invoked to explain the timing of puberty, especially in girls. Menarche closely follows the attainment of a critical level of body fat (Frisch, 1983a), as well as a certain pelvic diameter (Worthman, 1993). Other milestones of girls' puberty development are also highly correlated with body weight, including the start and end of the growth spurt, the peak of weight gain, and the onset of ovulatory cycles (Lancaster, 1984). In other mammals, too, the onset of reproductive maturity is associated with the level of body fat (Frisch, 1983a). Some scholars argue that fat levels do not actually trigger menarche and that other pubertal measures, such as completion of the growth spurt, are more closely tied to menarche. However, the close parallel between levels of body fat and pubertal development doubtless is adaptive, that is, ultimately even if not proximately causal (see Chapter 10). In fact, a hormone called **leptin**, which registers the magnitude of fat stores, has recently been found to accelerate maturation in rodents.

Other Environmental Factors

High altitude may retard pubertal development even if nutrition is adequate and temperature is controlled for (R. E. Jones, 1991). Greater energy expenditure may be involved.

The season of the year can affect growth. Children gain height faster in summer than in winter in temperate latitudes (Bogin, 1988). Growth in height when food is abundant would be adaptive. The effect of height seems to be mediated by day length. Abundant sunlight means plenty of ultraviolet light, which aids synthesis of vitamin D_3, which promotes bone growth. However, children gain more weight in winter than in summer, provided that food is ample. Weight gain as a protection against cold and scarcity also makes adaptive sense. Girls in Germany and Czechoslovakia have been found to reach menarche most often in winter (Luce, 1971), perhaps because of an increase in weight then. Other environmental effects, especially those of SES, are difficult to tease apart. High SES is associated with better prenatal and postnatal medical care, better diet, and, often, reduced physical labor. Low-SES children in the United States have lower birth weight, smaller size, and smaller head circumference (Garn et al., 1984). These differences were present at birth and increased at least until age 7. Scores on the Bayley test of infant development and an IQ test were also affected. Low-SES girls also tend to have later menarche (E. E. Johnston, 1974). Only two countries, Norway and Sweden, have managed to eliminate social-class influences on growth (S. Jones et al., 1992), although an influx of immigrants has changed this in Sweden (Greta Ågren, personal communication, 1992).

Height

The fact that tall individuals tend to achieve a higher SES also is difficult to explain precisely. Belgian and Polish studies (Bogin, 1988) reveal that even within the same family, taller children became better educated. In a U.S. study, taller men earned more money even after education, occupation, IQ, and marital status were taken into account. Among the Mehinaku Indians of Brazil, taller men had more wealth, prestige, wives, and lovers (Gregor, 1979). In Belgium, upwardly mobile sons tended to be taller as well as more clever than economically stable sons (Cliquet, 1968).

A well-documented bias exists favoring taller job candidates and employees, but this bias may have some validity in that taller individuals tend to be more intelligent and healthier (Tanner, 1978). Part of the reason why tall children are more intelligent is that they tend to be more neurologically mature, but some correlation between intelligence and height is still seen in adults. Taller individuals probably tend to have had a more favorable development than shorter ones, some of whom will have had their growth stunted by adversity.

Height seems to provide an SES advantage to women, too. Taller Scottish women tended to work at more skilled jobs (Scott et al., 1956). Schreider (1964) found that, taking father's occupation into account, taller British women married men with more skilled jobs— although perhaps they married taller men, who tend to have high-skilled jobs.

Family Factors

One variable that has been studied carefully is family size. Menarcheal age tends to be directly proportional to family size, as reported in Romania and French Canada (Surbey, 1998b). Large family size reduced height, independent of SES and urbanization, in a Polish study (Bielicki et al., 1981). A negative correlation between the number of children sharing a bed and height has also been reported in Britain, controlling for other factors (Worthman, 1993). Siblings, although disposed to be altruistic toward each other because of their genetic relationship, compete for parental resources.

In another British study, in addition to a family size effect, older siblings were found to grow faster than younger ones (H. Goldstein, 1971). Similar results have been reported in Canada, Italy, and the United States (Surbey, 1998b). A firstborn child has a period of time in which she is the only child in the family. Twins tend to mature somewhat later than singletons, probably because of prenatal competition for resources.

However, caring for younger siblings has been found to delay a girls' maturation in a study of a Caribbean village (Flinn, 1988) and to reduce her fertility in a study in Micronesia (Turke, 1988). In the latter study, mothers whose first child was female had more children overall.

Stress

Psychological stress can affect growth, even when there is an adequate food intake (Mascie-Taylor, 1991). Stress can interfere with the secretion of digestive enzymes and hence the absorption of food (Parisi & de Martino, 1980). Chronic anxiety can also elevate caloric expenditures (Hopwood et al., 1990). In a famous study of **psychosocial dwarfism** in post–World War II Germany, children in an orphanage who were berated by a hostile supervisor at mealtime gained less weight than another group despite receiving vitamin supplements (Widdowson, 1951). When the supervisor was replaced, the former group then surpassed the latter in growth.

Psychological stress can cause amenorrhea in women. For example, before a performance, ballerinas sometimes cease menstruating, independent of intense training or dieting (Scott & Johnston, 1982). Also, dancers who sharply reduced their exercise regimen resumed menstrual cycling even without any change in body weight or composition (Warren, 1980).

Stressors of any sort, including crowding, fear, noise, pain, defeat, heat, cold, and exercise, produce a fairly similar set of hormonal adjustments in mammals, known as the General Adaptation Syndrome (Selye, 1956). Levels of the adrenal hormone cortisol rise in order to mobilize the organism to confront the stressor. Cortisol then reduces the levels of growth hormone and gonadal hormones. Growth and reproductive maturation are inhibited. In addition, the functioning of the immune system is depressed as the body defers the less urgent processes of fighting infections and tumors and healing wounds. In full-grown animals, stress can also interfere with reproductive functioning, including fertility in both sexes, gestation, and lactation.

Interestingly, mild or short-term stress in infancy tends to enhance growth (Worthman, 1993). Cross-cultural research reveals that genital mutilation, scarification, and brief maternal separation lower the age of menarche and increase adult height (Surbey, 1998b). For example, cultures in which fathers are frequently absent tend to have tall men (Belsky et al., 1991), although these may have been polygynous cultures, which are known to have taller men than monogamous ones (Low, 1979). Acceleration of maturation under conditions of brief early stress has been reported in other mammals as well. It may be adaptive for organisms undergoing stress to mature early because they may not live long and therefore need to begin reproduction quickly. However, prolonged stressors, such as long-term maternal separation, tend to delay maturation and stunt growth.

Weight loss can stop menstrual cycling (Warren, 1983). Thus, dieting can interfere with reproductive health. But obesity can cause amenorrhea, too (Frisch, 1983a).

Girls who exercise very hard and regularly, such as ballet dancers and track athletes (Frisch, 1983a), tend to have later menarche. Similarly, women who are serious joggers can cease menstruating. Research on prepubertal ballet dancers reveals that their gonadal hormones and bone age are affected (Warren, 1983). Either the stress of hard exercise, the conversion of fat to muscle, or both may be involved.

Hard labor constitutes a physiological stressor for organisms. With hard labor, metabolic energy is diverted from growth, reproductive functioning, and other bodily processes. Therefore, animals tend to rest and conserve energy when possible—the law of economy (Stanley, 1898). Exercise can increase the efficiency of the muscular and skeletal systems, and appearing muscular may enhance men's sexual attractiveness, but benefits to other bodily systems are dubious. One big methodological problem in research on exercise is that people who are healthy to begin with are more likely to follow an exercise regimen. The actual health benefits of exercise, particularly of any exercise beyond the most minimal, appear to be small (Wooley & Garner, 1994).

Ambient Light

Although disease generally retards development, blindness constitutes an exception. Blind girls tend to reach menarche earlier than sighted ones (Magee et al., 1970). Evidently, the onset of puberty in girls is influenced by changes in illumination; similar effects have been reported for rodents (Austin & Short, 1972; see Chapter 9). Another possible explanation is reduced exertion; bedridden girls tend to mature early (Warren, 1983), as do those with cerebral palsy, epilepsy, deafness, and diabetes (Surbey, 1998b; R. E. Jones, 1991).

But ambient light is probably involved. Boys with lesions of the light-sensing pineal gland can develop precocious puberty (Bogin, 1988; J. S. Perry, 1971). Fewer girls reach menarche in the spring, when light is abundant, than in the fall (Becker et al., 1992; see Chapter 9). Moonlight helps regulate the menstrual cycle. Guenon monkeys cycle with the full moon (H. Ellis, 1936), and most other female primates have approximately lunar (monthly) cycles. Women with irregular cycles have been treated by exposing them to light at night from days 14 through 17 of their cycles (Dewan, 1967).

Social Contact

Lastly, social effects influence reproductive maturation in mammals. Generally speaking, *potential mates* accelerate maturation. In female mice that are caged with adult males or exposed to adult male odors, maturity is reached earlier than among those with no such exposure (Vandenbergh, 1969). In some studies, the urine of subordinate males was ineffective in achieving this effect; the male had to be dominant (Lombardi & Vandenbergh, 1977). Acceleration of maturity by potential mates has also been demonstrated in prairie voles, pigs, cows, and saddle-backed tamarins (Sanders & Reinisch, 1990). Likewise, adult females accelerate reproductive maturation in male mice and (provided the female is subordinate) in bonnet macaques (Rosenblum & Nadler, 1971).

By contrast, *sexual rivals* delay pubertal onset. The presence of numerous adult females delays puberty in female mice (Drickamer, 1974), probably also because of a pheromone (scent signal). Analogously, the presence of adult male prairie deer mice slows the maturation of juvenile males (Huntingford & Turner, 1987). Even dominant female mice can delay maturation in male mice (Svare et al., 1978). This may plausibly be viewed as an effect of competitive stress or as an adaptive response to poor conditions for reproducing successfully.

Puberty is sometimes delayed by the presence of *opposite-sex adult kin*. In prairie dogs, first ovulation is delayed if the female remains in contact with her father (Hoogland, 1982); similarly, female voles that remain in their natal burrows delay puberty (Lidicker, 1980). In some New World monkeys, reproduction is delayed or inhibited in juvenile females that remain in the family group (A. Jolly, 1985). Primate parents may sometimes benefit from delaying their juveniles' maturation in order to retain the services of the latter in caring for younger siblings and to reduce sexual and food competition among family members (Surbey, 1998b).

Evidence for comparable social effects in humans is accumulating. In the Oneida Community of New York in the nineteenth century, prepubertal girls practiced frequent sex and reached puberty about 2 years earlier than girls in surrounding communities (R. E. Jones, 1991).

Several studies also suggest that father absence influences pubertal development. In an Australian study, women who had experienced the absence of their fathers before age 6 matured earlier than those whose fathers were present until menarche (S. Jones et al., 1972). In a Canadian replication of this study, girls who had experienced father absence before age 10 matured 6 months earlier than girls from intact homes (Surbey, 1990). Moreover, the earlier the father's absence began and hence the briefer the daughter's exposure to him, the earlier menarche occurred. Moffitt et al. (1992) reported the same effect of father absence in the United States. Similarly, in polygynous societies, in which fathers generally have less contact with their children than in monogamous ones, girls tend to reach menarche earlier (Bean, 1983).

There may be other ways in which the father's absence might speed menarche. One possibility is that the presence of a stepfather—a potential mate—might accelerate puberty. Girls whose fathers were absent but who had stepfathers did not reach menarche significantly earlier than those without stepfathers in Surbey's (1990) and Hetherington's (1993) research. By contrast, B. J. Ellis (1998) found that stepfather presence did accelerate menarche.

Another of the many possibilities adroitly discussed by Surbey (1990, 1998b) rests on the appreciable heritability of pubertal timing. Early-maturing mothers have early-maturing daughters and are prone to marry early and to divorce, which of course leads to father absence. This factor seems to have operated in Surbey's (1990) sample, but not in B. J. Ellis's (1998). Heritability is seldom considered by social scientists as an explanation for individual differences in behavior, but it is often a strong possibility (see Chapter 14).

Yet another possible mechanism is stress. Accelerated maturation in girls whose fathers are absent may reflect early exposure to stress, which sometimes accelerates maturation, as described earlier. In Surbey's (1990) study, high scores on a life-events stress inventory were associated with the duration of the father's absence and with early puberty. The moderately consistent finding, in cross-national research, that family conflict also accelerates puberty in both sexes (Kim et al., 1997) supports the stress hypothesis. B. J. Ellis (1998) discovered that a mother's psychopathology acted as a stressor to accelerate her daughter's maturation, partly by driving the father out of the home.

In sum, social conditions, particularly the presence of mates and rivals, can affect reproductive maturation. The possible adaptive value of these adjustments is discussed further in Chapters 13 and 14.

Mating opportunities can also influence reproductive functioning in mature animals. When the highest-ranking male rhesus monkey in a group is removed, the others undergo surges in testosterone level (Bernstein et al., 1983), perhaps because their rank and hence mating prospects have improved. Also, the introduction of females raises testosterone levels in male rhesus monkeys, as does gaining high rank (Bernstein et al., 1983). And in female Celebese black apes (which are actually monkeys), the absence of adult males lengthened menstrual cycles, thereby delaying ovulation (Bernstein et al., 1982). In adult female rodents, the presence of adult males induces estrus, but the presence of the father delays it (Hoogland, 1982). The presence of a dominant female suppresses ovulation in some marmosets and tamarins (Sanders & Reinisch, 1990).

Comparable effects of social contact on reproductive physiology have been reported for humans. Taking on a regular sex partner tends to shorten and regulate menstrual cycles (Surbey, 1990). Similarly, sexual contact with men was associated with a higher rate of ovulation (Veith et al., 1983). Pheromones are probably involved: When male axillary (armpit) secretions were applied to the upper lips of women with variable cycles in this effect, menstrual cycles became more regular after 14 weeks (Cutler & Preti, 1986).

In college women, menstrual cycles tended to become synchronized with those of roommates, close friends (McClintock, 1971), or lesbian lovers (Sanders & Reinisch, 1990). Women given female axillary secretions tended to synchronize their cycles with those of the donors (Preti et al., 1986). McClintock's recent research suggests that one such pheromone, produced during the follicular phase of the menstrual cycle, speeds ovulation by 2 days; another, excreted during ovulation, slows it by 1.5 days. However, Baker and Bellis (1995) have disputed the existence of menstrual synchrony, and pointed out that such a phenomenon has no clear adaptive value.

In conclusion, physiology, anatomy, behavior, function, and development are interrelated. This is well illustrated by the phenomenon of puberty. The same theme will be followed in the next two chapters in regard to the specific changes of puberty—their mediation and adaptive value.

Summary

Delayed maturation allows time for learning through play, observation, and instruction, but it often requires prolonged parental care. Primates benefit greatly from learning because their behavior is highly flexible due to the fact that they are arboreal and omnivorous. By conserving energy, slow juvenile growth affords protection from starvation. Juvenile primates are prone to starvation because they spend time and calories on play. Then, too, a juvenile competes with adults for food because it needs to stay close for protection. Small size is also tolerable in juvenile primates because they can forage onto thin branches and thereby eat food that adults cannot, and can also escape from heavier predators. The primate growth spurt is mainly a compensation for slow juvenile growth. The growth spurt of the human female is unusually pronounced. It may reflect compensation for the large size (especially the head size) of human newborns. The large size of the human newborn's brain and our long period of immaturity allow the assimilation of knowledge necessitated by the complexity of hominid technical and social adaptations.

Size dimorphism and bimaturism are explained mainly by selection pressure that favors large males in polygynous or promiscuous species. Humans have a moderate degree of both, consistent with our modicum of polygyny. In animals generally, masculine traits attract females and intimidate males. These and other features that appear at reproductive maturation usually have some direct or indirect reproductive function.

The sex-specific order of pubertal events is highly invariant (Bogin, 1994), but the rate of pubertal maturation can be affected by various genetic, environmental, and metabolic factors. Most stressors delay puberty, but early adversity sometimes accelerates it. Pubertal maturation is influenced by contact with adults of the same or opposite sex and by whether the opposite-sex adults are kin. For example, the father's absence speeds menarche, possibly by acting as an early stressor. The presence of suitable mates in mammals accelerates reproductive maturation and enhances reproductive function. Sexual contact with men can induce ovulation in women by a pheromonal effect, and it may accelerate menarche. The presence of same-sex competitors or opposite-sex adult kin retards maturation in mammals.

9 Pubertal Changes in Boys

Pubertal changes in each sex will be described system by system in the next two chapters. Most pubertal changes can be understood in terms of the evolutionary principles developed in previous chapters. The present chapter will deal with pubertal changes that are more prominent in boys, but it will also include comparisons with girls, as well as some general information on both sexes.

Few pubertal changes are **monomorphic**, that is, occurring similarly in the sexes. One of these is the development of amorousness, described under the heading Nervous System. Another is the gradual increase in logical ability, or so-called fluid intelligence. Also, as described in Chapter 8, both sexes undergo a growth spurt and a concomitant increase in appetite, although these features are more pronounced in boys. Thus, both sexes have an increase in physical and mental powers, which contributes to their greater independence from parents and prepares them to be parents themselves. Adolescents' independence is enhanced by their drawing away from their parents and toward their peers—another monomorphic pubertal change (see Chapter 14).

Endocrine System

Since this system influences most of the others involved in the changes of puberty, it will be described first. The endocrine glands produce biochemicals called hormones that travel in the blood. They are carried throughout the body, but each hormone acts selectively on its particular target tissues. Hormones are catalysts. They activate particular metabolic processes in these target tissues. Various hormones promote tissue growth, maturation, secretion, and other metabolic processes. The endocrine system orchestrates relatively long-term bodily adjustments, whereas the nervous system is generally faster acting. Hormonal effects can be brief or chronic, quick or slow, cyclic or steady. They can be triggered by maturation, by internal bodily changes, or by external events, including social stimuli.

The "master" endocrine gland is the *pituitary.* The anterior lobe of the pituitary gland controls many other endocrine glands. The pituitary, in turn, is controlled by the *hypothalamus,* which is concerned with motivation (see Chapter 2). The hypothalamus is involved in various motivated behaviors, such as aggression, flight, and sex; in emotional expression; and in the visceral adjustments that often accompany emotion. Thus, the part of the brain that is central to emotion and motivation oversees the endocrine system, and hormones are important in motivation. The hypothalamus directs the endocrine system to prepare the body for particular motivated behaviors. Certain hormones have been implicated in various motivated behaviors, such as sex, aggression, fear, and parental behavior.

Prenatal Sex Differentiation

Hormones are involved in sexual differentiation of the body and behavior. Much of this differentiation occurs at puberty, but it actually begins in early fetal life. *The main hormonal cause of sexual differentiation before birth is the presence or virtual absence of fetal testosterone.* If the fetus is male and testosterone is present, male differentiation of the genitalia and brain occurs. If the fetus is female and testosterone is absent, then female differentiation takes place. Masculine differentiation occurs as follows.

Males have a Y chromosome. A gene on this chromosome produces a substance that induces the undifferentiated gonads to become testes. This occurs at 7 to 8 weeks of fetal life. The testes produce testosterone, which masculinizes the undifferentiated external genitalia into the penis and scrotum (Figure 9.1). Testosterone itself is less effective than its metabolite, **dihydrotestosterone** (DHT). The enzyme necessary for this conversion, 5α-reductase, is absent in rare cases, leading to female development in genetic males until puberty, when masculinization occurs due to sufficient amounts of testosterone (Ganong, 1997). At this point, these girls assume the gender identity of boys, and some are capable of coitus.

Male and female fetuses possess the forerunners of the internal genitalia of both sexes. In boys, only the male structures develop; in girls,

UNDIFFERENTIATED STAGE

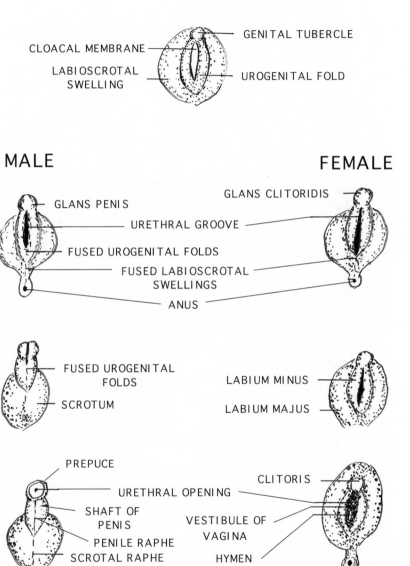

Figure 9.1   Prenatal Development of External Genitalia.

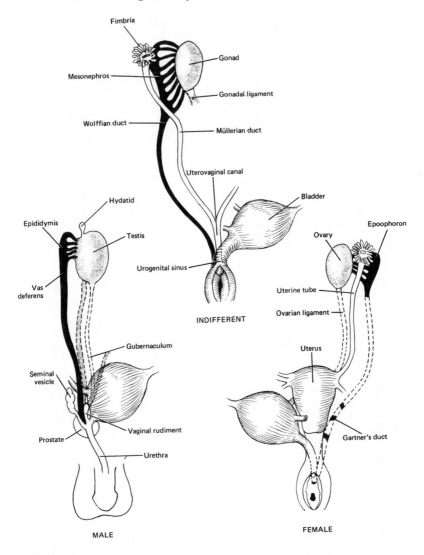

Figure 9.2   Prenatal Development of Internal Genitalia. Source: Ganong (1997). Reprinted with permission.

only the female. The testes secrete **Müllerian inhibiting substance** (or **MIS**, also known as Müllerian regression hormone), which suppresses development of the female internal genitalia, the **Müllerian duct system.** Testosterone promotes development of the primordial male internal genitalia, the **Wolffian duct system.** The primitive Wolffian ducts

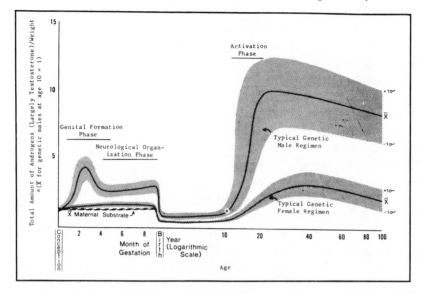

*Figure 9.3   Androgen Levels in Males and Females over the Life Span.
Source: L. Ellis (1982). Reprinted by permission.*

become the vasa deferentia (singular vas deferens), prostate gland, seminal vesicles, and other structures that transport sperm and add ingredients to the seminal fluid (Figure 9.2). Differentiation of the internal and external genitalia occurs during the first peak of testosterone levels in fetal life (Figure 9.3). Descent of the testes into the inguinal (groin) region occurs under the influence of MIS. Further descent into the scrotum before birth is caused by different factors.

A second surge in testosterone organizes the male brain in the masculine direction, around the fifth and sixth months in utero. Some of the resulting behavioral sex differences will be seen before puberty, such as more roughhousing among boys. Others, such as sexual orientation, do not occur until activated by the hormonal changes of puberty. Some morphological changes also involve two stages: one fetal, the other pubertal. For example, the prostate gland is organized (or induced) in early fetal life by testicular hormones, but it is only activated by testosterone at puberty.

Pubertal Sex Differentiation

During infancy and childhood, both sexes have low testosterone levels, and little further sex differentiation occurs then (Figure 9.3).

However, at puberty, testosterone levels diverge greatly. At maturity, men have about twenty times the testosterone level of women, and women's estrogen levels are about ten times those of boys (Hoyenga & Hoyenga, 1993). Male pubertal changes are due to this rise in testosterone and other **androgens** (masculinizing hormones) from the testis. DHT is mainly responsible for enlargement of the penis and prostate and the increase in facial hair. Testosterone causes libido and increased muscle mass.

Throughout life, the production of gonadal hormones and some other hormones is regulated by a feedback system that works as follows. Various **releasing hormones** from the hypothalamus travel by blood to the anterior lobe of the pituitary gland. They stimulate the pituitary to produce their respective hormones, called **tropic** (Gr. "turn toward") **hormones**. Tropic hormones travel by blood to particular endocrine glands, which are stimulated to produce their hormones. These latter hormones exert their effects on various target tissues. They also inhibit further production of releasing and tropic hormones by acting on the hypothalamus and the pituitary. These negative feedback systems keep the level of each hormone fairly constant (except for the female's menstrual cycling, which complicates matters)—see Figure 9.4.

Negative feedback controls the production of hormones from the gonads, thyroid gland, and adrenal cortex. There is a corticoid-releasing factor (CRF), which prompts the pituitary to secrete adrenal corticotrophic hormone (ACTH), which stimulates the adrenal cortex to produce **corticosteroids**, such as cortisol. Similarly, there are a thyroid-releasing hormone (TRH) from the hypothalamus, a thyroid-stimulating hormone (TSH) from the pituitary, and thyroid hormones from the thyroid gland. And a growth hormone–releasing hormone from the hypothalamus triggers the release of growth hormone from the pituitary.

The gonadal hormones are even more complicated. A single releasing factor from the hypothalamus, **gonadotropin-releasing hormone (GnRH)**, prompts the production and secretion of both the **gonadotropins** from the pituitary: **follicle-stimulating hormone (FSH)** and **luteinizing hormone (LH)**. The gonadotropins, FSH and LH, stimulate the gonads to produce gonadal hormones. High levels of **gonadal hormones** (androgens and estrogens) inhibit further production of GnRH, FSH, and LH (Figure 9.5). Another gonadal hormone, **inhibin**, also inhibits FSH release by the pituitary in both sexes.

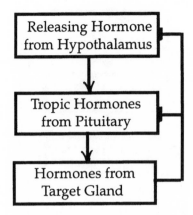

Figure 9.4   Negative Feedback Control of Hormone Secretion via Anterior Pituitary. Releasing hormones from the hypothalamus stimulate production of tropic hormones by the anterior lobe of the pituitary gland. Tropic hormones stimulate hormone production by target glands: the adrenal cortex, thyroid, and gonads. Hormones of target glands (adrenal corticosteroids, thyroid hormones, and gonadal hormones, respectively) inhibit further hormone production by the hypothalamus and pituitary. Blood levels of these hormones therefore have stable baselines. Production of posterior pituitary hormones (oxytocin, vasopressin) is stimulated via neural connections from the hypothalamus.

In both sexes, FSH and LH stimulate the gonads to perform two functions: gamete production and gonadal hormone production. **Gametes** are the germ cells—the sperm and ova. Sperm production is stimulated mainly by FSH. FSH stimulates **Sertoli cells** to promote the development of sperm within the seminiferous tubules of the testis. Sertoli cells also produce inhibin. LH promotes testosterone production, resulting in high concentrations in the testes. This local buildup of testosterone fosters sperm maturation. Testosterone, produced by testicular **Leydig cells** under LH influence, also has general bodily effects. It promotes and maintains masculinization before birth and after puberty. Men who take high levels of androgenic (anabolic) steroids can become infertile because gonadotropin production, necessary for spermatogenesis, is suppressed by intense negative feedback. These drugs are discussed further in a later section, Musculoskeletal System.

In both sexes at puberty, the pituitary-gonadal feedback system is reset at a higher level, resulting in greater production of gonadal hor-

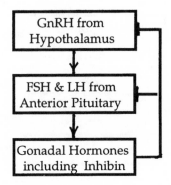

Figure 9.5 Negative Feedback Control of Gonadal Hormone Production via Anterior Pituitary. Gonadotropin-releasing hormone(GnRH) from the hypothalamus stimulates production by the pituitary of the tropic hormones, follicle-stimulating hormone (FSH), and luteinizing hormone (LH). FSH and LH stimulate the testes and ovaries to produce their characteristic hormones—androgens in the testes and estrogens and progesterone in the ovaries. These gonadal hormones inhibit further production of GnRH and FSH and LH. Inhibin, produced by the gonads, inhibits production of FSH in both sexes.

mones. LH and FSH levels rise, as do gonadal hormone levels (androgens in the male, estrogens in the female). *The gonadal hormones are chiefly responsible for the bodily and behavioral changes of puberty in both sexes.*

It is still unclear just what triggers the hormonal changes of puberty. The pineal body of the brain is sensitive to fluctuations in daylight and may act as a biological clock to suppress pubertal development until the proper time (Kolata, 1984). Rats raised in constant light mature early (Becker et al., 1992), as do blind girls (Chapter 8). The decline in melatonin production by the pineal may release the changes of puberty. Pineal tumors, which inactivate the structure, are associated with **precocious puberty** in boys—although perhaps only when there is secondary damage to the hypothalamus (Ganong, 1997). The hypothalamus is involved in pubertal onset because it produces GnRH; tumors of this structure can cause precocious puberty in both sexes (Hopwood et al., 1990). Another possible factor is the level of body fat, especially in girls; see Chapter 8.

Precocious puberty occurs with premature production of gonadotropins (Ganong, 1997). **Precocious pseudopuberty,** without gametogenesis, is caused by early exposure to exogenous hormones or by a masculinizing or feminizing adrenal cortical or gonadal tumor. Normally, the first endocrine changes of puberty occur at about 7 years of age in well-fed populations. Pituitary ACTH secretion increases, followed by an elevation in the level of **adrenal androgens**, the masculinizing hormones produced by the adrenal cortex in both sexes (Nottelmann et al., 1990). Pubertal activation of the pituitary-adrenal axis is termed **adrenarche**. Adrenal androgen production peaks in late adolescence. Being the main masculinizing influence on women, *adrenal androgens cause the masculinizing pubertal changes of girls*, such as hair growth (see Chapter 10). Adrenal androgens are secreted in about the same amounts in both sexes but are unimportant in males, since their effects are swamped by those of testicular androgens.

The gonadotropins (FSH and LH) begin to rise at about 9 years of age in well-nourished girls and at 10 in boys (Katchadourian, 1977). Pubertal activation of the pituitary-gonadal axis is termed **gonadarche**. Testosterone levels in boys typically begin to rise at 11 or 12 years (Bogin, 1988) and peak at age 17. The bodily changes of puberty begin at 10 or 11 in girls, at 11 or 12 in boys. Pubertal development in boys is correlated with blood levels of testosterone and other androgens.

Stages of pubertal development in boys are conventionally defined in terms of Tanner's five stages of genital development (Figure 9.6). Adolescents' reports of their own stage of pubertal development are highly correlated with direct observations made by physicians (Morris & Udry, 1980). All children seem to follow the same stage sequence, whether they are early or late maturers; only the speed varies **(pubertal timing)**. The term **pubertal maturity (or pubertal status)** refers to the stage of pubertal development of an individual. Thus, an early maturer reaches a given stage of maturity before a late maturer of the same chronological age.

The role of the **adrenal cortex** in puberty will be described now. The adrenal gland sits atop the kidney (adrenal = L., "next to the kidney"). The inner **adrenal medulla** (L., "marrow") is part of the sympathetic division of the autonomic nervous system. It produces adrenalin (epinephrine) and noradrenalin (norepinephrine) in emergencies—the flight-or-fight response. It bears no specific relation to puberty. The outer adrenal cortex (L., "rind" or "bark") secretes three families of hormones, known collectively as the corticosteroids, or corticoids:

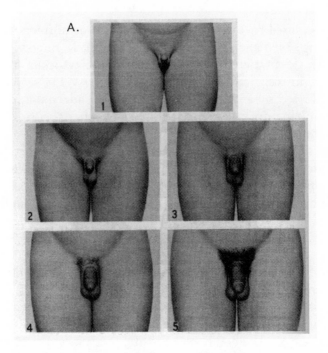

Figure 9.6   Tanner's Stages of Male Pubertal Development. Source: Tanner (1978). Reprinted by permission.
A. Genitalia Standards
B. Pubic Hair Standards

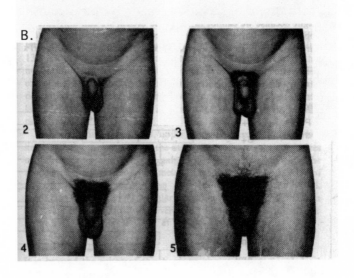

1. The *mineralocorticoids* (e.g., aldosterone) are involved in regulating blood ion concentrations (especially sodium) and have no specific bearing on puberty. They are regulated independently of the pituitary.
2. The *glucocorticoids* (mainly cortisol and corticosterone) are regulated by ACTH from the pituitary. They influence glucose metabolism and, with the mineralocorticoids, mobilize the body to meet stressors. Under stressful conditions, less urgent physiological processes are suppressed. As mentioned in Chapter 8, stress can suppress growth, reproductive maturation and function, and immune system activity. For example, an athlete may be given an injection of cortisone in his injured knee during a football game to suppress swelling, which is part of the healing process. He can then go back onto the field and really wreck his knee.
3. The *adrenal androgens* (mainly dehydroepiandrosterone [DHEA] and androstenedione) have masculinizing effects. Their levels are similar in both sexes, so their masculinizing effects are mild. Levels rise at adrenarche (at around age 9), plateau at about age 40, and fall at menopause. As explained earlier, the adrenal androgens are important only in the female. Adrenal androgens are regulated by ACTH and possibly other factors (Nottelmann et al., 1990).

The corticosteroids belong to a chemical family called **steroid hormones**, which include the androgens, the estrogens, and progesterone. Many different steroid hormones are produced by each of the endocrine glands: the testes, ovaries, adrenal cortices, and placenta. For example, the testes produce estrogens, and the ovaries produce androgens. However, the testes specialize in androgens, the ovaries produce high levels of the estrogens and progesterone, and so forth.

Because of their common basic structure, the steroid hormones sometimes have similar effects. For example, a synthetic progesterone and a synthetic estrogen (diethyl stilbestrol, DES) that were given to pregnant women both proved to have masculinizing effects on their daughters' behavior (see the discussion later in this chapter and Chapter 13). Similarly, estrogens injected directly into the rat brain masculinize behavior. But steroid hormones, especially the androgens and estrogens, can also have opposite effects because of competition for the same cellular receptor sites. *Estrogens and androgens generally have opposite effects on the same tissue,* since they are the hormones mainly responsible for sex differentiation. For example, androgens promote growth of the prostate gland, and so estrogens have been prescribed to men with prostatic cancer. Likewise, an inoperable uterine tumor may be treated with androgens.

There seems to be some truth to the common belief that adolescents are troubled by hormonal changes. Behavioral problems have been associated with gonadal and adrenal cortical hormone levels in both sexes (Nottelmann et al., 1990). For example, late-maturing adolescent boys sometimes have adjustment problems and manifest low levels of testosterone and high levels of stress hormones (cf. Chapter 11). However, adolescents' moods also shift in response to external events and activities (Csikszentmihalyi & Larson, 1984).

Reproductive System

Just as the common features of puberty rites provide clues about the nature of adolescence, so do the pubertal changes, as the remainder of this chapter will show. As an obvious example, at puberty the organism prepares for reproduction. The internal and external genitalia mature. Fertility is low at first—the phenomenon of **adolescent sterility** (or **adolescent infertility**)—but in neither sex can this be safely relied upon for contraceptive purposes. The onset of sperm production is called **spermarche**. Sperm become more numerous and viable as puberty proceeds.

As explained in Chapter 6, testis size is related to sperm production. The human testis is relatively small, consistent with our being a pair-bonding species with comparatively minor sperm competition. Sexual frequency, however, seems to have little to do with testis size. Male chimpanzees copulate almost daily and have large testes. Married men likewise have sex almost daily cross-culturally (Ford & Beach, 1951), but their testes are much smaller.

Musculoskeletal System

Growth

Skeletal growth occurs throughout maturation. **Growth hormone (GH)** does not increase much at puberty; the growth spurt is due mainly to the gonadal hormones (see later discussion). GH is pro-

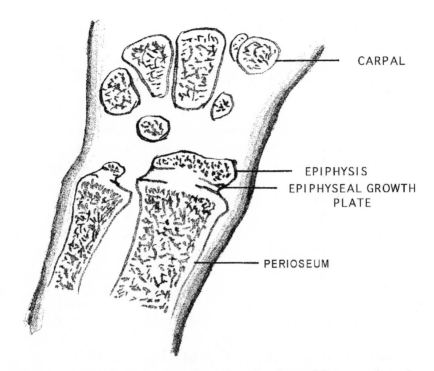

CARPAL

EPIPHYSIS
EPIPHYSEAL GROWTH
PLATE

PERIOSEUM

Figure 9.7   Bone Growth. Long bones lengthen by proliferation of cartilage in the epiphyseal growth plates at each end; cartilage cells become mineralized into bone and are deposited in the shaft end of the epiphysis. A fracture at the growth plate can permanently stunt growth. At the end of puberty, gonadal hormones seal the growth plates completely with bone, leaving the sexes with their characteristic proportions. Long bones widen by depositing bone on the outside of the shaft (in the inner layer of the periosteum) but without mediation by cartilaginous growth plates. Growth of the skull bones and most of the facial bones occurs in the same way. Small bones such as the epiphyses themselves and the carpals (wrist bones) have concentric growth plates and grow from the outside in toward their centers. Bone growth is influenced by stresses and strains imposed by muscles. For details, see Tanner (1978).

duced by the anterior pituitary and stimulates the liver to release growth factors called **somatomedins**. Somatomedins act on the growth plates of the bones where cell proliferation occurs to enlarge them (Figure 9.7). GH promotes growth of most of the other bodily tissues also, through other growth factors. A childhood excess of GH (also known as **somatotropic hormone, STH**) causes **gigantism**. A shortage of GH causes shortness of stature but with adult bodily proportions. An excess after puberty when the long bones can no longer lengthen causes the thick skeletal and facial features of **acromegaly**.

Thyroid hormones mediate maturation in the vertebrates, such as metamorphosis in amphibians. In humans, they transform the infantile body into one with adult proportions. Thus, in chronic hypothyroidism during childhood (**cretinism**), both short stature and juvenile proportions result. Other symptoms include immature dentition and mental retardation. Hypothyroidism in adulthood causes lethargy because thyroid hormones raise the basal metabolic rate (BMR); hyperthyroidism causes an elevated BMR.

The *pubertal growth spurt in both sexes is caused mainly by androgens*, with a contribution by estrogens in the female. These gonadal hormones stimulate long-bone growth and then terminate it at the end of the growth period by closing the epiphyseal growth plates. Thus, boys who take anabolic steroids can stunt their final height. These two effects—stimulation and inhibition of growth of the long bones—mold the male and female body. Girls grow almost as much as boys during the growth spurt, so their adrenal androgens are quite effective. It is in fetal life that males are organized to undergo the more prominent masculine growth spurt (Coe et al., 1988).

Strength

Androgens promote growth partly through their general facilitation of protein synthesis; in other words, they are **anabolic**. Bone and muscle are protein rich; their growth is promoted by testosterone and other anabolic steroids. Estrogens are relatively **catabolic**. They break down tissue protein into carbohydrates (sugars and starch) and fats. Thus, estrogens cause women to have less muscle and more fat than men, and androgens cause the opposite tendency in men.

Growth at puberty involves the muscles as well as the skeleton. At puberty, testosterone greatly increases muscle mass and hence strength. By age 17, the average boy has about twice the arm strength of the average girl, with the curves still diverging (Tanner, 1978). In males, muscle mass and strength increase until the late twenties; in females, they increase only until 10.5 years of age (Katchadourian, 1977).

Petersen and Taylor (1980) have suggested that exercise may play a major role in the sex difference in strength. However, the fastest running times of well-trained women are still about 12 percent slower than those of men (Åstrand, 1985). Contests that require upper body strength produce an even greater differential. Women tend to be better long-distance swimmers than men, but that is because of greater buoyancy rather than greater strength or endurance.

The sex difference in adult strength seems to be due mainly to the muscle-building effect of testosterone, rather than to practice or training. Before puberty, when the testosterone levels of the sexes are similar, girls are close to boys in strength (Tanner, 1978). For example, girls can throw as far as boys when the nondominant arm is used to control for sex differences in practice (Åstrand, 1985). After puberty, however, boys surpass girls in this regard even with their untrained arms.

Other related traits also show sex differences. The greater length and thickness of men's bones contribute to strength and durability (Katchadourian, 1977). This durability is important, since boys suffer more skeletal fractures than girls even with this advantage. In addition, men show greater endurance at strenuous activities. For example, men's superiority over women in running (unlike swimming) is proportionally greater at the longer distances (Åstrand, 1985).

Why do males tend to be stronger than females? Strength and endurance were probably selected for in males to promote success in fighting against rivals. In human evolution, size and strength were probably also advantageous in hunting, in repelling predators, in working with heavy and hard materials, and in warfare—all male specialities. Males are undoubtedly more interested in warfare and hunting than are women, as well as in sports (e.g., Omark et al., 1975). Males' interest in sports, which is virtually universal, may reflect selection pressure for practicing the skills used in fighting and hunting, such as running, throwing, wrestling, and teamwork.

The supposed awkwardness of adolescents is sometimes attributed to contretemps in the development of coordination, size, and strength. However, coordination improves as strength increases (Katchadourian, 1977). Moreover, ungainly children tend to become ungainly adolescents, so puberty is not causal in this regard.

Bodily Proportions

Other aspects of pubertal growth also permit interesting functional interpretations. The legs reach their growth peak first, followed by the trunk and shoulders (Tanner, 1978). For both sexes, the ability to keep up with the group would have been important among semi-nomadic foragers. Moreover, selection may have placed a premium on running ability in early-adolescent boys to allow them to observe hunting and combat close up but to flee when necessary. In late adolescence, boys develop the upper-body strength to participate more actively in combat and hunting.

Another interesting question is why the sexes diverge so markedly in the width of the shoulders and hips. The greatest sexual dimorphism of the skeleton occurring at puberty concerns these dimensions (Tanner, 1978). Men and women differ markedly in this measure: three times the width of the shoulders minus the width of the hips. In boys, the peak of muscle growth coincides with the peaks of trunk and shoulder growth. The growth of heart muscle shows a similar curve. The common developmental pattern of these changes suggests a common function. This function is probably to prepare the male for fighting, which depends on upper-body strength and endurance (N. Barber, 1995). Concomitantly, the female is prepared for childbearing, which depends on the widening of the pelvis.

The growth of fat—especially limb fat and especially in boys— shows an inverse curve. This can be interpreted as an investment in strength and endurance in exchange for protection against starvation. At puberty, boys become less dependent on their fat reserves and more capable of competing for food.

Another skeletal sex difference concerns the prominence of the eyebrow ridges. At puberty, they grow appreciably in boys but not in girls (Tanner, 1978). Brow ridges presumably protect the eyes from injury. Thus, prominent brow ridges indicate selection for frequent and successful combat. Animals that are intimidated by large brow ridges probably enjoyed a selective advantage in their evolutionary past. Therefore, prominent brow ridges probably constitute another threat or dominance feature that other animals, through evolution, came to heed. This interpretation is strengthened by the observation that the eyebrows are lowered in anger, thus accentuating the brow ridges, and raised in friendship (Eibl-Eibesfeldt, 1989). The eyebrows are less arched in men, which means the resting signal is "angrier" in men than in women. Lowering the eyebrows in anger occurs in other primates, too, especially those with little hair on the forehead (Guthrie, 1976). In most cultures sampled by Keating and colleagues (1981), lowered eyebrows increased judgments of a man's dominance.

Lowering the eyebrows may be a partially deceptive signal. By themselves, eyebrows do not protect the eyes and therefore do not render the animal less vulnerable. However, the presence of this threat signal does imply that this animal's ancestors often chose to fight rather than to flee. Hence, the animal may indeed be a good fighter and worthy of respect, especially since testosterone increases aggressiveness and strength as well as eyebrow thickness.

The lower jaw (**mandible**) becomes more prominent at puberty, especially in boys (Tanner, 1978). This accentuates the main primate weapon, the teeth. Again, this feature is accentuated by the facial expression of anger. The mandible is thrust forward, and the teeth are bared, as in other primates.

The canine teeth enlarge at puberty in most male primates (Tanner, 1978). In humans, the canine is only slightly larger in the male, perhaps reflecting its functional replacement by manmade weapons. However, the permanent canine teeth erupt 11 months later in boys than girls, as compared with 2 months later for the first molars. The extreme sexual bimaturism of the canine teeth may reflect their original importance as hominid weapons.

Another male pubertal change is the broadening of the chest (Tanner, 1978). Guthrie (1976) has argued that this is another threat sign. He pointed out that an animal's broadest dimensions are usually presented toward an opponent. Hoofed mammals and most fish are broader when viewed from the side, but bottom-dwelling scavengers such as catfish look larger from above. Male gorillas threaten each other by standing erect and facing each other. They have broad chests, which they accentuate by beating them. Likewise, men threaten each other frontally and have unusually broad chests for a primate.

Men's hands and feet are disproportionately larger than women's. Men's larger hand size is probably associated with manipulation of heavy, hard materials, such as weapons. Even before puberty, males have stronger forearms than females (Tanner, 1978). The male forearm is also longer, relative to height, than the female's (Katchadourian, 1977).

Other skeletal sex differences are harder to explain functionally. Women's arms and legs flare outward more than men's, on average. The index finger is longer than the ring finger more often in women than in men (Tanner, 1978). Since this sex difference is present at birth, the explanation is unlikely to relate to reproduction—but men and women with pronounced sex differentiation of these fingers tend to be highly fertile and to have high LH levels (Manning, 1998). Further complicating the issue, the masculine digital pattern tends to occur in women who rate themselves as assertive and competitive (Wilson, 1983). The trait is controlled by a single gene, which causes the ring finger to be longer than the index finger. The gene is dominant in males and recessive in females, accounting for the observed sex difference in the frequency of the two patterns.

Cardiovascular and Pulmonary Systems

Compared with girls, boys at puberty develop a larger heart, a higher systolic blood pressure, a lower resting heart rate, a greater oxygen-carrying capacity of the blood, and a greater ability to neutralize the waste products of exercise (Tanner, 1978). Likewise, lung size and respiratory capacity increase during puberty, and oxygen exchange is more efficient, especially in boys (Katchadourian, 1977). These sex differences can be parsimoniously explained in terms of a greater advantage to males of strength and endurance. "In short, the male becomes more adapted at puberty for the tasks of hunting, fighting, and manipulating all sorts of heavy objects" (Tanner, 1978, p. 76).

The larynx undergoes a growth spurt at puberty, causing the vocal cords to lengthen and the voice to deepen irreversibly, especially in boys (Tanner, 1978). Since large animals tend to have large larynges and hence deep voices, selection has probably favored animals that are intimidated by low voices. Thus, deep voices are a threat or dominance signal. Another reason why large animals have deep voices is that low tones carry long distances and are easy to localize; a large animal is willing to reveal its position far and wide because it can defend itself well. By contrast, alarm calls tend to be high pitched so as not to reveal the sender's location to the predator. Sirens are designed to be high pitched in order to evoke a fear response.

Integumentary System

Guthrie (1976) studied the functions of various forms of hair in mammals and identified the following categories:

(1) *Course, curly hair* on males typically covers body parts that contribute to fighting ability. This hair puffs out and therefore exaggerates the size of the underlying musculoskeletal structure—at a far lower metabolic cost to the organism than real additional muscle would require. For example, the gorilla has "epaulets" that accentuate its shoulders. Another indication that bushy mammalian hair can act as a threat signal is provided by piloerection: The hair puffs out under

sympathetic activation when the animal is afraid or angry. In men, the jaw, brow ridges, chest, arms, legs, and sometimes shoulders and back are covered with dark, curly, coarse, and hence conspicuous hair. These structures are (or were) relevant to fighting ability.

(2) *Long, thin, straight hair* is typically found near a mammal's scent glands. This hair floats in the wind and wafts the pheromones produced by these glands. The odors of mature males of many mammalian species, like other masculine traits, repel rival males and attract females. In humans and especially males, hair of this form appears in the axillary, pubic, and perineal (anal) regions at puberty, as do **apocrine sweat glands**.

Men's apocrine sweat seems to contain pheromones. By contrast, exocrine (or eccrine) sweat glands are present from birth, cover the whole body, and serve to cool it. Apocrine sweat, which includes the steroid **androstenol**, is almost odorless, but bacteria thrive on it. These bacteria produce an odoriferous substance, especially in the warm, moist armpit, that acts as a pheromone when dispersed by hair. The odor is stronger in men, and it acts as a *threat signal*. Once they reach puberty, boys produce and also recoil from this odor, whereas when younger they cannot detect it. Thus, apocrine sweating is "offensive." It occurs in fear or anger—when fighting is likely to erupt— in adult male chimpanzees as well as men.

Apocrine sweat is also involved in *mate choice*. Specifically, it guides mate choice in order to enhance the future offspring's ability to fight off infectious disease. Apocrine sweat contains odorous proteins that vary with the person's **Major Histocompatibility Complex** (**MHC**), which detects and fights microbes (Furlow, 1996). Individuals with different histocompatibility genes have different axillary odors. If mates differ in these odors, they will have offspring with many different genetic weapons for fighting infection. Indeed, female mice and women do prefer the odor of males whose MHCs differ from their own. Moreover, infertile couples often have similar MHCs.

Axillary sweating has additional pheromonal functions, as mentioned in Chapter 8. Exposure to men's armpit odor shortens and regularizes menstrual cycles (Cutler & Preti, 1986), which hastens the period of fertility; similarly, in many mammals, the female ovulates only in the presence of the male. The ability to detect male sexual smells develops at puberty in girls as well as boys, and it is most acute in women at ovulation (M. A. Baker, 1987). Moreover, women who are ovulating are less repelled by male odors than women at other menstrual stages (Grammer, 1996). In one study, women who had worn an androstenol-soaked pad during the night engaged in more social interactions with men the next day than did controls (Cowley & Brooksbank, 1991). Thus, this male pheromone *hastens ovulation and draws the sexes together.*

Substances known as vaginal fluid **copulines** change in composition at ovulation, when they become effective in *raising men's testosterone level.* Among other effects, this increases the sex drive and sperm production in some males. Thus, at least on some neural level, ovulation is not completely concealed from men (see Chapter 6).

(3) Pubic hair—that which covers the pubic bones, not the straight, thin hair between the thighs—is dark and conspicuous. It seems to act as a maturity marker, appearing in both sexes at puberty. In males, the pubic hair distribution (**pubic escutcheon**, Gr., "shield") eventually extends up toward the navel, thus providing a sex marker also. The scrotum becomes more pigmented and corrugated in pubertal males, and therefore more conspicuous.

All of the conspicuous pubertal changes, including body odor and voice change, probably act as *maturity and sex markers.* Pubic hair may be especially important in this respect, however, because it appears early in puberty. It may also serve to protect the skin during intercourse (Guthrie, 1976). In fact, this is likely to be its original function; bodily signs often evolve out of previously serviceable traits (Darwin, 1872/1965).

Also at puberty, the **sebaceous glands** proliferate, especially around the eyelids, ear canals, mouth, nose, anus, vulva, and face. This distribution and the fact that the fatty sebum collects dirt suggest that these glands function to keep orifices and eyes clear of debris. That the palms and soles are free of sebum may relate to arboreality, for grease would interfere with the gripping of tree limbs. Why sebum production for hygienic purposes increases at puberty, especially in boys, is unclear— unless it is nature's way of punishing obnoxious adolescents by giving them acne. Perhaps the increase, especially in males, is tied to the rise in testosterone, which reduces the efficiency of infection fighting.

Functional Overview of Bodily Changes

Thus, puberty brings maturation of the **primary sexual characteristics**, that is, the internal and external genitalia. Reproductive maturity is attained. The male's **secondary sex characteristics** function mainly in fighting or intimidation. In many other species, too, the maturing male repels rivals and attracts females with **epigamic** (extragenital) **displays**. The male body becomes larger, stronger, hardier, and more formidable. The male looks, sounds, feels, and even smells tough and, at midcycle, not entirely repellant. As in other species, females that were attracted to these masculine traits would have raised their reproductive fitness. These traits connote success in fighting and hence genetic quality. In addition, strength in a man communicates potential as a provider and protector. Hominid females that were attracted to mature, muscular males would have enhanced their fitness because these men would have been good *providers, protectors, and progenitors*. Various masculine traits raise the perceived dominance status and sexual attractiveness of their bearers. These traits include height, a beard, prominent eyebrows and brow ridges, and a large mandible (Freedman, 1979; Keating, 1985; Jackson, 1992); see Chapter 13.

The developmental sequence of male pubertal changes is consistent with this functional interpretation. First to develop is *fertility*—spermatogenesis, the genitalia, and maturity markers. There is no point in competing for mates before fertility begins. The testes begin to grow at about 11.5 years in the West, and the penis, prostate, and pubic hair begin to grow at 12.5 years (Tanner, 1978). Spermatogenesis begins at about 11, although fertility only builds up gradually. Ejaculation of seminal fluid commences about a year after penile growth starts, but before this, the capacity for (dry) orgasms has been reached.

Next, *strength* increases to enhance the ability to compete for mates. Muscle growth and arm strength accelerate, and the shoulders begin to widen. The peak of the strength spurt occurs at age 15. The limbs grow first; they are important in gaining leverage for fight and flight. Then the trunk lengthens, and the shoulders broaden; these features lend strength for fighting. Concomitantly, heart growth peaks, for endurance. As the male becomes stronger, he increases in *formidability*. Before becoming strong, he could not afford to antagonize other males, but as he grows in strength, he can safely threaten rivals. Thus, axillary hair appears at 14, facial hair grows at 16, and the voice changes in late puberty (Tanner, 1978). The increase in strength and hairiness, especially of the torso, may continue well into the twenties.

Thus, boys seem to resemble those male songbirds that reach reproductive maturity early and have some limited success in attracting females (Daly & Wilson, 1983). Later, these birds become more formidable—both threatening to males and attractive to females. Similarly, the male baboon's characteristic mantle and long jaws do not develop fully until late in puberty (Baldwin, 1969).

In girls, unlike boys, *growth precedes fertility* (Lancaster, 1986). Fertility begins at about 14 in well-nourished girls, when the growth spurt is ending. As mentioned in Chapter 6, fertility must be deferred until body size is sufficient to carry a full-term fetus. Even so, the caloric requirements of pregnancy compete with growth to some extent in adolescent girls who became pregnant while still growing (Bogin, 1988; see Chapter 13).

Nervous System (Behavior)

Behavior must be functionally compatible with anatomy and physiology. The animal must eat what it can capture and digest, it must be motivated to seek mates with which it is fertile, and so forth. Developmental changes, too, must occur in concert, and behavioral changes must occur apace with anatomical and physiological ones. Evolved behavioral changes at puberty doubtless serve the same functions as the anatomical ones, and they unfold in a parallel manner. Similarly, since sex hormones influence behavior as well as the body, individuals who are highly sex differentiated somatically tend to be so behaviorally as well.

Sexual Behavior

This section will describe the development of male sexual behavior. Sexual behavior will also be treated in Chapter 13, which will describe the development of sexual orientation, sex differences in mate choice and sexuality, and adolescent pregnancy.

When ejaculations begin, the capacity for *orgasm* has been present for many months. Perhaps the human male becomes sexually competent before fertility begins so he can practice sexual behavior. Presumably, it is important that the capacity for orgasm not begin too early, however. Being very pleasurable, sexual play might become obsessional and detract from the learning of other skills. For this reason, it is unlikely that the genital pleasure that younger children experience approaches the ecstasy of true orgasm, which is clearly a pubertal event.

Primate sex seems to require quite a lot of learning. This is especially true for the male, who must learn to juxtapose his body to the female's. Peer-isolated male rhesus monkeys and chimpanzees do very poorly when presented with a receptive female once they are mature (R. R. Baker & Bellis, 1995). Thus, if the evolving hominid was a typical primate in this respect, some of the social skills of sex were learned in childhood, probably by observation, practice, and instruction. Then at puberty, orgasm provided an opportunity for fine-tuning these motor skills shortly before the onset of fertility.

Since adolescent boys have relatively few sexual opportunities, sexual frustration is doubtless a major form of discomfort and distraction for them. U.S. male university students reported that sexual arousal frequently interfered with their studying; women reported this only infrequently (Singer, 1985b). Further, college men were far less willing to volunteer for a study entailing a month of sexual abstinence than were women. None of the 15 male volunteers completed the study, whereas all 300 of the women did! Katchadourian (1977) surmised that early-maturing boys suffer more sexual frustration than later maturers, but this is not necessarily true because early maturers tend to begin their sex lives at a younger age (Udry & Billy, 1987).

The strength of the sex drive is related to testosterone level, but there is a ceiling effect beyond which more testosterone does not increase libido (Udry, 1988). In adult men, testosterone level is correlated with libido only in hypogonadal men—those with low levels of sex hormones. Young adolescent boys, albeit with testosterone levels ten to twenty times those of girls (Udry, 1988), have not yet reached full testosterone production and are within the sensitive range. In a U.S. sample of 13- to 16-year-olds, testosterone level was related to sexual motivation, measured as self-reported orgasmic frequency and arousability.

Based on his research results, Udry developed a "biosocial model" to account for adolescents' variation in self-reported sexual motivation. For boys, testosterone level explained a whopping 47 percent of the variance in libido. The only other significant factor, parental permissiveness about sex, accounted for only 12 percent. For girls, testosterone and two weaker androgens explained 14 percent of the variance; girls' (and women's) testosterone levels are low enough to be within the range for affecting libido. Parental permissiveness affected girls' sexual motivation about as strongly as did hormones. Girls' pubertal development also contributed to sexual motivation as an attractiveness factor; perhaps the attentions of boys arouse them.

Presence of the biological father in the home (see Chapter 8) and the girl's participating in sports somehow neutralized the effect of testosterone. Thus, *for boys, sexual motivation was governed mainly by testosterone. For girls, hormones (mainly testosterone) increased sexual motivation but so did pubertal maturity and parental values.* This U.S. study suggests that the sexual motivation of girls is more controllable by socialization than that of boys. This is one of the few studies that contrast both hormonal and socialization influences on the same behavior.

Udry and Billy (1987) found that the age of U.S. white males at *initiation of coitus was dominated by hormonal effects and by attractiveness to girls.* Social controls had no measurable effect on the onset of coitus. The hormonal effects operated independently of pubertal status or age. Therefore, these were direct hormonal effects on libido, rather than indirect effects mediated by others' perceptions of boys' pubertal maturity. Social scientists are sometimes reluctant to consider that hormones can act directly on behavior, rather than just through bodily perceptions, or "stereotypes" (Udry, 1988). But in Udry's research, direct hormonal effects on behavior have been demonstrated.

Girls' initiation of coitus was dominated by the effects of social controls, with pubertal maturity (i.e., bodily appearance) and age playing minor roles. Social controls included a general sexually permissive attitude, engaging in other "deviant" behaviors, and poor school performance. There were no effects of attractiveness or hormones.

Thus, boys' sexual motivation and onset of coitus were influenced mainly by hormones and attractiveness. Girls' sexual behavior was affected mainly by hormones, pubertal maturity, and social values. These sex differences are consistent with sociobiological principles (see Chapter 5). Males' sexual opportunities reflect their appeal to girls (cf. the predominance of female choice). Females' sexual activity is more closely tied to the onset of fertility, in order to maximize their reproductive span. Females' sexual activity also varies with the value of remaining chaste in a given social environment.

Sexual frequency in adolescents has been studied far less than sexual initiation. Sorensen's (1973) survey of the sexual behavior of a national sample of U.S. adolescents ages 13 to 19 seems to be the most detailed source of information on adolescent sexual behavior. Sorensen classified adolescents as virgins, serial monogamists, sexual adventurers (three or more partners in the previous month), inactive nonvirgins, and others. Of the entire sample, 24 percent of the boys and 6 percent of the girls were adventurers, 15 percent of the boys and 28 percent of the girls were monogamists, and 41 percent of the boys and 55 percent of the girls were virgins. The median and modal age of sexual initiation for all nonvirgins was 15 for both sexes. Although sexual adventurers reported multiple partners, they tended not to have intercourse as frequently as monogamists. Thus, adventurers were trading sexual frequency for variety. Sexually active adolescents had intercourse about once a week.

Sorensen's data suggest that males tend to be more promiscuous, that is, motivated to seek sexual variety, whereas females are more motivated than males to confine their sexual activity to one partner at a time. As explained in Chapter 5, a woman, once pregnant, cannot have more offspring by copulating with additional men, whereas a man can fertilize multiple women in rapid succession. More generally, in most species, physiological factors limit the female to a certain number of offspring in her lifetime. Males, by contrast, are limited only by their attractiveness to females; sperm are abundant. Thus, males tend to be more promiscuous than females in most species. These physiological and behavioral sex differences result in greater variance in lifetime reproductive success for males than for females (the **Bateman effect**). Simply stated, this principle means that some males have high mating success and some males have none, but most females are intermediate. For example, Bateman (1948) demonstrated that some male fruit flies had huge numbers of offspring, many males had none, and most females had intermediate numbers. Thus, males tend to be big winners or big losers in the reproductive sweepstakes. Being a male constitutes a bigger gamble for reproductive success, and so, with more at stake, more effort theoretically will be expended in gaining sexual opportunities. In other words, males are the more competitive sex (see Chapter 5). This also explains the Trivers-Willard effect on the sex ratio, discussed in Chapter 8.

Being largely unregulated by marital conventions, adolescent boys are probably more promiscuous than adult men. In Sorensen's study, 7 percent of the boys had had intercourse with at least 16 partners, whereas only 1 percent of the girls were that promiscuous. Similarly, Hass (1979) reported that 11 percent of U.S. boys 17 to 18 years old had had more than 10 partners, as compared with only 2 percent of girls. Thus, *adolescence is a time of great competitiveness* for boys and also for girls, who presumably are competing for the same few highly attractive boys. Promiscuity declines through adolescence, as pair bonding increases. Of nonvirgins aged 13–15, adventurers outnumbered monogamists by a ratio of 3 to 2 (Sorensen, 1973). Of nonvirgins aged 16–19, monogamists outnumbered adventurers by a ratio of 8 to 7.

Promiscuous adolescent sexual behavior may serve several functions. It may help young people determine their mate preferences and their own mate value, practice mate attraction strategies and sexual techniques, and (mainly for girls) gain resources in exchange for sex (Buss, 1994; R. R. Baker & Bellis, 1995). Obviously, sex may also help a girl to gain the affection of a boy. Sexually inactive girls may seek to undermine the reputation of sexually active rivals (see Chapter 13).

It should be noted that in sex surveys, males seem often to overreport their sexual activity and females to underreport it (Steinberg, 1996). For example, Hayes (1987) reported that by age 15, only 5 percent of girls had had intercourse but 17 percent of boys had. Since girls tend to initiate sex with older boys (Sorensen, 1973), with whom are these 15-year-old boys having sex? There are a few adventurous girls who presumably are initiating multiple boys, but there are many more adventurous boys who presumably are deflowering even more of the girls. Even among older subjects, it is unlikely that prostitution accounts for much of this discrepancy (Einon, 1994). Rather, it appears likely that females tend to downplay their sexual activity, in keeping with social expectations, and that males exaggerate their own. Male bragging sessions are common cross-culturally (Freedman, 1967), whereas women lower their mate value by appearing promiscuous.

Amorousness

Amorousness functions to allow cooperative care of offspring but also perhaps to promote mate guarding. Amorousness is present in many prepubertal children (see Chapter 3), but it is not directed toward the object of sexual interest until puberty (Money & Ehrhardt, 1972).

Thus, mature amorousness is a pubertal phenomenon. Early maturers tend to date earlier, to report falling in love earlier, and to have sex earlier than later maturers in both sexes, controlling for chronological age (Higham, 1980). Hypogonadal boys usually manifest little sexual or romantic interest. If the problem lies with the testes themselves, then testosterone therapy usually induces sexual and romantic behavior. If the problem involves the pituitary gland, then testosterone therapy only produces a low level of sexual interest and little in the way of falling in love.

Boys with early, or precocious, puberty tend to be sexually mature but do not report dating or falling in love (Money & Ehrhardt, 1972). Similarly, girls with precocious puberty do not begin erotic and sexual activities early. However, it is still possible that these precocious individuals possess the necessary hormonal factors for romantic motivation. They may lack a suitable social context for expressing their romantic inclinations; for example, they may lack a suitable partner or be reluctant to admit to these feelings.

Few sex differences in amorousness have been reported, except that men tend to fall in and out of love more quickly (Money & Ehrhardt, 1972). This sexual monomorphism may reflect the mutuality of the relationship; it could not be unilateral (i.e., coercive) and be easily maintained. Thus, both sexes must gain similarly from pair bonding.

Recent research has shed some light on the hormonal basis of amorousness. Orgasm results in the release of the pituitary hormone oxytocin, which promotes mother-child bonding and other social bonds in mammals (see Chapter 10). Therefore, this hormone may contribute to the romantic attachment that often accompanies a sexual relationship; it has been implicated in postcoital cuddling (Zeifman & Hazan, 1997). The exhilaration of infatuation may be mediated by the natural stimulant phenylethylamine. Long-term bonding, or attachment, seems to rely on endorphins, natural opiates whose addictive properties are consistent with the acquired need for particular individuals. In various species, exogenous opiates relieve the separation distress of offspring.

Aggressiveness, Competitiveness, and Self-Confidence

Because these traits are closely related and show the same sex difference, they will be considered together here. Males are generally more aggressive than females, but the type of aggression matters greatly. Females exhibit more parental (maternal) aggression than males in most mammals. Further, women seem to experience just as much anger as men, as when someone steps ahead of them in line (G. Mitchell, 1981; Deaux, 1976). It makes adaptive sense for both sexes to resist being exploited, although women are less prepared to fight and may instead respond with appeasement behavior (Hokanson, 1970); see Chapter 10.

Most research on sex differences in aggression concerns dominance aggression, which is the type most closely related to the concepts of competitiveness and self-confidence. The sex difference in aggression is clearest in regard to dominance aggression (L. Ellis, 1986; Lauer, 1992) and play fighting (Blurton Jones, 1967; Boulton, 1994); the latter may likewise contribute to the formation of dominance hierarchies.

This research strongly suggests the existence of an evolved sex difference in dominance aggression and competitiveness. Males initiate and receive more aggression than females (Daly & Wilson, 1988). Moreover, boys are more aggressive and competitive than girls from a young age cross-culturally (Rohner, 1976; Freedman, 1974; Hoyenga & Hoyenga, 1979). In their Six Culture study, Whiting and Whiting (1975a) reported a consistent sex difference in physical and verbal aggression in childhood. In none of the 240 cultures studied by Schlegel (1995) were adolescent girls more competitive than boys. German boys show off more than girls at about 5 years of age (Hold-Cavell, 1985).

Other findings are consistent with the greater competitiveness of males, which is explained in terms of the Bateman effect. Males are more achievement motivated (i.e., self-confident) and have higher levels of aspiration, self-esteem, and self-confidence (Hutt, 1972; C. C. Weisfeld, 1986). They risk failure more often (Ginsburg & Miller, 1982), including rising to intellectual challenges (Maccoby, 1966), and persist longer at tasks at which they have previously failed (Crandall & Rabson, 1960).

The greater self-confidence of males, whatever its origins, may also help to explain why men tend to take credit for success and shift the blame for failure. When men succeed, they typically attribute their success to high ability (Hoyenga & Hoyenga, 1979). When they fail, they blame lack of effort or bad luck, rather than admitting lack of ability. By contrast, when women succeed, they tend to attribute their success to hard work or luck; when they fail, they cite lack of ability. Therefore, when men fail, they tend to redouble their effort, since they continue to believe that they are capable of success. Women who fail, by contrast, are more prone to give up.

One indication of self-confidence is the overrating of self. Young boys overrate themselves more than girls do on a variety of qualities, including toughness rank (Omark & Edelman, 1976; Pollis & Doyle, 1972). Self-confidence may serve to maximize competitiveness in the crucial early going, prompting boys to issue and accept challenges, intimidate rivals, and hence rise in rank (see Chapter 11). Overrating declines subsequently; if it did not, formation of a consensual hierarchy would be impossible. By about age 6, self-ratings of toughness have become more realistic and consensual (Omark & Edelman, 1976). Similarly, overrating of self on reading ability declined starting at age 6 (Ruble, 1983). However, even adults tend to overrate themselves compared with the ratings of them given by acquaintances (Wylie, 1979), probably to provide the self-confidence necessary to compete (see Chapter 4).

Thus, a variety of research conclusions about sex differences in competitiveness, achievement motivation, and attribution theory can be explained parsimoniously in terms of the male's greater competitiveness. It should be noted, however, that the types of competition used in this research may reflect a male bias. Perhaps girls and women are more competitive than males in areas such as effective caregiving and sensitivity to others.

The basis for specieswide sex differences is usually hormonal. This seems to be the case with respect to the sex difference in aggression. As explained previously, testosterone can act during fetal life to masculinize behavior after birth. Fetally masculinized female rhesus monkeys show high levels of threat behavior and rough-and-tumble play as infants, as well as more aggression as adults (Mazur, 1983). Male rhesus monkeys that were given androgens in utero showed more rough-and-tumble play before and after puberty than did controls.

Clinical research on children has shown the same sort of influence of prenatal hormones on aggression. Girls who were exposed in utero to abnormally high masculinizing hormones (due either to a synthetic steroid drug the mother received during pregnancy or to androgens produced by a tumor of the fetal adrenal cortex [**congenital adrenal hyperplasia, CAH**]) tended to have elevated levels of roughhousing behavior in childhood (Money & Ehrhardt, 1972). A prenatal estrogen given to pregnant women was found to lower sons' aggressiveness compared with that of controls (Yalom et al., 1973).

Because of its implication that hormones can influence sex differences in human behavior, this research on fetally masculinized girls has been severely criticized. One objection has been that the girls behaved differently because their genitalia were masculinized, causing them to be perceived differently even after surgical treatment. However, the girls whose mothers received hormones did not have masculinized genitals and did not require drug therapy, as did the girls with CAH. Another objection is that the girls' parents, knowing their daughters' history, would have been more tolerant of their masculine behavior. However, interviews of the parents (Ehrhardt & Meyer-Bahlburg, 1981) indicated that they did not encourage their daughters to exhibit masculine behavior. Yet another criticism, that the controls were not adequate, is refuted by the fact that, in some samples, the unaffected sisters of the subjects served as the controls. The Money and Ehrhardt findings have been confirmed by other researchers. For example, Reinisch (1981) reported that fetally masculinized children were more aggressive than their control siblings between ages 6 and 8.

Although prenatal androgens are probably the most important hormonal contributors to the sex difference in aggression (L. Ellis, 1986), pubertal androgens likely also play a role. Testosterone injections increase aggression in many mammals, in both sexes and at all ages (Hoyenga & Hoyenga, 1979), probably via vasopressin, a pituitary hormone (Panksepp, 1993). Studies of men have shown increases in assertiveness after testosterone treatment (Mazur, 1983). Testosterone also seems to enhance strength, coordination, and concentration, which would help explain why it rises when male mammals are about to compete (Mazur & Booth, 1996). Testosterone tends to rise to higher levels in men who win rather than lose competitions such as chess or tennis matches (see Chapter 4). Presumably, testosterone keeps winners prepared for further contests, whereas losers withdraw from competition and so have less need to remain mobilized by testosterone.

Early in puberty, individual differences in boys' antisocial behavior and aggressiveness mainly reflect pubertal maturity rather than testosterone levels per se (Drigotas & Udry, 1993; Mazur & Booth, 1998). That is, a mature appearance seems to trigger aggressiveness by male rivals.

Once boys reach late adolescence, however, they all look mature, and individual differences in behavior become more closely correlated with testosterone level (Mazur & Booth, 1998). From then on, males show consistent evidence of a correlation between testosterone level and various antisocial behaviors, including trouble with the law and at work, marital disruption, and violence. For example, the peak of testosterone corresponds with the peak of aggressiveness and antisocial behavior, in the late teens and early twenties. Questionnaire research has usually given weaker results than more direct, ethologically valid behavioral measures.

Why does aggression increase in pubertal boys? To analyze a behavior functionally, we must consider its distribution. As noted in Chapter 5, rivalry increases in maturing males of many species, including dogs (Tinbergen, 1951) and chimpanzees (D. A. Hamburg et al., 1975). During adolescence, male primates in various species become more assertive, strutting in "macho" fashion. They move up the dominance hierarchy, taking their places among the adult males (D. A. Hamburg, 1971). In these diverse species, the males are competing for females. At maturity, a supremely important resource—access to fertile females—suddenly becomes available to them. Therefore, rivalry increases markedly. In many primates, the female also shows an increase in aggression at puberty, although that increase is smaller than that in males (G. Mitchell, 1981).

In our species, too, males seem to become more aggressive at adolescence, as expected (see Chapter 5). Boys become much more aggressive than girls at puberty (Hoyenga & Hoyenga, 1979). Although peer fighting gradually declines in children up to age 12 (Cairns, 1979), serious fighting seems to rise at adolescence (see Chapter 11). Criminal assaults by men in the United States and Canada peak in the late teens, and homicides peak in the twenties (Daly & Wilson, 1988). Young males are disproportionately represented among violent criminals worldwide.

Disputes frequently concern access to women, as illustrated by a Detroit study by Wilson and Daly (1985). The majority of homicides occurred in social conflict situations between acquaintances; most commonly, two unrelated men were involved in a public dispute over status, or "saving face." "Trivial altercations" over an insult or a small amount of money seem improbable causes of murder, but the loss of status carried momentous consequences for these subjects. A man who became the butt of public ridicule would be prone to a loss of girlfriends and property. Moreover, the average length of imprisonment was only about 1 year, whereas the risk of getting killed if one did not shoot first was, presumably, rather high. Homicides arising out of robbery attempts (to secure wealth to attract women) and out of jealousy were frequent as well. Thus, aggression usually occurred as a means of securing reproductive success.

Less violent forms of rivalry also seem to rise at adolescence, such as teasing, ridicule, and athletic competition, especially in boys. Adolescent boys are more likely to drive recklessly with a male passenger than a female one (Daly & Wilson, 1983). Around puberty, U.S. boys participate in more verbal dominance contests than girls (Goodwin, 1980). This repartee is sometimes called "ranking." Humorous repartee, like social competition in general, is especially common in adolescent boys and men cross-culturally (Apte, 1985). By contrast, female adolescents mainly use less aggressive humor to exchange information about peer norms and sexuality (Sanford & Eder, 1984). However, in Savin-Williams's (1987) research on adolescent campers, both sexes frequently employed ridicule in their dominance relations.

Males exhibit more dominance displays than females. They show more expansive postures and less smiling, especially in situations in which smiling connotes deference (G. E. Weisfeld & Linkey, 1985). Females show more eye contact than males; a direct gaze can be a threat display but also can express intimacy, which females often do. Males seem to exhibit dominance but to avoid threat displays. At puberty, boys (but not girls) maintain greater distance between each other, and they avoid standing face to face (G. Mitchell, 1981).

Mazur and Booth (1998) have suggested that a positive feedback cycle can lead to high levels of testosterone and competitiveness in males living in "cultures of honor." As mentioned earlier, testosterone rises in competitive situations, as though to mobilize the male. In cultures of honor, in which male competition is common, testosterone levels would tend to be high, leading to greater aggressiveness and perpetuation of the cycle. Consistent with this model, testosterone tends to be high in young inner-city black males but not in preteen or older black males.

These investigators also discovered that testosterone tends to fall in men who are approaching marriage and then marry; these men are withdrawing from the competitive world of batchelorhood. However, divorcing and divorced men experience a rise in testosterone, which may reflect competition with the spouse or ex-spouse as well as with male rivals. This model underscores the point that hormones and behavior interact reciprocally. The endocrine and nervous systems are interrelated, mainly through the hypothalamus and pituitary.

Spatial Perception

Spatial perception is usually defined as the ability to recognize an object that has been rotated into another orientation or to orient oneself in space. Boys tend to surpass girls in spatial perception beginning before puberty (Kimura, 1998). Although practice effects and sex bias doubtless explain some of the sex difference in spatial perception, pure socialization explanations are refuted by the fact that this difference is observed in other mammals, too (L. Ellis, 1986), and in various human cultures (Kimura, 1998).

This sex difference is partly hormonal. Spatial ability can be altered by prenatal testosterone treatment in rats. Pubertal hormones also play a role. Boys with delayed puberty due to androgen deficiency suffer a permanent decrement in spatial ability that is not corrected by later androgen treatment (Hier & Crowley, 1982). Likewise, early-maturing, masculine-appearing men, who tend to have higher androgen levels, have somewhat low spatial ability. Androgen levels in the lower range of those exhibited by normal males seem to maximize spatial ability. Late-maturing, androgynous-appearing women, who have higher androgen levels, have greater spatial ability than other women. Spatial ability is higher in women at menstruation, when estrogens are low (Silverman & Phillips, 1993). And in men, it is higher in the spring and in the evening, when testosterone is low (Kimura, 1998).

Consistent with this, various pathological conditions that alter sex hormone levels tend to distort spatial ability. Females with congenital adrenal hyperplasia (CAH) produce high levels of androgens and have better spatial skills than controls (Hoyenga & Hoyenga, 1979). Highly feminized individuals (i.e., individuals subject to relatively strong estrogenic influences) tend to be low in spatial perception. These include girls with **Turner's syndrome** (a single X chromosome rather than two), who tend to have normal verbal ability but poor spatial and numerical skills. Low spatial ability also characterizes girls with **testicular feminization** (target tissue insensitivity to testosterone in a chromosomal male, resulting in a phenotypic female, also known as **androgen insensitivity syndrome**). In addition, boys whose mothers had been given an estrogen during pregnancy had low spatial skills (Yalom et al., 1973). Lastly, low spatial ability and high verbal ability typify male victims of **kwashiorkor** (a protein deficiency accompanied by high estrogens and low androgens).

If males' relative proficiency in spatial tasks has any evolved basis, its adaptive value may be related to the male need to range widely in search of mates. In support of this explanation, Gaulin and FitzGerald (1986) predicted that the sex difference would be greater in a polygynous species, in which males range widely in search of mates, than in a monogamous one, in which the sexes range about equally. Testing two closely related rodent species on maze running, they found that the promiscuous male meadow vole surpassed the monogamous pine vole, as expected. If additional research confirms this hypothesis, then the sex difference in spatial ability in humans probably reflects the general mammalian pattern.

Men's spatial skills may also aid them in hunting—in orienting themselves and in hurling projectiles accurately. The latter ability has been correlated with spatial skill (Jardine & Martin, 1983), and again a sex difference emerges before puberty (Kimura, 1998).

But women may possess a different type of spatial skill that is useful in foraging activity. Women surpass men at recalling the location of objects, a spatial skill that would be well suited for gathering plant food (Silverman & Phillips, 1993). Female superiority in location memory begins at puberty. Research supports the notion that the sexes have complementary skills that were exchanged by hominid pairs.

Risk Taking

Adolescent and adult males tend to be more sensation seeking, exploratory, and accident prone than females (L. Ellis, 1986). This may relate to the male tendency to range widely in search of women and game, and to challenge others to combat. Men are more aggressive experimental subjects when observed by other men than by women (Daly & Wilson, 1983; van der Dennen, 1992). Young men also tend to be risky drivers because they overestimate their own skills (overrating of self) and underestimate dangers (Daly & Wilson, 1994). Evidence cited by Daly and Wilson indicates that much dangerous and violent behavior by young men functions as social display, and that successful risk taking is admired.

However, both sexes may be prone to taking risks at adolescence. It makes sense for adolescents to act as though they are relatively invulnerable to injury and disease, since *adolescence is the healthiest stage of life*. It is adaptive for the individual to be healthiest when just entering the reproductive years, that is, when reproductive value is greatest. Families whose mortality rates are highest among the very young and very old will leave more offspring than will populations that suffer high adolescent mortality. Perhaps reflecting these considerations on some level, evidence indicates that parents grieve the loss of adolescent children more intensely than of younger ones (Crawford et al., 1989).

The greater risk taking of males extends to the physiological level. Polygynous birds and mammals tend to show a consistent sex difference in longevity and morbidity, with females being favored (Daly & Wilson, 1983). In effect, males trade some of their life expectancy for enhanced short-term mating opportunities. Male animals compete for mates by accumulating muscle mass for fighting. However, muscle is metabolically costly to maintain; even at rest, muscle fibers contract and use up energy, thus wearing down the male. The function of muscle shrinkage with disuse is doubtless to divert energy to other tissues, in accordance with the law of economy.

Consistent with this explanation of the metabolic cost of muscularity, castration reduces muscle mass and increases longevity. Institutionalized men who had been castrated because they were mentally retarded were found to live 13 years longer than intact controls (Hamilton & Mestler, 1969). The advantage in longevity was greatest if castration had occurred before puberty, perhaps because after puberty, the men had developed masculine muscularity. Other research has established that the sex difference in mortality is greatest just after puberty (Childs, 1965).

Hoyenga and Hoyenga (1979) provide a table on sex differences in susceptibility to particular diseases in humans. Castration reduces susceptibility to infectious disease, and intact men are more prone than women to infectious diseases and cancer.

Incidentally, sexual activity lengthens the life span of male rats (Hoyenga & Hoyenga, 1979), and there are comparable reports on men. It appears that the tension of sexual frustration is more wearing than is any extra morbidity due to the fact that copulation raises testosterone levels in men (Daly & Wilson, 1983).

One proximate mechanism proposed for the greater morbidity of males is sex-linked disease. Indeed, males suffer more sex-linked disease than females throughout the mammals. For example, men have hemophilia more often than women because the condition is carried on the X chromosome. If a woman has the hemophilia gene on one of her X chromosomes, she is almost certain to have a normal **allele** (corresponding gene) on her other X chromosome that will offset the bad one and protect her from getting the disease. But if a man has the defective gene, he has no second X chromosome to offset it, and he will get the disease. Nevertheless, sex-linked disease is not the main physiological reason for the sex difference in morbidity. In birds, it is the females that have the smaller sex chromosome, which accounts for the fact that they are more vulnerable to sex-linked conditions—yet the males tend to die younger (Daly & Wilson, 1983). The physiological key to the sex difference in morbidity is the male's higher testosterone levels.

Summary

Masculine differentiation begins with a gene on the Y chromosome that causes the gonads to differentiate into testes. The Leydig cells of the testes secrete testosterone and other androgens. These androgens cause male differentiation first of the internal and external genitalia and then of the brain. Maturation of the primordial female internal genitalia is suppressed by Müllerian Inhibiting Substance from the testicular Sertoli cells. Testosterone causes the Wolffian duct system to differentiate into the male internal genitalia. Some of the effects of fetal testosterone lie dormant until puberty, when high levels of androgens activate the changes that have been organized before birth. At puberty, gonadotropin levels (FSH and LH) rise steadily, bringing increases in testicular androgens and production of mature sperm. Testicular hormones cause the masculine bodily and behavioral changes of puberty, some of which were organized by prenatal hormonal exposure. Prenatal hormones also influence prepubertal behaviors, including play fighting and spatial skills (see Chapter 10).

The adrenal cortex releases adrenal androgens, which cause the moderately masculinizing changes of puberty in girls, such as the lowering of the voice. The adrenal cortex also secretes stress hormones, which can suppress growth, maturation, and other less urgent bodily processes (see Chapter 8).

The growth spurt is superimposed on normal growth (regulated mainly by growth hormone) and on maturation (regulated mainly by thyroid hormones). In both sexes, androgens are mainly responsible for the growth spurt. Estrogens or androgens, respectively, feminize or masculinize the skeleton and other structures.

Adolescent boys undergo the same radical changes in morphology and behavior as occur in many other species at sexual maturity. They compete intensively with other males for dominance, which, in turn, enhances their reproductive opportunities. They become larger, stronger, and more aggressive and intimidating. Males' strength and endurance also improve the capacity for hunting, warfare, and heavy labor.

In the first stage of male puberty, fertility gradually rises. Once reproduction is possible, muscle and bone development and stamina accelerate, so that running and, later, fighting are enhanced. Concomitantly, formidability increases, so that rivals are intimidated and females are attracted. By contrast, fertility follows bodily growth in girls. Hormones probably induce mature amorousness at puberty in both sexes.

Many of the other pubertal changes in voice, skeleton, pheromones, and hair in boys likewise function to attract females and intimidate males. Male **hirsutism** (hairiness) increases apparent body size, conveys maturity, protects the pubic area during sex, and disseminates pheromones that repel males and induce ovulation in females. Vaginal copulines raise men's testosterone level, and axillary odors guide mate choice. The aggressive humor, dominance displays, and risk taking of adolescent boys reflect the heightened dominance competition of males trying to enter the breeding pool. Aggressive, "antisocial" behaviors in early puberty are due somewhat to individual differences in bodily maturity, which triggers aggression by rivals. Thereafter, antisocial rivalrousness is attributable more to testosterone level, which tends to be high in males living under competitive conditions such as cultures of honor or bachelorhood.

The male libido appears early in puberty, paralleling the early onset of fertility. In adolescent boys and girls, the strength of the sex drive increases as androgen levels rise. The male sex drive is generally stronger, more distracting, more under hormonal as opposed to socialization control, and more directed at a variety of sex partners than is the female libido. Boys' sexual activity partially reflects their attractiveness, whereas girls' sexual activity reflects socialization and pubertal maturity. Male promiscuity declines as puberty proceeds, paralleling the establishment of pair bonds in the breeding pool. Concomitantly, sexual competition presumably declines.

Many sex differences in cognitive ability emerge or increase at puberty, and they have a hormonal basis. Spatial skill is associated with moderate masculine hormonal influences at puberty. Male spatial ability may reflect selection pressure to range great distances in search of mates. Women surpass men at recalling the location of objects, an aptitude that may have enhanced their ability to forage for plants.

Whereas females maximize their fitness by having a long reproductive span, males sacrifice some longevity in favor of greater reproductive success through competition. They sustain higher morbidity because they maintain greater muscle mass for fighting against rivals, but other bodily systems are taxed as a result. Morbidity and mortality are especially high in males compared with females just after puberty, when muscle mass is growing and rivalry is high. Nevertheless, this period, when reproductive value peaks, is the healthiest part of the life span for both sexes.

We may be reluctant to recognize the blatantly sexual and aggressive connotations of these developmental changes and their parallels in other cultures and species. We may wish to downplay the role of hormones in behavior, to minimize sex differences by regarding them as cultural artifacts or roles, as products of "stereotypes" about bodies and behavior. If we focus on individual and cultural variation rather than on universal sex differences, however, we will ignore the patterns that do exist in men's and women's behavior. Moreover, we will fail to appreciate the adaptive value of these specieswide sex differences, which are profound in adolescence (Bogin, 1994).

10 Pubertal Changes in Girls

Some of the pubertal changes in girls will now be reviewed systematically. Some of these changes have already been described in the previous chapter and so for the most part will not be repeated here.

Endocrine System

Sex Differentiation

As explained in Chapter 9, the absence of a Y chromosome is the factor initially responsible for female sex differentiation in utero. The outer layer of the undifferentiated fetal gonad develops and becomes an ovary, whereas in males the inner layer develops into a testis. Without fetal testes, the female genital tract (the Müllerian duct system) develops, forming the uterus, vagina, and oviducts, and the male (Wolffian) duct system degenerates. In the absence of fetal androgens, the undifferentiated phallus becomes a clitoris instead of a penis, and the genital folds become the labia majora instead of the scrotum. (See Figure 9.1.) In the absence of fetal testosterone, the brain is feminized, too. For instance, the fetal hypothalamus is organized to secrete GnRH cyclically once menstruation begins, rather than tonically, as happens in mature males.

As in boys, puberty begins in girls when the sensitivity of the hypothalamus to gonadal hormones decreases. The low level of childhood estrogens no longer inhibits the hypothalamus from producing much GnRH. More GnRH is produced, the pituitary produces more FSH, and the ovaries produce much higher levels of estrogens (Tanner, 1978). In addition, the pituitary becomes more sensitive to

GnRH, especially in girls, which may explain why they undergo puberty earlier than boys (Hoyenga & Hoyenga, 1993).

Subsequently, estrogens rise and cause the feminizing pubertal changes of girls, that is, those changes not caused by adrenal androgens. Androgens cause masculinizing changes in girls, bringing increased hair growth, voice change, libido, and oily skin (Tanner, 1978). The growth spurt in girls is due mainly to androgens, although the feminizing skeletal modeling is caused by estrogens. The first feminizing event is breast development, **thelarche**, followed by the development of pubic hair, **pubarche**. Adrenal androgens bring about the female sex drive at puberty and also the peak in female-initiated sexual activity in the middle of the menstrual cycle, which is the time of greatest fertility (Persky et al., 1978; Morris et al., 1987; Udry, 1988). Androgens increase the sensitivity of the penis and clitoris, and they may also influence motivation by acting on brain centers.

Menstrual Cycling

Late in puberty, when a girl's estrogens reach adult levels, the estrogen sensor in the hypothalamus undergoes another change. Suddenly, estrogen levels no longer always turn off the production of GnRH; at high levels, they instead turn it on. The feedback system changes from negative to positive at high levels. The more estrogen there is, the more GnRH and hence the more FSH and the more estrogen is produced. This change in the hypothalamus is what activates menstrual cycling. Before puberty, FSH and LH levels are about equal in the two sexes. At puberty, LH levels rise twofold in boys and fivefold in girls. FSH levels rise only slightly in boys and twofold in girls (Chumlea, 1982).

The endocrinology of the menstrual cycle is complex. When menstruation ends, FSH levels rise. FSH stimulates the follicle of the ovary to produce estrogens. The **ovarian follicle** is an endocrine tissue capsule that encases an immature ovum in a woman's ovaries (Figure 10.1). Each month, one ovum and its follicle grow under the influence of FSH and later of LH.

The follicular cells release estrogens (**estradiol, estriol,** and **estrone**) into the blood. These same estrogens have produced the earlier pubertal changes before their release became cyclic. Now that menstrual cycling has begun, these estrogens complete the feminizing changes of puberty and also play a part in menstrual changes.

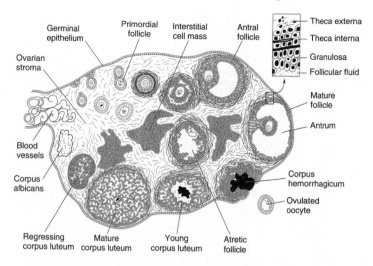

Germinal epithelium — Primordial follicle — Interstitial cell mass — Antral follicle — Theca externa — Theca interna — Granulosa — Follicular fluid — Ovarian stroma — Mature follicle — Antrum — Blood vessels — Corpus albicans — Corpus hemorrhagicum — Ovulated oocyte — Regressing corpus luteum — Mature corpus luteum — Young corpus luteum — Atretic follicle

Figure 10.1   Time-Lapse Diagram of Development of an Ovarian Follicle. A primary follicle develops into a vesicular follicle and then a mature follicle. This ruptures at midcycle, yielding an ovulated oöcyte (ovum) and a corpus hemorrhagicum, which develops into a corpus luteum that degenerates into scar tissue (corpus albicans). Source: Ganong (1997). Reprinted by permission.

The estrogens from the follicle peak late in the first half of the cycle (Figure 10.2). They cause the uterine lining (**endometrium**) to thicken in preparation for the implantation of a fertilized egg; they plump the cushion. Estrogen production continues to rise, triggering a burst of LH secretion by the pituitary. Estrogen levels then decline.

This midcycle burst of LH triggers ovulation. The ovum breaks out of the follicle and ovary, and floats in the fluid of the abdominal cavity. There, wavelike movements of the fringe at the opening of the **oviduct** (fallopian tube) usher the ovum inside, where fertilization normally occurs. Sperm survive for about 48 hours and the ovum for about 72, but the ovum is capable of being fertilized for only 12 to 24 hours (Hyde & DeLamater, 1997). The most fertile period is 48 hours before ovulation (Ganong, 1997).

After ovulation, the follicle undergoes structural and metabolic changes. The hollow area where the ovum was ensconced fills with blood (**corpus hemorrhagicum**). This minor bleeding may irritate the peritoneum, resulting in midcycle pain (**mittelschmerz**). The endocrine tissue of the follicle then proliferates, replacing the blood, and the now-solid structure secretes progesterone as well as estrogens. Rich

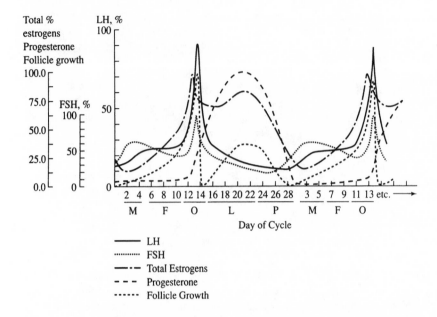

Figure 10.2 Hormonal Fluctuations over the Menstrual Cycle. Hormone levels are represented as a percent of maximum secretion. M = menstrual, F = follicular, O = ovulatory, L = luteal, P = premenstrual stage. Source: Schnatz (1985). Reprinted by permission.

in fat, the structure is now called the **corpus luteum** (L., "yellow body"). If fertilization does not occur, the corpus luteum degenerates into glistening scar tissue (**corpus albicans**, L., "white body"). The endometrium then breaks down and is partially sloughed off, accompanied by 3 to 5 days of bleeding (**menses**). The first day of bleeding is conventionally called the first day of the new cycle.

The first phase of the menstrual cycle is called the **follicular phase** because the follicle is present and actively secreting hormones. It is also called the **proliferative phase** because the endometrium is thickening. The length of this phase is elastic; if a woman's cycles are long, it is usually because of the lengthening of the follicular phase only. The second phase of the cycle, after ovulation, is the **luteal**, or **secretory** (referring to secreting glands in the endometrium), **phase**. It is usually 14 days long.

Pregnancy and Labor

If fertilization and implantation do occur, the corpus luteum persists. Estrogen and progesterone levels rise further. They maintain the en-

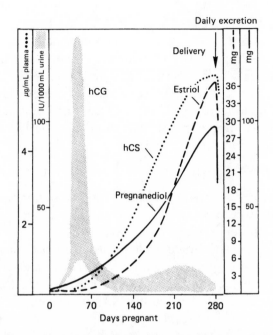

Figure 10.3   Levels of Pregnancy Hormones. HCG = human chorionic go-nadotropin, HCS = human chorionic somatomammotropin. Estriol is one of the three estrogens in women (along with estrone and 17β-estradiol); pregnanediol is the metabolic product of progesterone. The placenta also secretes relaxin. Source: Ganong (1997). Reprinted by permission.

dometrium for the developing embryo and then mediate other changes of pregnancy (the term *progesterone* means "for gestation"). High levels of estrogens and progesterone inhibit gonadotropin production, and so cycling stops. Progesterone is produced in men, too, but its function is unknown. The persistence of the corpus luteum in the face of declining FSH production by the pituitary is due to a placental gonadotropin known as **HCG**, or **human chorionic gonadotropin** (the chorion is a layer of the placenta).

Production of estrogens and progesterone shifts from the mother's corpus luteum to the placenta between 6 and 12 weeks of gestation (Warren & Shortle, 1990), but the corpus luteum persists through pregnancy (Ganong, 1997). Figure 10.3 shows the levels of some of the pregnancy hormones. **Human chorionic somatomammotropin** (**HCS**, also known as **human placental lactogen**) causes some metabolic adjustments in pregnancy. The placenta also produces **relaxin**, which softens the pelvic ligaments to facilitate delivery (**parturition**).

Labor may be initiated by oxytocin from the fetus's pituitary. The ensuing labor contractions dilate the cervix, sending nervous signals to the mother's hypothalamus, which, in turn, sends nervous (not hormonal) signals to her pituitary, which then releases oxytocin. Oxytocin levels rise, dilation increases, and still more oxytocin is secreted into the bloodstream. Thus, the fetus's and mother's pituitaries act sequentially to trigger parturition. A fall in progesterone may also be involved in labor (LeVay, 1993).

Breast-Feeding

Milk production does not begin until 1 to 3 days after delivery. In the meantime, **colostrum**, which is rich in antibodies, is produced by the breasts right after delivery.

Milk production occurs as follows. At puberty, estrogens cause breast enlargement by triggering growth of mammary ducts and of fat. During pregnancy, high levels of progesterone, estrogens, HCS, and prolactin cause full development of the milk-producing lobules. **Prolactin**, produced by the pituitary and placenta, finalizes activation of the breast and converts it into its fifth and final stage of maturity, when the pigmented areola (L., "halo") flattens down to become flush with the surrounding tissue (Tanner, 1978). The areola doubtless aids the nursling in locating the nipple; estrogens cause it to grow and darken conspicuously at puberty and, further, at pregnancy (Ganong, 1997). During pregnancy, estrogen molecules block the access of prolactin to breast tissue. When estrogen levels fall with expulsion of the placenta at birth, prolactin is free to induce milk production, which ensues (Warren & Shortle, 1990). Prolactin may also enhance sperm production in men (Becker et al., 1992). In both sexes, prolactin secretion by the pituitary is controlled by a negative feedback system via the hypothalamus.

Milk delivery, or **ejection**, or **let-down**, is mediated in the following way. Suckling triggers a nervous reflex that causes the pituitary to secrete oxytocin. This hormone causes milk ejection (the **let-down reflex**), and milk is transported from the **alveoli** (little sacs of glandular tissue) in the lobules through the ducts to the nipple.

Thus, oxytocin stimulates labor contractions and milk ejection. It also causes the orgasmic contractions of the uterus and vagina during sex. For this reason, women sometimes experience orgasmic sensations while nursing. This may serve as a natural reward to encourage nursing, in addition to the relief from painful breast enlargement.

Some women reportedly are reluctant to nurse because these orgasmic sensations make them feel guilty (Elissa Walsh, personal communication, 1989). Prolactin also enhances feelings of well-being (Dettwyler, 1995b). Both hormones promote maternal feelings and behavior, leading to more appropriate maternal behavior and feelings of acceptance in the child. For example, breast-fed babies receive more affection and are left alone less often (Fleming, 1990).

Suckling maintains and augments milk production by the reflexive stimulation of prolactin production by the pituitary. Research has shown that newborns whose mothers received anesthetics or analgesics sucked and ate less than controls in the first four days (Stuart-Macadam, 1995a). The infant actively participates in nursing by means of its sucking drive, rooting reflex, sucking reflex, hunger cry, and expressions of satisfaction. At weaning, oxytocin and prolactin levels decline because of less suckling, and milk production and ejection wane. Thus, the milk supply is maintained as needed by means of a positive feedback system. Only in girls do prolactin levels rise at puberty. Prolactin levels then rise 100-fold during pregnancy, and they increase further with each successive birth, possibly contributing to the improved competence of experienced mothers (Warren & Shortle, 1990).

The composition of the milk of a species precisely meets its particular nutritional needs—which is an obvious argument for breast-feeding. Human milk is very low in protein and very high in both lactose (milk sugar) and lipids (metabolic fats); because of the high sugar content, it is sweeter than cow's milk. This nutritional content reflects the fact that although the human infant grows rather slowly, its brain grows very quickly, almost reaching adult size by age 4 (Dobbing, 1974). High levels of lactose are needed to fuel the brain; in fact, during the first year of life, the brain uses up 65 percent of the body's energy (Holliday, 1978). The fat composition of milk changes through the nursing bout, so babies should be allowed to regulate cessation (Woolridge, 1995), as they do in traditional cultures, in which mothers nurse their infants on demand and even sleep with them. Co-sleeping is typical of primates, including traditional human cultures (McKenna & Bernshaw, 1995); see Chapter 6.

Breast-feeding has innumerable benefits for the child and mother alike. It is clean and convenient, requiring no sterilization, shopping, refrigeration, or heating. Human milk contains white blood cells, immunoglobulins, benign bacteria, and lactoferrin, all of which reduce the incidence of respiratory and intestinal infections. However, milk may also contain toxins, such as nicotine and alcohol, and the AIDS virus. Specific growth-enhancing factors for the intestine and other tissues are also present. Breast-feeding reduces the child's risk of a range of health problems, including: allergies, juvenile diabetes, obesity, atopic disease, ulcerative colitis, lymphoma, otitis media, poliomyelitis, liver disease, reduced bone mass, breast cancer, Sudden Infant Death Syndrome, dental malocclusion, slow initial weight gain, slow motor development, and inferior cognitive development (Stuart-Macadam, 1995a; A. S. Cunningham, 1995).

Breast-feeding benefits mothers by lowering the probability of breast, uterine and ovarian cancer, and osteoporosis (Stuart-Macadam, 1995a). Through the release of oxytocin, which helps the uterus shrink back to normal size (**involution**), breast-feeding also diminishes the risk of postpartum hemorrhage.

U.S. hospitals often thwart breast-feeding by routinely providing pacifiers or bottles of water or formula. Stuart-Macadam (1995a, p. 28) cautioned that "nature has crafted a unique two-way system for the health and survival of mothers and infants. . . . Because of our evolutionary history mothers and infants need each other for optimum physiologic and metabolic functioning and breast-feeding provides the key to achieve this."

After birth and loss of the hormone supply from the placenta, the hormonal effects of nursing (probably those related to prolactin) continue to suppress gonadotropin production. Cycling is inhibited, resulting in a fairly effective form of natural contraception. If nursing ceases (for example, if the baby dies), then cycling resumes. In traditional cultures, nursing lasts for 2 to 3 years (Stuart-Macadam, 1995b). Solid foods are introduced around the end of the second year, consistent with eruption of the deciduous teeth from 6.5 to 24 months of age. Weaning earlier than this can detract from the health of modern humans (Dettwyler, 1995a). Cycling becomes more likely to resume the longer it has been inhibited and the less regularly nursing occurs; births typically occur about 3 years apart in these populations. In the West, 50 percent of nursing mothers ovulate before their babies are weaned.

Reproductive System

Pubertal maturity in girls is usually measured by referring to Tanner's (1975) stages of breast development and pubic hair development (Figure 10.4). As with boys, girls' self-ratings are highly correlated with ratings

A.

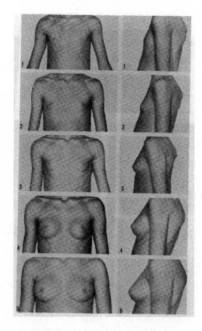

Figure 10.4 Tanner's Stages of Female Pubertal Development. Source: Tanner (1978). Reprinted by permission.
A. Breast standards
B. Pubic hair standards

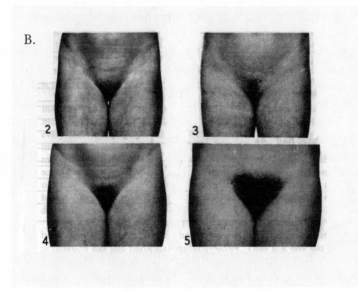

by physicians (Morris & Udry, 1980). A simpler, equally valid method is
to record the age of menarche. Maturation of estrogen-dependent structures, such as the breasts, is correlated with maturation of androgen-
dependent structures, such as pubic hair (E. A. Smith, 1989).

At puberty, the genitalia grow and mature. The uterus increases in
size and strength. The vagina lengthens and thickens. The clitoris develops sexual sensitivity. A capacity for orgasm emerges that depends
on the presence of the clitoris, at least initially. If the clitoris is absent
before puberty, orgasm never develops, but if it is removed after orgasm has been established, orgasmic capacity often persists. This suggests that some sort of priming effect operates with respect to orgasm
in females.

This notion of a priming effect in female sexual pleasure may be related to some other observations. Unlike boys, girls often take some
time to acquire a full appreciation of sexual pleasure (Kinsey et al.,
1953), as though crucial neural connections must be built up through
experience. (However, male castrates who are sexually experienced
retain some sexual capacity longer than do the inexperienced [Rathus
et al., 1997].) About one-half of U.S. girls do not begin to masturbate
until they have become sexually active with boys (Kinsey et al., 1953;
Arafat & Cotton, 1974). In contrast to boys, few adolescent girls report feelings of sexual deprivation (Kinsey et al., 1953).

Moreover, women have less intense sexual drives than men cross-
culturally (Davenport, 1977). They masturbate less often than men
(Ford & Beach, 1951), and they generally endure sexual abstinence more
easily than men (Kinsey et al., 1953; Symons, 1979); see Chapter 9.

Early adolescence is a time for romantic and sexual experimentation in most cultures and for premarital sex with a succession of potential spouses (Broude & Greene, 1976; Shostak, 1981). Adolescent
girls often fixate on evaluating boys; natural selection would have
strongly favored women's ability to choose mates wisely. Sexual behavior begins in most cultures well before fertility. Accordingly, the
genitals mature prior to menarche (R. R. Baker & Bellis, 1995). This
includes the development of the corrugations (**rugae**) that line the
vagina and stimulate the penis, and of the protective pubic hair. Later
on, as the sex drive becomes more insistent, regularity of sex may become more important than variety of partners, a change that would
be more suitable for marriage.

The breasts develop well before fertility. Since lactation will not be
possible for years, it is likely that the breasts serve as sexual lures.

Various observations are consistent with this hypothesis. The breasts are cited explicitly as attractive features in about one-third of traditional cultures (Ford & Beach, 1951). Even in some cultures that do not cite the breast as alluring, the breast is stimulated in foreplay (N. Barber, 1995). The sexual significance of the breasts is underscored by the fact that they are often covered only in unmarried women of reproductive age, as among the Nepalese and the Dogon of Mali (Low, 1990).

The pendulous human breast is unusually conspicuous; the mammary tissue of most nonlactating primates, by contrast, is barely protuberant. The human breast is composed mainly of fat tissue, so its conspicuousness does not reflect the amount of mammary tissue. Thus, conspicuous breasts do not seem to be necessary for adequate lactation. Breasts are prominent even during the menses and pregnancy and after menopause. It seems as though nature has deposited an abundance of fat tissue in the breasts to render them more conspicuous to men.

But is large breast size a valid indicator of lactational potential? In well-nourished populations, breast size is not closely related to lactational ability, since size differences are due mainly to fat rather than mammary tissue. However, in poorly nourished women, body fat is probably related to the ability to nurse efficiently, given the enormous metabolic cost of lactation. Even in modern societies, severe mammary tissue insufficiency results in nutritional deficits (Low, 1990). Therefore, men who chose wives on the basis of fat reserves would be at a selective advantage.

But why should large breasts be more attractive than overall adoposity? Perhaps breasts, being a female sex characteristic, already acted as sexual attractants in hominid evolution because they signaled emerging femininity. Perhaps breasts played this role in hominids and not in other primates because our hairlessness and bipedalism made breast development easy to observe (R. R. Baker & Bellis, 1995). This would also explain why women accumulate fat around the hips, for the wide pelvis is another feminine trait that is attractive to men and easily observed; by contrast, male hormones concentrate fat in the upper body.

Then, too, women may have favored men who were attracted to large breasts because these men would have stayed with pregnant women who had lost their slim waists. That is, women may have been selected to choose men who chose women with large breasts, setting off a spiral both of larger breasts and of a growing preference for them. Women are, in general, the more selective sex, and so they could have exercised strong control over men's preferences.

Fat deposits in the breasts may be a partially deceptive signal; they may exaggerate the woman's mammary tissue—the lactational ability that originally attracted males (Low et al., 1987). Pelvic fat may be another deceptive signal; it may exaggerate the apparent width of the birth canal and deceptively attract men. But why don't women have large breasts made up entirely of mammary tissue—true signals—instead of breasts composed mostly of fat? Wouldn't such women have better-nourished children than "deceptive" women? Perhaps the answer is that fat is more versatile than excess mammary tissue, since it can be converted to energy used for nursing but also for survival. A male would be less biologically interested in a female's lifetime reproductive potential than in her short-term fertility, that is, her reproductive success only so long as he is mated to her. A female, however, would want to maximize her lifetime fitness—her reproductive success with her future mates as well as the present one.

Selection pressure favors the ability to detect deception, so men probably evolved ways of identifying women with abundant mammary tissue. Men tend to be attracted to the "hourglass figure," in other words, to women with large breasts and slim waists (N. Barber, 1995). Such women would have a high ratio of mammary tissue to body fat, and so such men would not be deceived. Furthermore, because fat tends to accumulate around the abdomen with age, a slim waist is a sign of youth, which would also have attracted men.

Next, the role of bodily fat in pregnancy and lactation will be described. The main function of fat is to provide stored energy. Figure 10.5 illustrates a fat cell. It is almost all fat, a light-weight reservoir of energy. A gram of fat yields about twice the calories as a gram of protein or carbohydrate. Energy storage is especially important for pregnancy and lactation. During these states—which constituted the majority of the female's adult life in prehistory—a woman is relatively incapacitated and easily fatigued. She may have difficulty procuring and digesting food, and yet she has a great need for calories. The 16 kilograms of fat deposits of an adult woman are sufficient for her either to nurse for 1 year without further caloric intake or to complete a pregnancy (which consumes about 50,000 calories) and 3 months of lactation (1,000 calories per day) (Frisch, 1983b). During pregnancy, fat accumulates around the hips and thighs, where it tends to be re-

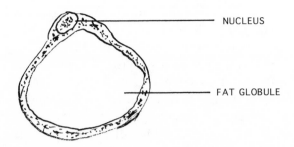

NUCLEUS

FAT GLOBULE

Figure 10.5   Adipose Cell. Note size of fat globule, which makes the cell a bundle of energy.

tained if breast-feeding does not occur (R. R. Baker & Bellis, 1995). This fat is of a special type that is only mobilized during lactation (Caro & Sellen, 1990)—a good point to mention if one is trying to persuade young women to breast-feed.

Thus, fat accumulation is very important for women's reproduction. Intermediate levels of fat optimize fertility and gestation. In most mammals, the female is only slightly fatter than the male, especially when not breeding (Pond, 1977). In our species, however, the sex difference in adiposity is very large (Lancaster, 1986). Young women are about 80 percent fatter than young men, whereas young men are only about 30 percent more muscular than women. Girls have more body fat and fat cells than boys from childhood on.

Fat has some additional advantages. Women survive starvation better than men, as was observed during the siege of Leningrad in World War II. Perhaps women in our species, being protected by males, have evolved the luxury of fat accumulation as a hedge against starvation. Subcutaneous fat also acts as an insulator against heat loss. Thus, subcutaneous fat is concentrated on the buttocks in some African tribes (**steatopygia**) but is more evenly distributed in Eskimos (Low et al., 1987).

Skeletal and Integumentary Systems

The hormonal basis of the growth spurt in both sexes is described in Chapter 9. Because of the earlier onset of the growth spurt in girls, females are generally taller than their male agemates between 11 and 14 years of age (Chumlea, 1982). This female advantage is primarily confined to the legs; girls do not undergo a growth spurt in the upper body to the extent that boys do. The epiphyseal plates of the long bones close at about age 18 in girls in the West, preventing further lengthening. In boys, this occurs at about 20 years.

Estrogens feminize the growing skeleton. They widen the pelvis so that it winds up about as wide as a man's, whereas the rest of a woman's skeleton is smaller than a man's. In addition, the pelvic outlet (birth canal) widens at puberty (Low et al., 1987). Even in newborns, a girl's pelvic outlet is wider than a boy's (Tanner, 1978). Women's hands are smaller than men's, enhancing manual dexterity (Hoyenga & Hoyenga, 1979); cross-culturally, women predominate at sewing, cooking, and gathering plant food.

In this and many other respects, a woman's skeleton and face are more like a baby's than are a man's. At puberty, a man's body matures more than a woman's, digressing further from the juvenile (**pedomorphic**) form. A woman is smaller than a man. Her eye orbits are taller, making the eyes more prominent, again like a baby's. Her brow ridges and mandible are smaller (cf. Tanner, 1978). A woman's skin is soft, smooth, thin, hairless, and lightly colored compared to a man's, and her hair soft like a baby's. Her cheeks are chubby, her forehead large and rounded, her mouth and teeth small, her voice soft and high-pitched.

Women may gain protection and care as a result of their relative pedomorphism. Starting with the work of the Nobel laureate Konrad Lorenz, research has demonstrated that babyish facial features are attractive and endearing (Eibl-Eibesfeldt, 1989). The appeal of pedomorphic features extends to men's reactions as well as women's (Sternglanz et al., 1977), perhaps because of the paternal behavior of our species. "Disarming" infantile features, which often include a distinct coat color, inhibit attack by male simians, too, even in species without paternal care (Rowell, 1972). At maturity, male primates develop masculine traits that threaten rivals. Thus, *women possess an appealing immature appearance and also lack threatening masculine features.* They are disarming as well as endearing.

Women who exaggerate their immaturity or femininity seem to intensify the effect of pedomorphism. Observational and questionnaire research has shown that women are less likely to be targets of aggression in a given situation than are men (van der Dennen, 1992), especially if they act femininely (G. Mitchell, 1981). Cosmetics that accentuate the eyes cause women to be perceived as more submissive and warmer (Berry & McArthur, 1986). Cross-culturally, flirtation by women includes submission displays, which are characteristic of immature, less aggressive animals (Eibl-Eibesfeldt, 1989). In courtship, both sexes may be inspired by the nonthreatening, even childish behavior of the other to exhibit nurturant behavior. For example, hand feeding is an element in both child rearing and courtship, and cuddling, babyish expressions, and pet names are common features of both (Singer, 1985b). Many animal courtship displays evolved from submissive or infantile displays that presumably are disarming.

The appeal of pedomorphism, or the "infant schema," continues beyond infancy. Abused children possess less babyish craniofacial dimensions than matched controls (McCabe, 1984). Throughout childhood, the younger a face appears, the more it is perceived as defense-provoking (Alley, 1983). This tendency may help mediate both the gradual withdrawal of parental help as offspring mature and the abrupt decline in sympathy that people seem to feel toward (obnoxious) adolescents. Not only are adolescents less dependent than children, they also possess mature characteristics that may instill competitive feelings in adults. Children's facial features have been found to become more threatening and less submissive with age in both the United States (McArthur, 1982) and Korea (McArthur & Berry, 1987). These effects were independent of perceived age and attractiveness; they reflected features such as eye size and forehead size (McArthur & Apatow, 1983–1984). Because boys depart further from the pedomorphic form than do girls, they may be even more off-putting than girls. Masculine traits, such as apocrine sweat, are essentially "offensive." Boys are, in effect, doubly obnoxious. In a questionnaire study, U.S. and Japanese respondents of both sexes said they would be more helpful to female subjects than to males, and to younger subjects than to older ones (Burstein et al., 1994).

It is important to recognize that these effects are not "stereotypes" in the sense of being incorrect perceptions. Children actually are more helpless and less threatening than mature individuals, especially mature males, and females do tend to be less aggressive and competitive than males. Nature may have endowed us with these perceptual biases so that we recognize these developmental and sex differences. Additional evidence that these facial characteristics convey accurate information comes from studies of adults whose faces vary in babyishness and masculinity/femininity. People whose faces were judged to be dominant and powerful scored higher on behavioral scales of aggressiveness and dominance (Berry, 1995). Facial babyishness was negatively related to self-reported aggression and to aggression and assertiveness as rated by close friends. However it comes about, behavior and anatomy tend to be functionally correlated.

Nervous System (Behavior)

Endearment

Because of their relative pedomorphism, women may utilize a somewhat different general behavioral strategy from that of men. Since women are less capable of using aggression to gain their ends, they may use gentle persuasion, or endearment, more than men. Endearment behavior would complement women's anatomical pedomorphism. It might function to elicit sympathy and hence assistance. Women could then return this assistance and continue to benefit from these relationships of reciprocal altruism. In other words, females might benefit from giving and eliciting help, that is, from being cooperative, rather than being threatening or competitive. Similarly, Rosenthal and DePaulo (1979) referred to an "accommodation hypothesis": Women are more motivated than men to please others. Cross-culturally, women and girls are more dependent and nurturant (i.e., mutually helpful, or cooperative), and more pleasant and agreeable, than males (Hall, 1984). In all 45 cultures surveyed by Barry and colleagues (1967) and all 56 reported by Zelditch (1955), girls were more nurturant and obedient, and boys were more achieving and independent. And in none of 82 cultures were girls more self-reliant than boys (Barry et al., 1967). Perhaps because they do not evoke much sympathy, boys are encouraged to be self-reliant. Of course, this is only a relative sex difference. Men participate with women in exchanging various forms of help; indeed, the specialization of labor between the sexes means that men and women are dependent on each other. And women *can* be aggressive, for example, toward their husbands (Campbell & Muncer, 1994).

Research on adolescents supports the notion of this average sex difference in social strategies. At a U.S. summer camp, boys helped as much as girls, but boys' assistance tended to be instrumental (e.g., fixing a broken bicycle), whereas girls' help was mainly expressive (e.g., comforting an injured victim) (Savin-Williams, 1987). In another study, adolescent girls reported experiencing more emotion in affiliation situations, and boys experienced more emotion in achievement settings (Stapley & Haviland, 1989). At adolescence, girls become even more concerned than boys with being popular and having a good marriage, whereas boys focused on personal and occupational success (Hoyenga & Hoyenga, 1979). Indirect evidence that hormones are involved in the sex difference in affiliative behavior is provided by research showing that early-maturing girls (who are more feminine) and late-maturing boys (who are less masculine) tend to rank high for their sex in terms of the need for affiliation (M. C. Jones & Mussen, 1958).

It makes sense that women did not take their inferior muscular strength lying down. Natural selection would have worked just as hard on them as on men to enhance their success in social situations. Social power is not simply a matter of intimidating or overpowering others; being helpful is also a means of influence. In particular, the stronger sexual needs of men give women an important means of exercising power; Hrdy (1981) elaborated this idea with respect to female primates. In general, a helpful, cooperative strategy has notable advantages over a competitive, self-reliant one. It tends to be less dangerous and uncertain, and it permits the exchange of skills and favors. Moreover, even if not reciprocated, helpfulness can raise one's fitness if directed at kin.

The social effectiveness of endearment has been amply demonstrated. Gazing and smiling can enhance persuasiveness (Vrugt, 1987); girls and women exhibit more of these displays than boys and men (G. Mitchell, 1981). Affiliative nonverbal behavior creates a positive impression and evokes reciprocal affiliation from the other person. Indeed, in one study, having women friends to talk to reduced self-reported loneliness for adults of both sexes, but having male friends did not (Argyle & Henderson, 1985).

Endearment seems to require communication skills at which females excel. Women are more accurate at sending and perceiving nonverbal signals than men (Hall, 1984; Deaux, 1976) and at recognizing faces, starting at an early age (H. D. Ellis, 1975). By 4 months of age, girls are more interested in faces than are boys (Kagan, 1970). Women also surpass men at most verbal skills, starting before puberty (Kimura, 1998). This may relate to the fact that women are usually their child's main language teacher, or it may relate to the general endearment and nurturance strategy of women. Both sexes would benefit from social sensitivity (Tiger, 1969), but women's greater involvement in child care would at least explain their superior comprehension of infants' nonverbal signals. In discriminating the emotional expressions of infants, female university students surpassed males for all 11 of the emotional expressions studied; child-care experience did not affect performance (Babchuk et al., 1985).

Although the cross-cultural and developmental data suggest that the sex difference in social strategies has an evolved basis, individual experience can modify behavior. In one study, experimental subjects were mistreated, causing a rise in systolic blood pressure, which correlates with self-reported anger (Hokanson et al., 1968). Male subjects typically retaliated aggressively—disparaging their tormentor—and then showed a prompt fall in blood pressure, indicating reduced anger. Females experienced a rapid drop only if they reacted in a friendly manner toward their tormentor, as they tended to do. However, males could be conditioned to react in a friendly way by being rewarded for doing so and being punished for aggression; likewise, females switched to aggression when rewarded for doing that. Thus, the original tendency of the female subjects to use endearment apparently can be modified by experience and instruction; so, too, can the males' intimidation propensity. Nevertheless, these initial sex differences might have a biological basis. They might provide a starting point for experience to modify, just as prepotent fears (e.g., of snakes) can increase or decrease as a result of experience.

Nurturance

As suggested earlier, the basis for the sex difference in endearing behavior may be female predominance in child care. Does the universal sex difference in nurturance have an evolved basis? Are hormones involved?

In most female mammals, maternal behavior is primed by pregnancy and lactational hormones (estrogens, progesterone, prolactin, and oxytocin [Coe, 1990; Hrdy & Carter, 1995]), and it is released by features and signals of the young of the species (Becker et al., 1992; see Chapter 3). Thus, maternal behavior can be provided even before a specific bond to the mother's own offspring forms; the mother will care for any newborn placed before her.

At some point, however, an individual bond forms in most mammals. The bond is usually reciprocal, and relies on multiple sensory modalities; redundancy typifies important biological systems. The mother-offspring bond develops at birth or hatching, as by imprinting, in **precocial** species, which are independently mobile early on and might otherwise get lost. This early bonding allows mother and offspring to find each other if separated. In slowly developing, or **altricial**, species, such as those that keep their young in a den or carry them about as do primates, bonding develops slowly because the young cannot wander off. The ability of the mother and newborn to recognize each other by odor, voice, and sight occurs shortly after birth, but bonding intensifies gradually.

The slow formation of the bond in altricial species may permit continued parental assessment of the baby's viability, so that the mother can adjust the extent of her care according to the baby's potential fitness (see Chapter 3). However, an assessment of viability would best be performed as soon as possible, at birth. Indeed, mothers examine their newborn's body in a stereotypic sequence cross-culturally (Eibl-Eibesfeldt, 1989). The mother-infant bond may be weak if this assessment during the early-contact period is prevented. Evidence from several controlled studies suggests that mothers who did not experience immediate social contact with their newborn were less likely to breast-feed, less inclined to interact with the baby later on, and more likely to abuse the baby (Daly & Wilson, 1988), although this effect wore off by 6 weeks (Fleming, 1990).

Postpartum depression may reflect a lack of opportunity to make this early assessment, or an adverse emotional reaction to the baby's features or social circumstances (Daly & Wilson, 1988). Postpartum depression is most common in young, single mothers (Rathus et al., 1997), who, cross-culturally, are also most likely to kill their newborn (Daly & Wilson, 1988). Depressed mothers have been observed to interact less with their babies than do normal mothers (Fleming, 1990).

Parturition may itself enhance maternal care. As a lamb is born, it stimulates the mother's cervix and vagina to trigger the release of oxytocin, one of the hormones of maternal care (Becker et al., 1992). Cervical-vaginal stimulation also prolongs the ewe's acceptance of alien young. Perhaps women who deliver by cesarean birth experience less maternal motivation.

As described in Chapter 3, primate mothering is relatively flexible and extensive, but lactation, at least, is influenced by female hormones. Little evidence exists about other pregnancy hormonal effects on primate mothering (Fleming, 1990; Warren & Shortle, 1990). Pregnant women do tend to respond to a baby's pain cry with a heart rate acceleration that is typical of new mothers (Fleming, 1990). Feelings of attachment to the offspring usually increase between 3 and 5 months of gestation, and then they rise sharply after delivery and contact with the newborn. Maternal feelings and satisfaction continue to rise thereafter. Similarly, in other mammals, maternal tendencies increase with exposure to a normal offspring and with the number of previous offspring.

Although the role of pregnancy hormones in primate maternal care is unclear, the mother's prenatal hormones probably play a role, since sex differences in parental behavior emerge before puberty (G. Mitchell, 1981). Female primates are more interested in neonates than are males from early in life. Research on fetally masculinized girls has shown that childhood doll play and interest in marriage and in having children were reduced (Money & Ehrhardt, 1972; LeVay, 1993). These girls even exhibited less desire for frilly clothes than did controls, and they showed more of an interest in having a career (see Chapter 9). By contrast, women who are highly feminized hormonally, such as those with Turner's syndrome or androgen insensitivity syndrome, are exceptionally nurturant (e.g., Hoyenga & Hoyenga, 1979).

Why does interest in infant care emerge before puberty in primates? Primate maternal care is complex and takes time to learn. Accordingly, young females observe mature females caring for infants, and often try to handle these infants themselves. In many primate species including chimpanzees, interest in infants increases sharply before sexual maturity, and peaks in the season before the first birth (Higley & Suomi, 1986). **Alloparenting** (caring for another's offspring) probably enhances subsequent skill in raising one's own offspring (Daly & Wilson, 1983). It may also constitute a form of "helping at the nest": In some birds and mammals, a juvenile defers the start of her own reproduction in order to help care for a young sibling. Thus, kin altruism is a possible explanation when alloparenting is directed toward younger siblings (see Chapter 6).

A similar pattern of sex differences and development in alloparenting occurs in humans. Sex differences in parental behavior were reported at ages 3 to 6 and 7 to 11 in a cross-cultural study (B. B. Whiting & Edwards, 1973). Bogin (1988) confirmed that prepubertal children, especially girls, tend children worldwide. However, Berman's (1980) review revealed that sex differences in responsiveness to babies were most pronounced in preadolescence and adolescence. The preference for infants' photos over photos of other age groups has been found to increase at menarche, controlling for chronological age and various experiential factors (Jacobson & Kriger, 1978; Gold-berg et al., 1982). Similarly, girls who were more advanced in pubertal development, controlling for age, showed a stronger preference for pictures of infants (J. Chandler, 1977). And girls' attraction to pedo-morphic features rose sharply between ages 11 and 13; boys' attrac-tion rose less sharply and occurred 2 years later (Fullard & Reiling, 1976). These developmental patterns suggest a hormonal basis be-cause boys proceed through puberty about 2 years after girls.

If we are typical mammals in that mothers are attracted to infants, probably infants are attracted to mothers, too. Infants are particularly drawn to the female voice (Freedman, 1974). Other female features may also be attractive to infants; for example, babies seem to enjoy fingering their mother's hair. This tendency may have evolved in or-der to motivate primate infants to grasp their mother's fur when being carried, and it may have been retained in humans because it helped to draw infants to their mothers. This may be the reason that females tend to have longer hair than males, even before puberty.

Fearfulness

Other human sex differences are consistent with the distinction be-tween the relatively intimidating male and the more vulnerable fe-male. In most vertebrate species, the female is smaller and more fear-ful than the male. It makes adaptive sense to be quick to flee if one is not very formidable in a fight. Moreover, female primates, including women, accompany or even carry their offspring, who are even more vulnerable. Then, too, women can usually leave the fighting to their husbands or kinsmen. Men have more upper body strength, for fight-ing; women's strength is more in the legs, for flight.

Many studies indicate that primate females are more fearful than males, insofar as females tend to defer to males in dominance encoun-ters (Gray, 1971). This includes human adolescents (Ekehammer, 1974). Even as babies, girls smile more than boys (Freedman, 1974). The primate smile is basically an appeasement signal (Van Hooff, 1969). It makes sense for the more vulnerable sex to make more fre-quent use of this ingratiating display.

One of the problems with self-report studies of fear is that women may be more willing to admit being afraid than men. To overcome this problem, researchers have sought sex differences in experiencing visceral changes associated with anxiety, such as sweating palms and fast heart rate. In a study of 16-year-olds, girls reported experiencing

12 of 18 anxiety symptoms significantly more often than males (Eke-hammer et al., 1974).

Male hormones have been associated with lower fearfulness. Androgens depress avoidance conditioning (L. Ellis, 1986). In mammals, fear can sometimes be reduced by administering prenatal or postnatal androgens (L. Ellis, 1986). Jacklin et al. (1983) reported that timidity in infant boys was inversely proportional to testosterone levels in umbilical blood.

Sensory Acuity

Likewise, good sensory acuity is typical of prey species. Women surpass men in sensitivity to sound, the four basic tastes, touch, color, temperature, and pain (M. A. Baker, 1987; Hoyenga & Hoyenga, 1979; Hutt, 1972). Sex differences in olfaction are complicated; they depend on the substance, the menstrual phase, and the species. Women surpass men in night vision; as a diurnal species, we are more vulnerable at night. Men outstrip women in day vision, perhaps because they hunt then. It would, of course, be best to see as well as possible at all times, but no species' eye, like no camera, is perfectly versatile.

Most of these sex differences are present throughout life, but the female superiority for touch may first appear at puberty (Robinson & Short, 1977). Women are more sensitive to the smell of musk but only after puberty. Women are particularly sensitive to several types of stimuli—visual, temperature, tactile, auditory, and painful—during the luteal phase of the menstrual cycle (M. A. Baker, 1987). Since the hormonal profile of the luteal phase is a miniature version of that of pregnancy, it may be that sensitivity is greatest when a woman is most vulnerable: when pregnant.

Summary

The fetus differentiates as a female in the absence of testicular hormones. The brain as well as the internal and external genitalia are feminized. The hypothalamus is induced to orchestrate the menstrual fluctuations of hormone levels that are activated at puberty.

Breast-feeding is regulated by several hormones and is advantageous to both the infant's and the mother's health. The mother-offspring bond is as old as mammals, some 50 million years, and evidently has evolved to their mutual benefit. For example, morning sickness seems to be induced by the early fetus in response to foods that are toxic to it. Because the fetus is small, is in the process of differentiating, and is poor at detoxifying poisons, it is highly vulnerable to toxins that pass the placental barrier.

At puberty, a girl becomes attractive to males well before she is fertile. Evidently, early sexual and romantic experience aided prehistoric females in mate choice or mate retention. The lower initial intensity and the priming effect exhibited by the female sex drive, the widespread prevalence of prefertile sex, the trend from promiscuity to monogamy, and the early maturation of the breasts, vaginal rugae, and pubic hair are consistent with this notion of prolonged and experimental sexual experience. The female's prominent breasts, wide hips, general adiposity, and other sex-differentiated traits associated with fertility attract males.

The relative pedomorphism of women is consistent with the idea that the social influence of the "gentle sex" comes more from endearment than from intimidation. Cross-culturally, females are more nurturant and cooperative, and males are more independent and competitive. Female traits, such as soft hair and skin, high voice, and prominent breasts, attract infants as well as men.

Maternal behavior is enhanced by prenatal and pubertal hormonal changes, as well as by the hormonal events of lactation. Alloparenting, which allows prolonged practice at mothering and which intensifies at puberty, is a widespread simian and human feature.

Other behavioral sex differences reflect various anatomical and social specializations. Women exhibit greater sensory acuity, fearfulness, manual dexterity, memory for object locations (see Chapter 9), communication skill, attention to detail, and ability to shift attention (Hutt, 1972) than men. These sex differences are consistent with Trivers's theory of sexual selection, but they go beyond it to accord with the division of labor between the sexes and their emergent social aptitudes. Women's ability to shift attention may have been adaptive for alternating between child care and other tasks.

The evidence in favor of evolved behavioral sex differences in general and hormonal influences in particular continues to mount. Sex differences in various areas of the brain itself are now demonstrable (Becker et al., 1992; Hoyenga & Hoyenga, 1993; Kimura, 1998). Further, women's performance on verbal, object-location, and dexterity tasks peaks during the follicular phase, when estrogen levels climb.

A purely sociocultural explanation for human behavioral sex differences does not address the great stability of perceptions of sex-typed personality traits. Lueptow et al. (1995) reviewed 18 longitudinal studies of gender stereotypes and self-ratings, and also conducted their own survey. They found that despite an increase in avowed tolerance for women and men working in nontraditional roles since the 1960s in the United States, sex typing—regarding the traditional characterstics of each sex as normal or desirable—has not declined noticeably. They concluded that the persistence of these expectations cannot be explained without acknowledging their evolved bases. Another meta-analysis (Feingold, 1994) gave similar results.

As stressed in Chapter 1, to recognize that human behavior and sex differences have an evolved basis is not to deny the importance of socialization factors (Hoyenga & Hoyenga, 1993). Nature and nurture generally work in concert, and both are essential. For example, socialization tends to exaggerate differences between the sexes (i.e., to socialize children into sex roles consistent with evolved sex differences) because this differentiation has apparently been adaptive (see Chapter 6). For this reason, male and female "stereotypes" are similar across cultures (Williams & Best, 1986). As another example, consider cultural variation in the attractiveness of obesity in women. In cultures with food shortages, obesity tends to be desirable in a wife (Low, 1990)—for an adaptive, not an accidental, reason.

Analyzing the function of universal and local traits and sex differences provides a way to make sense out of chaos. Those who are receptive to the notion of somewhat different behavioral predispositions in the sexes have a chance to appreciate the powerful, new view of humankind now emerging in the behavioral sciences. Nowhere does this revolution promise to be more radical than with respect to adolescence because of the profound role that sex hormones—including those of pregnancy and lactation—play at this stage of life.

11 Boys' Peer Relations

Chapter 9 described universal, hormonally based, and hence evolved pubertal changes in boys. Most of these morphological and behavioral changes can be understood as enhancing success in competing for females. Boys become larger, more muscular, more intimidating, and more competitive in adolescence. These pubertal changes would aid the individual in gaining a high dominance rank and its attendant prerogatives, especially mating opportunities. Because young males start off with no mate, they need to assert themselves in order to break into the breeding pool.

In Chapter 4, it was argued that peer competition in humans resembles dominance behavior in other primates in many ways and therefore probably evolved from it. In the present chapter, the dominance hierarchy model of peer relations will be applied to the data on boys' social competition. The chapter will address questions such as: Why are adolescents so concerned with peer status? Why does appearance—their own as well as that of others—take on such importance? What traits raise a boy's social status among his peers and why?

No claim is made that competitive peer relations in adolescence can be reduced to this single model of heightened sexual competition. Obviously, a huge amount of cultural and individual variation must be accounted for. However, given the absence of any alternative explanation for the universal aspects of this competitiveness, this model may serve as a means of organizing the data. Peer competition in males will now be described in childhood, adolescence, and adulthood in light of the dominance model. After this, implications of peer competition for personality development will be addressed, followed by a discussion on peer-group dynamics.

Dominance Behavior in Childhood

In most mammals, physical prowess is the most important determinant of rank. Just as juvenile primates establish ranks through play fighting, children also seem to compare themselves on their fighting ability. Omark et al. (1975) studied children at free play in Switzerland, the United States, and Ethiopia. Children who were rated by peers as "tough" tended to exercise leadership. When asked what "tough" meant, the children assumed boxing postures or flexed their muscles. Fighting for dominance began at about age 3 and peaked at about age 5. Dominant children exercise various prerogatives, such as assigning roles at play; they exhibit more threat or dominance displays (Camras, 1977); and they receive more attention than their subordinates (Hold, 1980).

By age 6, agreed-upon dominance hierarchies emerged in groups researched in the United States and Switzerland (Omark et al., 1975). Likewise, stable, linear hierarchies formed rapidly in free play groups in North America (Coie & Kupersmidt, 1983; Strayer & Strayer, 1976). Omark and Edelman (1976) noted that before age 6, many children lack the cognitive ability of **transitivity** that permits them to conceptualize rank ordering. Transitivity refers to the logical implication that if A > B and B > C, then A > C. Omark and Edelman suggested that once children are able to infer who can defeat whom, they do not need to fight as often, and fighting diminishes. (See also Sluckin [1980].)

In this research and that of others, boys tend to outrank girls. Greater male dominance motivation makes sense for species in which high-ranking males gain more mating opportunities (see Chapter 5). But why should sex differences in dominance and competitiveness emerge well before puberty? Perhaps this can be explained by the importance of initial outcomes. If one animal defeats another, the former will be more aggressive when they meet again, and the latter will be less aggressive. This differential in aggressiveness (or competitiveness, or self-confidence) will contribute to repetitions of the first outcome and hence to the permanent dominance relationship of the two animals. As mentioned in Chapter 9, this primacy effect, called **conditioning to success**, has been demonstrated for several species (G. E. Weisfeld, 1980). Success breeds success, which breeds breeding success!

Prepubertal boys, like male simians in most group-living species, also play fight more than females. Research indicates that play fighting, or rough-and-tumble play, involves different behavior patterns from aggressive behaviors and hence is probably a separate motive (Blurton Jones, 1972), which is called *interest* in Chapter 2. Children's play fights can often be distinguished from angry aggression by the facial expressions employed—although children at play may "look" fierce because they are fantasizing. Play-fighting partners often are friends, so play fighting is not generally antagonistic (Pellegrini, 1995). Its main function seems to be to provide practice in fighting (Boulton, 1994). Despite these different forms and functions of play fighting and aggression, it is likely that knowledge of each other's strength and fighting ability, and hence dominance ranks, emerge from play fighting.

Dominance ranks in childhood do tend to carry over into adolescence, thus confirming the primacy explanation for childhood fighting. Longitudinal research on 25 of Omark's original U.S. subjects showed that boys' dominance ranks remained remarkably stable into adolescence (Figure 11.1). Toughness ranks at around 7 years of age were correlated by 0.71 with dominance, by 0.70 with popularity, and by 0.71 with leadership at about age 16 (an average interval of 9 years). Tough young boys also exhibited the erect posture of dominant individuals when they reached adolescence (G. E. Weisfeld & Beresford, 1982). In another longitudinal study that used interview ratings of dominance/passivity, Bronson (1966) reported a correlation of 0.41 between ages 5 to 7 and 14 to 16 for boys. In a third study, dominance was stable from ages 3 to 6 to ages 10 to 14 for both sexes (Kagan & Moss, 1962); furthermore, boys' (but not girls') competitiveness at ages 6 to 10 predicted competitiveness in adulthood. Lastly, Coie and Dodge (1983) found stability in negative peer status from ages 8 to 13 and from ages 10 to 14. Thus, if a boy builds up a history of successful competitive encounters, his resulting self-confidence may carry over into adolescence and beyond.

This striking stability of dominance is probably due, at least in part, to the importance of early outcomes, but genetic factors probably also play a role. Dominance has been found to be highly heritable— 0.49 as reported by Gottesman (1966). Dominance, in turn, may depend largely on strength, which is another stable, highly heritable trait (Klissouras, 1984). Finally, a favorable environment, such as one that promotes health, may enhance development and contribute to dominance status. Aggressiveness in boys, with heritability of about 0.40 (Turner, 1994), has also been shown to be stable from kinder-

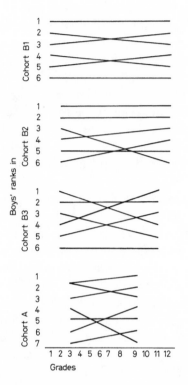

Figure 11.1 Stability of Dominance Ranks in Boys over Longest Available Intervals. U.S. first-graders are about 6 years old. Here, boys are rating boys. Source: G. E. Weisfeld, Muczenski, Weisfeld, & Omark. (1987). Reprinted by permission.

garten to adolescence (Olweus, 1984); however, the relation of aggressiveness to dominance and popularity is complex, as will be explained later in this chapter.

Dominance Behavior in Adolescence

As noted in Chapter 9, competitive behavior among males increases at maturity. Cairns and Cairns (1986) reported a rise in physical coercion in early adolescence, especially for boys. In the United Kingdom, Boulton (1994) found that some of his 13- to 16-year-old boys reported an increase, with age, in the roughness of their play fighting and a greater motivation to win. Strength and endurance in males increase sharply at puberty, and young men are strongly motivated by competition (Daly & Wilson, 1994).

Given this apparent increase in dominance motivation, it is not surprising that, like children, groups of adolescent boys form dominance hierarchies. Sherif and Sherif (1964) observed that adolescent boys from various socioeconomic backgrounds all spontaneously formed groups with recognizable, increasingly stable hierarchies. High-ranking boys exercised control over group decisions, that is, they enjoyed the prerogatives of rank. Rank was related to perceived manliness and success with girls. In sports groups, athletic skill was highly valued. In poorer neighborhoods, they observed, "'toughness' was a general prerequisite of standing in a peer group" (p. 159). Thus, physical prowess seemed to be salient for male adolescents' peer relations, just as it was among children and animals.

In adolescent groups where adult-imposed social values are weak, as in street gangs and prisons, fighting is important. Although clever verbal bantering is respected, it is often trumped by the use of force. Observers of boys' street gangs have long noted the importance of toughness and success in fighting for securing material resources, achieving leadership, and being popular with girls (Feldman & Weisfeld, 1973; Thrasher, 1926; Yablonsky, 1966). Aggressive behaviors and displays, such as threats, swaggering, profanity (a sign of anger), and spitting (salivation is inhibited by fear), are constantly exhibited to indicate one's readiness to fight. (I once worked as a community organizer with a white street gang in Chicago. The gang members sometimes jostled an organizer to provoke a fight, an invitation that, of course, was declined. In explaining this reaction to the gang leader, one organizer, David Feingold, explained that middle-class types fight with their mouths, not their fists. Fortunately, Feingold was not hit in the mouth!)

Even among middle-class U.S. adolescent boys, fighting prowess is sometimes respected. In a classic ethological study, Savin-Williams (1987) observed adolescent boys and girls at a summer camp. He and his collaborators, employed as counselors, clandestinely recorded the behavior of cabin mates. The boys as well as the counselors ranked each camper's "dominance," using a questionnaire. These intuitive rankings were validated by the observational data: Boys who were regarded as "dominant" were, in fact, observed to win more verbal and physical dominance encounters. These dominant boys also tended to be the best athletes and to be good-looking. Like primates in other species, they possessed physical traits that lent them high rank.

Savin-Williams's research confirmed a number of other predictions based on studies of dominance hierarchies in monkeys. Dominant boys exercised prerogatives, such as food choices, bed choice, and directing of activities. Especially in boys, fighting declined within the first few days of camp, and ranks remained consistent until the end of camp several weeks later. Pellegrini (1995) also documented a decline in aggressive interactions in the second year after a group of boys came together in middle school. Thus, on several counts, the dominance hierarchy model of peer relations has been supported (see Chapter 4).

Other studies of boys' peer groups have confirmed the importance of physical traits in adolescent boys' peer relations. Many of these studies have measured popularity or leadership rather than dominance. However, boys who are dominant also tend to be popular leaders (Wagner & Asarnow, 1980; G. E. Weisfeld et al., 1987), so the particular term used for peer social success is of comparatively minor importance. What is important is that highly regarded boys tend to be attractive athletes who were tough and attractive as children (e.g., see Dodge, 1983). In other words, whether measured as leadership, popularity, or dominance, boys' social status tends to be related to physical traits—toughness, attractiveness, and athletic ability.

It should also be noted that the criteria for social success in adolescence are similar whether the subject is being judged by male peers or female peers (G. E. Weisfeld et al., 1983, 1984a). If an adolescent is highly regarded by one sex, he or she is usually highly regarded by the other, too. This suggests that dominance ranks are relevant for relations with the opposite sex, that is, that they mirror mate choice (see Chapter 13).

One other methodological issue must be addressed. Measures of "dominance" that reflect frequent fighting tend not to be associated with popularity. In fact, older children and adolescents who fight a lot are often unpopular, as Pellegrini (1995) showed for 13- to 15-year-old boys who bullied weaker ones (also see G. E. Weisfeld, 1994). For this reason, it may be better to define dominance in the traditional ethological sense of gaining resources in conflicts of interest (G. E. Weisfeld et al., 1980). A bully who fights frequently may not even win many fights or may be defeating only very weak opponents. A dominant animal is seldom challenged and so may fight infrequently, but it does not back down. Thus, dominance over an opponent is reflected best by success in either securing contested resources or in fights.

Next, some psychological, rather than ethological, studies of boys' peer relations will be reviewed. The classic study of the criteria for peer success in adolescence is that of J. S. Coleman (1961), who studied popularity at ten representative U.S. high schools. The boys reported that athletic success and good looks were more important for membership in the "leading crowd" than was academic success. Another two schools were studied because they were very academically oriented and had few interscholastic sports teams. In these two atypical U.S. schools, academic success allegedly was valued about equally with athletic ability and good looks. This suggests that intelligence can influence boys' popularity in U.S. schools—but only under extraordinary circumstances. Physical traits are usually paramount.

This conclusion has been confirmed for U.S. boys by many studies, stretching back 40 years. These include investigations by Gronlund and Anderson (1957), Eitzen (1975), G. E. Weisfeld et al. (1987), Williams and White (1983), and Kennedy (1990). Tannenbaum (1960) even found that being studious detracted from a boy's popularity at one U.S. high school. If a boy did well in school without trying, this did not detract from his popularity, as though he was not responsible for his success and so was blameless! Intelligence is often cited as important to peer success in the United States (e.g., see Hartup, 1983), but it pales in comparison with physical traits. Savin-Williams's (1987) data on four adolescent boys' groups, for instance, revealed that dominant boys tended to be good athletes ($r = 0.60$, $p < .05$) rather than especially intelligent ($r = 0.37$, n.s.).

In a study of six U.S. high school classes (G. E. Weisfeld et al., 1987), athletic ability and attractiveness were significantly correlated with popularity, leadership, and dominance (getting one's way in a conflict of interest), as judged by male peers throughout high school (ages 14 to 17). Attractive, athletic boys were also ranked as desirable dates and party guests by girls. A boy's intelligence had little or no effect on any of these measures of social standing.

U.S. adolescents, especially those at academically excellent high schools such as this one and Coleman's two, may believe—as some of our other subjects revealed when interviewed (G. E. Weisfeld et al., 1980)—that intelligence is highly valued by their peers. But objective research methods usually reveal that the popular boys are the athletes and that intelligence is no great social boon. One reason for this misapprehension may be that the values of school officials and parents are assumed to influence the peer culture, whereas, in fact, adult values have little impact in this domain (J. R. Harris, 1995). Another possibility is that U.S. adolescents accurately perceive and assimilate adults' admiration for physical traits. Adults' values do seem to have a great impact on adolescents' self-esteem, which is affected by the judgments of adults as well as of peers (Coopersmith, 1967).

The salience of athletic ability for adolescent boys' peer relations is not universal, however. In research in Beijing, academic success contributed much more strongly to the dominance, popularity, and leadership of both sexes than did athletic ability (Dong et al., 1996). In China, scholarship has long been valued, as it is by contemporary high school students. Athletic ability was only modestly respected, evidently because of the students' belief that weak students focus on sports. Physical attractiveness was associated with social success for Chinese boys and girls, however. Findings regarding English adolescent boys proved to be intermediate between those for boys in the United States and China. At a rather downscale school in London, athletic ability, attractiveness, and intelligence were weighted about equally (Boardway & Weisfeld, 1994). In a Canadian replication of Coleman's research, more students preferred to be good students than good athletes (B. Brown, 1990).

This limited cross-national research suggests that the criteria for dominance among boys vary, presumably as a result of societal values, but that physical attractiveness may be salient everywhere. The notion that *physical traits influence boys' peer social status* in childhood and adolescence is supported by cross-cultural research that has included boys in Japan, the Hopi Indian culture of the U.S. Southwest, Ethiopia, Switzerland, Mexico, England, Australia (reviewed by G. E. Weisfeld et al., 1987), and Canada (Friesen, 1968). Sheldon's original results concerning the social value of the mesomorphic somatotype (Sheldon et al., 1940), once dismissed out of hand by behaviorists, have been broadly confirmed (e.g., see Staffieri, 1967).

What about factors other than physical traits—don't they also influence adolescent boys' peer status? Traits such as personality and reputation are also correlated with social success among peers, but the terms "personality" and "reputation" are vague and derivative. "Social skills" are often found to be correlated with peer social standing.

However, like "personality" or "charisma," they may largely reflect the consequences of being physically attractive, as suggested in the section on personality development that follows.

All of this suggests that a physical factor strongly influences boys' social success among peers. Just as various measures of social success seem to overlap, so do bodily measures. This cluster of traits includes strength, athletic ability, and physical attractiveness, which are highly correlated (e.g., G. E. Weisfeld et al., 1980), heritable, and stable (e.g., Klissouras, 1984; Tanner, 1978).

Physical traits also influence appeal to the opposite sex (see Chapter 13). For example, in a U.S. study, attractive adolescents of both sexes were more likely to have a steady dating partner (Chess et al., 1976). Why are females attracted to strong, virile, athletic, and courageous males? In a hunting economy, these men would have been good providers, progenitors, and protectors. Moreover, males who chose these prestigious men as companions and sought their favor presumably would have had a selective advantage over those with no such allies (cf. Barkow, 1989). This sensitivity to the physical prowess of other males probably evolved originally to allow male animals to "size each other up" so as not to challenge insuperable opponents. The salience of male pulchritude to other males would explain why boys seem to agree closely with girls in judgments about other boys' attractiveness (G. E. Weisfeld et al., 1980).

But why are women—and perhaps men, too—awed by an attractive male face? Attraction to facial pulchritude may have evolved to provide an additional set of clues about a potential mate's fitness. Most genes are pleiotropic: They influence multiple traits. A single gene might hypothetically influence both the attractiveness of the mouth, say, and cardiac efficiency. Natural selection would have favored women that were preferentially attracted to males with facial features that connoted genetic quality and healthy development, in addition to bodily features such as muscularity. Indeed, judgments of boys' attractiveness are highly correlated with judgments of athletic ability (e.g., G. E. Weisfeld et al., 1980), so faces do seem to reflect bodily traits. Then, too, dominant facial features in men tend to attract women (Jackson, 1992), to increase the sexual opportunities of male adolescents independently of their attractiveness, and to reflect testosterone levels accurately (Mazur et al., 1994). Attractive bodily (nonfacial) features also connote health. Bilateral symmetry of somatic features, which is thought to reflect an unperturbed developmental course, is perceived as attractive, and such symmetry reflects health and reproductive success (Thornhill & Gangestad, 1994; Grammer & Thornhill, 1994). For women, a low waist-to-hip ratio is correlated with health and fecundity, and is attractive to men (Singh, 1993). In general, facial attractiveness is correlated with bodily attractiveness. Facial appearance was found to be a better predictor of psychosocial functioning than bodily attractiveness in 12-year-olds in the United States (Perkins & Lerner, 1995).

An ability to judge a man's physical prowess at a glance would be valuable to males in dominance competition and to females who are seeking a mate. Similarly, women and men who could judge their rivals' attractiveness would be better able to strategize in mate competition. In various ways, it would have benefited both sexes to be able to distinguish good physical specimens at a glance. Attractiveness remains an important determinant of social success throughout life for both sexes (Elder, 1968). For example, attractive West Point cadets went on to gain the most promotions (Mazur et al., 1984).

It is sometimes claimed that "beauty is in the eye of the beholder," that is, that standards of attractiveness are highly variable. If so, this would argue against the notion that the body reflects objective health and genetic quality. But contrary to platitudes about the relativity of attractiveness, people in one culture are able to judge reliably the attractiveness of people from another (Jackson, 1992). Local and individual standards most certainly do apply, and experience does shape our tastes, but at the same time, universal standards operate as well. Consistent with this, children begin to look longer at attractive faces (as so judged by adults) as early as 3 months of age—before standards of beauty are likely to be acquired by socialization (Jackson, 1992). Likewise, even newborns evoke more parental care if they are attractive (see Chapter 3). Finally, judgments of attractiveness are made in a fraction of a second, further suggesting the operation of an evolved sensitivity. This is all the more remarkable given that these judgments involve multiple features and proportions (N. Barber, 1995). The fact that average, or normal, features are more appealing than idiosyncratic ones (Buss, 1994), even to newborns, suggests that humans possess mental templates of ideal male and female faces.

There is another element in the constellation of physical traits that seems to enhance an adolescent boy's social status and well-being: *pubertal timing*. It has long been known that early-maturing adolescent boys enjoy many social advantages, including dominance, popularity, leadership, self-confidence, being relaxed, acting maturely, and being pleasing to parents (M. C. Jones & Bayley, 1950; Mussen & Jones, 1957; Weatherley, 1964; Savin-Williams & Small, 1986).

Early pubertal maturity predicts social success well into adulthood. In the Oakland Growth Study, it was correlated with traits such as dominance and making a good impression as late as age 30 (M. C. Jones, 1965). Early-maturing U.S. boys became relatively assertive and held more supervisory positions at 30 to 40 years of age (Mussen & Jones, 1957). In their early forties, they were more poised, responsible, achieving in conformity with society's expectations, self-controlled, and sociable, and less neurotic (M. C. Jones, 1965; Livson & Peskin, 1980). Late maturers were judged at interviews to be more humorous, fearful, tolerant of ambiguity, and creative, and less conforming. Late maturity may have some compensations, but they do not appear to rival those of early maturity.

Most textbooks on adolescence emphasize early maturity as a predictor of social success in boys. However, indications are that pubertal maturity does not directly influence peer status very strongly despite the fact that the two factors are correlated. Early maturity is associated with attractiveness, athletic ability, strength, and mesomorphy (M. C. Jones & Bayley, 1950; Tanner, 1978)—traits that are correlated with social success throughout development. Thus, these latter traits can better account for males' social success; early puberty per se (which peers can not observe directly) can probably be discounted. In fact, Jones and Bayley (1950) found no consistent differences in peer success between the earliest-maturing and latest-maturing 16-year-old boys they studied. In Weatherley's (1964) research, late-maturing boys were disadvantaged socially, but boys who matured at the average age were as well off as those who matured early. Savin-Williams (1987) reported the average correlation of pubertal maturity with dominance to be 0.35. By contrast, athletic ability showed a correlation of 0.71 with dominance, across the 52 groups studied. Dominance was more closely related to maturity in early adolescence than in late adolescence, when all the boys had matured (Savin-Williams, 1987). Aside from a temporary head start in strength and attractiveness, whatever advantage early-maturing boys enjoy seems due mainly to their having been large, strong, and athletic, and therefore dominant, all along.

Furthermore, as described earlier, dominance remains quite stable from childhood through adolescence, so pubertal events do not transform boys' social ranks in stable groups (G. E. Weisfeld et al., 1987; G. E. Weisfeld & Billings, 1988). Therefore, the event of early pubertal maturity probably does not affect dominance status very much. Along the same lines, maturity itself is quite stable. Early pubertal boys tend to have been early maturers from age 2 on, as judged by bone age and by weight/height (Tanner, 1978), so again, *pubertal timing probably has little causal impact on boys' peer status.*

The timing of puberty can be understood in terms of life-history strategy. In most species, early maturity is advantageous to a male animal only insofar as he gains breeding opportunities (see Chapter 8). In male primates, for example, breeding success rests less on early fertility than on size and strength (G. E. Weisfeld & Billings, 1988). At the same time, it is in the interest of strong juvenile males to mature early. There is no advantage to delaying maturity once one is ready to compete successfully for mates. This explains why early-maturing boys become early-maturing adolescents. For whatever genetic and environmental reasons, they are ready at a young age to compete successfully with other males. As expected, size and dominance rank tend to be stable from early in life among males of other species, too, including red deer, African hunting dogs, and the lizard *Anolis garmani* (Trivers, 1985). Health and high rank when young lead to advantages in size and rank at maturity.

Consistent with the dominance hierarchy model, body image is very important in adolescents' peer evaluations (Tobin-Richards et al., 1983). The psychoanalyst Hall (1904) popularized the idea that the changes of puberty are traumatic. However, it does not appear that adolescents are traumatized by undergoing puberty and the slow but dramatic changes their bodies undergo. Rather, it is the individuals whose pubertal development is delayed who tend to have severe psychological problems, not those whose maturation is normal (Higham, 1980). Adolescents who feel that they are not developing into attractive, appealing adults are more likely to be troubled (Weatherley, 1964; Tanner, 1978). For example, low-ranking boys (who mature late) tend to have high levels of stress hormones (corticosteroids); see Chapter 9.

Dominance Behavior in Adulthood

By young adulthood, men's social success is related to both bodily appearance and other factors, such as wealth, age, social class, lineage, intelligence, skill, and character (e.g., Hyman, 1942; Barkow, 1975). It appears that adult male dominance is influenced by two sets of factors: physical and cultural.

Developmentally, the cultural factors may increase in importance late in adolescence. In one longitudinal study, the salience of intelligence gained ground over athletic ability and attractiveness at the transition to college (G. E. Weisfeld et al., 1987). In the sophomore year of college, women weighted a man's intelligence and expected earning power about equally with his athletic ability and attractiveness when considering his potential as a husband.

There is another reason why cultural factors should increase in importance with age. As young women mature, they evaluate men more seriously as possible husbands rather than merely as dating partners. Factors such as a man's wealth and character therefore may become more salient in women's judgments. A woman can raise her reproductive success by marrying a rich, powerful man; wealth is valued in a husband the world over (Daly & Wilson, 1983; Buss, 1994). Therefore, it is to be expected that a woman would desire such a man as a husband or even just a lover, and that her parents likewise would urge such a choice on her. When a girl is younger, her parents' entreaties to seek a good, sober wage earner may fall on deaf ears. Sexual motivation may be paramount early on, and the features that render males sexually attractive during adolescence strongly reflect primordially salient attributes such as strength. Even in the university women referred to earlier, physical traits largely determined judgments of a man's sex appeal, rather than his potential as a husband.

Personality Development Through Peer Relations

As children's dominance hierarchies begin to stabilize around age 4, physical aggression declines. Presumably, as ranks become apparent, there is less need to "fight it out." At the same time, verbal aggression rises—for example, threatening, ridiculing, and directing others (Cairns, 1979; Hartup, 1974, 1983; LaFrenière & Charlesworth, 1983; Kagan & Moss, 1962; Strayer & Trudel, 1984). Apparently, children learn how to compete without risking injury or adult disapproval. Socialization of middle-class U.S. children tends to increase the frequency of prosocial behaviors, such as generosity (Charlesworth & Hartup, 1967). However, this progression from aggressive to prosocial behaviors does not always occur in the U.S. lower class (Schroeder &

Flapan, 1971). The basic, default criterion for organizing male peer groups seems to be physical prowess. Normal socialization seems to move children away from aggression toward socially approved means of gaining and defending their status and prerogatives.

Nevertheless, a boy's physical attributes may have lasting value in his social development. Recall that peer status tends to be quite stable in boys. This means that dominant, popular, attractive boys build up a history of gratifying peer interactions. They are attended to, deferred to, listened to, and obeyed. Peers and teachers (Algozzine, 1977) treat them prosocially and are less severe in punishing them (Berkowitz & Frodi, 1979). They gain experience as active participants (Dodge, 1983), leaders (Coie & Kupersmidt, 1983), and conflict mediators (Hold, 1976, 1977). Their positive social encounters lead them to seek still more active social participation, thus honing their social skills. Attractive children tend to be verbally skilled (Chaiken, 1979; Goldman & Lewis, 1977) and verbally assertive (LaFrenière & Charlesworth, 1983).

Treated respectfully by others, these popular boys tend to behave more prosocially than rejected boys (Charlesworth & Hartup, 1967; Hartup et al., 1967; J. M. McGuire, 1973; Coie & Kupersmidt, 1983), even independently of their attractiveness (Dodge, 1983). That is, they reciprocate the favorable treatment they receive. They make suggestions, establish norms, direct activities, and remind others of the rules. Popular boys engage in little aggression, in large part because they are seldom challenged (Dodge et al., 1982; Dodge, 1983). They do not hesitate to defend their rights, however (Lesser, 1959); angry aggression is useful for enforcing social norms, and within bounds, it may be healthy. Retaliatory, angry aggression at age 14 did not predict criminality at age 20 in a study of Finnish males, but offensive, unprovoked aggression did (Pulkkinen, 1987).

The benefits of high rank seem to carry over to adulthood, although some of this stability doubtless stems from the substantial heritability of social dominance. Male seniors in U.S. universities who were attractive tended to interact more with women and fear rejection less, to enjoy social interactions more, and to be more socially competent (Reis et al., 1982). Attractiveness is very important throughout the life span (Huston, 1974), even in older married couples (Margolin & White, 1987).

Low-ranking, rejected boys seem to experience the opposite social dynamics. They tend to be socially withdrawn (Dodge, 1983), anxious, low in self-confidence, poor in social skills, depressed, aggressive, and lonely (D. G. Perry et al., 1992; G. E. Weisfeld et al., 1980). How does this pattern come about? It has been established that rejected boys tend to interpret peers' acts as hostile; they sometimes perceive ill will even when it is absent. Consequently, they exhibit frequent "retaliatory" aggression even against accidental slights (Dodge & Frame, 1982; Langlois & Downs, 1979). Peers then perceive them to be aggressive and antisocial, and they are rejected all the more. Gradually, these boys withdraw from social interactions. However, the pessimistic outlook of these rejected boys seems to be generally realistic, not inaccurate. Rejected boys are, in fact, treated with less tolerance than accepted ones, by definition. Peers react more favorably to a popular boy who commits an antisocial deed than to a rejected boy who does the same thing. Rejected boys seem to have a chip on the shoulder because of actual mistreatment (Coie & Kupersmidt, 1983).

What causes these boys to be rejected in the first place? Dodge (1983) and Coie and Kupersmidt (1983) suggested that unpopular boys may receive unkind treatment because they tend to be less attractive. Indeed, unattractiveness comes first, then aggressiveness, by 5 years of age (Langlois & Stephan, 1981). Thus, unattractiveness seems to cause unkind treatment and the downward spiral of antisocial behavior and social withdrawal, rather than poor social skills arising out of some cognitive deficit that mysteriously targets unattractive boys.

Rejected boys are at risk for developing adjustment problems (Rutter & Giller, 1983). Some rejected boys resort to bullying (G. E. Weisfeld, 1994). Typically, these generally unpopular children settle on a passive victim and direct ambiguous rough play toward him. Having provoked a fight, they ignore the victim's submission displays. Research has shown that bullying can be reduced by increased adult supervision and by more frequent breaks from classroom work (Pellegrini, 1995; P. K. Smith & Thompson, 1991). However, aggressive retaliation against the bully by the victim may be a more effective remedy (G. E. Weisfeld, 1994); an example is described by Savin-Williams (1987).

Recent research on serotonin may fit with the dominance hierarchy model of personality development. As mentioned in Chapter 4, serotonin levels tend to be low in subordinate vervet monkeys and depressed people (M. T. McGuire et al., 1984). Children who exhibit impulsive aggression tend to have low levels of this neurotransmitter, as do violent criminals and suicides (Kalat, 1992), so perhaps these behaviors are responses to chronic low rank.

Juvenile delinquency can be predicted from behavior toward peers in childhood. For example, peer-rated aggressiveness at 8 years remained stable to age 18 in an English sample (Lefkowitz et al., 1977). Similarly, antisocial behavioral tendencies that had been observed in adolescence were still in evidence 30 years later (Robins, 1978). If childhood peer relations cause delinquency rather than merely predicting it, this may occur partly because rejection by peers leads to moralistic aggression directed at targets who cannot easily retaliate.

It has also been established that juvenile delinquency is more likely to develop if a boy changes residence often (Rutter & Giller, 1983). This may be a case of heightened aggressiveness due to the fact that the boy must work his way into and up the hierarchy in his new neighborhood (J. R. Harris, 1995), just as simians transferring troops engage in frequent fights. Juvenile delinquency is discussed further in Chapter 14.

Similar developmental effects of peer status seem to operate in girls. Attractive girls have been found to receive more help, physical affection, and prosocial comments (G. Smith, 1985). Perhaps as a consequence, attractive females tend to be highly prosocial and sociable (Adams & Read, 1983). Attractive university students of both sexes tend to be more nonverbally expressive, a trait that seems to enhance popularity independent of this correlation (Sabatelli & Rubin, 1986). Attractive men and women were more skilled at sending nonverbal messages but less skilled at receiving them. Sabatelli and Rubin suggested that those who have an easy time in social relations need less skill at decoding the expressions of others. Consistent with this, subordinate children (like low-ranking animals) attend to dominants more than vice versa (Hold, 1980). Subordinates presumably need to monitor dominant individuals carefully, and they may learn how to discern their intentions accurately.

It may be impossible to do much about unpopularity. Dominance competition is a zero-sum game with as many losers as winners; perhaps adults can only control the level of aggression and insults. In addition, it may be helpful to encourage a low-ranking boy to accept his situation; those who accept their station tend to be less disliked than those who continue to resist it (Pierce, 1990). A low-ranking child can then be steered toward activities at which he does well and thereby be able to gain some pride and develop his aptitudes.

Put another way, the dominance motive is harnessed to promote different parental or societal values in different social groups. Adolescents are not born with the particular values of their "subculture"; they assimilate them from peers, parents, and other adults. For example, the unusual preoccupation with school sports and the long-standing anti-intellectualism in the United States (Tocqueville, 1835/1969) reflect spending priorities of adult-controlled institutions. By contrast, interscholastic sports are virtually nonexistent in Asian and European high schools and universities. Back in 1961, Coleman recommended that U.S. high schools emphasize academic achievement by staging interscholastic academic competitions on a scale typical of today's sports events, but this would require a change in the general values of the society. Admiration for attractive bodies seems to take care of itself, but the U.S. case suggests that respect for learning requires cultural support.

Group Dynamics

So far in this chapter, competitive relations among peers have been described. But adolescent boys also exhibit strong affiliative tendencies. Even in preadolescence, during the gang stage around age 9, boys spontaneously band together everywhere. This affinity is formalized in cultures with male puberty rites (see Chapter 7). Later on, after being initiated into adult society, young men in some societies join a warrior society or otherwise fraternize in male solidarity groups. The principles of dominance hierarchization, together with some generalizations from social psychology, may help to explain this class of behavior. At the same time, an analysis of group behavior may shed light on the functional operation of human dominance hierarchies.

Leadership of animal dominance hierarchies and human groups often shifts as the group passes from one setting to another (Barnlund, 1962; Sherif & Sherif, 1964). For example, in Savin-Williams's (1987) research, the dominant boy in one cabin of campers usually allowed a subordinate with some expertise in religion to lead the religious discussions, while still reserving the right to terminate them. At the same time, leadership is somewhat stable across situations. Whyte (1943) observed that when a low-ranking gang member excelled at bowling, the other boys harassed him until his performance declined. It would seem to be utilitarian for leadership to depend both on aptitude for the task at hand and on general leadership tendencies reflecting social skill, ability to command attention, calmness, health, vigor, and so forth.

One of the functions of groups is to improve the members' abilities. The leader is usually the most capable member, and so she can serve as teacher and model. Research on small groups has indicated that the most capable individuals usually exert the greatest influence (Webster & Sobieszek, 1974). In an observational study of evaluative remarks between male volleyball teammates in a U.S. high school class, the best players gave the most evaluation and received the least (G. E. Weisfeld & Weisfeld, 1984). These evaluative remarks included praise, criticism, and instruction. Thus, the prerogative of evaluation was exercised by the highest-ranking players, an arrangement with obvious utility for group performance. More generally, high-status individuals are permitted to evaluate others, but it is considered presumptuous to evaluate a superior.

Another essential function of a group is simply to stay together—to cohere. Mutual liking is enhanced by similarity, a tendency referred to as **homophily** (Kandel, 1978). This principle applies to choices of friends and lovers as well as to group cohesion. Any means of enhancing similarity will increase group coherence and solidarity. Toward this end, armies and other institutions impose conformity of dress, behavior, ritual, and so forth. Group members seem to adopt their own insignia, apart from any that are imposed from above. Sherif and Sherif (1953) described the adoption of group names, emblems, and ideals by preadolescent boys at a summer camp who organized themselves into factions, and similar behavior is observed in street gangs. Conformity enhances similarity and hence solidarity, and it peaks in early adolescence (Costanzo & Shaw, 1966; Gardner & Thompson, 1963). At this same time, friendship choices become more stable and increasingly mutual (Gronlund, 1959).

Solidarity is also enhanced by the presence of a common adversary, goal, or plight. Likewise, in animals, group cohesion is heightened by the presence of a hostile threat (Hall & DeVore, 1965; Marler, 1976). This tendency is exploited by military trainers, who deliberately antagonize recruits in order to mold them into a cohesive unit (Dyer, 1985). Surviving boot camp also provides a common goal and plight. Actual combat conditions will later provide a common enemy, goals, and adversity. Sherif and Sherif (1956) demonstrated the effect of a common goal in a naturalistic experiment. They fabricated various crises for their campers; one example was a supposedly malfunctioning water pump. The boys responded by working cooperatively across factional lines to repair it.

Successful groups, such as those that train and practice, cohere more than unsuccessful ones (J. C. Turner, 1982). Savin-Williams (1982) observed that male adolescent volleyball players on losing teams exhibited more dissension, in the form of critical remarks, than did winners. This was especially true of early (as opposed to middle) adolescents. The experience of surviving military training camp thus would increase cohesion. Basic training requires mastering unfamiliar tasks that appear difficult but can actually be accomplished by most recruits (Dyer, 1985). In combat, excessive losses can precipitate retreat, which may be adaptive for the individual. Grossman (1995) concluded that when fatalities exceed 50 percent, combat units usually become ineffective.

The military enhances group self-esteem by the patriotic exaggeration of the virtues of their army and the disparagement of the enemy. Dehumanization of enemy tribes occurs in other cultures, too (Eibl-Eibesfeldt, 1989). Furthermore, aggressiveness is enhanced by dehumanizing the target. Social psychologists have demonstrated that subjects delivered stronger electric shocks to targets who had been disparaged than to those who had been described favorably (Bandura et al., 1975). Similarly, the loss of a companion sometimes triggers moralistic anger that results in acts of heroism by his comrades (Rachman, 1978). For this reason, the military has learned to mold soldiers into small, face-to-face combat units whose members remain closely attached, often for life (Dyer, 1985). There is usually a strong ethic not to let down one's buddies. This feeling of solidarity is typically essential if the combat unit is to be effective (Grossman, 1995).

For the same reason, fraternization with the enemy is strictly prohibited, as among the Tsembaga of New Guinea (Eibl-Eibesfeldt, 1989). As individuals spend time together, attraction increases, perhaps in part because of a reduction in **neophobia**, fear of the unfamiliar. Eibl-Eibesfeldt (1989) discussed Lorenz's (1966) idea that modern weapons allow killing at a distance so that the victim's human features and appeasement gestures cannot be perceived. Thus, Lorenz suggested, the technology of weaponry, a cultural feature, has overridden evolved, biological safeguards against aggression. After all, our biological heritage promotes empathy and altruism, not just aggressiveness.

Military practices have been described at some length because they furnish good examples of functional behavior. Armies sustain stringent, mortal "selection pressure" for efficiency. Like any other behavior, culturally dictated actions are subject to natural selection. However, since cultural values change quickly, selection does not have as much time to perfect these behaviors as it has to perfect genetically based behaviors, which have slower mutation rates. Another reason to discuss the military is that textbooks on adolescence usually say nothing about it despite its profound effects on many adolescents and young adults. For an exception, see Rutter and Rutter (1993) on developmental consequences of U.S. military service.

In analyzing warfare ethologically, one should recognize that armies are a modern institution that does not predate the beginning of agriculture. However, collective aggression has primate roots, being demonstrated by groups of marauding male chimpanzees, and it was probably common in our prehistoric past, judging from the behavior of contemporary foragers (Chagnon, 1992) and fossil evidence of manmade wounds (Eibl-Eibesfeldt, 1989). Although the behavior of large, modern military units therefore does not admit of direct evolutionary analysis, smaller-scale military behavior does. For example, Eibl-Eibesfeldt (1989) identified various motives as animating soldiers, such as desire for prestige (or dominance), fear of criticism for not fighting, hatred of the enemy or desire for revenge (moralistic anger), pugnacity (perhaps deriving from the atavistic form of dominance competition), and desire for the spoils of war, including land, livestock, water access, and women. Concerning competition for women, Chagnon (1988) has shown that Yanomami men who have killed have more wives and children than those who have not—although, of course, there is the risk of being killed oneself. Eibl-Eibesfeldt also discussed the necessity for face saving (i.e., reconciliation) in dispute resolution.

Summary

In children, consensual dominance hierarchies emerge that reflect toughness, strength, fighting ability, and attractiveness. Boys usually dominate girls. Similarly, terrestrial primates form male-dominated hierarchies based on aggression, starting as juveniles. Dominant individuals are monitored more closely than subordinates—they are paid more attention—and they exercise various prerogatives.

In U.S. adolescent boys' peer groups, physical traits remain salient. Dominant, popular leaders tend to be attractive, athletic boys whom girls find desirable. These physical attributes all show developmental stability, as do dominance ranks themselves. As in other species, these masculine, testosterone-dependent facial and bodily traits attract females. Attractiveness is perhaps a more general indicator of genetic quality than is muscularity, athletic skill, or current dominance rank. However, dominance rank is an indicator of current resource-holding power and hence of potential nuptial gifts, and so it may also constitute a useful criterion for mate choice by females (see Chapter 13). Early maturity does not directly influence peer status; dominant adolescent boys tend to have been dominant early maturers in childhood, too. Early maturity, size, and high rank indicate a favorable developmental course and fitness advantages at maturity.

The appeal of attractive physical features may be universal. However, in Europe, China, and Japan, it appears that scholastic achievement is also respected in adolescence. Intelligent individuals are rated as dominant leaders by their classmates, and they manifest dominance displays.

Not until adulthood is social standing in the United States heavily influenced by cultural standards as well as by physical features. A man's mate value seems to depend not only on his attractiveness but also on his expected economic success. Parents seem to stress the importance of these material values; great differentials in wealth occurred only with the advent of agriculture about 10,000 years ago and hence probably did not shape the human genome appreciably. Other males may seek out, defer to, and pay tribute to high-ranking males in order to secure effective, competent, vigorous, healthy, and courageous leaders in hunting and warfare.

Attractive, dominant boys enjoy various social prerogatives. Peers defer to them; they receive few dominance challenges. Peers and teachers treat them prosocially. Dominant boys generally reciprocate and so are perceived as prosocial. Their positive social experience renders them more outgoing, and they gain practice at exercising leadership. They experience ample pride and little loneliness. Less attractive boys have the opposite sort of experience. They may become angry and aggressive in response to harsh treatment, and they are at risk for delinquency.

Social groups, such as juvenile play groups, military units, and other male solidarity groups, can be analyzed by applying principles of dominance hierarchization and concepts from social psychology. Because of their competence, leaders are often imitated, but their influence sometimes declines in settings in which they do not excel. One prerogative that leaders often exercise is evaluation of other group members. Group coherence is enhanced by similarity, a common goal, a common threat, success, and group self-esteem.

The roots of human warfare are found in collective attacks by male chimpanzees. Observational studies reveal that human aggression is not particularly frequent in comparative perspective but is deadly because of technological "advances."

12 Girls' Peer Relations

Dominance Behavior Among Female Primates

Female primates devote less effort to competitive peer relations, or dominance competition, than do males (see Chapters 5 and 9). Nevertheless, being dominant does tend to enhance a female primate's fitness. Dominant females of various primate species enjoy feeding advantages, which result in earlier maturity, earlier first pregnancy, more offspring, fewer spontaneous abortions, and greater offspring survival (Hrdy, 1981). Furthermore, in many simian species, dominant females sometimes harass subordinates, just as dominant males may harass subordinate males trying to copulate. Another benefit of high rank for a female is that (in chimpanzees, for example) she can effectively raise her offspring's ranks by supporting them in confrontations. This is especially true for daughters' ranks. Daughters of high-ranking chimpanzee mothers tend to reach puberty early and to raise more offspring. Similarly, in some primates, a female may rough up another female's offspring, which can cause the latter's death. Yet another advantage is the tendency of high-ranking females to mate with high-status males.

Dominance relations among female primates are complicated by various factors. In many species, such as rhesus macaques, the female hierarchy is less clear-cut than the males'. Female ranks are often labile because estrus can raise a female primate's rank, perhaps because males defer to receptive females in hopes of copulating with them. Another reason individual ranks are hard to determine is that in many species, the mother, and sometimes other matrilineal kin as well, support the daughter in dominance encounters. For example, Japanese macaque and rhesus macaque mothers favor daughters who are undergoing their first pregnancy, which is the riskiest, over other daughters (Hrdy, 1981). In some species, such as rhesus macaques, the male consort supports the female. In chimpanzees, females are often supported by male kin (Goodall, 1986). In several primates, female rank peaks during the early reproductive years, when fertility is highest. The rule that age and size confer status holds better for male primates than females (Walters, 1987). Thus, although dominance competition among females may not be as intense and straightforward as among males, female rank is associated with reproductive success, partly because it is related to reproductive condition.

Dominance Behavior Among Girls and Women

Consistent with this primate model, girls tend not to be as competitive for dominance as boys. Even in preschool, being tough is more salient for boys, who tend to outrank most girls (Omark et al., 1975)—although if a girl is dominant, she exercises leadership and other prerogatives like a boy (Hold, 1976). Shepher and Tiger (1978) found little evidence for female hierarchies in Israeli kibbutzim or elsewhere. If anything, the presence of dominance behavior indicated strained relations among kibbutz women.

Observational research on U.S. adolescent campers supports the notion that female dominance relations are less clear-cut than males' (Savin-Williams, 1987). Hierarchies in the girls' cabins were less distinct than among the boys, and girls' ranks were less stable. Further, girls' dominance behaviors increased over time, whereas boys' decreased. Girls competed for and expressed dominance with fewer acts of aggression or threats than did boys. Instead, girls indicated their higher status by behaviors such as giving unsolicited advice and shunning; subordinate behaviors included asking advice, seeking favors, and imitation. Extending advice and favors seems to reflect a theme of cooperation rather than the competition that typifies male interactions. However, the competitive nature of this "cooperation" among girls is apparent from the fact that extending and receiving advice and favors reflected social rank. Moreover, in both sexes but especially in girls, ridicule, a competitive behavior, was the most frequent means of indicating dominance. Similarly, in a British study of adolescent girls in gangs, insults, gossip, and fighting were common, especially regarding accusations of promiscuity (A. Campbell, 1995). This sort of behavior is also common between adolescent girls in Finland and Norway (Ahmad & Smith, 1994).

Physical assertiveness may actually be disadvantageous to an adolescent girl's social standing. In research on early adolescents, tough girls tended to be less popular with boys (Cronin, 1975). Also, fifth- and sixth-grade girls were more successful at persuading same-sex peers if they used coaxing rather than aggressive commands, whereas the results were mixed for boys who used that technique (Dion & Stein, 1978). Similarly, shy girls experienced less tension in their relations with their mothers than did nonshy girls, but shy boys experienced more (Hinde, 1987). And girls with more need for approval—that is, those with low self-confidence—were more popular, whereas boys with low self-confidence were less popular (Tulkin et al., 1969).

Because physical assertiveness may confer fewer advantages on girls rather than more, the term *dominance* may have disadvantages in questionnaire research with female subjects. Also, in Savin-Williams's (1987) research, dominant adolescent girls exhibited little in the way of distinctive traits; they were only average in attractiveness, for example. Alternatives to the dominance concept are popularity, which may represent general success in gaining resources in social contexts, and attracting others' attention. Attracting attention characterizes high-ranking primates, including children (Hold, 1976), although the fitness advantage of this trait is less obvious than that of gaining resources. But attracting the attention of group members may constitute a first step in garnering resources.

Which girls, then, are popular? Perhaps the best single predictor of popularity among U.S. girls is attractiveness, which doubtless is due to the consequences of this trait for reproductive success. As is true for males, attractive females tend to be popular throughout development (Adams, 1977). Among U.S. adolescent girls, appearance is consistently related to popularity and leadership (e.g., Kennedy, 1990; Adams, 1977). This includes dressing fashionably and being well groomed as well as physical attractiveness (Allen & Eicher, 1973; J. S. Coleman, 1961; G. E. Weisfeld et al., 1984a). Other traits have been correlated with girls' popularity, including social skill, intelligence, and athletic ability (but *not* team sports participation [Eder & Kinney, 1995]), but attractiveness seems to be paramount. In China, the dominant, leading adolescent girls and boys tended to be intelligent as well as attractive (Dong et al., 1996). This contrasted with the results of a U.S. study in which the correlation of girls' popularity with intelligence for an excellent suburban high school was precisely 0.00 (G. E. Weisfeld et al., 1984a). Culture can, of course, impose additional values that influence peer evaluations, but attractiveness seems to carry some universal appeal. For example, attractive Hopi adolescent girls tended to be popular (G. E. Weisfeld et al., 1984b).

Despite the fact that girls do not seem to compete for dominance very much in aggressive terms, the dominance model does help to explain nonverbal behavior in adolescents of both sexes. For example, popular, leading, dominant U.S. adolescent girls and boys were perceived by peers as exhibiting the dominance displays of erect posture, direct gaze, and relaxation (G. E. Weisfeld et al., 1983, 1984a). Dominant, leading Chinese (Dong et al., 1996) and English (Boardway & G. E. Weisfeld, 1994) adolescents were judged to exhibit the same displays, even though the criteria of dominance varied across countries. Similarly, in an observational study of U.S. college students, attractive women and men tended to exhibit erect posture (G. E. Weisfeld & Laehn, 1986). Lastly, Moore (1995) observed that younger adolescent girls paid attention to older, dominant, attractive females, evidently to learn successful courtship tactics.

Pubertal Timing

Reaching puberty early is less consistently correlated with social success, self-esteem, and other positive traits for girls than for boys (M. C. Jones & Mussen, 1958). This famous finding has been replicated many times. For example, Clausen (1975) reported that early maturation was correlated with high self-confidence in a middle-class sample of girls but with low self-confidence in a lower-class sample.

Girls who reach puberty before their peers sometimes experience embarrassment about their height, menstruation, breast development, or poor complexion (Stolz & Stolz, 1944; Tobin-Richards et al., 1983; Simmons et al., 1983). In another U.S. study, early-maturing 11-year-old girls tended to be rather unpopular with other girls (Faust, 1960). However, any negative effects of early puberty for girls seem to be short-lived. Later in puberty and in adulthood (at age 30), peer status and self-confidence tend to be somewhat higher for early-maturing girls than for late maturers (M. C. Jones & Mussen, 1958; Peskin & Livson, 1972). In the Faust study, early-maturing girls between the ages of 12 and 14 were actually more popular with female classmates than were late-maturing girls. Similarly, in a German study, early-maturing girls tended to have higher self-esteem (Silbereisen et al., 1989). Thus, on balance, early maturity is a boon to girls in their same-sex peer relations, although not as markedly as it is for boys. Moreover, early-maturing girls tend to be popular with boys throughout pubertal development (Simmons et al., 1983). In the Faust research, early maturers were popular with boys in all 4 years studied. Early-maturing girls also tend to be popular with adults (Simmons et al., 1983). Thus, *early maturity has moderate social benefits for girls.*

One tentative explanation for this pattern is the following. Initially, at around 11 years of age, early-maturing girls are not very popular with same-sex peers because they are not deemed especially attractive in the United States (Elder, 1968). Early-maturing U.S. girls tend to be dissatisfied with their bodies, which are often short and chubby (Tobin-Richards et al., 1983; Simmons et al., 1983). Since attractiveness largely determines popularity, especially for females (Tobin-Richards et al., 1983), early-maturing girls are at no particular advantage among their female peers. Initially, too, other girls regard them as "different." At this early age, children are still in the throes of the gang stage and its conformism, and being different can be upsetting. For obvious reasons, however, they are popular with boys throughout puberty. Moreover, since early-puberty girls tend to begin dating early in the United States and elsewhere, they become more experienced with boys than are other girls. This may help to explain the fact that they are subsequently respected by other girls. Furthermore, early-maturing girls tend to be more feminine (Terman & Miles, 1936), and their feminine traits may eventually contribute to their attractiveness and popularity.

The most common explanation for the initially low status of early-maturing girls is that they are extremely "off time" developmentally (M. C. Jones & Mussen, 1958). They are ahead of most of the other girls and all of the boys. Being off time may indeed be awkward, especially at an age when conformity is so important. Consistent with this explanation, early-maturing boys are the most popular, since they are near the average in maturity for boys and girls combined. But then, why do the early-maturing girls soon become more popular with other girls? And why aren't late-maturing girls the most popular, since they are closest to the average maturer among boys and girls combined? And don't boys compare their development with that of other boys only, not with that of both sexes—and likewise for girls?

Yet another explanation is that female sexual development is threatening to sexually conservative U.S. society (Tobin-Richards et al., 1983). This may explain the low initial popularity of early-maturing girls, but it does not explain the popularity of early-maturing boys, whose sexuality should also be threatening. It also does not explain the subsequent popularity of early-maturing girls.

For these reasons, the best explanation may be related to attractiveness (G. E. Weisfeld & Billings, 1988). Early-maturing girls are more feminine and hence more attractive to boys. These girls initially may feel they are not attractive, at least in the United States, perhaps because of a squeamishness about sexual development or the high prevalence of obesity. And other girls may not view them as attractive for the same reason. Later on, however, these early-maturing girls' greater femininity, popularity, and experience with boys may enhance their status in the eyes of other girls (cf. Moore, 1995).

Early puberty carries other implications for girls. It leads parents to grant them more independence, as in babysitting (Simmons et al., 1983; Magnusson et al., 1986). *Early-maturing girls date earlier, have sex earlier, go steady earlier, marry earlier, and have their first child earlier* across cultures, including Sweden, the United States, Finland, Belgium, Pakistan, and Malaysia (Udry & Cliquet, 1982; Dwyer & Mayer, 1968–1969; Aro & Taipale, 1987; Magnusson et al., 1986). They view themselves as more mature and more romantic (Magnusson et al., 1986; M. C. Jones & Mussen, 1958). Since early-maturing girls tend to have longer reproductive spans and higher fertility, as among the agropastoral Kipsigis of Kenya (Borgerhoff Mulder, 1989), early maturity is advantageous biologically.

Yet early-maturing girls in the West tend to be more "antisocial" than late maturers. They do less well in school in the United States and Sweden (Simmons et al., 1983; Magnusson et al., 1986), even though early maturers of both sexes perform somewhat better on aptitude tests. They are less achievement-motivated (i.e., less competitive), and they show less school leadership (M. C. Jones & Mussen, 1958). They are less likely to enter college and to have a career. Early-maturing Swedish girls were more likely to violate parental rules concerning school attendance, drinking, smoking hashish, petty theft, and curfews (Magnusson et al., 1986). Early-maturing Finnish girls had more alcohol problems and psychosomatic symptoms (Aro & Taipale, 1987). Early-maturing U.S. girls have been found to have worse relations with parents (Savin-Williams & Small, 1986) and to exhibit behavior problems in school (Simmons et al., 1983). In the study by Simmons et al., 12-year-old girls were especially prone to low self-esteem if they negotiated three events simultaneously: early puberty, changing schools, and the onset of dating.

Most of these effects of early development can be explained by the fact that *early girls are more feminine, just as early boys are more masculine* (Terman & Miles, 1936). Early puberty and a short, chubby physique are themselves feminine developments; why should these girls' behavior not also tend to be relatively feminine? This would account for their greater romanticism and nurturance (cf. Chapter 10), and their lesser competitiveness, leadership, and academic aspirations (cf. the observation that fetally masculinized girls are more career-orientated and less maternal, discussed in Chapter 9).

These are apparently not all direct hormonal effects, however. In Sweden, early-maturing girls violated parental rules only if they socialized with older schoolmates, which led them to expect greater leniency from their parents. However, hormones probably exerted an indirect effect; the mature appearance of these girls and their dating behavior probably inclined older girls to accept their company (Magnusson et al., 1986). Similarly, early-maturing girls tended to use alcohol if they had older friends. This effect did not last into adulthood. In contrast, late-maturing boys were more likely to use alcohol, an effect that did last into adulthood (Andersson & Magnusson, 1990). Perhaps some early-maturing Swedish girls drink to be part of the group, and perhaps some late-maturing boys drink because they are low in social status (see Chapter 11).

Lastly, early-maturing girls report more distress during menstruation (Brooks-Gunn & Ruble, 1983); feeling that one is "on time" is associated with having the least distress (Greif & Ulman, 1982). The degree of distress experienced at the first menses seems to influence subsequent distress. Not being psychologically prepared for menstruation was also associated with more symptoms, perhaps because the anxiety associated with neophobia aggravated the experience.

Obesity

Early-maturing girls are often chubby. For one thing, they attain the critical level of body fat at a young age. Furthermore, they are more feminized, and that may mean possessing more body fat. As discussed in Chapter 10, fat development is a normal feminine change.

238 / Girls' Peer Relations

Obesity is very hard to overcome, especially if present since childhood (Rodin, 1977; Wooley & Garner, 1994). It is usually refractory to dieting—there may be an initial weight loss with dieting, but in almost all cases, the lost weight is regained within 2 years. In fact, obese people typically eat little more food than average-weight individuals (Logue, 1991). Similarly, weight lost through exercise is usually regained within 2 days (Rodin, 1977). Moreover, exercise regimens, like diets, are seldom maintained (Logue, 1991).

The permanence of obesity and the fact that body weight tends to be very stable for most people suggest that adherence to the body's set point has some adaptive value. Indeed, obesity and a stocky, heat-retaining shape are common in populations (e.g., Eskimos and Arctic mammals) that have evolved in cold climates or where food was scarce (Bogin, 1988), suggesting that obesity is an adaptation, at least in part, to starvation (Hoyenga & Hoyenga, 1984). This would explain why repeated bouts of dieting often result in rebound increases in appetite and greater weight than before. It would also account for the lowered metabolic rate and lethargy of obese people, whose bodies are trying to conserve energy. Their relative lethargy makes obese people less inclined to exercise than are controls (Logue, 1991). Moreover, obese people tend to be opportunistic feeders, eating a lot when high-calorie food is available that requires little energy to prepare, such as snack foods (Hoyenga & Hoyenga, 1984). Normal-weight individuals respond more to bodily cues, such as mealtime. Similarly, rats made obese by brain lesions are highly responsive to the properties of food.

The notion that obesity is an adaptation to starvation is supported by other observations. Organisms that have little need for bodily agility are prone to obesity—women, the elderly, infants, sedentary populations, and domesticated animals. In effect, these organisms trade some fleetness of foot for protection against starvation. Similarly, rodents that have been starved subsequently hoard food; even rats whose pregnant mothers were starved hoard food. Women's need to lactate, which requires a great deal of caloric energy, also helps explain their greater tendency toward obesity (Hoyenga & Hoyenga, 1984).

Consistent with this evolutionary interpretation, obesity does not seem to be caused by a personality problem; rather, any personality difficulties that obese individuals suffer seem due to social rejection (Rodin, 1977). Also consistent with the notion that this widespread phenomenon is not pathological, mild obesity does not jeopardize health very much (Wooley & Garner, 1991), and most obese people succeed in getting married—often to other obese individuals. Parental attitudes toward physical "imperfections" may influence the adolescent's attitude more than the imperfections themselves (Bruch, 1943). The best preventive for obesity is good nutrition, starting with breast-feeding and proceeding to a diet with ample fresh fruits and vegetables and nutrient-rich dairy products, eggs, and meat. If nutrients are insufficient, the body compensates by calling for more food, resulting in weight gain. Still, the heritability of body weight is around 0.66 (Plomin et al., 1990), so experience has a limited influence. For example, obesity in the United States is most common in the Midwest, where many residents have Eastern European ancestors whose ancestors, in turn, originated in starvation-prone Central Asia.

Female Inhibition in Mixed-Sex Competition

Horner (1972) concluded that women have a "fear of success." Subsequent research has revealed that this tendency is quite complicated. First of all, females are generally less competitive than males (see Chapters 9, 11). But beyond this, many females perform below their ability when competing against males specifically.

C. C. Weisfeld et al. (1982, 1983) referred to this phenomenon as **female inhibition in mixed-sex competition**. It occurs specifically in the presence of males; for example, girls in a coed elementary school were less likely to overrate their own toughness than girls in an all-girl school (Parker & Omark, 1980). And women were observed to exhibit more subordinate body posture in mixed-sex group discussions than in same-sex group discussions (Aries, 1982). Female inhibition is seen more often in naturalistic, face-to-face studies than in artificial laboratory situations, and in adolescent and adult (reproductive-age) females rather than in children (C. C. Weisfeld, 1986).

A simple socialization explanation in terms of it being "unladylike" in our culture to defeat a man is a dubious explanation for this phenomenon. First, the phenomenon has been reported in various cultures, namely, among Hopi Indians and African Americans (C. C. Weisfeld et al., 1982). Second, subjects who inhibit their performance are often not aware of doing so, and they often vehemently deny that they are not trying their hardest (Mausner & Coles, 1978; C. C. Weisfeld et al., 1982). Third, the phenomenon even occurs in female-biased tasks such as spelling (Cronin, 1980)—tasks at which girls are encouraged to succeed and in which they usually surpass boys. The phenomenon typically occurs in women with traditional, feminine interests. For example, Peplau (1976) found that a traditional woman was inclined to perform more poorly when working with her boyfriend on an intellectual task than when performing alone. Moreover, the hormonal profiles of inhibited women differ from those of women who do not show this effect (C. C. Weisfeld, 1986). The latter respond with the typical male hormonal pattern to competitive situations: Their adrenalin levels increase (Frankenhaueser, 1982). These women tend to be androgynous in their sex-role behavior; they often enter masculine fields such as engineering and bus driving, and they tend to be less interested in marriage and parenthood. In inhibited females, who tend to have feminine interests, adrenalin levels usually do not to rise in competitive situations. This is a fascinating case of a possible polymorphism, that is, of two developmentally distinct and adaptive forms.

How might female inhibition be functional? The disadvantage of lowering one's performance may be offset by the advantage of attaining greater harmony with one's husband (Callan, 1970). Note that the phenomenon is cross-cultural, is confined to reproductive-age females interacting with potential or actual mates, has hormonal correlates, and is more pronounced for successful women who might defeat their male competitors. For example, women in married-couples group therapy were observed to exhibit more submissive behavior toward their husbands than toward the other men (McCarrick et al., 1981). In another study, women who expected to find a husband to support them were less likely to display their own financial resources than those with lower expectations in that regard (Cashdan, 1993).

In theory, it would not matter which spouse dominated decision-making, but perhaps males were preadapted to be intimidating and hence came to take this role. Also, since male competition is more consequential for family welfare than female competition, the wife would not benefit by undermining her husband's public status (C. C. Weisfeld & Weisfeld, 1996). At a more basic level, females in many species (including our own) tend to prefer dominant males (see Chapter 13). Therefore, women may inhibit their competitiveness in order to encourage a potential mate.

In terms of actual (as opposed to perceived or alleged) decision-making power, wives typically wield considerable influence and, cross-culturally, predominate in decision-making regarding domestic matters (Stephens, 1963). It would make no adaptive sense for men to decide matters about which they knew little, such as child care. The wife's public deference to her husband may be a convenient fiction that aids him in his competition with other males. Consistent with this explanation, favoritism of males (the **male supremacy complex**) is especially pronounced in warlike cultures (Divale & Harris, 1976), perhaps also to ensure the health of the warriors on whom the rest of the society depends. See also Chapter 13.

Friendship

Another important aspect of peer relations is friendship. In childhood and preadolescence, peers provide partners for play and models for learning sex-specific behavior. Boys' and girls' friends and playmates tend to be of the same age, sex, and rank throughout development; the same is true for simians' play partnerships. Peers are also likely to be interested in the same activities. Then, too, same-age peers are roughly equal in ability and hence are interesting play partners because the outcome of competitions between them is uncertain. Thus, friendships are relatively egalitarian, and they are usually undermined if they are not. For example, some highly attractive women complain that other, envious women harass them around desirable men.

A friendship may be viewed as a relatively permanent partnership with a peer for mutual learning and support. Various primates, including chimpanzees (de Waal, 1982) and preschoolers (Grammer, 1992), form coalitions for mutual support in dominance competition. In Grammer's study of German kindergartners, both sexes supported girls who were being attacked by boys, but neither sex supported girls being attacked by girls. Support was usually tendered by children who outranked both the attacker and the victim. Help seemed to solidify friendships and also raised the rank of the helper, who was perceived as gaining respect. Long-term relationships such as friendships presumably are conducive to reciprocal altruism, since mutual trust takes time to engender. By contrast, it is advantageous to abandon a relationship that is unsatisfying.

Although friendships in childhood are mainly concerned with play, they become increasingly stable and then more altruistic. Friendship stability has been found to increase from age 6 to 9 but not from 9 to 16 (T. Berndt, 1981). Between ages 9 and 13, children begin to perform favors preferentially for friends as opposed to other classmates (T. Berndt, 1982). This may reflect the emergence of relationships of reciprocal altruism rather than simple play partnerships.

Adolescent friendships entail the disclosure of more intimate information than children's friendships (Buhrmester & Furman, 1987), especially among girls. From ages 11 to 13, U.S. girls' friendships seemed to revolve around play, whereas from ages 14 to 16, girls emphasized the loyalty of friends (Douvan & Adelson, 1966). For both sexes, insecurity about friendships peaked at 15 years; from age 17 on, friendships were less intense and less important. Similar results were obtained in Britain (J. C. Coleman, 1974). Friendship may decline as opposite-sex relationships become preoccupying.

Some consistent sex differences concerning adolescent friendship have been reported. Insecurity about social matters peaks in midadolescence for both sexes, but it seems more profound and longlasting for girls (Douvan & Adelson, 1966; Powell, 1955; J. C. Coleman, 1974). For example, a small group of female friends were more rejecting of a newcomer than were males (Sones & Feshbach, 1971), and girls expressed more concern than boys about a friend's sensitivity (Douvan & Adelson, 1966). Boys seem less concerned about a friend keeping confidences and more concerned about having mutual interests, backing one up when in trouble, and not quarreling over property or girlfriends (Douvan & Adelson, 1966; J. C. Coleman, 1974). There is no clear sex difference in friendship stability.

Douvan and Adelson suggested that the trust issue is intense for middle-adolescent girls because they usually start to date at that time and wish to share confidences. Trust may be more of an issue for girls for several reasons. Perhaps males, being generally more self-confident than females, have fewer self-doubts to reveal. Also, sexual activity, if revealed, tends to enhance the status of a male and lower that of a female; therefore, females may be more worried than males about the betrayal of this sort of secret. In a study of female adolescent gang members in the United Kingdom, Campbell (1995) discovered that the main cause of fights was insults to sexual reputation, which might consist of the betrayal of sexual secrets. Then, too, mate choice is more important for females than males, so perhaps girls gain more than boys from exchanging confidential information about the opposite sex. Lastly, males may socialize in larger and less intimate groups because of the function of the male solidarity unit in hunting and combat. There has been little cross-cultural research on adolescent friendship by which to test such explanations.

Summary

In general, female primates compete for dominance less intensively than do males. Their ranks fluctuate somewhat with their reproductive condition. However, once this lability is taken into account, ranks may be quite important for female primates. They do predict reproductive success.

For girls as well as boys, success among peers reflects attractiveness to a very great extent and probably universally. Peer success is largely a unitary phenomenon, in that attractive individuals tend to be popular, self-confident, dominance-displaying leaders, as judged by both sexes. Moreover, peer success is developmentally stable, at least insofar as it rests on attractiveness, which is highly stable. Assertiveness seems to reduce girls' popularity, contrary to the case for boys. Dominant adolescent girls typically dispense advice to, are imitated by, and shun subordinates.

Early maturity connotes a favorable developmental trajectory and a long reproductive span. In tribal societies, early-maturing girls undergo puberty rites early, marry early, and reproduce early. They therefore experience more reproductive years; in addition, menopause tends to come late for early maturers.

Since early maturity is generally advantageous to females' reproductive success, it is appealing to the opposite sex. Girls who reach puberty early suffer, at most, only a temporary social disadvantage; they are generally more popular than later maturers.

Just as early-maturing boys are more masculine, early-maturing girls are more feminine. Early-maturing girls who associate with older peers tend to become sexually involved at a younger age than late maturers, and accordingly, they sometimes neglect scholastic pursuits. Their greater femininity may incline them to early reproductive activities rather than to studying for a career.

Being highly feminine, early-maturing girls tend to be somewhat plump. Obesity is highly heritable and may constitute an adaptation to starvation pressure or an evolved response to a diet low in nutrients. It is generally permanent and is aggravated by bouts of dieting, which mimic starvation conditions.

Female inhibition in mixed-sex competition may reflect an evolved tendency to defer to potential mates for the sake of harmony. As Chapter 13 will describe, female-dominated mateships tend to be unstable.

Primate play partnerships and dominance coalitions provide comparative models for human friendship. Young children sometimes aid each other unilaterally, but reciprocal friendships tend to emerge in early adolescence. Many human friendships are distinguished by the verbal exchange of sexual information, especially between adolescent girls. Trustworthiness is a major ingredient in adolescent friendships, especially for girls.

13 Sexual Relations

This chapter will begin with analyses of sexual orientation in men and women, and then address sex differences in sexuality. Next, the criteria for mate choice in the sexes will be described. Lastly, the causation and prevention of unmarried adolescent childbearing and of divorce will be discussed.

Sexual Orientation in Men

Sexual preference is a fascinating developmental issue, since it involves diverse genetic and experimental factors. The issue is also of great interest to evolutionists, who are puzzled by the 3 percent prevalence of a male homosexuality, a condition of obviously low reproductive fitness and of appreciable heritability. In one report, the identical twin of 50 out of 57 male homosexuals was also homosexual (Puterbaugh, 1990). Most heritable pathological conditions, that is, those that lower fitness, are rare. They appear because of random mutations, and they are selected against, so they tend to occur in far fewer than 1 percent of individuals. But male homosexuality is probably evolutionarily stable—it likely is a variant with some adaptive value for humans rather than a pathological variant or a product of unusual environmental conditions. A low rate of exclusive male homosexuality is found around the world, rather than being confined to certain locales (Ford & Beach, 1951; L. Ellis, 1996a). It is rare in most species in the wild but is common in captive rams, rhesus monkeys, and bonobos (pygmy chimpanzees).

One recent study provided a possible functional explanation for homosexuality in men: Gay males are more likely than straight males to have a certain genetic marker on the X chromosome (Hamer et al., 1993). This might explain the higher incidence of homosexuality in men with Klinefelter's syndrome; these men have one or more extra

X chromosomes (LeVay, 1993). Hypothetically, an X-chromosome gene might be evolutionarily stable if it reduced males' fitness by making them gay but raised the fitness of females. Moreover, because twice as many females as males would have the gene (since women have two X chromosomes), the benefit to females would only have to equal half the cost to males for the gene to be neutral (Trivers, 1994, 1997).

Explanations that emphasize socialization are doubtful, given the appreciable incidence of homosexuality across cultures. After all, why would different cultural experiences produce the same outcome? Furthermore, male homosexuals in different societies tend to resemble each other with respect to behavioral interests and occupational choices (Whitman, 1983), which implicates genes in these interests and choices as well as in homosexuality. Although no culture completely approves of a man who spends his whole life as a homosexual (Gadpaille, 1980), male homosexuality is tolerated more in some cultures than in others. Nevertheless, cultures that tolerate boyhood homosexuality do not produce disproportionate numbers of adult homosexuals (Singer, 1985a). In these cultures and under certain circumstances, such as imprisonment, men may engage in optional, or facultative, homosexuality (or, roughly speaking, bisexuality). Obviously, environmental conditions play a role in this form of homosexuality.

By contrast, little evidence supports a socialization explanation for exclusive, or obligate, homosexuality. The favorite psychoanalytic theory of male homosexuality—a domineering mother, a weak father—has no good research support. Father absence in childhood was more common among gays than straights, but most gays had had the father present (Saghir & Robins, 1973). Although most homosexuals, unlike the heterosexuals, had an unsatisfactory relationship with the father and identified primarily with the mother, these family dynamics could have been due to (1) the boy's preexisting effeminacy alienating the father, (2) the father's effeminacy alienating the son, (3) the father and son sharing genes for effeminacy, or (4) the son's effeminacy drawing him closer to his mother.

Socialization explanations are weakened further by the poor record of psychotherapy in changing sexual orientation, especially of exclusive homosexuals (Mellen, 1981). Similarly, cross-national research indicates that childhood seduction seldom, if ever, contributes to exclusive homosexuality. **Pedophilia** (attraction to children) is rare even in gay men, although male homosexuals are often attracted to adolescent boys, and children raised by lesbians seldom become homosexual (L. Ellis, 1996a). Then, too, most homosexuals report that they "felt different" from a young age, and many were effeminate as children (Bailey, 1996)—even at 1 or 2 years of age (LeVay, 1993).

Another socialization explanation cites a lack of heterosexual fulfillment. Gallup (1986) suggested that adolescent boys resort to homosexuality because of sexual failure with girls. He noted that one study found the average homosexual man had had only 1.3 female partners before becoming gay. This finding may explain some facultative male homosexuality, but it is inconsistent with the high heritability and immutability of exclusive homosexuality. Perhaps effeminate boys are simply less attractive to girls.

So far, the best-established experiential influence is prenatal stress. Pregnant rats that were subjected to stress gave birth to sons that subsequently became bisexual. Prenatal stress resulted in lower testosterone levels during sex differentiation of the male's brain (Ward & Weisz, 1980); stress hormones can depress gonadal hormone production, even before birth (see Chapter 9). At maturity, the male rats showed a tendency toward estrous cycling; presumably, their hypothalami had been partly feminized during early development.

Research on exclusively homosexual men is consistent with this mammalian model. L. Ellis et al. (1988) showed that during the second trimester alone, when the human brain is differentiating sexually, the mothers of male homosexuals reported that they had experienced twice the stress of mothers of heterosexuals. Similarly, pregnant German mothers who gave birth to male homosexuals experienced more stress (being raped, widowed, or bombed out in World War II) than the mothers of heterosexuals (Dörner et al., 1983). In addition, more homosexual men were born to German women during World War II than before or after it.

It appears, then, that testosterone exerts an organizing effect on sexual orientation during the sensitive period for sexual differentiation of the brain. Some alterations in hormones are also observed in male homosexuals in adulthood. Lifelong gay males exhibit a hormonal menstrual cycling response that is intermediate between those of heterosexual men and women, and they show altered levels of some neurotransmitters (Gladue et al., 1984). Also, male homosexuals differ from heterosexuals in corticosteroid metabolism, the size of several brain structures, fingerprint pattern, and sex-differentiated cognitive aptitudes (L. Ellis, 1996b).

This research may explain the inconsistency of reports of lower testosterone levels and decreased muscularity in adult male homosexuals, as well as the fact that hormone treatment in adulthood does not change sexual orientation. Low prenatal testosterone seems to be the crucial factor for the development of male homosexuality, but in gay men testosterone may sometimes be low postpubertally, too, leading to less muscularity. It is also easy to see how homosexuality might be highly heritable: Some males (or their mothers) might be genetically predisposed to suffer this effect of stress. Exposure to prenatal stress is an environmental effect, but reactivity to it may vary with the mother's or the fetus's genes.

Prenatal factors may also influence some other sexual variants. Pedophiles have an abnormal LH response to GnRH (Gaffney & Berlin, 1984). And in male-to-female transsexuals, a structure in the stria terminalis (connecting the amygdala and hypothalamus) was as small as that of females (Zhou, 1995). Thus, sexual identity (self-perception as a boy or girl), sexual orientation, and sex role (masculinity or femininity) are all apparently influenced by prenatal hormones.

Sexual Orientation in Women

Female homosexuality is less of an evolutionary conundrum than male homosexuality for two reasons. The incidence is only 1 or 2 percent, perhaps within normal limits for a fitness-reducing variant, especially if the woman is heterosexual for part of her reproductive life. And a woman can reproduce without being sexually aroused by the partner, whereas a man normally cannot.

Socialization explanations for lesbianism encounter many of the objections raised in regard to male homosexuality. Lesbians may tend to have had disturbed relations with their parents, but the direction of causation is not clear.

Gallup's (1986) explanation for lesbianism posits that lesbian women had little problem attracting sex partners but found sex with men unsatisfying. He reported that the average lesbian had had 5.3 male partners previously; almost half of those women had been married. But lesbianism shows appreciable heritability (LeVay, 1993). Experience may play a major role in facultative homosexuality but perhaps not in the obligate form.

Prenatal stress is not associated with lesbianism (L. Ellis et al., 1988). Stress lowers gonadal hormones; lower testosterone would only enhance feminine differentiation. However, prenatal masculinization might promote lesbianism. Female rats that were given testosterone at birth mounted males at maturity. Women who were fetally masculinized by either congenital adrenal hyperplasia (CAH) or therapeutic diethyl stilbestrol (DES) had elevated rates of lesbianism (L. Ellis & Ames, 1987). Lesbians have been found to be intermediate in adult menstrual hormonal cyclicity between heterosexual men and women. Some but not all studies show that lesbians have masculine hormonal profiles, corticosteroid metabolism, body build, cognitive abilities, childhood play preferences, and neurotransmitters (L. Ellis, 1996b; Durden-Smith & deSimone, 1983).

Sociobiologists have suggested that the study of homosexuals' behavior may enlighten us about the extent of sex differences in heterosexuals, inasmuch as homosexuals do not have to compromise with the opposite sex and can therefore behave with fewer inhibitions. For example, concerning sexual variety, many male homosexuals report having had more than 1,000 lifetime partners (Symons, 1979). In this light, future research on gays' and lesbians' motivation to care for children, to experience jealousy, and so forth may reveal a great deal about sex differences in heterosexuals as well.

Research up to this point, however, shows that homosexuals are not simply heterosexuals with the motives of the opposite sex. In some respects, they possess the inclinations of same-sex heterosexuals. For example, male homosexuals, despite their attraction to males, show a typically masculine interest in sexual variety, youthful partners, and frequent sex (Mellen, 1981). But they tend to dislike effeminate partners (Kim & Bailey, 1996). Lesbians show the opposite, feminine pattern on most of these dimensions. However, although they exhibit a slight preference for partners who are feminine in appearance, they generally prefer women who are masculine in interests. For additional information on the developmental aspects of homosexuality, consult Savin-Williams and Cohen (1996).

Sex Differences in Sexual Behavior

Some additional sex differences in sexual behavior will now be described. It is important not to overdraw these differences in sexual strategy. Women show some tendency toward extrapair copulations (see the discussion that follows), and most men seek marriage, even though they are tempted by extrapair sexual opportunities.

It can even be argued that men are more romantic than women. Young U.S. men fall in love earlier and more frequently than young women (Kanin et al., 1970), although they may fall out of love somewhat sooner; intense infatuation seldom lasts more than 2 years for women or more than 1 1/2 years for men (Money & Ehrhardt, 1972). In other studies of U.S. college couples, the woman usually broke up the affair (C. Hill et al., 1979). In addition, the man tended to report more unhappiness after the breakup than did the woman, and he was less able to remain friendly with the woman if he was rejected as a lover. Furthermore, women are more likely than men to marry someone they do not love (Kephart, 1967).

Why might it make adaptive sense for men to be more romantic than women? One possibility is that only a genuinely romantic man would be able to convince a woman of his sincerity. Another is that, because of polygyny, more men than women will be left unmarried; therefore, men need to be more highly motivated to secure a pair bond than women. Yet another possibility is that since men have greater sexual motivation than women, they desire the sexual component of a relationship more than women do. Thus, men may not be more romantic than women—they may just be more highly motivated to become mated.

One contentious issue is the question of sex difference in physiological sexual arousal in response to erotica. In reviewing the literature on this issue, Symons (1979) pointed out that, although the sexes may respond similarly to erotica once exposed to it, males are much more highly motivated to seek it out. The market for erotica for heterosexual females is minuscule compared with that for males. Symons also noted that in Heiman's (1975) research, although there was only a small sex difference in responsiveness to erotica, there was a huge difference in responsiveness to "control" tapes that depicted casual conversation between a man and woman. This may indicate that men respond even under conditions of low stimulation, whereas at conditions of high stimulation, the sexes respond more similarly.

A recent Austrian study shed further light on these sex differences (Jütte et al., 1998). Women as well as men usually reported genital sensations in response to a film depicting sexual intercourse. And in both sexes, testosterone level rose—more sharply in men but more lastingly in women. But women, unlike men, reported stronger sensations if they were in a romantic relationship than if unpaired. Moreover, women were much less likely than men to experience the affect of sexual arousal. The authors speculated that women need to be physiologically prepared for sex whenever the possibility appears, but they must not be emotionally aroused too readily.

Thus, women are more selective, and what they are looking for is a romantic, pair-bonding man. Many U.S. research findings can be explained by hypothesizing a sex difference in the linkage of sex with romanticism. For example, the first sexual experience of a boy typically has little romantic attachment; that of a girl typically involves someone she loves or expects to marry (Carns, 1973; Kallen & Stephenson, 1982). The boy will probably have sex with his first partner a few more times, but the girl will probably have sex with her first partner many times and actually may marry him. Typically, losing his virginity has no impact on a man's feelings toward his partner, but a woman typically reports feeling more love for the man who was her first sex partner (Peplau et al., 1977). A man, however, usually reports heightened love for a woman who loses her virginity with him. Thus, for both sexes, the girl's loss of virginity is often momentous for both partners, almost like an imprinting effect, and it may be dramatized by the existence and penetration of that curious structure, the hymen. Furthermore, males tell more friends about their first sexual experience than do women (Carns, 1973), presumably because a girl does not wish to appear promiscuous, whereas a boy's status may rise if he is viewed as having many sex partners.

Once a romantic bond is established, women's sexual responsiveness tends to increase, consistent with the notion of a priming effect in female sexuality (see Chapter 10). Adolescent girls who had a single partner were more often orgasmic than girls with multiple partners (Sorensen, 1973). Also, women are more likely to be orgasmic in happy marriages, and to be more often orgasmic when married rather than single (Laumann et al., 1994). Elderly men reported higher chronic sexual arousal when not partnered, but women felt more arousal when partnered (Pfeiffer & Verwoerdt, 1978). Women's sexual responsiveness within a pair bond would help to solidify the bond. As the bond persists, women have been found to become progressively more attracted to the partner (Singer, 1985b). In motivational terms, men seem to be driven more by an internal, periodic need for sex, and women more by reactivity to the external stimulus of a pair-bonding male.

Many women who engage in frequent episodes of casual sex seem to drift away from this practice, apparently in response to negative emotional reactions. Townsend et al. (1995) studied an undergraduate sample of such women, who seemed to proceed through three stages. In the first stage, they experimented with their sexual attractiveness and power. They sought the ego satisfaction (pride) derived from competing successfully with their female peers for the attention of attractive males. This stage may correspond to the sexual experimentation observed in adolescents in most traditional cultures. The next stage involved trying to balance the degree of sexual access they allowed the men against the investment they provided. Even in these sexually liberal women, insufficient attention from a man was aversive; women reported feeling "used" (anger? shame?), vulnerable (fear?), and other negative emotions. This stage may represent maturation of the pair-bonding motive, perhaps mediated by the hormonal connection between copulation and bonding (see Chapter 3). In the last stage, women reached a decision to cease engaging in casual sex because they were deterred by feeling "used," "vulnerable," and "bonded." Ziegenhorn and Schubiner (1997) reported that, for adolescent girls, the number of sex partners was positively correlated with depression and suicidal ideation. However, for boys, the correlations were negative, and the sex difference was statistically significant.

The content of sexual fantasies is a rich source of information about sex differences because such fantasies presumably are less subject to social acceptance than actual behavior is. In research by Miller and Simon (1980), 75 percent of U.S. college men but only 22 percent of women reported that their sexual fantasies sometimes involved a stranger. The percentage of women who acknowledged fantasies about nonsexual activities with a lover (74 percent) was approximately the same as the percentage who cited sexual activities with him (79 percent). In contrast, only 48 percent of men cited nonsexual activities.

In research on sexual arousal, adolescent boys were aroused by nudity, and girls were aroused by romantic books and films, with virtually no overlap between the sexes (Singer, 1985b). Adolescent girls devour these formulaic books with a passion perhaps approaching that of boys consuming male pornography. Across cultures, pornography for men consists mainly of depictions of a variety of sexually aroused women (Ellis & Symons, 1990). Pornography for women consists mainly of romance novels with a similarly invariant theme—love, fidelity, and mate selection in the context of a broader plot. Where sexual arousal is described, the heroine is aroused by touch, the hero's passion, and her response to him. Male fantasies are more frequent, visual, varied, anonymous, and active; women's are more personal, tactual, and passive.

The perplexity or even moral indignation that male pornography arouses in some women may stem, in part, from their own emotional response to such material. Applying their own sex-specific standards for erotica, they are indifferent to or even repulsed by male pornography. "The absence of romantic themes rather than the conjunction of genitalia depicted precludes the investment of erotic meaning in this genre of pornography for all but the exceptional female," whereas for men, "the explicitly sexual is endowed with erotic meaning regardless of the emotional context" (Miller & Simon, 1980, p. 403). Similarly, the arousing potential of romantic novels for adolescent girls, in which the hero is invariably described as rich as well as handsome, probably baffles many males.

Consumption of pornography is highest for males in their twenties and females between 18 and 20 (Abelson et al., 1970). Studies of men in adult bookstores and movie theaters have revealed that these men tend to have had relatively little sexual experience in adolescence (Buck, 1988). Thus, pornography may provide some satisfaction of sexual curiosity.

Arguments that nonviolent erotica leads to sexual crimes are not persuasive (Buck, 1988). Liberalization of pornography laws in Denmark did not raise the incidence of sex crimes. In fact, rapists and pedophiles reported less exposure to pornography in adolescence than normal males, especially to depictions of heterosexual intercourse (M. J. Goldstein et al., 1971). The authors suggested that these depictions help channel sexual impulses along normal lines. But exposure to violent pornography, like violent media content in general, is associated with violent crime.

It should also be noted that men's behavior is driven by emotion just as much as is women's. Sexual feelings, such as interest in sexual variety, are just as much an emotion as is amorousness, and they are just as understandable in adaptive terms. The sexes are probably equally motivated and hence equally emotional, but they probably have different mixes of emotional thresholds. Consequently, the same sex act may arouse a different set of affects in the man and in the woman. Table 13.1 illustrates some sex differences in the emotions underlying Colombian adolescents' first act of coitus.

The "scoring" motif plays a major part in organizing a boy's sexual behavior. Male bragging sessions about sexual conquests are very

254 / Sexual Relations

TABLE 13.1   Reasons Colombian Adolescents Engaged in First Coitus

Reason	Males (N = 169)	Females (N = 40)
Sexual desire	60.9%	32.5%
Love	10.7	47.5
Curiosity	27.2	17.5
Other	1.2	2.5

Source: Useche, Villegas, & Aizate (1980). Reprinted by permission.

common cross-culturally (Freedman, 1967). A man with a reputation for sexual prowess may intimidate rivals and capture the attention of women. If admiration for sexual success is respected everywhere among males, it may have an evolved basis. Vervet monkeys that observed another male copulate experienced a fall in serotonin, a neurotransmitter associated with high rank. Thus, the observing male was evidently "put down" by his cagemate's sexual triumph. But gaining a romantic success may be inherently satisfying and enviable for both sexes. Individuals who registered a burst of pride when they gained such a reproductive advantage may have enjoyed greater fitness than those whose pleasure did not include pride. Much of the appeal of romance novels may lie in their providing adolescent girls with fantasies about such triumphs; analogously, boys fantasize about success at sports and other competitive pursuits. Mentally replaying past and anticipated scenarios probably improves future performance (see Chapter 2).

Sexual behavior represents a sort of compromise between the differing motivations of the man and woman. Such a compromise is often facilitated by the use of deception. The man may feign a stronger bond to the woman than he actually feels, or a woman may act more sexually aroused than she actually is. These deceptions probably cause us to underestimate the extent of the true sex differences in these matters. A man, for example, may try to represent himself as "different" from other men, that is, more concerned with love than sex. A woman may act sexy when her real motive is to find love.

One area of sexuality in which deception abounds is infidelity. A small but appreciable percentage of **extrapair copulations** *(EPCs)* occur in modern society. In a British study, 4 percent of married women's copulations were EPCs (R. R. Baker & Bellis, 1995). On theoretical grounds, Russell and Wells (1987) placed the estimate somewhat higher for prehistoric populations. The existence of various adaptations for infidelity in both sexes confirms its significance. Men typically engage in EPCs opportunistically; those who do are just as satisfied with their marriage as those who do not (Buss, 1994). In contrast, women involved in EPCs tend to be dissatisfied with their husbands, and they often intend to leave them.

Women may engage in EPCs for a variety of adaptive reasons: infertility of the mate, trading sex for resources, and superiority of the extrapair male. In their ground-breaking analysis of physiological and behavioral adaptations in sexual behavior, Baker and Bellis (1995) provided support for the last factor. A woman may be able to gain superior genes for her offspring by means of an EPC, which tends to involve a male who is higher in social status or more attractive than the regular mate. Moreover, EPCs frequently result in fertilization: They are more likely than **intrapair copulations** (IPCs) to occur during the woman's fertile period, and more sperm are retained in her genital tract (rather than flowing back out) than following an IPC. Sperm retention is enhanced by simultaneous orgasm, which tends to characterize EPCs, and sperm rejection is promoted by precoital masturbation, which women practice more often before an IPC than an EPC.

Men have evolved various adaptations to increase their likelihood of fertilizing women, such as mate guarding. Women whose husbands spend more time with them engage in fewer EPCs. These mate-guarding men also tend to have smaller testes than men who pursue a more promiscuous sexual strategy, suggesting that the "cad" and "dad" strategies have distinct physiological and behavioral manifestations. Also, when a man has been absent from his wife for a time, he then produces more sperm per ejaculation in order to oppose sperm from an EPC. The function of male masturbation seems to be to keep sperm fresh and hence more likely to be retained in the vagina.

Various anatomical and physiological adaptations have been identified for promoting effective sperm competition. Semen coagulates upon insemination, forming a barrier to any sperm that are introduced subsequently. This "soft copulatory plug" forms from fluid introduced at the end of the ejaculation; this fluid, from the seminal vesicles, also contains a spermicide. The first spurts of ejaculate contain a great deal of prostatic fluid, which buffers the sperm against a previous male's spermicidal fluid and also stimulates orgasm in the woman. Comparative analysis suggests that the size and shape of the human penis function to remove a previous male's copulatory plug during sexual thrusting. Lastly, "kamikaze sperm" are incapable of fertilizing an ovum, but they specialize in destroying the "egg-getting" sperm of rivals.

Mate Choice by Males

The criteria and tactics that operate in mate selection will now be described for each sex. As a general rule, traits that attract the opposite sex are traits that are relevant to same-sex competition. That is, *peer competition is mainly competition for mates.* If peer competition did not enhance reproductive fitness, it would be energy wasted. The congruence between peer and sexual competition also accounts for the general agreement found between social ranks by adolescents' same- and opposite-sex peers (G. E. Weisfeld et al., 1980).

In this section and the next, sex differences in criteria and tactics will be emphasized, but it is important to remember that the sexes agree on the desirability of numerous traits in a mate. In the United States, for example, kindness and understanding are valued very highly (Buss, 1988a). Similarly, both sexes try to keep their mate mainly by being nice and affectionate (Buss, 1988b). Cross-culturally, industriousness is usually prized in a bride, not just in a groom (Symons, 1979).

Homogamy

Another joint criterion of mate selection is similarity, or **homogamy**. Couples tend to be similar, and similar couples tend to stay together (G. E. Weisfeld et al., 1992). The benefit of similarity for married couples is not simply a matter of compatibility of beliefs, since matching occurs even for blood-group factors and other genetic traits, and homogamy is widespread in animals, too. In one study on humans, genetic similarity predicted whether or not a randomly matched man-woman pair were sexually involved, and in cases of disputed paternity, genetic similarity predicted actual paternity as established by independent means (Rushton, 1988).

Several evolutionary explanations for homogamy have been proposed. Homogamy increases relatedness to offspring, thereby adding to the effectiveness of parental care in ensuring the survival of one's genes. For similar reasons, homogamy would also increase kin altruism among siblings. Another possible functional explanation is that homogamy preserves adaptive genetic complexes; it reduces the rate of miscarriage (Rushton, 1988). But since close inbreeding is detrimental (see Chapter 9 on the advantage of genetic differences in histocompatibility), only a moderate degree of homogamy is ideal. Consistent with data on mate choice in birds and mammals showing a preference for a moderate degree of relationship (Andersson, 1994), first-cousin marriages are often sought in human forager cultures (Coon, 1971). These marriages may optimize the degree of genetic relatedness. Of course, homogamy may partly reflect matching for mate value; couples tend to resemble each other on desirable traits such as attractiveness, intelligence, and social-class background (Tharp, 1963).

Women's Attractiveness

So homogamy and some other traits are sought by both sexes. But certain sex differences in mate selection criteria seem to operate, too. Consistent with Trivers's theory (see Chapter 5), men seek wives who are good potential breeders, that is, those who are attractive and promise sexual fidelity. Research stretching back 40 years shows that U.S. males desire attractive females as dates and wives (Buss, 1987). A study at an upper-middle-class high school showed that boys wished to date girls whom others had rated as attractive, well groomed, fashionably dressed, and feminine (G. E. Weisfeld et al., 1984a). Intelligent or high-achieving girls were not especially desirable. Boys judged girls on the same criteria by which girls judged each other. This was also seen in China, where, however, intelligence as well as attractiveness was valued in adolescent girls (Dong et al., 1996).

Some researchers have tried to specify the physiognomic features that make a woman attractive. Symons (1979) argued that women (and, presumably, men) with average features for their sex will be the most attractive. Individuals of average features presumably are the fittest and carry the best genes. Indeed, composite photos in which several faces are blended tend to be perceived as more attractive than any of the individual faces (Symons, 1979; Langlois & Roggman, 1990). Evidence for the attractiveness of bodily symmetry (Gangestad & Thornhill, 1997) is consistent with the notion that regular features are appealing.

Women's Youth

Symons also posited that an ideal female mate will be newly fertile (having ovulatory menstrual cycles), will have ample body fat, and will be in apparent good health. In other words, *the ideal bride is healthy, has good genes, and is young but mature.* Across cultures, women who are young are prized as brides, presumably because of their high reproductive value—their long-term breeding potential (Daly & Wilson, 1983). The likelihood of the bride having already borne another man's child is also less if she is young. In monogamous cultures, the average groom is 19 and the bride 17; in polygynous cultures, the average groom is 25 and the bride 15 (J.W.M. Whiting, 1968). Moreover, men seek young brides, not just any bride younger than they. Men in their twenties prefer women of the same age, but men in their fifties prefer women in their thirties or forties (Buss, 1989).

Femininity

Besides health, genetic quality, and youth, another characteristic seems to enhance female attractiveness: femininity. A woman who is well differentiated sexually will have greater reproductive success than a more androgynous women who is equally healthy, carries the same good genes, and is equally mature. She will have more body fat to support childbearing. An average-looking person of the opposite sex may be normal and healthy, but she is, well, average. But a woman who is highly sex differentiated probably experienced low stress during development and was able to divert much bodily energy to reproductive development. A man who then chooses her when she is mature can take advantage of her healthy history.

This principle—that rather pronounced *sex differentiated traits attract the opposite sex*—is supported by comparative analysis. In sexually reproducing species in general, males are attracted to feminine features, and females are attracted to masculine ones. Thus, women tend to choose men with well-developed secondary sex characteristics, traits that may even interfere with survival. The peacock's tail is an example of such "runaway" sexual selection, and the energy-expensive muscularity of men is another (see Chapter 9). Then, too, women dislike high voices in men, just as men dislike low voices in women (Daniel & McCabe, 1992). Dominant behavior in men is valued more highly by women than men, and femininity in women is valued more highly by men than women (Urberg & Labouvie-Vief, 1976). The next major section offers additional examples of the appeal of masculine features to women.

Another advantage of being attracted to highly sex-differentiated mates is that they tend to be early maturers, which means that they have more reproductive years ahead of them than late maturers do. For example, early-maturing Kipsigis women had more children than late maturers and, accordingly, brought higher bride prices (Borgerhoff Mulder, 1989). Similarly, early-maturing U.S. girls and boys tended to begin their sex lives earlier, by virtue of their attractiveness (Udry & Billy, 1987).

Why would this not lead to runaway selection for extreme sex differentiation? Energy devoted to sex differentiation doubtless comes at some cost to health and vigor. This is why animals are not born fully sex differentiated. Stated somewhat differently, there is only one ideal form for a species' habitat, and so the designs for the two sexes will tend to converge. This convergence is offset by the advantages of sexual differentiation; that is, monomorphism and dimorphism are opposing tendencies that confer advantages and disadvantages. Because monomorphism is more important before reproductive maturity, it predominates then. At maturity, dimorphism becomes important.

When an animal chooses a mate, it is choosing a mature sex partner and hence will seek dimorphism. And, practically speaking, full dimorphic development may have been compromised by exposure to stressors during immaturity. If so, this was a price that the stressed individual had to pay to survive, but a potential mate will not wish to choose such an individual with which to reproduce (see Chapter 5).

Several studies of bodily proportions suggest that women of above-average femininity are attractive to men. U.S., British, and Israeli subjects judged breasts that are somewhat larger than average to be the most attractive (Eysenck & Wilson, 1979; Singh & Young, 1995). U.S. men prefer women with feminine bodily proportions: large breasts and a low waist-to-hip ratio (Singh & Young, 1995). Waist size is an especially good predictor of a woman's estrogen level and hence femininity. Another feminine pubertal change is an increase in body fat, especially around the hips. Several cross-cultural studies indicate that men prefer somewhat plump women, particularly women with fatty legs and hips—the feminine distribution pattern (P. J. Brown & Konner, 1987). Singh and Young expressed doubt, however, that true obesity is desirable in traditional cultures, since it is so rare; rather, thinness is less desirable than average weight. Consistent with this interpretation, U.S. men—even recent immigrants from Indonesia and India—found heavy women to be less attractive than average-weight ones (Singh & Young, 1995). Thus, although feminine bodily characteristics are attractive to men, there may be an upper limit to the desirability of feminine bodily features: Really large hips were found not to be attractive.

The notion of the attractiveness of femininity is also supported by research on facial features. U.S. beauty contest winners had more pedomorphic, feminine facial features than a same-aged sample of university women (M. R. Cunningham, 1986). These features included large eyes, small nose, and small chin. In another U.S. study, the pedomorphic features of large eyes, thin eyebrows, small mandible, and thick lips rendered drawings of female faces more attractive (Keating, 1985).

Girls' appearance becomes relatively feminized at puberty by two processes. First, estrogens feminize some features; for example, they thicken the lips (V. Johnston & Franklin, 1993). Second, girls also become more feminine than boys by not undergoing masculinization. For example, boys' skin darkens at puberty, and most men prefer women with relatively light skin (N. Barber, 1995). In addition, androgens change the facial dimensions of boys radically at puberty. This renders men less pedomorphic than women, and women are therefore more feminine.

Pedomorphic features per se do not make women attractive to men, however, since prepubertal children do not appeal sexually to most men. Rather, men find feminine features in general desirable, of which some but not all are pedomorphic. That is, men are attracted to young but sexually mature women. For example, men prefer large breasts even though they raise the woman's estimated age. Singh and Young (1995) suggested that small breasts are less attractive because they sometimes indicate a not-yet-fertile condition. Thus, femininity is crucial, not pedomorphism.

Consistent with this interpretation, some attractive feminine features are not pedomorphic. These include raised eyebrows and wide smiles (M. R. Cunningham, 1986), features that are more characteristic of women than of men but not particularly of children. Women raise the eyebrows when flirting or greeting in various cultures (Eibl-Eibesfeldt, 1989), perhaps in order to accentuate this feminine feature; also, raised eyebrows may signal friendliness, since the eyebrows are lowered in anger.

Other attractive features may be neither pedomorphic nor feminine. Cunningham (1986) found that dilated pupils, a sign of interest, were attractive. European women have used belladonna (Ital. "beautiful lady") as a cosmetic; also known as atropine, it dilates the pupils.

Chastity

Another widespread and perhaps universal ideal in a bride is chastity (Daly & Wilson, 1983). Chastity does not necessarily mean virginity, which may be scarce in sexually permissive cultures and will not matter in a sense before fertility. But once a girl reaches menarche, a man typically seeks assurance that she is not yet pregnant and will not engage in extramarital affairs if he marries her. Wealthy men tend to marry less-promiscuous women.

Women's Courtship Tactics

Women's courtship tactics offer clues to the criteria of mate choice being used by men. U. S. university women relied heavily on appearance enhancement (Buss, 1988a). Likewise, Tooke et al. (1990) found that U.S. undergraduate women used appearance enhancement to attract men and to intimidate rival women.

Buss and Schmitt (1993) distinguished between tactics used for gaining short-term and long-term partners. Women used indications of sexual access effectively for attracting short-term partners, but signs of sexual restraint were perceived as more effective for attracting long-term mates. They used appearance enhancement for securing both long-term and short-term partners. Women desiring a short-term relationship sometimes resorted to calling a rival ugly, frigid, or a tease. Those seeking a long-term affair labeled rivals ugly and promiscuous. Finally, in a study of mate-retention tactics, women were more likely than men to use infidelity threats (i.e., to provoke jealousy) and to do so effectively (Buss, 1988b).

A woman's reluctance to become sexually involved serves several functions. She can gain time to evaluate the male. Female birds sometimes use "coy" behavior to defer copulation until they have determined that the male is not already mated (Tinbergen, 1951). Coy behavior by a woman can preserve her reputation for chastity if the match dissolves. She can also gauge the male's commitment by his willingness to persist in courting her, and she can perhaps elevate her perceived mate value by being "hard to get." But, of course, she also risks losing him to a more compliant rival. Not surprisingly, U.S. undergraduate women played hard to get more often than men, although this tactic was not judged to be very effective (Buss, 1988a). Inflating one's mate value may intimidate potential mates, or, if the deception is detected, even repel them. One way that a girl can remain chaste but chased is by gradually escalating sexual involvement with a boy, thereby giving him the impression of progress. Attractive women may be in a stronger position to withhold sex without losing their courtiers; U.S. undergraduate women who rated themselves as attractive reported fewer sex partners (Walsh, 1993).

Interestingly, in Sorensen's (1973) research, more adolescent girls (43 percent) than boys (29 percent) believed that a boy would lose respect for a girl who went to bed with him. This belief was twice as common in girls and boys aged 13 to 15 than in those aged 16 to 19, so it seemed not to stand the test of time. In general, research suggests that a boy does not want a virgin; what he wants is a girl who will go to bed with him but no one else—which certainly makes adaptive sense. Also, a study of dating relationships revealed no association between having sex early (in the first month) or late (after 6 months) and the permanence of a relationship (Peplau et al., 1977).

Another characteristic female tactic is subtlety. Women's sexual overtures tend to be vague and nonverbal everywhere (Ford & Beach, 1951), whereas men are the overt sexual initiators (Stephens, 1963). As the choosier sex, women need not issue overt invitations that may be publicly and unequivocally rebuffed. Similarly, men tend to begin physical intimacy by ambiguous, "accidental" touches (Symons, 1979; Moore, 1985). Female subtlety also reduces the risk of appearing promiscuous.

Women sometimes cooperate in assessing males. At a singles' dance, U.S. women tried to form alliances in order to exchange information about men (Berk, 1977). Atrocity stories were an important topic of conversation among the women. Similarly, adolescent girls spend much time discussing the virtues and vices of boys.

Mate Choice by Females

Men's Attractiveness

It has often been reported that women are less concerned with a man's attractiveness than vice versa (Ford & Beach, 1951; Buss, 1989). This may be due, in part, to women's greater reluctance to acknowledge an interest in men's bodies, especially when women have been interviewed by male ethnographers. Also, women usually list more criteria for attractiveness than men. A woman's third criterion may prevent more pairings than a man's first, since women tend to be more selective than men. It makes adaptive sense for females to choose mates for their apparent genetic quality because, as the more heavily investing sex, women would suffer more than men from an unwise mating. Moreover, attractive males will have male descendants who will also gain many mating opportunities, that is, they will have sexy sons.

Research that specifically addresses the issue of males' attractiveness in female mate choice often confirms its salience. G. E. Weisfeld et al. (1983) had suburban Detroit high school girls rank boys in terms of their desirability as a date; the boys had already been ranked by others on various attributes. Thus, independent choices were made among actual acquaintances. Desirability to girls was more highly correlated with the boy's athletic ability and attractiveness than with his intelligence, fairness, or financial prospects. The ascendancy of physical over mental traits was even greater in an academically elite Chicago high school (G. E. Weisfeld et al., 1980). Similarly, in a study of university students, trained observers rated the attractiveness of subjects' dates (Berscheid & Walster, 1974). The correlation between physical attractiveness and the subjects' liking their date was much higher for women rating men than the reverse. In research such as this, in which the subjects are young, attractiveness is about as important for females choosing males as for males choosing females. But when older subjects are included, the woman's attractiveness is somewhat more important than the man's because youth is a better indicator of reproductive value for females than males. Thus, older women are deemed less attractive than older men (see the previous major section). Insofar as attractiveness reflects genetic quality apart from youth, however, women may be just as interested in a potential mate's attractiveness as are men.

Men's Dominance

As in many other species, dominance in a man attracts women. Because dominance is associated with fighting ability even in humans, it is confounded with athletic ability, strength, and physical attractiveness (see Chapter 11). A strong, energetic, athletic, and dominant mate would have been a good fighter and hunter in prehistory, that is, a good provider and protector (G. E. Weisfeld et al., 1992).

Considerable research indicates that females desire dominant males. Dominance includes a variety of traits, including androgen-dependent, intimidating bodily features; dominant facial and bodily displays; ability to prevail in conflicts of interest (e.g., high social standing); and associated dominant behaviors such as competitiveness, self-confidence, and sociability. Some of this research supporting the notion that dominance appeals to women will now be described.

With regard to dominant, masculine bodily features, it has been found that a large mandible, thin lips, and prominent brow ridges made male faces more attractive (Keating, 1985). However, the appeal of pedomorphic features such as large eyes, small noses, and smiling may exert some countervailing effect (M. R. Cunningham et al., 1990). Adolescent boys with dominant faces had sex earlier; facial dominance was related to testosterone level and as such was an indicator of masculinity (Mazur et al., 1994). In most studies, beards render men's faces more dominant and attractive to women (N. Barber, 1995). Research on height preferences suggests that women prefer tall (or at least taller) men. In addition, shoulder width proved to be a very strong predictor of men's attractiveness. Aside from these masculine features, signs of health and genetic quality, such as clear skin and a symmetrical, normal appearance, enhance a person's desirability everywhere (Ford & Beach, 1951).

In research on dominance displays and other behaviors, it has been reported that adolescent boys whom girls found appealing tended to win conflicts of interest, have erect posture, maintain eye contact, exhibit self-confidence, be competitive, be sociable, and avoid being ridiculed (G. E. Weisfeld et al., 1983). Men who were depicted in dominant roles were rated as sexier by women (Kelley et al., 1983). Both sexes dislike submissive men (Costrich et al., 1975; Sadalla et al., 1987). Dominant "body language" rendered men sexually attractive to women (Sadalla et al., 1987). Similarly, dating couples preferred the man to be dominant (Curran, 1972).

With respect to dominance as high social standing, another common criterion of mate choice by women is the man's wealth, or "nuptial gifts." Rich men are desirable as husbands worldwide, and are more likely to be polygynous and hence to have more children (Daly & Wilson, 1983). Even in monogamous cultures, wealthy men tend to have prettier wives and more children (Barnard, 1989; Voland & Engel, 1990). Cross-cultural research confirms the effect of the male's financial resources and social status on his desirability (Buss, 1994) and reproductive success (Betzig, 1986).

But does wealth appeal to women because they have an evolved affinity for it? Since wealth takes various forms around the world, "wealth detectors" are unlikely to have been selected for. The desire for a wealthy husband may be primarily imposed by cultural values. Parents who socialized their daughters to seek a high-status husband probably had more grandchildren. This cultural influence may increase over development. In a longitudinal study, wealth was of little importance to U.S. adolescent girls, but it became salient for them as young women (see Chapter 11). Similarly, when mate choice occurs relatively independently of parental influence, it tends to be based on physical attractiveness (Rosenblatt, 1974). And among the Hadza, younger women had fewer opinions about the reputations of various men as hunters than did older women, suggesting that younger women had to rely on older relatives for guidance in evaluating men on this criterion (see Chapter 6).

It is still possible, however, for natural selection (in addition to cultural selection) to favor women who choose a wealthy husband. A man of high status is likely to have a dominant bearing, which itself might inherently appeal to women (G. E. Weisfeld et al., 1992). Another indirect indicator of wealth is men's (but not women's) walking speed, which was correlated with attractiveness to women in an Austrian observational study (Schmitt & Atzwanger, 1995). Signs of vigor and athleticism may have betokened health, endurance, and hunting prowess in Pleistocene times, and they may still attract women today.

The fundamental, evolved appeal of dominance in men rather than wealth is suggested by several more observations. Adolescent girls tend to date older boys in Westernized countries. At this age, boys do not differ significantly in their wealth, but older boys are more dominant. Then, too, wealthy husbands are desired more by wealthy women than by poor women (Rathus et al., 1997), so something besides need is dictating women's preferences. Specifically, few women marry a poorer man. Also, women across cultures consistently prefer a man somewhat older than they, not an older man per se (Buss, 1989; Kendrick & Keefe, 1992), so perhaps it is not age or its privileges that women are seeking but a modicum of dominance. In addition, women value height in a man cross-culturally (Buss, 1994); size is associated with fighting ability and hence dominance.

Research on married couples also suggests that male dominance is sought by women. Female-dominant married couples are prone to sexual difficulties (C. C. Weisfeld et al., 1983), just as female primates tend not to copulate with a male they can dominate. Moreover, married couples in which the man is somewhat more dominant than the wife tend to be happier, more satisfied sexually, and less likely to divorce (G. E. Weisfeld et al., 1992). This is true if dominance is defined in terms of decision-making power (dominance by the wife is rated worst, but extreme husband dominance is bad, too), nonverbal behavior, or ratings of a spouse's dominance or success. Furthermore, it is the wife's more than the husband's satisfaction that is undermined by low husband dominance—women want a dominant husband more than men mind being subordinate (also see Kotlar [1965] and Corrales [1975]).

Of course, a man's wealth and protectiveness are of no utility to a woman unless he offers them to her. Therefore, signs of pair-bonding motivation toward her, or commitment, are very important for sexual involvement, as explained previously.

Men's Courtship Tactics

Studies of U.S. men's courtship tactics confirm the salience of the mate choice criteria employed by females. Men's displaying of wealth and their spending of it on the woman were judged to be both prevalent and effective (Buss & Schmitt, 1993; Tooke et al., 1990). Men described their rivals as lacking wealth and ambition. At a singles' dance, men tried to demonstrate coolness (the low-anxiety characteristic of dominance?) and to claim a prestigious occupation (Berk, 1977). Both Kirkendall (1961) and Tooke et al. (1990) reported that men tried to show that they were popular. Kirkendall also found that men attempted to demonstrate their capabilities and to show off their clothes.

In an early U.S. study of mate-retention tactics, men were more likely than women to display resources, keep their mates away from rivals, and make concessions to their mates (Kirendall, 1961). Men also tried to show themselves to be emotionally committed to the woman, and to depict rivals as uncaring (Buss, 1988b). Declarations of love and caring, and a request for marriage, were more effective tactics when used by men than women. Women were more likely than men to raise the subject of marriage.

Unmarried Adolescent Childbearing

Sex, love, and a desire for a baby can draw together young people who are unprepared for parenthood. The problem of unmarried adolescent mothers is greater in the United States than in all other industrialized societies (Westoff et al., 1983). This section will begin by describing some of the problems stemming from births to unwed adolescents, and then discuss some possible preventive measures.

If the welfare of the next generation of children is our main concern, then we can summarize the developmental risk factors as follows. Unwed teen births are the worst, but married teen mothers are liable to divorce, which also poses risks to the child (see Chapter 14). Thus, the ideal is post-teen, enduring marriage and child rearing. It may be best to delay having children until after the peak in divorce rate, which occurs after 3 or 4 years of marriage (W. A. Fisher, 1989).

The problems created by births to unmarried adolescents can hardly be exaggerated (Rickel, 1989). These girls are at risk of dropping out of high school, depending on governmental support, having low-paying jobs (Furstenberg, 1976; Steinberg, 1996), being lonely and depressed, committing suicide (Petzel & Kline, 1978), and attracting only low-status males (Surbey, 1987). Adolescent boys and girls often make poor parents: They tend to be uninformed about babies, inconsistent, fatigued, negligent, harsh, and impulsive. Frequently, the child is given up and goes to a series of foster homes. Children of teenage mothers are more likely to be abused or neglected and insecurely attached, to have cognitive deficits (Konner & Shostak, 1986), to do poorly in school, to misbehave, to become delinquents, to get pregnant as unmarried teens (Furstenberg et al., 1987), and to have unstable romantic relationships (Belsky et al., 1991).

What are the medical risks of adolescent childbearing? The special problems of the babies of teen mothers are due more to improper prenatal nutrition and postnatal care than to the mother's reproductive immaturity, especially if she is at least 17 (Konner & Shostak, 1986). Low-SES girls and their infants are at risk for mortality because of maternal drug use, poor nutrition, and poor child care.

The optimal age for healthy childbearing is the twenties (B. A. Hamburg, 1986), but births to adolescent wives have long been normal, at least in well-nourished populations (Garn et al., 1986). Historical records indicate that menarche occurred in girls from 12 to 15 years of age in Europe during classical and medieval times, although these figures likely refer to well-nourished samples (Eveleth, 1986). Thus, the modern early onset of puberty is no anomaly, something to which nature has not had time to adapt. Fetal death is actually low in younger mothers because of the low number of mutations.

Even so, babies of teen mothers are at special risk medically because of two factors that lower birth weight (Garn et al., 1986). First,

268 / Sexual Relations

teen mothers tend to be small, so their babies are small. This effect is not specific to teenagers; smaller older mothers have smaller babies, too. The other effect, less weight gain by the fetus with the mother's weight gain, is specific to teenagers. Teen mothers convert less of their weight gain to fetal weight than do older mothers. This is an effect of immaturity, not age per se. Later-maturing teen mothers have smaller babies than early-maturing mothers of the same age (B. A. Hamburg, 1986). This immaturity effect does not seem to result from simple caloric competition between the growing mother and fetus—at least with good nutrition. Pregnancy does not normally retard the girl's growth, which has reached adult levels by 2 or 3 years after menarche (B. A. Hamburg, 1986). Perhaps the teenage girl's smaller pelvis is a limiting factor (Altmann, 1986); the birth canal does not reach final adult size until 17 or 18 even in well-fed girls (Lancaster, 1986). Indeed, pelvic size has been related to neonatal health (Moerman, 1982).

How can the rate of unmarried adolescent childbearing be reduced? These births will not occur if any of the following conditions, to be considered in turn, obtain:

1. The girl is not yet fertile.
2. The couple is married.
3. The couple abstains from sex.
4. The fetus is aborted.
5. The couple uses effective contraception.

(1) Adolescent Subfertility

The historical acceleration of pubertal maturation with improved health and nutrition (see Chapter 8) has greatly increased the risk of teen pregnancy. In less well-nourished populations such as the !Kung, adolescent infertility lasts until about 18, with the first birth typically occurring at 19 (Konner & Shostak, 1986). Menarche among the !Kung occurs at about 16 or 17.

Thus, less well-nourished populations can rely on adolescent subfertility to decrease the risk of early pregnancy, but we cannot. About 95 percent of girls in the West reach menarche between 11.0 to 15.0 years (Tanner, 1978). Adolescent sterility lasts 12 to 18 months after menarche—but it does not occur in all girls. Thus, some 12-year-old girls are at risk for pregnancy, especially since early-maturing girls tend to have a relatively short period of anovulatory cycles (adolescent infertility) (Reiter, 1986). Specifically, girls with menarche below age 12 begin to have ovulatory cycles about 1 year later.

(2) Age of Marriage

Age of marriage is another variable affecting the prevalence of unwed teenage pregnancy. In most cultures, marriage typically occurs before the end of the period of adolescent subfertility, usually around menarche. But in well-fed populations, this would mean marriage by about age 14. This is clearly impractical in a society with little child care provided by kin, many years of training necessary to perform adult labor, a high divorce rate for teenagers, and poor parental skills in teens.

However, to defer marriage is to defer fulfillment of the powerful, normal desires for sex, romance, and nurturance. Most adolescents want these things and, eventually, the state of matrimony that formalizes and legitimizes them. Cross-culturally, virtually all women marry, and virtually all men marry who can afford to do so. If sex, romance, and children are not available in the context of marriage, they will be sought extramaritally by many adolescents.

The issue can be viewed in terms of a window of vulnerability between the onset of fertility and the age of marriage. Fertility now occurs at the biological lower limit in industrialized societies. Marriage, by contrast, occurs late for our species, at least for women. This leaves a wide gap of about 10 years. In theory, accelerated education would be needed to prepare young people for economic independence and parenthood, and hence marriage, at younger ages.

Forced marriage seems a bad solution to pregnancy today (Rickel, 1989). Adolescent marriages typically last only 2 or 3 years in the United States. Adolescents often hold magical or idealized views of marriage (Tamashiro, 1979). Poverty and domestic violence are common, and the couple often entertain unrealistic expectations for life. The young mother's education and job prospects tend to be worse than if she had delivered without marrying.

(3) Sexual Abstinence

Sexual abstinence has been enforced in some places but has not been widespread; most cultures make little effort to curtail adolescent sexual experimentation. Surveying 114 societies, Broude and Greene (1976) found that premarital sex by girls was virtually universal in 49 percent of societies, common in 17 percent, occasional in 14 percent, and uncommon in 20 percent. The figures for males are slightly less restrictive: 60 percent, 18 percent, 10 percent, and 12 percent, respectively.

Those cultures that do try to restrict premarital sex often resort to rather drastic measures, perhaps attesting to the difficulty of this strategy. Genital mutilation is employed in polygynous cultures especially (see Chapter 7). Early betrothal is designed to preempt the formation of love matches by arranging a marriage before the girl becomes romantically inclined. Sex segregation is a very labor-intensive measure. Social pressure against premarital sex is less costly but tends to be unreliable. All of these measures have been employed by the Arabs, whose culture is among the most sexually restrictive (G. E. Weisfeld, 1990), but even the threat of death does not prevent transgressions completely. Among contemporary industrialized societies, only Japan seems to restrict teen adolescent sex effectively (Rohlen, 1983), but in recent years, more Japanese and Chinese adolescents have become sexually active.

In U.S. history, premarital pregnancy rates have fluctuated somewhat in response to changes in sexual norms (Vinovskis, 1986). In the puritanical Colonial period, fewer than 10 percent of brides were pregnant (Smith & Hindus, 1975). In the eighteenth century, the rate rose steadily, to nearly 30 percent at the time of the Declaration of Independence, as civil penalties for fornication declined. The first half of the nineteenth century brought religious revivalism and a decline in the rate to about 10 percent again. This was followed by a sharp rise in the second half of the nineteenth century (Figure 13.1). Through most of the twentieth century, sex was relatively restricted. In the 1920s, chaperones became less common and "dating" began (Dreyer, 1982), largely as a social competition because sex was generally limited to hand holding and kissing. Prostitutes were widely used. After World War II, dating was more "serious," in that relationships were more exclusive and longer term. "Going steady" became more important, and petting was common, including petting to climax. However, sexual intercourse remained rather infrequent.

The "window of vulnerability" notion does not easily explain these historical shifts. For instance, the sharp drop in premarital pregnancy during the early 1800s occurred while the window of vulnerability was widening. Therefore, sexual restrictiveness probably had an effect.

Nevertheless, even in puritanical days, a fair amount of premarital sex occurred. But its effects on children were mitigated by the fact

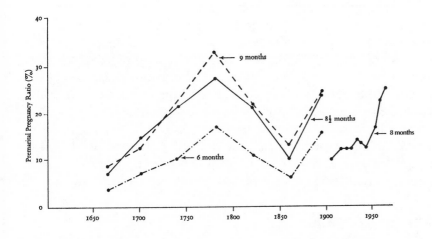

Figure 13.1 Percentages of Premarital Pregnancies in U. S. History. Births at various points after marriage. Source: Smith & Hindus (1975). Reprinted by permission.

that it usually involved couples who were courting. A conception simply expedited the anticipated marriage. Thus, the window was promptly shut before an unwed birth could occur, and children who had been conceived before marriage still had both parents. Moreover, the foreclosure of the mother's education probably produced few economic disadvantages (Vinovskis, 1986). Most nineteenth-century women did not continue to work outside the home once they married, and the divorce rate was low. Thus, the consequences of premarital pregnancy were much milder than they are today. The extended family also provided support, as it does in traditional cultures.

Sexual restrictiveness became less defensible when effective contraceptive techniques were introduced. When "the pill" became widely available in the United States around 1967, the rate of adolescent premarital sex rose sharply (Chilman, 1986). For the previous 40 years, rates had been stable; 10 percent of white female high school seniors were nonvirgins, as were 25 percent of college seniors. By 1979, however, 48.5 percent of female high school seniors were nonvirgins (Zelnick & Kantner, 1980), as were 74 perent of university women (Dreyer, 1982). Similar trends occurred in other developed and developing countries.

Consequently, in cross-cultural perspective, the sexual abstinence strategy seems to be difficult to impose successfully. Moreover, once an adolescent begins having sex, she or he almost always continues doing so (Sorensen, 1973). For females, this may reflect the priming effect of sex (see Chapter 10). It has also been argued that adolescents are entitled to sex and romance (E. Hamilton, 1971); a case for this is strengthened by cross-cultural data on adolescent sexual activity.

So adolescent sex has always been fairly common and has frequently resulted in nonmarital pregnancy. Given the wide window of vulnerability now existing and the continued advance of contraceptive techniques, this situation can be expected to continue indefinitely.

(4) Induced Abortion

Abortion is seldom viewed as an ideal solution to the problem of unwanted pregnancy. It entails health risks and is morally offensive to many individuals. The psychological consequences of abortion, however, are usually mild. There may initially be guilt, regret, or loss, especially if the girl was ambivalent about her decision (Institute of Medicine, 1975). However, 6 months later, 75 percent of girls reported being as well or better off emotionally than before the abortion (Perez-Reyes & Falk, 1973). At that point, the girls' mental health tends to be comparable with that of girls who have delivered.

Rickel (1989) reviewed the situational factors associated with the decision to abort. Choosing abortion is associated with the girl having a long-term, positive relationship with her boyfriend. Girls who choose to deliver tend to have poorer academic records and employment prospects, and to have girlfriends with babies. The availability of generous welfare payments does not predict unwed teenage pregnancy, but it does predict deciding to have the baby rather than having an abortion (Chilman, 1986). Placing a newborn for adoption is seldom done. Of course, ignorance of how to obtain an abortion may also affect the outcome. Another factor is that the girl may initially deny the possibility of being pregnant; this can delay confronting the issue until abortion is not an option.

(5) Effective Contraception

Several factors are related to the use of contraception, but sex education is a comparatively minor one. Many U.S. adolescents are ignorant of basic sexual knowledge, but sex education courses do not have much impact on knowledge (Chilman, 1986). In one study, only 33 percent of teens who had taken a sex education course knew the time of greatest risk for pregnancy over the menstrual cycle (Zelnick & Kanter, 1979). Most U.S. courses stress abstinence, and less than half tell the students how to get contraceptives (Rathus et al., 1997). Parents are not much better than educators at teaching about sex and contraception. Adolescents whose parents were their main source of sexual information knew no more than did adolescents who relied on their peers (Handelsman et al., 1987). Moreover, few U.S. parents talk to their adolescents about sex (Rickel, 1989); in contrast, a large majority of Swedish girls discuss contraception with their mothers (P. Brown, 1983).

Despite the obvious shortcomings of U.S. sex education, the basic problem may be motivation, not ignorance. Many girls express fear that if they are prepared with contraceptives, boys will think them promiscuous (Rickel, 1989). Many young men fear that a presex discussion of contraception will botch the sexual encounter, and they dislike condoms.

Another emotional barrier to the use of contraceptives is sexually restrictive attitudes, or **erotophobia**. Erotophobic male and female adolescents have been found to have less sex but, if sexually active, to use contraception less (W. A. Fisher, 1986). The net result is a greater risk of pregnancy than that of erotophiles. Likewise, individuals who report guilt about sex or are religious tend not to use effective contraception (Gerrard, 1987).

Given these emotional barriers to acquiring and using contraceptives, it is not surprising that sexually permissive Western countries such as Switzerland, Sweden, Denmark, and Finland have the lowest rates of teen births—around 10 percent compared with 25 percent in the conservative United States (Chilman, 1986). The United States consistently ranks as more conservative on sexual attitude surveys than Western Europe countries and Canada (Cook & McHenry, 1978), although U.S. adolescents begin their sex lives no later than, say, Swedes (P. Brown, 1983).

Liberal, erotophilic attitudes about adolescent sex in Europe have led to the development of the only highly effective type of preventive program: Sweden and other European countries have established confidential birth control clinics within their secondary schools. Confidentiality is strictly observed; Swedish law penalizes doctors who inform a girl's parents of her use of contraception.

Experiments with these clinics have proven successful in North America, too. Opening a clinic of this type dramatically reduced the rate of pregnancy among students at a Canadian university (W. A. Fisher, 1989), and there was a similar success in St. Paul, Minnesota, with the fertility rate cut roughly in half (Rickel, 1989). A school-based clinic in Baltimore resulted in a 30 percent decrease in pregnancy rate, compared with a 57 percent increase in control schools. Sex education without school-based contraception services produces little or no change in behaviors such as becoming sexually active or becoming pregnant (Chilman, 1986).

Another motivational factor may be even more far-reaching. Many U.S. adolescent girls want to get pregnant. Landry et al. (1986) reported that 86 percent of pregnant teens knew about contraceptives and 75 percent knew where to get them, but only 16 percent reported using them when they had got pregnant. Getting pregnant is not always a "mistake" that could have been averted if the girl knew more about contraception. In one study, 75 percent of pregnant girls acknowledged that they had wanted to have a baby (Lindemann & Scott, 1981); in another study, the figure was 35 percent (Zelnick & Kantner, 1978). Sorensen (1973) reported that 40 percent of sexually active girls "didn't care" if they became pregnant.

A motivational explanation for adolescent motherhood is supported by research on the characteristics of such girls. The attraction of motherhood seems to be strongest for girls with poor life prospects. Girls who get pregnant, like girls who decide against abortion, tend to have problems socially and academically or vocationally. They typically have no steady relationship with a boy, they have low self-esteem, they have poor relationships with their parents and an absent father—and they want to get pregnant (Chilman, 1986; S. T. Russell, 1994). For these girls, having a baby may be a fairly attractive option. A baby can provide someone to love and be loved by, and a means of gaining attention, support, and respect from peers and adults. Cross-culturally, having children elevates one's social status. Also, having a baby may provide an excuse to drop out of school without feeling obligated to get a job, or it may be a way to "catch" a particular boy (Buss, 1988b).

Not only may it be rational for a girl to get pregnant under these conditions, it is also likely that she will have more children—have greater reproductive success—than if she waits to reproduce until after adolescence (Surbey, 1987). African-American women suffer inordinately from health problems, so early reproduction may be especially adaptive for them (Burns & Scott, 1994). Any health problems that their daughters sustain in infancy may act as early stressors to accelerate puberty, thus perpetuating the pattern of early reproduction (see Chapter 8).

The leading role of motivation in adolescent pregnancy gains support from studies of low-income blacks (B. A. Hamburg, 1986). These girls have poor prospects for a stable, economically supportive marriage. Rather than waiting indefinitely for "Mr. Right," such a girl may do better to give birth as an unwed teenager. While still living at home, she and the baby can receive care from her mother and even stay in school. About five years after the first child is born, the girl typically establishes her own household. She is now more employable and can enroll the child in school. Far from being irrational, this reproductive strategy may be the girl's best opportunity, given her limited prospects. If there are few "Mr. Rights" with steady jobs available to become desirable husbands, mate choice will operate on other criteria. Occasional nuptial gifts may be sought in lieu of steady financial support (i.e., marriage). Women may choose as lovers men who are attractive and physically dominant because of the utility of force for protection in a violent environment.

This female reproductive strategy may occur in other cultures, too. Where there is a shortage of marriageable men, women may reproduce without marrying. Promiscuous behavior under such conditions might simply be learned, but it might also be an evolved, contingent reproductive strategy that all women potentially can exhibit (Barkow, 1984; Draper & Harpending, 1988). The hypothesis of an evolved reproductive strategy is supported by the fact that father absence and family conflict accelerate menarche, a physiological process (see Chapter 8). For example, family conflict and emotional distance from father before age 11 were associated with early menarche in Italy (Kim et al., 1997). In turn, early menarche was associated with dating at a young age. Around the world, in fact, early menarche is associated with early sexual involvement, early birth of first child, and having more children. This may very well constitute an adaptive response to family conflict or to a shortage of paternally investing men, which is assayed by father absence.

Various bits of evidence attest to the existence of this pattern in girls, in addition to those on early menarche and its sequelae. For example, Cashdan (1993) found that college women who expected low levels of paternal investment in their children reported acting more promiscuously. In an interview/observational study, father-absent girls flirted with the male interviewer more than did father-present ones (Hoyenga & Hoyenga, 1993).

In conclusion, the use of contraception may be enhanced over the short term by establishing confidential birth control clinics in secondary schools. In the long run, however, societal factors may need to be addressed, as will be discussed.

Marriage Maintenance

The problem of unmarried adolescent pregnancy cannot be analyzed without reference to the incentives to marry and stay married. The difficulty is not the timing of pregnancy so much as whether the child will grow up in a stable home with both biological parents (see Chapter 14). As discussed in the previous section, many adolescent girls will have children without being married if their marriage prospects are dim.

In the United States, the divorce rate is high—two or three times that in Europe (Burns & Scott, 1994)—and high from a cross-cultural perspective (Stephens, 1963). Almost half of current U.S. marriages are projected to end in divorce. The fundamental problem is not teen pregnancy, which was common in the 1950s but which usually occurred in the context of marriage or was followed by an enduring marriage (Steinberg, 1996). The anomaly is the low rate of enduring marriage. What, then, affects the stability of marriage?

Economic factors are prominent among the correlates of marital stability. High-income husbands tend to have lasting marriages everywhere (Goode, 1993). Among industrialized societies, divorce rates are high where wives' earnings rival husbands', such as in the United States, Eastern Europe (Scanzoni, 1972), and Sweden (Rathus et al., 1997). On the individual level, men who cannot contribute to the family finances are generally unmarriageable, and if the wife's occupational or educational achievements rival or surpass the husband's, the marriage often dissolves (G. E. Weisfeld et al., 1992). In a U.S. longitudinal study using a national sample, couples in which only the husband was employed full-time had the lowest chance of divorce (Tzeng, 1992). Couples in which only the wife was employed full-time had an even higher divorce rate than unemployed couples. In a recent U.S. study, wife beating was more common if the wife outearned the husband (Anderson, 1997).

Wives' growing economic independence has been offered as an explanation for the rising divorce rate in Western nations. Fisher (1989) suggested that this trend is related to the increase in women's paid employment since World War II. Goode (1993) noted that the trend goes back to the Industrial Revolution, when women's economic independence started to rise.

Cross-culturally, women's economic independence from husbands is related to a high divorce rate (Pearson & Hendrix, 1979; Seccombe & Lee, 1987; Trent & South, 1989). For example, matrilineal cultures, in which men often support their sisters' children (with whom they are sure to be consanguineous), tend to have high rates of promiscuity and divorce (van den Berghe, 1979). A related factor is the extent to which husbands and wives rely on each other's labor (Friedl, 1975). For instance, in horticultural societies, spouses perform different and complementary farming tasks, both spouses are essential to each other, and divorce rates are low. Where sex-role distinctions decline, divorce rates can be expected to rise.

These data on the effect of wealth can be interpreted in terms of women seeking socially dominant men, in terms of men offering nuptial gifts, or in terms of parental investment. It seems necessary also to invoke the notions of female inhibition and of economic independence to explain all of the findings.

The dominance interpretation, though, is perhaps the most powerful of these. Women not only seek dominance in a prospective husband, they also continue to seek it once married. For example, Hungarian marriages in which the husband was older and more educated than the wife lasted longer and resulted in more children than marriages exhibiting other patterns (Bereczkei & Csanaky, 1996b). However, according to a U.S. study, marriages in which the husband was more than 3 years older than the wife had a higher divorce rate than those of other couples (Tzeng, 1992). Extreme husband dominance may undermine similarity, which seems to be true for dominance in decisionmaking, too (G. E. Weisfeld et al., 1992).

Dominance and other criteria that operate in sexual competition and mate choice continue to be salient after marriage—the attractiveness and fidelity of the wife, kindness, romantic feelings, the husband's age at marriage, and so forth. The rules of the game remain essentially the same as young people compete with each other, choose a mate, and remain married. For example, similar couples tend to stay together, as well as to date and to marry. In addition, a long marriage is predicted by a lengthy courtship, good education, sexual satisfaction, sexual fidelity (especially by the wife), and the absence of drug abuse and spousal abuse (e.g., Amato & Rogers, 1997).

One correlate of marital stability that makes obvious adaptive sense is fecundity, or the production of offspring. Around the world, larger families are more stable (Goode, 1993). Similarly, birds that fail to raise young are more likely to seek new mates in the next breeding season (Daly & Wilson, 1983). Littlefield and Silverman (1991) likewise gave an evolutionary interpretation of the fact that the death of a child predicts marital discord, especially if a genetic factor in the spouse is thought to have been responsible. Declining health also tends to lower marital satisfaction (Booth & Johnson, 1994).

Another factor affecting marital stability is the sex ratio in a given society. When women are in short supply, as they were on the Western frontier of the United States, most women are able to marry (Goode, 1993). When men are scarce, men tend to pursue the "cad" strategy because they can more successfully be promiscuous. Thus, men as well as women seem to adjust their reproductive strategies to prevailing conditions in the sexual marketplace (see Chapter 14).

W. J. Wilson (1987) has applied this principle to U.S. blacks. He noted that many black men are unmarriageable due to high rates of unemployment, imprisonment, homicide, and drug addiction. Thus, the low sex ratio favors a male strategy of promiscuity, along with support of matrilineal kin (Burns & Scott, 1994). In comparative perspective, then, the low marriage rate of U.S. blacks today is readily understood in terms of black men's weak earning power and a low sex ratio. Under better economic conditions, such as those during World War II, most black men had steady jobs and 80 percent were married (M. Harris, 1980). In recent years, many black men have lost their jobs as factories closed.

Wilson recommended increasing the pool of marriageable males by providing jobs at good salaries—sufficient to help support a family—for all men. This would seem to be a more comprehensive remedy than providing income, jobs, or day care to women. To provide more jobs or services for single women without rehabilitating unemployed men does not address the problem of declining biparentalism and its associated ills (see Chapter 14). Moreover, it leaves women the burden of single parenthood. Providing jobs that allow women more economic independence from men would actually lower the marriage rate. For example, in a recent study of U.S. blacks, the husband's income stabilized marriage, but the wife's income destabilized it (Cready et al., 1997).

Other societal problems might also improve if men's economic needs were addressed. Child abuse and other violent crimes are disproportionately committed by unmarried men. Rape is more common in cultures with many unmarried men, such as polygynous ones (Thornhill & Thornhill, 1983). Rape also is more common wherever women live alone, which happens more often when the marriage rate is low.

The marriage rate would be raised by providing jobs for men at a rate of pay that allowed them to help support a family. For example, as the U.S. economy has improved in the 1990s, the divorce rate and the rate of unmarried childbearing have declined. Alternatively, the marriage rate would probably be raised by reducing disparities in men's wealth, in two ways: More men could afford to marry, and fewer men could afford to divorce in order to remarry. In other words, if wealth were more evenly distributed, fewer men would have the option of abandoning their wives and children in order to remarry. Most cultures with a high degree of economic stratification allow polygyny (Daly & Wilson, 1983). This means that a wealthy man can have more than one wife at a time, if he can afford them. The United States is unusual in having a pronounced (and growing) stratification but not allowing polygyny. This may result in a high rate of divorce and remarriage—serial polygyny—which, unlike simultaneous polygyny, does not allow for continued association with the first wife and her children (Eibl-Eibesfeldt, 1989).

Improved employment opportunities can be provided to men without denying women the same advantages. Women and men might both be offered more opportunities for full-time and part-time work. Providing a mother of young children with the chance to work part-time or to take parental leave might yield several benefits: She would be more dependent on her husband's income and so the marriage might be more stable, the children would receive more attention, and she might be happier spending more time with them.

If, however, single mothers receive government support but fathers are neglected, marriage rates can be expected to fall (Mackey, 1996). Higher welfare payments have been shown to decrease the probability of marriage in the United States (McLaughlin & Lichter, 1997). In Sweden, generous parental leave and child support policies have contributed to a low and falling marriage rate, although adolescent pregnancies are very infrequent (Burns & Scott, 1994).

Families, like society, are cooperative, homeostatic arrangements. If one member is neglected, the others are likely to suffer also. Reform measures that neglect husbands, wives, children, or other kin are likely to fail. The current U.S. policy of placing indigent mothers in jobs has left care of their children uncertain, and it writes off the fathers, thus undermining the family in two ways.

The family is truly the essential pillar of society, being universal (Rossi, 1987). Its strength was demonstrated by the failure of attempts to undermine it in the Soviet Union after the 1917 Revolution, and on Israeli kibbutzim. Political attempts to redefine the family are semantic legerdemain that offer no substitute for the kin ties upon which children of our species have always relied.

Some industrialized countries have adopted measures to bolster the family and enhance its beneficial effects. Hungary pays an allowance to a mother who stays home to care for her preschooler, an arrangement that may surpass day care provided by a hireling with several babies to tend. The Swedish government provides financial allowances for those who care for a sick child or other relative at home; caregivers are offered training in basic nursing. Some European countries offer compensation to grandparents who care for their grandchildren.

These policies are predicated on a recognition that most people live in families of kin, that the family has an evolved basis, and that children are usually and ideally raised by their own parents. Just as age and gender matter to human beings everywhere, so does kinship. Nevertheless, the family is not an arrangement that is impervious to social conditions; it does not just thrive because people are sentimental about it. In particular, economic conditions are very important to its form and prevalence. Work hours, wages, and parental-leave policies can, in theory, be adjusted to meet the needs of families, rather than families always having to adjust to employers' desires. Psychology, with its focus on the individual's adjustment to the social milieu, may sometimes neglect to point out the possibility of collective action to address collective problems.

Summary

Exclusive, or obligate, male homosexuality seems to be influenced by genes and prenatal hormonal factors. The main environmental factor may be prenatal stress, which can feminize male fetuses behaviorally.

Lesbianism is less well understood, but it seems to occur, in part, because of prenatal masculinization, and it is somewhat heritable.

Sex differences in romanticism and promiscuity are reflected by research on sexual fantasies and erotica. Males are highly romantic, but they do not require romantic imagery for sexual arousal to the extent that females do. Further, the sexual initiation of a girl seems to have more of a bonding effect on both partners than does a boy's.

The existence of various physiological and behavioral adaptations for promiscuity is consistent with the fact that a substantial proportion of copulations are extrapair copulations. Women as well as men would enhance their fitness by means of EPCs under certain circumstances.

In general, the traits that attract the opposite sex are those that raise one's status among peers (see Chapters 11 and 12). In other words, peer competition is essentially sexual competition. Mate value in a woman largely reflects genetic quality, health, youth (including early maturity), femininity, and sexual fidelity. Men seek good, faithful breeders. Mate value in men seems mainly to mean genetic quality, health, masculinity, dominance, wealth, and commitment. These traits signal a man's potential as a provider, protector, and progenitor. Women's attraction to men with the potential to offer nuptial gifts may be mediated by proxies for wealth, such as signs of dominance or vigor. In prehistory, athleticism may have signaled hunting prowess. The preference for a man richer, taller, and older than she suggests that a woman desires a more dominant husband.

Because mates exploit each other's reproductive systems, they tend to prefer rather pronounced sex differentiation in each other. Thus, many of the desiderata in a bride can be embraced by the term *femininity*, and many of the bodily and behavioral qualities in a groom are encompassed by *masculinity*. Yet both sexes desire mates who are kind, industrious, and similar to themselves. Homogamy may preserve locally adaptive gene combinations.

The importance for adolescents of attracting and choosing mates is underscored by observations of their informal behavior. Adolescent boys who act tough, exercise, brag, demean rivals, accost girls, and show off are behaving in ways that may enhance their mating success. Likewise, girls who discuss boys, flirt, enhance their appearance, and demean rivals are behaving normally in an evolutionary sense.

Unwed teen births are problematic mainly because of poor prenatal and postnatal care, and single parenthood. The risks imposed by a girl's small size and reproductive immaturity are minor. Various measures have been employed to lower the incidence of unmarried adolescent motherhood. Sexually restrictive attitudes are only modestly effective in discouraging sexual activity; the sex drive is hard to deny. Sexual abstinence is costly and difficult for a society to maintain, especially given the prolonged period of risk between puberty and marriage. Moreover, restrictive attitudes reduce contraceptive use, so that one barrier is lowered as another is raised, resulting in a net increase in pregnancies. The most effective public health measure is confidential clinics that dispense contraceptives in the high school. Sex education by itself has little impact on sexual behavior.

Often, an unplanned pregnancy is welcomed by the girl because its anticipated emotional benefits outweigh those of alternative life courses, such as the girl's marital prospects. Adolescent girls may even possess an evolved reproductive strategy for responding to rearing conditions that signal a low likelihood of marriage. Girls who experience family conflict or father absence tend to mature early and to embark on childbearing at a young age. Whatever its proximate causation, this behavioral option includes early menarche, early sex, promiscuity or early marriage, and early childrearing.

Thus, the more fundamental problem, in terms of the well-being of the next generation of children, is not adolescent pregnancy, which is normal from medical, historical, and cross-cultural perspectives. Rather, the main problem is the dim promise of a happy, stable marriage. Logically, marriage must be stabilized if more couples are to elect to bear—and raise—their children within families. Getting pregnant girls to marry is not a remedy for their children because of the high divorce rate of adolescent couples currently.

Various factors affect the marriage rate in humans. Comparative evidence suggests that marriage is strengthened by good employment opportunities for men, and it is weakened by the economic independence of women. For example, in the early 1980s, 68.2 percent of Dutch women were totally dependent financially on their husbands, and divorce and adolescent births were infrequent in The Netherlands (Burns & Scott, 1994). The marriage rate is reduced by a low sex ratio, which favors the "cad" strategy for men. Infertile marriages tend to break up, whereas those with many children endure. Marriage is weakened if spouses lack or lose the attributes of mate value, that is, if they are or become poor sexual competitors. For men, these attributes include wealth and dominance. The general appeal of male dominance is indicated by the fact that marriage is often weakened by the wife surpassing her husband in terms of education, income, or decisionmaking. Additional risk factors include drug abuse, a brief or tumultuous courtship, poor education, infertility, declining health, the husband being domineering or violent, the wife being unfaithful, and the spouses being dissimilar.

14 Parent-Adolescent Relations

This chapter will address some applied issues: parent-adolescent conflict, parental styles, juvenile delinquency, the effects of father absence and of divorce, and drug abuse. An attempt will be made to explain certain pathological phenomena in terms of normal processes. The medical model holds that pathological processes are best understood as departures from normality; physiology provides the theoretical basis for pathophysiology. The same reasoning would seem to apply to the study of behavioral pathology. Thus, what parents and other adults regard as adolescent misbehavior may, in many instances, be normal attempts at emotional satisfaction under constraining circumstances.

Parent-Adolescent Conflict

Despite the overlap of biological interests between parent and offspring, their genes are not identical. Therefore, a degree of **parent-offspring conflict** is to be expected (Trivers, 1974). In particular, conflict may arise over the distribution of parental resources to the offspring and its siblings. Each offspring can be expected to be biased in its own favor in such cases, since it shares only one-half of its genes with a full sib and one-fourth with a half sib. The parent, however, should be unbiased toward its offspring—hence the conflict. In other words, despite the fact that siblings are related to each other and so will tend to favor each other over nonrelatives, siblings are to some extent rivalrous, especially with regard to parental resources and attention (see Chapter 8).

At adolescence, dependence on the parent is diminished. A reordering of the parent-offspring relationship might be expected at this point, owing to a decrease in parental power over the offspring as well as an increase in the general independence of the adolescent (Trivers, 1985). Psychologically, emotional distance between them might increase. The distancing of parents may be caused, in part, by the decreasing pedomorphism of adolescents, especially boys (Chapter 10). This would be appropriate functionally, since attaining adult size contributes to independence.

Steinberg (1987) found that parent-adolescent distancing did occur (see Chapter 7). "Emotional distancing" increased with *pubertal maturity* and *chronological age*. Steinberg measured these two factors and *pubertal timing* (early versus late maturity) independently. Pubertal maturity produced the strongest effect on emotional distancing and other aspects of the parent-adolescent relationship. The greater the distance reported, the higher the level of androgens (testosterone in boys and androstenedione in girls) (Steinberg, 1988). Cognitive development showed no clear relation to parent-adolescent distance. Similarly, physically mature adolescents tend to spend relatively more time with other adolescents than with adults, so puberty may help shift interest away from the parents and toward peers (Steinberg, 1996).

In addition to this decrease in mutual aid at adolescence and any disputes that may arise from it, increased conflict with parents may result from the general rise in competitiveness at adolescence, especially in males (Borgia, 1980). Conflict with parents and siblings would be mitigated by kinship ties. Nonetheless, family members probably come into frequent conflict over resources, so the actual number of disagreements may be high. Montemayor and Hanson (1985) reported an increase in conflict between same-sex siblings at puberty, as well.

The ideal would seem to be to provide a gradual, appropriate transition to independence for adolescents. However, as expected from theoretical considerations, conflict often arises between adolescents and parents in our species. For example, running away has been reported for both sexes in 60 percent of traditional cultures (Schlegel & Barry, 1991).

The transition may be especially difficult in the West, which lacks several traditional mechanisms for easing this process. Because the extended family is weak in the West, young people are provided with few adult role models. For example, if the father is absent or a poor model, a son will probably not have an uncle or grandfather nearby as a substitute. In addition, occupational roles are more diversified in modern society, resulting in less commonality between parents and adolescents. The West also lacks formal puberty rites for distancing adolescents from their parents and providing them with a tutor (see Chapter 7). Then, too, many Western adolescents lack opportunities to contribute tangibly to the family economy (see Chapter 6).

Some aspects of parent-adolescent relations are sex-specific. These sex differences begin to make sense when seen in the light of two general principles concerning social status in our species (see Chapter 6). First, men have somewhat higher status than women everywhere. In all societies, men predominate in the highest formal political offices (van den Berghe, 1980). Men also are ascribed higher informal status than women everywhere (Stephens, 1963). Second, older individuals have higher status than younger ones. For example, in most societies, fathers remain dominant over their sons even after the latter marry. The son is usually in daily contact with his father, often living in the same dwelling, until the father dies or is incapacitated. The son must show submission to his father constantly. The same patterns are seen in other terrestrial primates: Most males dominate most females, and older individuals dominate younger ones.

Because men formally dominate women, however, at some point the son supplants his mother. This dominance reversal is likely to occur around adolescence, when the son attains maturity. This is what happens in chimpanzees, for example; adolescent sons begin to dominate their mothers (Goodall, 1986). Indeed, Steinberg (1996) and Paikoff and Brooks-Gunn (1991) concluded from the U.S. literature that parent-adolescent conflict is most acute between the son and mother. Similarly, Jacob (1974) reported that sons gained in influence in family decisionmaking between 11 and 16 years of age vis-à-vis the mother but not the father. Montemayor and Hanson (1985) found that conflict between mother and son increased at puberty. Likewise, in a German study, the mother-adolescent son relationship was the most troubled (Silverberg, 1989).

Steinberg's own work (1987, 1988) provides additional evidence of this sex difference. Observations of family discussions revealed an increase in conflict between mothers and sons with his maturation, an increase in his self-reported autonomy, and a decrease in cohesion reported by both parties. Mothers and sons explained themselves progressively less often and interrupted one another more often. As the son matured, he gave in less often. Once he had reached the peak of his growth spurt, his mother's rate of interrupting declined and she yielded to him more. In effect, the son displaced his mother in dominance. However, the father remained more influential than his son throughout the latter's pubertal development. For girls, conflict also rose during pubertal maturation, but neither the mother nor the father was displaced in dominance. As the growth spurt subsided, conflict usually diminished (Steinberg, 1996). Like most other pubertal changes, parent-adolescent distancing may occur earlier in girls. A Belgian study suggested that adolescent girls distance themselves from their parents sooner than boys do, gravitating toward girlfriends and others for intimacy (Marcoen & Brumagne, 1985).

In an important confirmation of Steinberg's model, Flinn (1988) observed father-daughter interactions in a Caribbean village. He reported more father-daughter conflict for girls between ages 11 and 15 than for older or younger girls. Fathers of daughters were also observed to have more conflicts with unrelated males than did fathers of sons. Further, girls with resident fathers stayed home more than girls without resident fathers or brothers. Girls with resident fathers had more stable marriages than those without, an example of a fairly direct contribution of paternal care to children's mating success.

Thus, the hormonal changes of puberty seem to promote parent-adolescent distancing in both sexes, directly or indirectly. Conflict increases with pubertal maturation and then declines (Laursen & Ferreira, 1994). This is distinct from the phenomenon (described in Chapter 13 for girls and later in this chapter for boys) of family conflict accelerating puberty. Whether an adolescent is an early or a late maturer, puberty seems to increase conflict with parents.

Following maturation of the adolescent, relations between the parents tend to improve also. Parents' marital satisfaction has been consistently found to increase in Western countries when the adolescent leaves home (see Chapter 6). When children are born, they demand parental investment, and relations between the parents tend to suffer. When adolescents mature, they require less care. Perhaps as a result, parents tend to each other's needs more assiduously.

Parental Styles

Different parental practices, or styles, seem to produce particular results in children (e.g., Steinberg, 1996). These effects can be understood in terms of some general behavioral principles that apply to adolescents as well as children. In this section, the main dimensions of parental style will be defined. Then the effects of the various parental practices on children's behavior will be described and interpreted.

Research on parental styles suggests the utility of recognizing three main dimensions. Parents can be warm or cold, controlling or permissive, and authoritarian or democratic. Many other terms have been used to characterize various parental styles, but most are reducible to one of these three dimensions. However, it may be helpful to mention some of the many alternative terms when each dimension is described.

Warm Versus Hostile

Warm parents are also described as "nurturant," "loving," and "warmly attached." They provide the child with a preponderance of rewards, such as praise, smiles, attention, and caresses. Cold, hostile, or punitive parents stress punishment, such as criticism, frowns, and ignoring. The important thing is the relative frequency of rewards and punishments, not so much their form.

Parental warmth is ideal. This does not mean that the child is rewarded for misbehaving; misdeeds should be recognized as such. However, with warm child rearing, rewards outweigh punishments. Warmth seems to raise the child's social and cognitive competence. It also reduces the incidence of psychosomatic symptoms.

These effects can be parsimoniously explained by noting that receiving rewards rather than punishment lowers fear, or anxiety. High levels of fear can interfere with social and cognitive performance, and they are a major cause of psychosomatic symptoms. Warm parents also tend to be more influential over adolescents (Elder, 1968), perhaps because a rewarding parent will be sought out and because low anxiety is conducive to absorbing the parents' lessons. Furthermore, children imitate nurturant models more than hostile ones, although the mechanism involved in this imitation is not clear.

Frequent punishment has the added liability of lowering self-esteem in children and adolescents (B. K. Barber et al., 1992). Individuals with low self-esteem are especially vulnerable to criticism; they fear criticism and hence may avoid challenging situations in which they might otherwise learn. They need a great deal of praise and encouragement for their efforts. Individuals high in self-esteem, by contrast, benefit from occasional criticism, which prevents them from becoming complacent. In sum, praise should predominate over criticism, but the child should be encouraged to improve continually (cf. Chapter 4).

Feedback should guide the child toward challenges of appropriate difficulty, so that progress is promoted. Individuals with high self-esteem tend to seek out realistic challenges and to persist in their efforts, so self-esteem should be cultivated to abet this process. At the same time, children need to learn what their strengths and weaknesses are. Again, the preponderance of feedback should be rewarding.

As Leach (1989) pointed out in her superb book on child care, the value of praise is sometimes neglected because the child is already doing the right thing. But the child may be uncertain that she is doing the right thing, so praise can provide useful information as well as warmth and encouragement.

Leach noted that most children want to do the right thing. If they err, it is usually out of ignorance, not malice. These good intentions should be cultivated by ample expressions of praise, which strengthens the child's view of himself as a good person. A suspicious, hostile parent will erode these good intentions. If the child or adolescent hears only criticism, he may despair of receiving credit for good behavior and stop trying. He may eventually come to accept the view that he is incorrigible and act accordingly.

Parental warmth is a major component of **parental responsiveness,** a concept applied to the care of infants. It means reacting promptly, appropriately, and consistently to the child's needs. That is, responsive parents are quick and competent in rewarding the child. They accurately diagnose the child's needs and respond in a manner appropriate for him. Research indicates that parental responsiveness, like parental warmth, is associated with a generally favorable developmental outcome. The children of responsive parents tend to excel in cognitive and social development. This is thought to occur, in part, because a warm, **secure** mother-infant bond is usually formed, as opposed to an **anxious,** or **insecure,** style of attachment (Ainsworth, 1979). Secure attachment to the mother seems to provide the warmth and protection from fear that enhance development, as explained earlier. Security of attachment in infancy is associated with favorable development 10 or more years later (Bradley et al., 1988).

On sociobiological grounds, one would expect that hired child-care workers would not generally be as warm and responsive as the biological parents. Indeed, infants in a variety of child-care arrangements are at risk of developing an insecure attachment to the mother and of exhibiting disobedience, aggressiveness, academic difficulties, and poor social adjustment in childhood (Belsky, 1990; Belsky & Eggebeen, 1991; Hoffman, 1974). If nothing else, a day-care worker supervising several children cannot respond as promptly and appropriately as a mother who has only her own child to monitor.

As the ethologist Bowlby (1969, 1973) theorized, the early social bond to the mother carries over to influence the child's later social bonds (Rutter & Rutter, 1993). For example, in a prospective study, warm and affectionate parental behavior in early childhood was associated with having a long, happy marriage and close friendships 36 years later (Franz et al., 1991). Secure attachment has been linked to stable romantic relationships, including marriage, in adulthood (Hazan & Shaver, 1987). In Hill et al.'s (1994) research, men's anxious attachment to their mothers was associated with briefer romantic relationships, and women's anxious attachment to their mothers was linked with early first romance and brevity of courtship.

Recent research on attachment styles suggests that anxiously attached individuals vary in their characteristic approach to romantic relationships (Zeifman & Hazan, 1997). Those who are further classified as **ambivalently attached** tended to focus on the amorous aspects, enjoying physical affection more than sex. Those in the anxious subcategory **avoidantly attached** showed the opposite pattern. By contrast, securely attached adults derived pleasure from both amorousness and sex.

Like younger children, adolescents seem to benefit from warm treatment. For example, parental warmth is associated with reduced parent-adolescent conflict (Rueter & Conger, 1995). Parental warmth seems to protect adolescents against developing antisocial tendencies. Adolescents with cold parents are at greater risk for delinquency (Montemayor, 1986; G. E. Weisfeld & Aytch, 1996) and drug abuse (Barnes et al., 1986), perhaps in part because peers compete effectively with parents for the youth's allegiance. Parental warmth reduces the risk of adolescent pregnancy, depression, and suicide (Belsky, 1990). In an observational study of aggressive adolescent boys from middle-class homes, Patterson (1982) found that aggression was reduced if the father merely paid attention to his son. Other researchers stress the importance of listening to and acknowledging the views of the adolescent, as during mealtime discussions. Furthermore, adolescent self-esteem was associated with father's interest (Amato & Ochiltree, 1986).

Adolescents are not too old to need parental attention. When Belgian students made the transition to secondary school, their parents seemed to pay more attention to their academic progress, and the students reported lower levels of parent-related loneliness (Marcoen et al., 1987). Boys tended to experience more loneliness than girls toward parents (especially the father), evidently because they were expected to be independent (Marcoen & Brumagne, 1985).

Violence is an intense form of punishment that very effectively produces the detrimental consequences of hostile treatment. For example, parental violence greatly increases children's anxiety. Research indicates that a child who has been struck is usually too upset, in fact, to absorb any parental instruction. Also, of course, many children are injured in the process.

Moreover, violence by parents is passed on to children. Children who have been physically punished are more likely to strike their peers (Belsky, 1990), to hit their own children, and to become delinquents and criminals (Straus et al., 1980). U.S. and Canadian couples who fought tended to have children who fought with their siblings.

Like parental violence, societal violence is also readily imitated. Observing television violence tends to increase aggression, rather than displacing the viewer's aggressive impulses (Rutter & Giller, 1983). Cultures that engage in aggressive sports tend to exhibit high levels of warfare (Eibl-Eibesfeldt, 1979), and U.S. historical periods when aggressive sports were popular tended to be followed by warfare (Rutter & Giller, 1983). "Competitive sports may have many values, but . . . the general reduction of aggressive tendencies is not one of them" (Moyer, 1976, p. 283).

Physical punishment is relatively common in the United States compared with, say, Norway (Werner, 1979). In Sweden, it is illegal to strike a child, and rates of physical punishment are lower there (Straus et al., 1980). In a national survey, 70 percent of married U.S. parents approved of spanking a 12-year-old "as necessary" (Herbert, 1986). The percentage was higher for those with less experience in raising children: men, the childless, and younger respondents. Adolescent parents are at risk to be child abusers. Asked about their own children, 63 percent of U.S. parents admitted having struck them in the past year; 3 percent had used a knife or gun! The average child was kicked, bitten, or punched 9 times per year, hit with an object 9 times, and beaten up 6 times.

Striking a child is tempting because it is an easy and effective deterrent. But in the long run, it erodes the child's confidence in parent and self. Alternatives to physical punishment are always available, such as depriving the child of a favorite pastime or simply explaining why the behavior was unwise. People sometimes argue that young children should be spanked to keep them from approaching dangers that they are too young to understand. But it is far safer simply to block access to stoves, poisons, and the like.

Many cultures succeed in raising their children without ever striking them, and members of such cultures are appalled at the thought. The same is true of many U.S. parents. When children are brought up with kindness and affection, they seldom require more than an occasional mild rebuke—shame is a very powerful punishment, and it is sufficient for most situations.

Controlling Versus Permissive

Controlling parents are sometimes referred to as "restrictive," as opposed to "permissive" or "laissez-faire." They tend to limit their children's range of action strictly. Parents may restrict their child's activities for different reasons: out of a desire to punish the child or because they are overprotective. Regardless of the parents' motivation, a restricted child tends to be incompetent, presumably due to a dearth of learning experiences. Children need to have a chance to make their own mistakes, to learn directly from the environment instead of just through parental instruction (Leach, 1989).

Adolescents often reject advice merely because they resent not being given credit for being able to handle a given matter themselves. Restricted adolescents are prone to various difficulties. The risks of suicide (Kerfoot, 1980), drug abuse (Gantman, 1978), male aggression (Bandura, 1960), and female running away (Wolk & Brandon, 1977) may be increased also. Black and white U.S. adolescent girls whose parents valued responsibility were less likely to give birth out of wedlock (Hanson et al., 1987).

Likewise, the motivation of permissive parents may vary. The parent may simply be indifferent to the child's activities, which seems frequently to give rise to delinquency (Conger & Miller, 1966) and to running away by boys (Wolk & Brandon, 1977). Alternatively, the parent may be indulgent and not want to deny the child anything. Regardless of the parent's motivation, the results for the child are again similar. Competence is low, presumably because the child has been exposed to overly difficult situations that overwhelm her capacities and self-confidence. Self-esteem tends to be low, too, perhaps because of these failures and a lack of parental attention. Parents who are overly permissive, like those who are overly controlling, are liable to have adolescents who use drugs (Barnes et al., 1986) or are delinquent (Rutter & Giller, 1983).

The ideal seems to be a moderate, appropriate level of autonomy for the child or adolescent (Baumrind, 1971). This means that the child will experience appropriate challenges, which maximize learning. Just as our curiosity naturally draws us toward tasks of moderate novelty and complexity (see Chapter 3), a wise parent provides appropriate learning experiences for the child. Similarly, high school students prefer classes that are moderately difficult for them (Csikszentmihalyi & Larson, 1984). Another indication of the desirability of an appropriate level of autonomy is the finding that parents who provide their adolescent with a moderate amount of control tend to experience little conflict with them (Montemayor, 1986).

Democratic Versus Authoritarian

A "democratic" parent relinquishes some power to the child. This parental style is associated with high self-esteem in the child, perhaps because of the parental implication that he is worthy. Academic performance tends to be good, self-confidence is high, and few behavior problems result (Steinberg, 1996). These effects may occur in a number of ways, such as via a social tone of rationality and respect for others' rights. Democratic decisionmaking entails rational discussion, and so parents who are democratic also tend to be rational, that is, to be **inductive**. This term, from the same root as that of "educate" (*ducere*, L., "to lead"), refers to the practice of providing reasons for one's statements. An inductive parent may exercise more control than the adolescent, but she explains her position and is receptive to criticism. The children of inductive parents tend to be generally competent and to resist antisocial peer pressure (Devereux, 1970).

Authoritarian, or "rigid," parents, by contrast, seldom provide explanations for their positions, and instead set down rules that are to be obeyed implicitly. This situation sometimes leads to adolescent defiance (Steward & Zaenglein-Senger, 1982). Younger children may accept their parents' rules and edicts without question, but adolescents often demand reasons. The authoritarian style eventually tends to produce a child who has difficulty functioning independently, that is, who has trouble thinking rationally (Leach, 1989). This failure probably occurs due to the lack of an example set by rational parents as well as the lack of practice and encouragement at independent problem solving. Memorizing and following a list of rules does not seem to equip a child for the many situations that do not fall neatly under a single, simple rule. Authoritarian parental practices are associated with less contraception use by sexually active teens (Cvetkovich & Grote, 1983; Olson & Worobey, 1984).

Flexible thinking seems to require absorbing some general, abstract principles rather than specific, concrete formulas. For example, the habit of systematically considering all alternatives and their consequences—formal operational thinking—would be generally useful for problem solving, at least in the absence of a time limit. Another principle of widespread utility is to anticipate the reactions of others and take others' feelings into account (Leach, 1989). This principle, the Golden Rule, is universal (Gouldner, 1960). Adolescents with behavior problems have often been found to lack this skill in planning, and as a result, they are often surprised when they offend someone (M. J. Chandler, 1973).

Since adults generally have higher status than adolescents, they are tempted to deal with teenagers in a peremptory, authoritarian manner. But adolescents usually do not like to be told what to do or to be otherwise pressured; they much prefer having the consequences of various alternatives shown to them so they can take their own decisions. Adolescents seem to respond best to a respectful approach—addressing them politely, showing that one wants to help them, being straightforward, and so forth.

In general, these dimensions and principles of parental style seem to hold cross-culturally. Children with warm parents tend to be less aggressive, more skilled and independent, warmer, more generous, less attention seeking, and higher in self-esteem (R. L. Munroe & Munroe, 1975; Werner, 1979). These children tend to emerge from cultures in which fathers are home daily and spend time with their children, and in which there is a high ratio of adults to children in the home. Mothers who are overwhelmed by child-care responsibilities are prone to reject their children. In fact, cross-cultural research has shown that infanticide of a newborn is most likely if the father is absent and the mother is young and otherwise poorly prepared to raise the child (Daly & Wilson, 1988).

Democratic, inductive parental practices seem optimal for middle-class children. However, the authoritarian style tends to characterize traditional societies, where questioning of time-honored practices can be a liability. For example, U.S. rural and working-class parents are less inductive than middle-class parents, reflecting the types of jobs available to them (Hoffman, 1984). A worker who repeatedly questioned the foreman, or a farmer who gambled on a new time for planting, would run a great risk. Also, parental explanation is time-consuming, and so it is less typical of families with many children (Elder, 1968). Similarly, physical punishment is more typical among working-class parents than middle-class parents in the United States and among middle-class parents under duress. Parental patience declines and anger increases as a function of limited resources (Belsky, 1984).

An important study by Lesser and Kandel (1969) compared parental styles and their consequences in the United States and Denmark. Particular parental styles had the same effects on adolescents in both countries. However, Danish parents tended to be warmer. As a result, Danish adolescents reported feeling closer to their parents than adolescents in the United States, and they were more willing to ask them for advice. U.S. fathers seemed to be particularly distant from their adolescent sons. Most sons reported feeling closer to their mothers in the United States, whereas in Denmark, most sons felt closer to their fathers.

Also, parents were more controlling in the United States than in Denmark. More Danish than American adolescents were content with the degree of independence they were granted. In both countries, satisfaction with one's independence was associated with positive interactions with parents, so the Danish adolescents were more satisfied with their degree of independence than were the Americans. Lesser and Kandel and others have concluded that U.S. parents are more restrictive in regard to their adolescents than are Europeans, but more permissive toward their children. Many U.S. children are indulged with material possessions but denied much personal attention and guidance. They enter adolescence ill equipped to function independently, and so their parents then try to impose restraints on them. In Europe, by contrast, independence is meted out progressively as children develop socially and proceed into adolescence.

Finally, in this research, most U.S. parents were found to be authoritarian, whereas most Danish fathers and mothers were democratic.

Danish parents typically provided reasons for their policies, whereas American parents merely issued demands. American adolescents were subject to more rules at age 18 than Danes were at age 14. In both countries, authoritarianism was associated with poorer parent-adolescent relations.

In summary, Danish parents were warmer, less controlling, and more democratic than American parents, and they consequently had more contented, cooperative adolescents. The prevalence of hostile, controlling, authoritarian parental habits in the United States may help explain the high rate of adolescent problem behavior.

Additional principles of good child rearing are noted by Leach (1989) and others. The parent's example is usually more effective than her advice; parental modeling effects are powerful, as noted earlier with respect to parental violence. For example, parents who treat each other warmly and democratically tend to have children with good social skills (Lamb, 1981). Parents who use drugs (including alcohol and tobacco) tend to have adolescents who use drugs, although not necessarily the drugs used by the parents (Steinberg, 1996). And parents who never admit a mistake can expect to have a child with the same habit.

It is also important to be consistent. Adolescents are sometimes defiant if they are rewarded or punished haphazardly (Steward & Zaenglein-Senger, 1982). To reward or overlook a behavior one day and punish it another is confusing for the child, as is parental disagreement about an issue. Parents need not fear honestly disagreeing in the child's presence, as long as they discuss the matter calmly and try to see each other's point. But they should reach agreement before addressing their child. Consistency of treatment may be compromised if child-care workers and the parents do not reach agreement on their practices and policies.

Leach (1989) recommended that parents remember that an honest effort needs to be encouraged even if the actual result is imperfect. Children need to be encouraged sufficiently for them not to give up on tasks.

A related point is that if a child admits to a wrongdoing, this admission should be acknowledged appreciatively. Similarly, a sincere apology should be treated as what it is, an appeasement gesture, and criticism should stop at once. Even chimpanzees know enough to exhibit a reconciliation gesture under such circumstances (de Waal, 1996). Adolescents are particularly sensitive to humiliation, since they are so competitive; consequently, they need to be allowed to make amends for mistakes and to regain their lost status. When we register a success, we rise in status; when we commit a misdeed, we fall (see Chapter 4).

Needless to say, parents cannot teach what they do not know and what they cannot explain clearly. For example, a study of knowledge of child development revealed that U.S. adolescents knew very little in this regard, especially if they lacked younger siblings or babysitting experience. Further, the less they knew, the more likely they were to favor punitive methods of child care (C. Johnson et al., 1982). Training improved these teenagers' knowledge about child development but not their attitudes. Like poor parental practices, ignorance tends to be perpetuated across generations. Many poorly educated U.S. parents are incapable of helping even their young children with their homework, and many U.S. teachers cannot even write English properly.

These conclusions about the ideal parental style seem to apply to teaching style, too; after all, a good parent is a good teacher. Schools with teachers who give frequent praise and support, and set high but clear standards for comportment and learning, have students with higher test scores and attendance rates, and less delinquency and classroom disruption (Rutter & Giller, 1983). Schools in which students hold positions of responsibility also tend to have low delinquency rates. In Japan, the students are responsible for cleaning the schools at all levels, and vandalism is virtually nonexistent (Rohlen, 1983).

Recent research indicates that, surprisingly, parental behavior is not nearly as powerful an influence on behavior as has always been assumed (Plomin, 1990). Siblings often differ greatly in their behavior, despite having been raised by the same parents and sharing much the same environment. Genetic differences explain some of this variation, but **nonshared environmental factors**—those that affect siblings differentially—are also influential. These factors, whose nature is unclear as yet, may include birth order, parental favoritism, the influence of particular friends and mentors, peer social rank, and health. The relatively small influence of **shared environmental factors**, including parental style and income, on personality and cognitive development means that our models of socialization are unbalanced.

In particular, relations with peers become increasingly important with age (J. R. Harris, 1995). Success among peers is ultimately translated into reproductive success. The peer value system closely resembles the adult value system in traditional cultures. But the age segregation of modern society creates a distinct peer subculture that diffracts adult values to some extent.

Another complication derives from the fact that parental style has appreciable heritability (Plomin, 1994). The high heritability of parental style and temperament means that this "environmental" influence on the child actually has a strong genetic basis. Likewise, the child's highly heritable temperament shapes the treatment she receives from her parents, as has been demonstrated in observational research. For example, a parent who is a worrier may reinforce the worrying habits of the child. In sum, environmental factors in parent-child interaction are often contaminated by genes. We tend to assume that parent-child similarities are due to the inculcation of parental values, but common genes are a far likelier explanation.

Juvenile Delinquency

Development of Delinquency

Observational studies of family interactions in the home have highlighted some of the parent-child behavior patterns associated with delinquency (e.g., Patterson, 1982). Parents of delinquent boys use frequent and violent punishment, issue numerous commands, provide little attention, are vague and inconsistent in giving direction, and practice little supervision of peer-group activities outside the home. That is, the parents of delinquents tend to be harsh, authoritarian, and lax in monitoring them, and they do not maintain consistent and high standards.

Other family variables also predict delinquency (Rutter & Giller, 1983). One is single parenthood, occurring through illegitimacy, separation, or divorce. Adolescent mothers are especially at risk for having delinquent children. In addition, extended families and neighborhoods are broken up by geographic mobility, which is prominent in the United States and is associated with juvenile delinquency. An aggressive neighborhood has been found to contribute to delinquency independently of family factors (Tolan & Lorion, 1988).

G. E. Weisfeld and Aytch (1996) tried to develop a model of delinquency that would account for the fact that delinquency often runs in families. They studied a triracial sample of male felons. Many of these felons reported having half siblings (45 percent) or stepsiblings (35 percent). According to sociobiological theory, these men would have quarreled frequently with these less-than-full siblings during childhood. This presumed family conflict may have led to punitive mothering of the subjects, since the presence of half siblings was correlated with a history of maternal punitiveness as reported by the subject. Maternal punitiveness, in turn, is known to be associated with anxious attachment (Rutter & Rutter, 1993). In the Weisfeld and Aytch study, anxious attachment, measured retrospectively, was correlated with the number of felony convictions.

Criminality might be transmitted to the next generation as follows. Anxious attachment predicts unstable romantic relationships (Hazan & Shaver, 1987). Unstable relationships, in theory, would generate many half and stepsiblings, thus perpetuating the cycle of maternal punitiveness, anxious attachment, and criminality across generations (Figure 14.1). The role of the father was also addressed by this model. Weisfeld and Aytch found that having had an attentive biological father was associated with fewer felonies; unstable marriages would, of course, weaken the involvement of the biological father.

Of course, economic factors, such as unemployment, are important in delinquency (Rutter & Giller, 1983). Crime tempts many impoverished male adolescents because it provides comparatively attractive economic rewards for little effort, and because the risks of incarceration are not very great, even for homicide (M. Wilson & Daly, 1985). Moreover, criminal behavior sometimes actually enhances a young man's neighborhood status through its economic rewards and independent, tough lifestyle (Feldman & Weisfeld, 1973). Poverty also tends to detract from desirable parental behavior (Belsky, 1984), and thus may indirectly predispose a child to delinquency.

Relatively little attention has been paid to the question of what happens to juvenile delinquents when they grow up. There are three possibilities. A great many of them die—from homicide, drug use, or other causes (W. J. Wilson, 1987; G. E. Weisfeld & Feldman, 1982). Some of them remain criminals, especially if they became involved in serious crime at a young age. Most of the rest eventually find a legitimate job and marry; in fact, marriage itself seems to have a palliative effect on criminality (Rutter & Rutter, 1993). The fact that criminality is greatest in adolescent boys suggests that much of it constitutes sex-

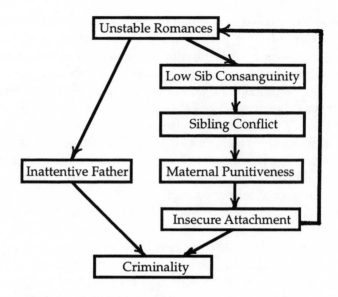

Figure 14.1   An Ethological Model of the Intergenerational Perpetuation of Criminality. Research by G.E. Weisfeld & Aytch (1996) revealed that male felons in a triracial sample committed more crimes if they reported having been insecurely (especially ambivalently) attached to their mothers. This maternal attachment status, in turn, was correlated with maternal punitiveness, as others have also reported. Many (45 percent) of these felons reported having half siblings. Sociobiological theory would predict that conflict between these low-consanguinity siblings would be higher than between full siblings, which might lead to more maternal punitiveness; indeed, in this study, maternal punitiveness was significantly greater for subjects with half siblings. Research by Hazan & Shaver (1987) revealed that insecurity of attachment is associated with unstable romantic relationships in adulthood, thus perpetuating the cycle across generations. Weisfeld & Aytch also found that extent of criminality was associated with having had an inattentive father, a situation likely to be more common in unstable romances.

ual competition among unmated males (Daly & Wilson, 1988). Although female criminality is highest in adolescence as well, the sex difference in criminality peaks in adolescence (Rutter & Rutter, 1993).

Prevention

Various individual factors are common in delinquents, such as aggressive temperament, poor peer relations, impulsiveness, hyperactivity, low intelligence, and mental illness (Rutter & Rutter, 1993). Neurological damage, such as that involving brain areas associated with aggression (the amygdala), impulse control (the prefrontal cortex), or guilt (the orbitofrontal cortex), is demonstrable in many cases of delinquency (e.g., see Raine, 1998). Brain damage can result from perinatal trauma or child abuse. Perhaps it is most practical to focus on variables that respond to intervention. For example, perinatal difficulty and maternal rejection have each been found to predict delinquency (Raine, 1998). Therefore, improved prenatal care and family-stabilizing economic policies, which enhance parental care and provide economic alternatives to criminality (see Chapter 13), might be fruitful goals for intervention. Such measures might be viewed as means of improving a son's capability to perform socially and economically, that is, to compete legitimately as opposed to illegally and violently.

It has long been known that recreational approaches provide no demonstrable benefits (McKay, 1949). One Chicago street gang was actually formed as a result of a sports program that drew a group of youths together (G. E. Weisfeld & Feldman, 1982). Likewise, Shanas (1942) reported a positive relation between participation in recreational programs and delinquency among boys in five areas of Chicago.

Rutter and Giller (1983) recommended making greater use of social pressure to curb delinquent behavior, specifically, public praise and criticism. This is the main method of social control in traditional societies (see Chapter 6), so it is not "unusual" punishment, nor is it any crueler than detention. Society would seem to need some intermediate level of punishment that does not involve the unwieldy, costly state legal apparatus.

Japan provides an example of an industrialized society that relies heavily on public acknowledgment of error to curb undesirable behavior (Braithwaite, 1989). The offender is pressured—gently—to admit his mistake and make restitution to his victim. If this is done, the offender is fully reinstated into the community, and punishment need not be escalated. The individual regains status (or saves face) and so is then treated with compassion and respect; compare this with the reconciliation displays between chimpanzees. Japan has very low rates of delinquency, drug abuse, and school assaults (Rohlen, 1983).

Remediation

Social-skills training has also been used effectively on delinquents. Efforts to teach parents to use rewards, monitor their children, be de-

cisive, negotiate social contracts with their children, and use other social skills have shown benefits lasting over a year (Rutter & Giller,
1983). However, many parents decline to enter such programs or
drop out of them.

As would be expected from the foregoing, juvenile offenders do
best under institutional conditions that provide warmth, respect, attention, high standards, firmness and consistency, a degree of autonomy, (democratic) behavioral contracts, and instruction in social
skills (Rutter & Giller, 1983; Gold & Petronio, 1980). For example,
Marenko (1955) used a demanding yet supportive approach to good
effect on postrevolutionary Soviet delinquents.

Most other types of program have not produced good results. Authoritarian, militaristic, unfocused counseling, and psychoanalytic approaches, accomplish little (Rutter & Giller, 1983). Punitive approaches, though they may satisfy the understandable desire of the
public and of crime victims for vengeance, are costly and ineffective. In
fact, penal institutions often act as "crime schools," where juveniles acquire criminal skills and attitudes (Feldman & Weisfeld, 1973). Likewise, token economies, in which chits are earned for good behavior and
can be redeemed for tangible rewards, are generally unsuccessful.

One difficulty with all of these rehabilitative programs is that there
is little carryover once the youth is released to his family and neighborhood. Adolescents who are treated kindly and fairly tend to reciprocate, but if they are treated as they originally were treated, they often reciprocate and revert to form. Likewise, probationary and other
community-based programs and family counseling have shown few
positive results for juvenile offenders.

To the extent that it is effective, punishment works best if it is
prompt and certain. Surveys of U.S. citizens show that a large percentage of people are victimized by crimes in a given year—many
more than show up in police statistics of reported crimes. Thus, it is
safe to conclude that many crimes go unpunished—even homicides
(M. Wilson & Daly, 1985). There is good evidence that court appear-
ances actually perpetuate delinquent activities by lowering respect for
the police and court officials and by convincing the offender that he
was merely unlucky to have gotten caught (Rutter & Giller, 1983).

Once crime becomes prevalent, prompt and certain punishment is
very difficult. Courts are crowded, prison space is scarce, and funds
are short. The criminal justice system must concentrate on the most
serious offenses, so minor offenses multiply. Turning a blind eye to

minor offenses, however, tends to promote even major crimes. Recently, New York has experienced a fall in major offenses following a crack-down on minor crimes. In keeping with the principle that misdeeds should carry consequences, Rutter and Giller (1983) concluded that most minor offenders ought to be admonished firmly and unequivocally by family and school. They felt that intervention by the courts is not called for, since juvenile offenses are widespread but usually petty and tend to drop out with maturity.

Father Absence

Once again, we return to the issue of maintaining the biological family. In this section, some additional problems will be mentioned that are associated with father absence.

Because fatherhood is universal, disruption of the father-child relationship can be expected to be problematic (Mackey, 1996). In addition to their economic contributions, fathers provide emotional warmth. Closeness to the father tends to affect psychological well-being even for adult sons and daughters (Amato, 1994). Cross-culturally, men's parental investment is somewhat different from and complementary to that offered by mothers. Fathers often tend to an older child when the mother has a nursling, and they spend more time with sons than daughters, whereas the reverse is true for mothers (Mackey, 1996).

Biller's (1981) review of research on father absence can be summarized as follows. Most effects are greatest if the father leaves before the child is about 5. This is true of cognitive as well as emotional effects. Father absence is especially bad for young boys who have little contact with same-sex adult models (Lamb, 1981). Biller (1981) recommended hiring more male teachers in the lower grades.

Father-absent boys and girls show poorer school performance and inferior math, spatial, and motor skills. Young adults raised by single parents tend to have less academic and economic success, even when family economic background is controlled for (Dubowitz et al., 1988). Adolescents from divorced families were less likely to finish high school than those from intact families (Astone & McLanahan, 1991). Thus, fathers typically provide more than just money; they teach, if only by example. But father absence usually does result in fewer economic resources, which often mean a worse school for the child.

Father-absent children also do worse in peer relations (Lamb, 1981). Warm, involved fathers tend to have masculine sons and feminine daughters (M. M. Johnson, 1963). Whatever the liabilities of being strongly sex differentiated may be, these individuals tend to have high mate value (see Chapter 13); sex differences provide much of the glue that keeps couples together (*vive la différence!*). Raising children with high mate value is perhaps the ultimate goal of parental behavior.

Father absence is associated with various behavioral problems. Father-absent boys and girls are prone to anxiety, illness (Kulka & Weingarten, 1979), dependency, impulsivity, aggressiveness, depression, suicide, running away, and drug abuse (Adams & Gullotta, 1989; Santrock, 1996). Whether their fathers are absent because of divorce or death, their own marriages are at risk for being unstable.

The greater aggressiveness of father-absent males may reflect an adaptive strategy—whether learned or evolved—for promiscuity and heightened mate competition where marriages are unstable (Draper & Belsky, 1990). Cross-cultural research has revealed that where fathers are away from the family for long periods, boys tend to develop macho behavior, including promiscuity and criminality (Biller, 1981; Katz & Konner, 1981; Bacon et al., 1963; Bereczkei & Csanaky, 1996a). Aggressiveness and promiscuity might be adaptive where marriages either are unstable or are interrupted by the father's absence. Under such conditions, men might benefit from being aggressive so as to intimidate rivals and offer protection to women, as well as to commit property crimes in order to trade gifts for sex.

A study in southern Italy indicated that boys from homes with marital conflict and emotional distance from the father tended to reach puberty early, as well as to be aggressive (Kim et al., 1997). Early spermarche, in turn, was associated with promiscuity—earlier dating and more sexual partners—as reported by others, too. If the finding on early puberty in boys from troubled homes is corroborated, then the case for an evolved developmental strategy would be strengthened. This male strategy would complement that of females maturing early and becoming promiscuous under similar circumstances of family conflict (see Chapters 8 and 13). However, Surbey (1998b) concluded from a literature review that family conflict does not usually accelerate puberty in boys.

Effects of Divorce

In some ways, divorce is a special case of father absence, but it carries its own consequences as well. In addition to suffering from the ill effects of father absence and reduced father closeness (Amato, 1994), the child is often neglected around the time of the separation (A. K. Mitchell, 1983). The family suffers economic and psychological stress, and it frequently moves to a poorer neighborhood. This entails adjustment to a new and usually inferior school, and to new schoolmates.

Compared with younger children of divorce, adolescents report less guilt about the divorce—they understand that they are not at fault—but more anger at the parents. Thus, a divorce when the children are adolescents may not be any easier than one when the children are younger, but only different. Adolescents are also often disturbed by the custodial parent's dating and sexual behavior.

The relationship between the divorced father and child usually deteriorates severely (Aquilino, 1994). Fathers often report this to be a major privation (Mackey, 1996). In a study of 15- to 19-year-olds in Edinburgh 5 or 6 years after their parents divorced, the father's meetings with the child were often awkward or boring (A. K. Mitchell, 1983). Many fathers failed to take the initiative in contacting the child, resulting in the latter feeling neglected. In one study of 12- to 16-year-olds, 44 percent never saw their father at all in the year after the divorce (Furstenberg et al., 1983).

The wounds of divorce often persist indefinitely. College students continue to feel that their parents' divorce is a stigma (Parish, 1981). Kurdek et al. (1981), studying upper-middle class children between ages 8 and 17, discovered that feelings were still typically negative 6 years after the divorce. In research by Wallerstein and Kelley (1980), 37 percent of children 5 years after divorce were still experiencing severe adjustment problems, such as shame, loneliness, anger, and academic difficulties. Follow-up research (Wallerstein & Blakeslee, 1989) revealed a similar picture at the 10-year point, plus negative effects on the grown children's marriages (this is consistent with Kulka & Weingarten, 1979). Similarly, Hetherington (1972) reported that daughters of divorcees were prone to marry inadequate men. In addition, adult children of divorce experience a lower level of well-being than do other adults (Amato & Keith, 1991). Lastly, only about 10 percent of divorced couples are both in satisfactory marriages 10 years later (Wallerstein & Kelley, 1980), so their subsequent children are at risk of family difficulties, too.

It is often stated that, because family conflict is damaging to children, divorce may be preferable to staying together. Surely there are such cases, but there must also be cases in which divorce made things worse. The only objective comparison is between the developmental prospects of children from representative samples of divorced and intact families. The former do much worse on the whole. Furthermore, if the main problem for the child were family conflict, then one would expect the effects of divorce to be brief, for once the parents part, fighting subsides. But as described earlier, the wounds of divorce persist; in fact, divorce tends to be more damaging to the children than death of the father (Rathus et al., 1997). Moreover, children of divorce typically remain loyal to the original family arrangement, which belies the notion that separations come as a relief.

It is also sometimes claimed that divorce is not harmful if certain conditions are met—if there is no loss of income, if the parents remain on good terms, if they do not criticize each other in the children's hearing, and so on. Unfortunately, these conditions are very seldom met. Overwhelmingly, it is best to be raised by both biological parents. Consistent with this, children of divorce often continue to hope, however unrealistically, that their parents will reconcile (Kurdek et al., 1981).

Are the effects of father absence mitigated by remarriage? In one study, the risk of delinquency was lessened by the mother's remarriage when the son was still young (Daly & Wilson, 1985). However, running away and child abuse were even more likely after remarriage than with single motherhood. The risk of child homicide in the United States, United Kingdom, and Canada is 40 to 100 times higher when the biological father is absent (Daly & Wilson, 1988). In a large U.S. national sample, children living with a single mother or with a mother and a stepfather experienced more school failure and expulsion, emotional or behavioral problems, injuries, and illness than those in intact families (Dawson, 1991).

Children are especially likely to be abused violently or sexually by stepfathers and boyfriends, that is, by nonkin. The heightened risk of sexual abuse by unrelated men is consistent with the absence of mutual social contact during the first several years of the child's life. Childhood cohabitation tends to prevent the development of sexual interest later (see Chapter 1). Incidentally, early social contact does not seem to suppress sexual play, just sexual intercourse (Bevc & Silverman, 1993).

The decision to adopt another person's child does not guarantee that the relationship will thrive. As would also be expected from sociobiological principles, only about 75 percent of adoptions are successful, and in the successful cases, the parents and child tend to resemble each other physically and behaviorally (Raynor, 1980). Relations between stepparent and stepchild are often strained. A. K. Mitchell (1983) reported that the stepparent typically was viewed solely as the parent's spouse, not as a substitute parent. Most of the adolescents in this study showed no net psychological gain, and some experienced a setback, partly due to increased competition for the parent's attention. Similarly, children older than 8 had greater difficulty accepting a stepfather than did younger ones (Wallerstein & Kelley, 1980). Studying adolescents in single-mother families, intact families, and stepfamilies, Carlson and Cooper (1989) found that the stepfather-adolescent relationship exhibited the most mutual dissatisfaction of all three combinations.

In a careful study, White and Booth (1985) reported that the presence of an adolescent stepchild accelerated his leaving home and also greatly increased the risk of divorce. Most of the couples studied complained about their relationship with the child rather than with each other. As long as they remained in the home, stepchildren caused tensions for both biological parent and stepparent. The authors concluded that remarriages are at heightened risk for divorce mainly because of the adverse effect of stepchildren. In addition, adolescents have been found to have special difficulty accepting discipline from stepparents (Lutz, 1983). The mental health of young people whose custodial parent has remarried is also worse than that of children of divorce (Adams & Gullotta, 1989). The risk of drug abuse is greater, too, which is the next topic to be addressed.

Drug Abuse

Adolescents who experience problems with their parents or in any other aspect of life are liable to have recourse to drug use (Steinberg, 1996). Euphoriant drugs tend to be used by all sorts of unhappy people, such as oppressed minorities. Beyond this, little distinguishes those who use drugs except perhaps a tendency to take risks and to engage in other delinquent behaviors. These drugs provide vicarious pleasure; for example, opiates reduce pain, induce general euphoria, and elevate self-esteem. The use of euphoriant drugs is very common cross-culturally, and it occurs in the wild in various mammals (Rosenzweig et al., 1996).

Confusion abounds concerning the definition of addiction. The time-honored medical definition holds that an addictive drug produces withdrawal symptoms and tolerance effects (Mook, 1996). **Withdrawal**, or **abstinence syndrome**, means illness upon abrupt cessation after prolonged use. **Tolerance** means that progressively higher doses of the drug are needed to get the same degree of effect. Since most drugs that exhibit a withdrawal effect also show tolerance effects, the crucial factor is withdrawal. Psychological dependency, or psychological addiction, is defined as a psychological need to take a drug (Santrock, 1996). Operationally, this only means that the person takes the drug regularly. By the same reasoning, an adolescent could be said to be dependent on television or Mom's apple pie. Alcohol, barbiturates, opiates, and nicotine are addictive in the medical sense. But marijuana, amphetamines, and cocaine are not: Because they do not induce a withdrawal syndrome, they can safely be discontinued abruptly. Cocaine, in fact, produces the opposite of tolerance—sensitization, whereby progressively smaller doses produce the same effect (Rosenzweig et al., 1996). But nonaddictive drugs can still be hard to quit and very unhealthy.

Illicit drug use by U.S. adolescents and adults is a major social problem and expense. Aside from the risk of contracting AIDS and other diseases, many drug users commit crimes in order to buy drugs (Fields & Walters, 1985). In a study of male heroin addicts in several U.S. cities, subjects admitted to an average of 178 crimes per year (Hanson et al., 1985). Great numbers of underclass adolescent males are involved in the drug trade, and many of them are imprisoned for possession of even small amounts of drugs. About half of U.S. property crime is drug related, and about half of prison inmates were convicted of drug offenses. Juveniles are seldom prosecuted as adults, and hence are often hired as drug couriers or assassins. Many murders occur over suspected attempts to cheat drug gang leaders. The legitimate employment prospects are so dismal for these unskilled, undereducated youth that they are tempted by the quick and sometimes exorbitant profits of drug trafficking. However, low-level dealers make very little money.

The United States has followed a law enforcement approach for the past 80 years, has spent the most money of any nation on its "war on drugs," and yet has by far the greatest drug problem in the world. Virtually all other Western countries have treated drug use as a public health problem, and they have lower prevalence rates. The **British**

system of narcotics control, begun in the United Kingdom in the 1920s, works as follows: Opiates are given—only to certifiable addicts—under proper medical conditions, so side effects such as abscesses, overdoses, and withdrawal symptoms are minimal (Stimson & Oppenheimer, 1982). Medically prescribed opiates are relatively safe drugs, and have a long history of therapeutic use. Above all, under the British system, drugs are administered at little or no cost to the addict. This undersells the black market and greatly reduces street crime, police corruption, and the attendant costs for police, courts, and prisons. Under the British system, addicts are treated as patients rather than criminals, and most hold jobs and lead normal lives. In short, the advantages of the British system resemble those that occurred when Prohibition was repealed in the United States. It is based on the well-founded assumption that the drug trade cannot be effectively interdicted but only driven underground. Obviously, it would be preferable for everyone to be drug free, but opiate addiction seldom responds to counseling and is virtually a permanent condition, at least until middle age, when usage usually stops.

The British system is one of decriminalization—a medical rather than a legal approach. **Decriminalization** does not mean government approval of drug use; rather, it shifts resources from the pursuit and incarceration of low-level users to prevention and treatment. Individual use is tolerated. However, trafficking in dangerous drugs is prosecuted, even in tolerant countries such as the Netherlands.

The great fear about decriminalization is that it would increase drug consumption. However, advocates such as Miller (1991) assert, drug use is so high in the United States compared with other countries that the present policy cannot be working. It is possible that drug use might increase somewhat after decriminalization; alcohol consumption fell slightly after Prohibition began but then rose to levels greater than before Prohibition (R. L. Miller, 1991). However, the associated social costs of Prohibition—in terms of crime and corruption—were so enormous that the country has never considered reinstituting the experiment.

According to Miller (1991), no experiments with decriminalization have resulted in a substantial increase in drug use. Adoption of the British system early in the century resulted in a steady fall in opiate addiction in the United Kingdom, whereas contemporaneous adoption of the punitive approach by the United States was followed by a steady rise in addiction (Robertson, 1987). The Netherlands has liberal drug laws and legal marijuana coffeehouses, but marijuana use there is no higher than in other Western European countries, and it is only 9 percent higher than that in the United States (R. L. Miller, 1991). Following Dutch decriminalization of marijuana use, the prevalence of marijuana, heroin, and cocaine stabilized or decreased. Experiments with the decriminalization of marijuana in Oregon and California likewise resulted in very slight increases in consumption.

Advocates of decriminalization also assert that instituting the British policy here would undercut U.S. hypocrisy about the use of alcohol and tobacco. No thinking adolescent can fail to see the inconsistency in a parent's condemning of marijuana as a drug taken for pleasure while enjoyed an evening's cocktail. Further, there is no documented evidence of permanent damage caused by moderate marijuana use (Julien, 1992; R. L. Miller, 1991). But the damage that alcohol and tobacco cause in the form of disease, accidents, fires, assaults, homicides, and suicides dwarfs the dangers of all other drugs combined (Rosenzweig et al., 1996). Alcohol and tobacco are by far the drugs most commonly used by adolescents (Steinberg, 1996). Moreover, they are the "gateway drugs" whose usage tends to occur first, around 12 or 13 years of age (Steinberg, 1996). Introduction typically occurs in the home, under parental supervision, despite the fact that consumption by minors is illegal in the United States.

Alternative approaches to curb drug use have been tried. Moralistic campaigns have been ineffective (Steinberg, 1996), but raising the price of cigarettes and alcohol does reduce adolescents' use of them. Needle-exchange programs have reduced the rates of infectious diseases such as AIDS dramatically, and have not raised rates of drug use.

Summary

Parent-offspring conflict usually intensifies at adolescence, probably due to a declining need for parents' help and hence for appeasing them, and because of a general increase in competitiveness and the need for independence that results from reproductive maturation. In most cultures, adolescents sometimes run away from home. Proximally, conflict with parents rises with pubertal maturity, especially between sons and mothers, and then it falls as an accommodation is reached. At the end of puberty, the son usually has displaced his mother in dominance.

The ideal parent, counselor, or teacher is warm, attentive, competent, consistent, and rather demanding. In modern, middle-class settings, an inductive, democratic parental style seems beneficial as well. This parental style generally optimizes social, emotional, and cognitive development, and it minimizes anxiety. A surfeit of punishment is harmful. The word *discipline*, it is good to remember, derives from the Latin *discere*, which means "to teach or to learn." Compared with Danes, U.S. parents are relatively punitive, violent, authoritarian, and permissive toward their children but restrictive toward their adolescents. U.S. adolescents are particularly poor at child rearing. Parental style seems to affect many cognitive and emotional traits, but it has only modest consequences compared with the impact of genes and nonshared environmental factors.

Various day-care arrangements have been found to reduce the likelihood of secure attachment to the mother, and to detract from social and scholastic development. A positive relationship with the mother portends stable romantic relationships; likewise, a contentious marriage can worsen the wife's treatment of her children. Cross-cultural research suggests that involvement of the father and other kin in child care has positive effects.

Delinquency is associated with adverse child rearing and poor economic opportunities. It is combatted by prompt, certain punishment and warm, attentive, demanding, respectful treatment. Public praise and criticism to control adolescent behavior are employed less in Western societies than in traditional cultures. Delinquency in girls often takes the form of prostitution, which can be viewed as a strategic alternative to marriage or property crime.

Father absence is associated with various educational, financial, emotional, and behavioral problems. Young boys are especially vulnerable. Boys living in poor areas high in marital instability may benefit from pursuing a mating strategy of criminality and promiscuity. One possible scenario is that poverty and a history of anxious attachment tend to destabilize marriage, resulting in father absence and low sibling consanguinity. The latter factors, in turn, increase family conflict and anxious attachment. Poverty, family conflict, father absence, and anxious attachment give rise to a behavioral strategy of promiscuity and criminality. Exactly how these alternative reproductive strategies come about in boys and girls is a current focus of research by evolutionists (reviewed by F. Kim et al., 1997).

312 / *Parent-Adolescent Relations*

Parental divorce and remarriage tend to bring lasting and multi-tudinous adverse emotional and economic difficulties for the adolescent. The adolescent's relations with the father and stepfather tend to be distant and acrimonious, respectively. Sexual abuse, homicide, school difficulties, behavior problems, and poor health are more likely to befall children living with an unrelated male than those living with their biological father.

Drug abuse is an especially bad problem in the United States, which has adhered to a punitive, criminological approach to this problem. The other Western countries have adopted the British system of decriminalization to varying degrees, with far better results in terms of health and crime prevention.

15 A Model of Human Adolescence

Psychologists usually acknowledge that their field lacks an accurate, general description of normal human behavior. To develop a general model of human behavior, it would seem necessary to use the naturalistic behavior of other species as a basis for comparison. Thus, human ethology appears to provide an approach uniquely suited for describing human behavior in broad outline. Since ethology is a biological science based on evolutionary theory, adoption of this approach would also allow psychology to be integrated with the other natural sciences (Segal et al., 1997). Behavior is a property of living organisms, so the study of behavior is fundamentally a biological science. This book provides a preliminary outline of a specieswide, biological model of human adolescence. This last chapter will summarize the principles of this model.

Adopting a biological, evolutionary approach means that Darwin's powerful, parsimonious, incontrovertible theory can be used in understanding human behavior. Darwinism allows us to understand function—the "why" of behavior, not just developmental sequences and mechanisms. Since Darwinism is the integrating theory of biology, it can also be used to assimilate the vast and interlocking fields of knowledge that comprise the biological sciences, especially endocrinology and the neural sciences. The theory can integrate data from the social sciences, too, if its functional approach is borrowed. Learned behaviors tend to be adaptive also—they raise the individual's fitness in concert with evolved tendencies. If learned behaviors or cultural values detract from individual fitness, they will be weeded out along with their adherents (cf. M. Harris, 1974).

The ethological approach stresses the study of observable behavior as it occurs under naturalistic conditions. This means that motivated behaviors—the emotions—are emphasized over more variable cognitive processes and learning experiences. Therefore, developing a description of human behavior entails identifying the basic emotions, that is, those that occur in all cultures. These comprise the elements of all voluntary behavior.

Several of these emotional modalities change profoundly in adolescence: sexual feelings, pair bonding, parent-offspring bonding, and dominance (pride and shame). To a large extent, human adolescence can be understood in terms of developmental changes and sex differences in these emotions. Specifically, the striking sex differentiation of adolescence makes sense in terms of the emergence of reproductive competence. As Darwin (1871, p. 916) put it, "Certain characters are confined to one sex; and this alone renders it probable that in most cases they are connected with the act of reproduction. In innumerable instances these characters are fully developed only at maturity."

Sex Differentiation

The evolutionary approach to the study of behavior was advanced dramatically by Trivers's (1972) theory of sexual selection and parental investment. This breakthrough analysis accounted for numerous widespread sex differences in motivated behavior and anatomy. Therefore, it has great utility for explaining adolescence, the life stage when sex differences are most marked.

This theory of sex differentiation recognizes that human sex differences resemble those in many other species and therefore have roots in biology. Accordingly, sex differentiation in humans, as in other species, is governed by hormonal factors. Sex differentiation occurs mainly in utero due to the presence or absence of testosterone, and at puberty due to the actions of androgens or estrogens. The brain and behavior are affected, as well as anatomy and physiology. For example, prenatal hormones influence sexual orientation, prepubertal play activities, and maternal tendencies, and pubertal hormones enhance pair bonding, libido, aggressiveness, and maternal behavior. Masculine pubertal changes, including hirsutism, deepening of the voice, the growth spurt, and libido in girls, are activated mainly by androgens. Feminine pubertal changes, including the temporary gynecomastia (breast development) of some boys, are brought about by estrogens.

The widespread sex differences of puberty include the following. In humans and other species, competition increases at reproductive maturity. This competition mainly takes the form of dominance contests in males. Accordingly, most of the pubertal changes of males, such as increased muscle mass, height, odor, and hair, function to promote effective fighting or intimidation. Boys' dominance ranks tend to be highly stable and to influence peer relations and attractiveness to girls. Competition among female primates consists primarily of nurturing young successfully. Accordingly, most of the pubertal changes of females, such as breast development, widening of the hips, fat accumulation, and interest in child care, promote effective childbearing, nursing, and nurturance, all of which likewise have a hormonal basis.

Temperamentally as well as anatomically, pubescent males are aggressive and competitive, and females are nurturant and cooperative (i.e., inclined to provide and accept help). Females, although less formidable in a fight, provoke less aggression. They possess many endearing, pedomorphic features, whereas boys are more intimidating and less disarming. Males compete with one another by seeking to be dominant by whatever criteria operate in a given group. Females compete by striving to be attractive to males and by choosing a mate wisely. Adolescent girls avidly trade information about boys, and in some cultures, they also guard their reputations for sexual chastity against betrayals of their confidences by other girls. This may help explain the importance of trust in adolescent girls' friendships.

Same-sex competition ultimately concerns mating success. The criteria of mate choice reflect this fact. Women seek a mate whose appearance connotes genetic quality and who is dominant enough to provide her with resources (nuptial gifts) and protection. Of course, the prospective mate must also be emotionally committed to offer his help specifically to her. A male seeks a mate who will be a faithful recipient of his help and who is high in reproductive value—possessing youth and good genes. Because they seek to exploit each other for reproductive purposes, women prefer relatively masculine men and men prefer feminine women. But because provisioning, raising, and protecting children is a highly cooperative enterprise in a biparental species such as ours, kindness, industry, and health in a mate are sought as well.

As in other species, sex-differentiated traits in humans attract the opposite sex and intimidate the same sex, leading to success in same-sex competition. Socially successful individuals enjoy various long-term advantages. They practice leadership, receive favorable attention, develop self-confidence, and gain tangible benefits. Presumably,

316 / A Model of Human Adolescence

it was adaptive for prehistoric males to follow and to curry the favor of strong, vigorous, successful hunters and warriors, and for females to imitate and to heed the advice of their successful peers.

The traits that render an individual attractive show some constancy across cultures, rather than being completely relative. Some of the facial and bodily dimensions that contribute to attractiveness in each sex have been identified. Sexually attractive individuals tend to be relatively sex differentiated and thus high in reproductive value. For females, this means youth, health, genetic quality, and femininity. For males, it means muscularity, health, genetic quality, and masculinity. Feminine girls and masculine boys tend to mature early, so early maturers are relatively successful socially. Early maturity, like bodily symmetry, connotes a favorable developmental course that allows full sex differentiation and hence renders the individual sexually attractive. However, early puberty does not in itself alter social rank very much; early-developing adolescents have been attractive and popular early maturers all along. Despite the general salience of bodily traits for mate value and hence for social success, cultural values, such as Chinese adolescents' respect for intelligence, can affect the criteria for peer competition and the manifestation of dominance displays.

Other human sex differences can also be understood in adaptive terms. In polygynous mammals, the males take longer than females to mature because they need extra time to grow strong enough to compete successfully. As a result, in our mildly polygynous species, boys mature 1 or 2 years later than girls, and they wind up larger and stronger. Male mammals are less selective in choosing sex partners because they have less to lose from an unwise mating than do females, and because they can increase their fitness by fertilizing multiple females in quick succession. Females are especially selective in a species such as ours, in which nurturance is long and costly and in which males are needed to provide parental assistance. Accordingly, the sex drive of adolescent girls is more prone to be controlled by social values than is boys', and most adolescent girls are serial monogamists. Rather than issuing overt sexual invitations and thereby appearing promiscuous, women covertly and coyly select their mates. Female mammals reproduce slowly and hence benefit from a long reproductive span. Early maturity and longevity are less important for males because a dominant male may fertilize multiple females over a brief period. Men's greater muscle mass, although adaptive for dominance competition, makes them more vulnerable to early death. The sex difference in mortality is greatest between ages 16 and 28, when male reproductive competition is most intense (Buss, 1994). In addition, men's greater strength prepares them for masculine pursuits such as hunting, fighting, and fashioning heavy materials. Men's superiority at spatial tasks enhances their throwing accuracy and their ability to track game. Women's greater sensory acuity, dexterity, and recollection of object locations are apt for detecting danger, gathering food, and performing other fine-motor tasks. In addition, their long hair, soft skin, gentle voices, nonverbal communication skills, and verbal fluency attract infants.

Again, Darwin (1871, pp. 867f) observed many of these and other sex differences:

> Man on average is considerably taller, heavier, and stronger than woman, with squarer shoulders and more plainly-pronounced muscles. . . . The superciliary ridge is generally more marked in man than in woman. His body, and especially his face, is more hairy, and his voice has a different and more powerful tone. . . . Man is more courageous, pugnacious, and energetic than woman. . . . In woman the face is rounder; the jaws and the base of the skull smaller; the outlines of the body rounder, in parts more prominent; and her pelvis is broader than in man. . . . She comes to maturity at an earlier age than man. . . . Male and female children resemble each other closely, like the young of so many other animals in which the adult sexes differ widely; they likewise resemble the mature female much more closely than the mature male.

Darwin explained these sex differences in comparative terms:

> The males are almost always the wooers; and they alone are armed with special weapons for fighting with their rivals. They are generally stronger and larger than the females, and are endowed with the requisite qualities of courage and pugnacity. They are provided, either exclusively or in a much higher degree than the females, with organs for vocal or instrumental music, and with odoriferous glands (p. 915).

Sex and Pair Bonds

Practice in sex and pair-bond formation begins early in adolescence in most traditional cultures, as attested to by the early appearance of pubic hair, penile development, vaginal rugae, and breasts. The capacity for mature pair bonding emerges at puberty, in response to hormonal changes. For the first time, romantic and sexual attraction are focused on one individual of the opposite sex, whereas unfocused sex play and infatuation often occur in childhood. The pair-bonding emotion seems to be more of a prerequisite for sex for girls than for boys. The sexual initiation of a girl appears to have more of a bonding effect on both partners than does that of a boy. Oxytocin, released during female orgasm, may promote bonding to the mate. Intense pair-bond infatuation seldom lasts more than 2 years, perhaps so that effort can then shift to care of a newborn, or to another mate in cases of infertility.

Adolescents' sexual pair bonds tend at first to be rather brief. With age and experience in mate selection, these bonds become more stable, and promiscuity declines in favor of sexual exclusivity. Adolescent boys' sexual experience is associated with their attractiveness to girls, but attractiveness is not a major factor in girls' sexual involvement. Because most adolescent boys are unmarried and a few of them have many sexual partners, sexual competition among adolescent males is intense. This may help explain their frequent use of ridicule as well as aggression. Young unmarried men commit a disproportionate amount of crimes of violence. But since a few adolescent boys attract many sex partners, competition among the girls is intense, also. Both sexes use various tactics to raise their own apparent mate value and to lower their competitors' access to their mate. Both sexes try to cultivate and maintain favorable reputations as potential mates.

In most traditional cultures, little if any restriction is placed on adolescent sexual behavior, especially if nuptial gifts are inconsequential. In cultures where females marry late, postmenarcheal girls often devote 1 or 2 years to courtship and live in special houses. However, girls are usually married by the time they become fertile, so premarital pregnancy is uncommon. If an unmarried birth does occur, extended family members help to raise the child. A wife's sexual fidelity is important everywhere, and paternity certainty is related to paternal investment.

Puberty and Puberty Rites

The growth spurt is a general primate characteristic. It seems, in part, to compensate for the growth plateau of juvenile primates, which maximizes the time and energy available for play and hence for learning. Small juvenile size is adaptive in arboreal primates for locomotion through trees and in terrestrial species because adults protect the young. The intense learning of the juvenile period is mediated by the buildup of synaptic connections in a brain that matures early relative to other bodily organs. The human female's growth spurt is especially pronounced, probably as an adaptation to large neonatal size, and perhaps also to permit intense and prolonged lactation.

Human children mature slowly because our technology and social adaptations are complex and take time to master. The long maturation of human children requires them to be cared for by both parents; older siblings and other kin also typically provide assistance. In most traditional cultures, adolescents perform child care and other useful labor for the family, in accordance with their developing strength, intelligence, and skill. This extensive child care proffered by family members prolonged the hominid life span and reduced interbirth intervals. Lactation itself lasts about 3 years in traditional cultures, and it provides innumerable health benefits to both mother and baby. The hormonal changes of parturition and breast-feeding may promote mutual mother-infant bonding.

Analogous to the growth spurt, a sociocultural growth spurt of concentrated learning prepares adolescents for adult responsibilities. In this and other respects, puberty rites provide a cultural analogue to pubertal maturation. They communicate adult status, enhance the acquisition of adult sex-role skills, confirm allegiance to the tribe, and play a role in sexual selection. Harsh ordeals at puberty rites are common for boys and exclude unmarriageable individuals from the breeding pool. Sex segregation is pronounced at adolescence in primates (and at puberty rites), apparently to aid in acquiring sex roles. This "gang stage" is universal. Conformity and incidental memory are high at this stage, too, perhaps to enhance the assimilation of skills. As reproductive maturity is attained, reasoning powers, gross brain myelination, and body size also reach their peak, to facilitate independence from parents and the transition to parenthood.

The timing of puberty rites confirms their relevance to sexual maturation. They occur around the onset of fertility in both sexes, at about age 14 in traditional cultures. Because girls' bodies must be fully grown before they can reproduce, girls attain fertility late in pubescence. Puberty rites usually occur at menarche for girls, as fertility approaches, so girls become marriageable at the peak of their reproductive value, when their mate value is highest. Puberty rites often occur collectively for boys; their coincidence with the onset of fertil-

ity is less important, since boys typically require additional years before they secure the strength, skills, and wealth to marry. Since fertility onset is an early pubertal event for boys, allowing them to gain
premarital fertilizations before they are fully grown, pubescence follows puberty rites in boys. In general, men marry when they can afford to, so in complex economies that require extensive training (or
during hard times), men tend to marry and to achieve adult status
rather late. Unmarried postadolescent youths serve as warriors in
many cultures, including modern societies.

Puberty can be delayed by various stressors, including exercise, numerous siblings, anxiety, and poor diet. However, blindness, deafness,
and mild stress can accelerate maturation. Under adverse conditions,
early maturation may be advantageous in ensuring that some reproduction occurs. Thus, in humans, family conflict may speed menarche, perhaps by acting as an early stressor. The absence of the father
and the presence of suitable mates also speed the maturation of
daughters, as occurs in other mammals. Under conditions that foster
unstable marriages, girls may maximize their reproductive success by
reaching puberty early and commencing to reproduce even without
marrying. Under the same circumstances, boys may pursue the "cad"
strategy of promiscuity and machismo, instead of investing as "dads"
in permanent pair bonds. High testosterone level may play a role in
mediating the cad strategy (Archer, 1998).

Recognition of the importance of olfactory communication in
mammals has led to recent discoveries about the role of pheromones
in human reproduction. Social contact with potential mates can induce ovulation in women through a pheromonal effect of men's apocrine sweat. Similarly, vaginal copulines produced around ovulation
raise men's testosterone levels. Body odors may also affect mate
choice, promoting moderate homogamy, which may preserve locally
adaptive genetic combinations and maximize resistance to pathogens.

Marriage and Divorce

Marriage, or human pair bonding, evolved to provide biparental care
and to institutionalize food exchange between the male hunter and
the female gatherer. The criteria of mate choice reflect this heritage
and continue to operate once marriage has taken place. In all cultures,
sex-role division of labor occurs, so that the sexes complement each
other and are interdependent. The father's direct contact with his

children, though never as extensive as the mother's, is correlated with the amount of work done by the mother, the father's proximity to the settlement, and monogamy. Fathers tend to spend more time with juvenile sons than with other age-sex categories, and to provide economic support and protection to the family.

A husband who is low in dominance (e.g., younger, lower-ranked, or less decisive than his wife) tends to dissatisfy his spouse; dominance may connote prowess as a provider and protector. In men, dominance is associated with high testosterone levels. However, men with low testosterone levels tend to earn more money and to have more stable marriages than those with high levels (Dabbs, 1992). High testosterone levels may increase impulsiveness and aggressiveness, which may hamper marital and workplace relations.

The appeal to men of signs of high reproductive value in a woman reflects the prehistoric importance of a lengthy and successful childbearing span. A wife's infidelity, which threatens his reproductive gains from paternal investment, detracts from the husband's happiness and, if suspected, often precipitates spousal abuse. Infidelity occurs at a fairly substantial rate in humans, reflecting the fact that a wife may be tempted by another man's genetic quality or resources. The existence of various adaptations in men (e.g., mate guarding, increased sperm production after mate absence, spermicidal seminal fluid, and kamikaze sperm) and in women (e.g., greater sperm retention and midcycle sex in extrapair copulations) confirms that wives' infidelity was a fact of prehistoric life.

The stability of marriage varies systematically with certain factors. Marriage tends to be unstable if there is a shortage of marriageable men, which generally means a dearth of economic opportunities for them. A shortage of women, by contrast, raises the marriage rate for women. Divorce is less likely the more children that there are in the family, just as ring doves seek a new mate if they have been infertile with their first mate. The death of a child can weaken a marriage. Cross-culturally, women's economic independence from the husband, as occurs in matrilineal societies and where spouses' labor is not interdependent, destabilizes marriage. Female inhibition in mixed-sex competition may have evolved to reduce spousal rivalry or as a consequence of the female preference for dominant mates.

Divorce carries harmful and enduring psychological consequences for children of any age, and adolescents often react to their parents' divorces with anger. Divorce removes one of the biological parents from the home and often substitutes an unrelated male, a situation that raises the risk of sexual and other abuse, another divorce, and other difficulties. Father absence is associated with various cognitive, social, health, and emotional problems, not just reduced economic resources. In traditional cultures, even in the event of divorce, adolescents are surrounded by biological kin rather than with same-age, unrelated peers. In the West, children likewise do best if they have both biological parents and additional kin caretakers.

Parent-Adolescent Relations

At adolescence, emotional distance from parents increases, perhaps to propel the adolescent toward final independence and into the company of potential mates. In effect, the adolescent's bond to the parents weakens in preparation for bonding to a mate and children. Parent-adolescent conflict rises along with the growth spurt and so has a hormonal basis. Because males tend to dominate females in ascribed status everywhere, there is typically a reversal of dominance as adolescent sons overtake their mothers. This also occurs in other primates at puberty. Because age takes precedence over youth, however, fathers remain dominant over their adolescent children, and mothers remain dominant over their daughters.

Puberty rites, which are typically conducted by an elder but not the parent, may facilitate parent-adolescent distancing. The same-sex parent continues, however, to provide most of the training in subsistence activities in most cultures, and is the main socializing agent overall. Both sexes are drawn to same-sex elders everywhere. Being about to enter reproductive life, adolescents may be especially demanding and selfish, as contrasted with "kindly" grandparents who will have no additional children and therefore devote themselves to their kin. For their part, parents may be less inclined to care for their adolescent children, who, as they become more independent, appear less endearing and more mature, especially boys. The weary parents may turn their attention to younger children or, if they have none, to each other. Marital satisfaction reaches its low point when the children are adolescents. In the West, when the children finally leave home, marital satisfaction tends to rise.

Research on parental style reveals that rewarding, attentive parents tend to have competent, healthy children and adolescents, partly because anxiety disrupts learning and self-confidence. A secure bond with the mother, fostered by warmth and responsiveness, heralds a favorable developmental trajectory. Ideal parents also provide appropriate but challenging and interesting tasks, offer clear explanations, and act as constructive models. Their policies are consistent, and their treatment of the adolescent is respectful. They instill general principles of conduct, rather than trying to enforce a set of narrow rules. These principles also seem to hold for schools and corrective institutions for juveniles. Nevertheless, parental style is a comparatively minor influence on development, and it is itself quite heritable. Genetic differences and nonshared environmental factors are more important than environmental factors shared by siblings.

Conclusion

Certainly, human beings are not merely monolithic representatives of our species. We exhibit great cultural and individual variation; that is, we adapt readily to our surroundings because of our inherent behavioral flexibility. Nonetheless, general biological principles of behavior pertain to our species as well as to others, and they explain a great many research findings, including cultural, individual, and gender differences. For instance, the individual's extent of sex differentiation predicts a variety of cognitive and social traits, such as spatial ability, mate value, and peer success. Another example is offered by the finding that economic stratification is associated with intense mate competition among young males and with polygyny. An evolutionary approach appears to have great heuristic value for all who are interested in organizing what we know of human adolescence, and, indeed, of human behavior in general, organizing our knowledge in comparative, functional terms. "There is no fundamental difference between man and the higher mammals in their mental faculties" (Darwin, 1871, p. 446).

Human adolescence is a developmental crossroads—the juncture of generations. Our ability as a world society to ease this metamorphosis from child to parent in a way that promotes the general welfare affects each new generation and reverberates indefinitely into the future. To understand and assist adolescents, we must view them as they are—that is, as cross-cultural, cross-species, and hormonal research reveals them to be. We must organize and extend these data on adolescence by functional analysis in the great Darwinian tradition.

References

Abelson, H., et al. (1970). National survey of public attitudes toward and experience with erotic materials. In *Technical Reports of the Commission on Obscenity and Pornography*, vol. 6. Washington, DC: U.S. Government Printing Office.

Adams, G. R. (1977). Physical attractiveness research: Toward a developmental social psychology of beauty. *Human Development, 28,* 217–239.

Adams, G. R., & Gullotta, T. (1989). *Adolescent Life Experiences.* Pacific Grove, CA: Brooks/Cole.

Adams, G. R., & Read, D. (1983). Personality and social influence styles of attractive and unattractive college women. *Journal of Psychology, 114,* 151–157.

Ahmad, Y., & Smith, P. K. (1994). Bullying in schools and the issue of sex differences. In J. Archer (ed.), *Male Violence.* London: Routledge.

Ainsworth, M.D.S. (1979). Attachment as related to mother-infant interaction. *Advances in the Study of Behavior, 9,* 2–51.

Alexander, R. D., & Noonan, K. M. (1979). Concealment of ovulation, parental care, and human social evolution. In N. Chagnon & W. Irons (eds.), *Evolutionary Biology and Human Social Behavior: An Anthropological Perspective.* North Scituate, MA: Duxbury Press.

Algozzine, O. (1977). Perceived attractiveness and classroom interactions. *Journal of Experimental Education, 46,* 63–66.

Allen, C. D., & Eicher, J. B. (1973). Adolescent girls' acceptance and rejection based on appearance. *Adolescence, 6,* 125–138.

Alley, T. R. (1983). Growth produced changes in body shape and size as determinants of perceived age and caregiving. *Child Development, 54,* 251–248.

Altmann, J. (1986). Adolescent pregnancies in non-human primates: An ecological and developmental perspective. In J. B. Lancaster & B. A. Hamburg (eds.), *School-Age Pregnancy and Parenthood: Biosocial Dimensions.* New York: Aldine de Gruyter.

Amato, P. R. (1993). Children's adjustment to divorce: Theories, hypotheses, and empirical support. *Journal of Marriage & the Family, 55,* 23–38.

_____. (1994). Father-child relations, mother-child relations, and offspring psychological well-being in early adulthood. *Journal of Marriage & the Family, 56,* 1031–1046.

Amato, P. R., & Keith, B. (1991). Parental divorce and adult well-being: A meta-analysis. *Journal of Marriage & the Family, 53,* 43–58.

Amato, P. R., & Ochiltree, G. (1986). Family resources and the development of child competence. *Journal of Marriage & the Family, 48,* 47–56.

Amato, P. R., & Rogers, S. J. (1997). A longitudinal study of marital problems and subsequent divorce. *Journal of Marriage & the Family, 59,* 612–624.

Anastasi, A. (1966). Heredity, environment, and the question, "How?" *Psychological Review, 65,* 197–208.

Anderson, K. L. (1997). Gender, status, and domestic violence: An integration of feminist and family violence approaches. *Journal of Marriage & the Family, 59,* 655–669.

Andersson, M. (1994). *Sexual Selection.* Princeton: Princeton University Press.

Andersson, T., & Magnusson, D. (1990). Biological maturation in adolescence and the development of drinking habits and alcohol abuse among young males: A prospective longitudinal study. *Journal of Youth & Adolescence, 19,* 33–42.

Apte, M. L. (1985). *Humor and Laughter: An Anthropological Approach.* Ithaca: Cornell University Press.

Aquilino, W. S. (1994). Impact of childhood family disruption on young adults' relationships with parents. *Journal of Marriage & the Family, 56,* 295–313.

Arafat, I. S., & Cotton, W. L. (1974). Masturbation practices of males and females. *Journal of Sex Research, 10,* 293–307.

Archer, J. (1998). Problems with the concept of dominance and lack of empirical support for a testosterone-dominance link. *Behavioral & Brain Sciences, 21,* 363.

Argyle, M., & Henderson, M. (1985). *The Anatomy of Relationships.* Harmondsworth, England: Penguin.

Aries, P. (1982). Verbal and nonverbal behavior in single-sex and mixed-sex groups: Are traditional sex roles changing? *Psychological Reports, 51,* 117–134.

Aro, H., & Taipale, V. (1987). The impact of timing of puberty on psychosomatic symptoms among fourteen- to sixteen-year-old Finnish girls. *Child Development, 58,* 261–268.

Astone, N. M., & McLanahan, S. S. (1991). Family structure, parental practices, and high school completion. *American Sociological Review, 56,* 309–320.

Åstrand, P. O. (1985). Sexual dimorphism in exercise and sport. In J. Ghesquiere, R. D. Martin, & R. Newcombe (eds.), *Human Sexual Dimorphism.* London: Taylor & Francis.

Atkinson, J. W. (1958). *Motives in Fantasy, Action, and Society.* New York: Van Nostrand Reinhold.

Austin, C. R., & Short, R. V. (1972). *Reproduction in Mammals.* 5 vols. London: Cambridge University Press.

Babchuk, W. A., Hames, R. B., & Thompson, R. A. (1985). Sex differences in the recognition of infant facial espressions of emotion: The primary caretaker hypothesis. *Ethology & Sociobiology, 6,* 89–101.

Bacon, M., Child, I. L., & Barry, H. (1963). A cross-cultural study of correlates of crime. *Journal of Abnormal Psychology, 66,* 291–300.

Bailey, J. M. (1996). Gender identity. In R. C. Savin-Williams & K. M. Cohen (eds.), *The Lives of Lesbians, Gays, and Bisexuals: Children to Adults.* New York: Harcourt Brace.

Baker, M. A. (1987). Sensory functioning. In M. A. Baker (ed.), *Sex Differences in Human Performance.* New York: John Wiley.

Baker, R. R., & Bellis, M. A. (1995). *Human Sperm Competition: Copulation, Masturbation and Infidelity.* London: Chapman & Hall.

Baldwin, J. D. (1969). The ontogeny of social behaviour of squirrel monkeys (*Saimiri sciureus*) in a seminatural environment. *Folia Primatologica, 11,* 35–79.

Baldwin, J. D., & Baldwin, J. I. (1976). Exploration and social play in squirrel monkeys. In J. S. Bruner, A. Jolly, & K. Sylva (eds.), *Play—Its Role in Development and Evolution.* New York: Basic Books.

Bancroft, J. (1990). The impact of sociocultural influences on adolescent sexual development: Further considerations. In J. Bancroft and J. M. Reinisch (eds.), *Adolescence and Puberty.* New York: Oxford University Press.

Bandura, A. (1960). *Relationship of Family Patterns to Child Behavior Disorders: A Progress Report.* Stanford: Standord University Press.

Bandura, A., Underwood, B., & Fromson, M. E. (1975). Disinhibition of aggression through diffusion of responsibility and dehumanization of victims. *Journal of Research on Personality, 9,* 253–269.

Barber, B. K., Chadwick, B. A., & Oerter, R. (1992). Parental behaviors and adolescent self-esteem in the United States and Germany. *Journal of Marriage & the Family, 54,* 128–141.

Barber, N. (1995). The evolutionary psychology of physical attractiveness: Sexual selection and human morphology. *Ethology & Sociobiology, 16,* 395–424.

Barchas, P. R., & Barchas, J. D. (1975). Physiological sociology: Endocrine correlates of status behaviors. In D. A. Hamburg & K. Brodie (eds.), *New Psychiatric Frontiers.* New York: Basic Books.

Barkow, J. H. (1975). Social prestige and culture: A biosocial interpretation. *Current Anthropology, 16,* 553–572.

———. (1984). The distance between genes and culture. *Journal of Anthropological Research, 40,* 367–379.

———. (1989). *Darwin, Sex and Status: Biological Approaches to Mind and Culture.* Toronto: University of Toronto Press.

Barkow, J. H., Cosmides, L., & Tooby, J. (1994). *The Adapted Mind: Evolutionary Psychology and the Generation of Culture.* New York: Oxford University Press.

Barlow, G. W. (1991). Nature-nurture and the debates surrounding ethology and sociobiology. *American Zoologist, 31,* 286–296.

Barnard, C. J. (1989). Sex, wealth, and productivity: The neo-Darwinian way. *Behavioral & Brain Sciences, 12,* 14–15.

Barnes, G. M., Farrell, M. P., & Cairns, A. (1986). Parent socialization factors and adolescent drinking habits. *Journal of Marriage & the Family, 48,* 27–36.

Barnlund, D. C. (1962). Consistency of emergent leadership in groups with changing tasks and members. *Speech Monographs, 29,* 45–52.

Barry, H., III, Bacon, M. K., & Child, I. L. (1967). Definitions, ratings, and bibliographic sources of child-training practices of 110 cultures. In C. S. Ford (ed.), *Cross-Cultural Approaches.* New Haven: Yale University Press.

Bartoshuk, L. M., & Beauchamp, G. K. (1994). Chemical senses. *Annual Review of Psychology, 45,* 419–449.

Bateman, A. J. (1948). Intra-sexual selection in *Drosophila. Heredity, 2,* 349–368.

Baumrind, D. (1971). Current patterns of parental authority. *Developmental Psychology, 4,* 1–103.

Bean, J. W. (1983). Cross-cultural variation in maturation rates in relation to marriage system. M.A. thesis, University of Chicago.

Becker, J. S., Breedlove, S. M., & Crews, D. (1992). *Behavioral Endocrinology.* Cambridge, Mass.: MIT Press.

Belsky, J. (1984). The determinants of parenting: A process model. *Child Development, 55,* 83–94.

_____. (1990). Parental and nonparental child care and children's socioemotional development: A decade in review. *Journal of Marriage & the Family, 52,* 885–903.

Belsky, J., & Eggebeen, D. (1991). Maternal employment and young children's socioemotional development. *Journal of Marriage & the Family, 53,* 1083–1098.

Belsky, J., Steinberg, L., & Draper, P. (1991). Childhood experience, interpersonal development, and reproductive strategy: An evolutionary theory of socialization. *Child Development, 62,* 647–670.

Benedict, R. (1934). *Patterns of Culture.* New York: Mentor.

_____. (1938). Continuities and discontinuities in cultural conditioning. *Psychiatry, 1,* 161–167.

Bereczkei, T., & Csanaky, A. (1996a). Evolutionary pathway of child development: Lifestyles of adolescents and adults from father-absent families. *Human Nature, 7,* 257–280.

_____. (1996b). Mate choice, marital success, and reproduction in a modern society. *Ethology & Sociobiology, 17,* 17–35.

Berk, B. (1977). Face saving at a singles' dance. *Social Problems, 24,* 530–544.

Berkowitz, L., & Frodi, A. (1979). Reactions to a child's mistakes as affected by his/her looks or speech. *Social Psychology Quarterly, 42,* 420–425.

Berman, P. W. (1980). Are women more responsive than men to the young? A review of developmental and situational variables. *Psychological Bulletin, 88,* 668–695.

Berndt, R. M. (1972). The Walmadjeri and Gugadja. In M. G. Bicchieri (ed.), *Hunters and Gatherers Today.* New York: Holt, Rinehart & Winston.

Berndt, T. (1979). Developmental changes in conformity to peers and parents. *Developmental Psychology, 15,* 608–616.

_____. (1981). Relations between social cognition, nonsocial cognition, and social behavior: The case of friendship. In J. Flavell & L. Ross (eds.), *Social Cognitive Development: Frontiers and Possible Futures.* Cambridge: Cambridge University Press.

_____. (1982). The features and effects of friendships in early adolescence. *Child Development, 53,* 1447–1460.

Bernstein, I. S., Bruce, K., & Williams, L. (1982). The influence of male presence or absence on the reproductive cycle of Celebes black ape females (*Macaca nigra*). *Primates, 23,* 587–591.

Bernstein, I. S., Gordon, T. P., & Rose, R. M. (1983). The interaction of hormones, behavior, and social context in nonhuman primates. In B. B. Svare (ed.), *Hormones and Aggressive Behavior.* New York: Plenum.

Berry, D. S. (1995). Beyond beauty and after affect: An event perception approach to perceiving faces. In R. A. Eder (ed.), *Developmental Perspectives on Craniofacial Problems: Insights into the Function of Appearance in Development.* New York: Springer-Verlag.

Berry, D. S., & McArthur, L. Z. (1986). Perceiving character in faces: The impact of age-related cranio-facial changes on social perception. *Psychological Bulletin, 100,* 3–18.

Berscheid, E., & Walster, E. (1974). Physical attractiveness. In L. Berkowitz (ed.), *Advances in Experimental Social Psychology,* Vol. 7. New York: Academic.

Betzig, L. (1986). *Despotism and Differential Reproduction: A Darwinian View of History.* Hawthorne, NY: Aldine de Gruyter.

Bevc, I., & Silverman, I. (1993). Early proximity and intimacy between siblings and incestuous behavior. *Ethology & Sociobiology, 14,* 171–181.

Bicchieri, M. G. (1972). *Hunters and Gatherers Today.* New York: Holt, Rinehart & Winston.

Bielicki, T., Szczotke, H., & Charzewski, J. (1981). The influence of three hormone secretory patterns in gonadal dysgenesis. *Journal of Clinical Endocrinology & Metabolism, 37,* 521–524.

Biller, H. (1981). Father absence, divorce, and personality development. In M. Lamb (ed.), *The Role of the Father in Child Development.* New York: Wiley.

Blurton Jones, N. G. (1967). An ethological study of some aspects of social behavior of children in nursery school. In D. Morris (ed.), *Primate Ethology.* London: Weidenfeld & Nicolson.

_____. (1972). Categories of child-child interaction. In N. Blurton Jones (ed.), *Ethological Studies of Child Behaviour.* New York: Cambridge University Press.

Blurton Jones, N. G., Hawkes, K., & Draper, P. (1993). Differences between Hadza and !Kung children's work: Original affluence or practical reason? In E. S. Burch (ed.), *Key Issues in Hunter-Gatherer Research.* Oxford: Berg.

Blurton Jones, N. G., Hawkes, K., & O'Connell, J. F. (1997). Why do Hadza children forage? In N. L. Segal, G. E. Weisfeld, & C. C. Weisfeld (eds.), *Uniting Psychology and Biology: Integrative Perspectives on Human Development.* Washington, DC: American Psychological Association.

Boardway, R. H., & Weisfeld. G. (1994). Social dominance among English adolescents. Poster presented at the International Society for Human Ethology congress, Toronto, August.

Bogin, B. (1988). *Patterns of Human Growth.* Cambridge: Cambridge University Press.

_____. (1994). Adolescence in evolutionary perspective. *Acta Paediatrica (Suppl.), 406,* 29–35.

Booth, A., & Johnson, D. R. (1994). Declining health and marital quality. *Journal of Marriage & the Family, 56,* 218–223.

Borgerhoff Mulder, M. (1989). Early maturing Kipsigis women have higher reproductive success than late maturing women and cost more to marry. *Behavioral Ecology & Sociobiology, 24,* 145–153.

Borgia, G. (1980). Human aggression as a biological adaptation. In J. S. Lockard (ed.), *Evolution of Human Social Behavior.* New York: Elsevier.

Boulton, M. J. (1992). Rough physical play in adolescents: Does it serve a dominance function? *Early Education and Development, 3,* 312–333.

_____. (1994). The relationship between playful and aggressive fighting in children, adolescents, and adults. In J. Archer (ed.), *Male Violence.* London: Routledge.

Bower, G. H. (1994). Some relations between emotions and memory. In R. J. Davidson (eds.), *The Nature of Emotion: Fundamental Questions.* New York: Oxford University Press.

Bowlby, J. (1969). *Attachment and Loss,* Vol. 1, *Attachment.* New York: Basic Books.

_____. (1973). *Attachment and Loss,* Vol. 2, *Separation, Anxiety, and Anger.* London: Hogarth.

Bradley, R. H., Bettye, M. C., & Rock, S. L. (1988). Home environment and school performance: A ten-year follow-up and examination of three models of environmental action. *Child Development, 59,* 852–867.

Braithwaite, J. (1989). *Crime, Shame, and Reintegration.* Cambridge: Cambridge University Press.

Bronfenbrenner, U., Moen, P., & Garbarino, J. (1984). Child, family, and community. In R. D. Parke (ed.), *Review of Child Development Research,* Vol. 7, *The Family.* Chicago: University of Chicago Press.

Bronson, W. C. (1966). Central orientations: A study of behaviour organization from childhood to adolescence. *Child Development, 37,* 125–155.

Brooks-Gunn, J., & Ruble, D. N. (1983). The experience of menarche from a developmental perspective. In J. Brooks-Gunn & A. C. Petersen (eds.), *Girls at Puberty: Biological and Psychosocial Perspectives.* New York: Plenum.

Broude, G. J., & Greene, S. J. (1976). Cross-cultural codes on twenty sexual attitudes and practices. *Ethnology, 15,* 409–429.

Brown, B. (1990). Peer groups. In S. Feldman & G. Elliott (eds.), *At the Threshold: The Developing Adolescent.* Cambridge, MA: Harvard University Press.

Brown, D. E. (1991). *Human Universals.* New York: McGraw-Hill.

Brown, I. C. (1963). *Understanding Other Cultures.* Englewood Cliffs, NJ: Prentice-Hall.

Brown, J. K. (1963). A cross-cultural study of female initiation rites. *American Anthropologist, 65,* 837–853.

_____. (1969). Adolescent initiation rites among preliterate peoples. In R. E. Grinder (ed.), *Studies in Adolescence.* New York: Macmillan.

_____. (1979). A note on the division of labor by sex. In S. W. Tiffany (ed.), *Women and Society: An Anthropological Reader.* Montreal: Eden Press Women's Publications.

Brown, P. (1983). The Swedish approach to sex education and adolescent pregnancy: Some impressions. *Family Planning Perspectives, 15,* 90–95.

Brown, P. J., & Konner, M. (1987). An anthropological perspective on obesity. *Annals of the New York Academy of Sciences, 499,* 29–46.

Bruch, H. (1943). Psychiatric aspects of obesity in children. *American Journal of Psychiatry, 99,* 752–757.

Buck, R. (1988). *Human Motivation and Emotion.* New York: Wiley.

Buhrmester, D., & Furman, W. (1987). The development of companionship and intimacy. *Child Development, 58,* 1101–1113.

Burke, R. S, & Grinder, R. E. (1966). Personality-oriented themes and listening patterns in teen-age music and their relation to certain academic and peer variables. *School Review, 74,* 196–211.

Burns, A., & Scott, C. (1994). *Mother-Headed Families and Why They Have Increased.* Hillsdale, NJ: Lawrence Erlbaum.

Burstein, E., Crandall, C., & Kitayama, S. (1994). Some neo-Darwinian decision rules for altruism: Weighing cues for inclusive fitness as a function of the biological importance of the decision. *Journal of Personality & Social Psychology, 67,* 773–789.

Buss, D. M. (1987). Sex differences in human mate selection criteria: An evolutionary perspective. In C. Crawford, D. Krebs, & M. Smith (eds.), *Sociobiology and Psychology: Ideas, Issues, and Applications.* Hillsdale, NJ: Erlbaum.

_____. (1988a). The evolution of human intrasexual competition. *Journal of Personality & Social Psychology, 53,* 1214–1221.

_____. (1988b). From vigilance to violence: Mate guarding tactics. *Ethology & Sociobiology, 9,* 616–628.

_____. (1989). Sex differences in human mate preferences: Evolutionary hypotheses tested in 37 cultures. *Behavioral & Brain Sciences, 12,* 1–49.

_____. (1994). *The Evolution of Desire.* New York: Basic.

Buss, D. M., & Schmitt, D. P. (1993). Sexual strategies theory: An evolutionary perspective on human mating. *Psychological Review, 100,* 204–232.

Cairns, R. B. (1979). *Social Development: The Origins and Plasticity of Interchanges.* San Francisco: Freeman.

Cairns, R., & Cairns, B. (1986). The developmental-interactional view of social behavior: Four issues of adolescent aggression. In D. Olweus, J. Block, & M. Radke-Yarrow (eds.), *Development of Antisocial and Prosocial Behavior.* New York: Academic.

Callan, H. (1970). *Ethology and Society.* Oxford: Clarendon Press.

Campbell, A. (1995). A few good men: Evolutionary psychology and female adolescent aggression. *Ethology & Sociobiology, 16,* 99–123.

Campbell, A., & Muncer, S. (1994). Men and the meaning of violence. In J. Archer (ed.), *Male Violence.* London: Routledge.

Campbell, B. (1966). *Human Evolution: An Introduction to Man's Adaptations.* Chicago: Aldine.

Camras, L. (1977). Facial expressions used by children in a conflict situation. *Child Development, 48,* 1431–1435.

Carlson, C. I., & Cooper, C. (1989). Variations in family process in early adolescent intact, single-parent, and stepparent families. Poster presented at the biennial meeting of the International Society for the Study of Behavior and Development, Jyvaskyla, Finland, July.

Carlson, E., & Stinson, K. (1982). Motherhood, marriage timing, and marital stability: A research report. *Social Forces, 61,* 258–267.

Carns, D. (1973). Talking about sex: Notes on first coitus and the double sexual standard. *Journal of Marriage & the Family, 35,* 677–688.

Caro, T. M., & Sellen, D. W. (1990). The reproductive advantages of fat in women. *Ethology & Sociobiology, 11,* 51–66.

Cashdan, E. (1993). Attracting mates: Effects of paternal investment on mate attraction strategies. *Ethology & Sociobiology, 14,* 1–23.

Caudill, W., & Plath, D. W. (1966). Who sleeps with whom? Parent-child involvement in urban Japanese families. *Psychiatry, 29,* 344–366.

Chagnon, N. (1977). *Yanomamö: The Fierce People.* New York: Holt, Rinehart & Winston.

Chagnon, N. A. (1988). Life histories, blood revenge, and warfare in a tribal population. *Science 239,* 985–992.

_____. (1992). *Yanomamö: The Last Days of Eden.* San Diego: Harcourt Brace Jovanovich.

Chaiken, S. (1979). Communicator physical attractiveness and persuasion. *Journal of Personality & Social Psychology, 37,* 1387–1397.

Chance, M.R.A., & Jolly, C. J. (1970). *Social Groups of Monkeys, Apes, and Men.* New York: E. P. Dutton.

Chandler, J. (1977). Sex differences in the nurturant responses of adolescent children. Ph.D. dissertation, University of Denver.

Chandler, M. J. (1973). Egocentrism and antisocial behavior. *Developmental Psychology, 9,* 326–332.

Charlesworth, W. R. (1986). Darwin and developmental psychology: 100 years later. *Human Development, 29,* 1–35.

_____. (1988). Resources and resource acquisition during ontogeny. In K. B. MacDonald (ed.), *Sociobiological Perspectives on Human Development.* New York: Springer-Verlag.

_____. (1992). Darwin and developmental psychology: Past and present. *Developmental Psychology, 28,* 5–16.

Charlesworth, W. R., & Hartup, W. W. (1967). Positive social reinforcement in the nursery school peer group. *Child Development, 38,* 993–1002.

Cheney, D. L., & Seyfarth, R. M. (1990). *How Monkeys See the World: Inside the Mind of Another Species.* Chicago: University of Chicago Press.

Chess, S., Thomas, A., & Cameron, M. (1976). Sexual attitudes and behavior patterns in a middle-class adolescent population. *American Journal of Orthopsychiatry, 46,* 689–701.

Childs, B. (1965). Genetic origin of some sex differences among human beings. *Pediatrics, 35,* 798–812.

Chilman, C. (1979). *Adolescent Sexuality in a Changing Society: Social and Psychological Perspectives.* Washington, DC: U.S. Government Printing Office.

Chilman, C. S. (1986). Some psychological aspects of adolescent sexual and contraceptive behaviors in a changing American society. In J. Lancaster & B. A. Hamburg (eds.), *School-Age Pregnancy and Parenthood: Biosocial Perspectives.* New York: Aldine de Gruyter.

Chumlea, W. C. (1982). Physical growth in adolescence. In B. B. Wolman (ed.), *Handbook of Developmental Psychology*. Englewood Cliffs, NJ: Prentice-Hall.

Cicirelli, V. G. (1994). Sibling relationships in cross-cultural perspective. *Journal of Marriage & the Family, 56*, 7–20.

Clausen, J. (1975). The social meaning of differential physical and sexual maturation. In S. E. Dragastin & G. H. Elder Jr. (eds.), *Adolescence in the Life Cycle: Psychological Change and Social context*. New York: Halsted Press.

Cliquet, R. L. (1968). Social mobility and the anthropological structure of populations. *Human Biology, 40*, 17–43.

Cobb, N. J. (1995). *Adolescence: Continuity, Change, and Diversity*. Mountain View, CA: Mayfield.

Coe, C. L. (1990). Psychobiology of maternal behavior in nonhuman primates. In N. A. Krasnegor & R. S. Bridges (eds.), *Mammalian Parenting: Biochemical, Neurobiological, and Behavioral Determinants*. New York: Oxford University Press.

Coe, C. L., Hayashi, K. T., & Levine, S. (1988). Hormones and behavior at puberty: Activation or concatenation. In M. R. Gunnar & W. A. Collins (eds.), *Development During the Transition to Adolescence*. Hillsdale, NJ: Erlbaum.

Cohen, Y. (1964). *The Transition from Childhood to Adolescence*. Chicago: Aldine.

Coie, J. D., & Dodge, K. A. (1983). Continuities and changes in children's social status: A five-year longitudinal study. *Merrill-Palmer Quarterly, 29*, 261–281.

Coie, J. D., Dodge, K. A., & Coppotelli, H. (1982). Dimensions and the types of social status: A cross-age perspective. *Developmental Psychology, 18*, 557–570.

Coie, J. D., & Kupersmidt, J. B. (1983). A behavioral analysis of emerging social status in boys' groups. *Child Development, 54*, 1400–1416.

Coleman, J. C. (1974). *Relations in Adolescence*. London: Routledge & Kegan Paul.

Coleman, J. S. (1961). *The Adolescent Society*. Glencoe, IL: Free Press.

Conger, J. J., & Miller, W. C. (1966). *Personality, Social Class, and Delinquency*. New York: Wiley.

Cook, M., & McHenry, R. (1978). *Sexual Attraction*. New York: Pergamon.

Coon, C. S. (1971). *The Hunting Peoples*. Boston: Little, Brown.

Coopersmith, S. (1967). *The Antecedents of Self-Esteem*. San Francisco: Freeman.

Corrales, R. G. (1975). Power and satisfaction in early marriage. In R. E. Cromwell & D. M. Olson (eds.), *Power in Families*. New York: Wiley.

Costanzo, P. R., & Shaw, M. E. (1966). Conformity as a function of age level. *Child Development, 37*, 967–975.

Costrich, N., et al. (1975). When stereotypes hurt: Three studies of penalties for sex-role reversals. *Journal of Experimental Social Psychology, 11,* 520–530.

Cowley, J. J., & Brooksbank, B. W. L. (1991). Human exposure to putative pheromones and changes in aspects of social behavior. *Journal of Steroid Biochemistry & Molecular Biology, 39,* 647–659.

Crandall, V. J., & Rabson, A. (1960). Children's repetitive choices in an intellectual achievement situation following success and failure. *Journal of Genetic Psychology, 97,* 161–168.

Crawford, C. B. (1989). The theory of evolution: Of what value to psychology? *Journal of Comparative Psychology, 103,* 4–22.

Crawford, C. B., & Anderson, J. L. (1989). Sociobiology: An environmentalist discipline? *American Psychologist, 44,* 1449–1459.

Crawford, C. B., Salter, B. E., & Jang, K. L. (1989). Human grief: Is its intensity related to the reproductive value of the deceased? *Ethology & Sociobiology, 10,* 297–307.

Cready, D. M., Fossett, M. A., & Kiecolt, K. J. (1997). Mate availability and African American family structure in the U.S. nonmetropolitan South, 1960–1990. *Journal of Marriage & the Family, 59,* 192–203.

Cronin, C. L. (1975). Observations of young girls prominent in their play group. Manuscript, University of Chicago.

_____. (1980). Dominance relations and females. In D. R. Omark, F. F. Strayer, & D. G. Freedman (eds.), *Dominance Relations: An Ethological View of Human Conflict and Social Interaction.* New York: Garland.

Csikszentmihalyi, M., & Larson, R. (1984). *Being Adolescent.* New York: Basic Books.

Cunningham, A. S. (1995). Breastfeeding: Adaptive behavior for child health and longevity. In P. Stuart-Macadam & K. A. Dettwyler (eds.), *Breastfeeding: Biocultural Perspectives.* New York: Aldine de Gruyter.

Cunningham, M. R. (1986). Measuring the physical in physical attractiveness: Quasi-experiments on the sociobiology of female facial beauty. *Journal of Personality & Social Psychology, 50,* 925–935.

Cunningham, M. R., Barbee, A. P., & Pike, C. L. (1990). What do women want? Facialmetric assessment of multiple motives in the perception of male facial physical attractiveness. *Journal of Personality & Social Psychology, 59,* 61–72.

Curran, J. P. (1972). Differential effects of stated preferences and questionnaire rate performance on interpersonal attraction in the dating situation. *Journal of Psychology, 82,* 313–327.

Cutler, W. G., & Preti, G. (1986). Human axillary secretions influence women's menstrual cycles: The role of donor extract from men. *Hormones & Behavior, 20,* 463–473.

Cvetkovich, G., & Grote, B. (1983). Adolescent development and teenage fertility. In D. Byrne & W. A. Fisher (eds.), *Adolescents, Sex, and Contraception.* Hillsdale, NJ: Erlbaum.

Dabbs, J. M. (1992). Testosterone and occupational achievement. *Social Forces, 70,* 813–824.

Daly, M., & Wilson, M. (1983). *Sex, Evolution, and Behavior* (2nd ed.). Boston: Willard Grant.

_____. (1985). Child abuse and other risks of not living with both parents. *Ethology & Sociobiology, 6,* 197–210.

_____. (1988). *Homicide.* Hawthorne, NY: Aldine de Gruyter.

_____. (1994). Evolutionary psychology of male violence. In J. Archer (ed.), *Male Violence.* London: Routledge.

Daniel, H., & McCabe, R. (1992). Gender differences in the perception of vocal sexiness. In J.M.G. van der Dennen (ed.), *The Nature of the Sexes: The Sociobiology of Sex Differences and the "Battle of the Sexes."* Groningen, The Netherlands: Origin Press.

Darwin, C. (1871). *The Descent of Man and Selection in Relation to Sex.* New York: Modern Library.

_____. (1872/1965). *The Expression of the Emotions in Man and Animals.* Chicago: University of Chicago Press.

Davenport, W. (1977). Sex in cross-cultural perspective. In F. Beach (ed.), *Human Sexuality in Four Perspectives.* Baltimore: Johns Hopkins University Press.

Dawson, D. A. (1991). Family structure and children's health and well-being: Data from the 1988 National Health Interview Survey on child health. *Journal of Marriage & the Family, 53,* 573–584.

Deaux, K. (1976). *The Behavior of Men and Women.* Monterey, CA: Brooks/Cole.

Dettwyler, K. A. (1995a). A time to wean: The hominid blueprint for the natural age of weaning in modern human populations. In P. Stuart-Macadam & K. A. Dettwyler (eds.), *Breastfeeding: Biocultural Perspectives.* New York: Aldine de Gruyter.

_____. (1995b). Beauty and the breast: The cultural context of breastfeeding in the United States. In P. Stuart-Macadam & K. A. Dettwyler (eds.), *Breastfeeding: Biocultural Perspectives.* New York: Aldine de Gruyter.

Devereux, E. (1970). The role of peer group experience in moral development. In J. Hill (ed.), *Minnesota Symposium on Child Psychology,* Vol. 4. Minneapolis: University of Minnesota Press.

de Waal, F.B.M. (1982). *Chimpanzee Politics.* London: Jonathan Cape.

_____. (1996). Conflict as negotiation. In W. C. McGrew, L. F. Marchant, & T. Nishida (eds.), *Great Ape Societies.* New York: Cambridge University Press.

Dewan, E. M. (1967). On the possibility of a perfect rhythm method of birth control by periodic light stimulation. *American Journal of Obstetrics & Gynecology, 99,* 1016–1019.

Diamond, A. (1991). Frontal lobe involvement in cognitive changes during the first year of life. In K. R. Gibson & A. C. Petersen (eds.), *Brain Maturation and Cognitive Development.* New York: Aldine de Gruyter.

Dion, K. K., & Stein, S. (1978). Physical attractiveness and interpersonal influence. *Journal of Experimental Social Psychology, 14,* 97–108.

Divale, W. T., & Harris. M. (1976). Population, warfare, and the male supremacist complex. *American Anthropologist, 78,* 521–538.

Dobbing, J. (1974). The later development of the brain and its vulnerability. In J. A. Davis & J. Dobbing (eds.), *Scientific Foundations of Paediatrics.* Philadelphia: Saunders.

Dodge, K. A. (1983). Behavioral antecedents of peer social status. *Child Development, 54,* 1386–1399.

Dodge, K. A., Coie, J. D., & Brakke, N. P. (1982). Behavior patterns of socially rejected and neglected preadolescents: The roles of social approach and aggression. *Journal of Abnormal Child Psychology, 10,* 389–409.

Dodge, K. A., & Frame, C. L. (1982). Social cognitive biases and deficits in aggressive boys. *Child Development, 53,* 620–635.

Dong, Q., Weisfeld, G., Boardway, R. H., & Shen, J. (1996). Correlates of social status among Chinese adolescents. *Journal of Cross-Cultural Psychology, 27,* 476–493.

Dörner, G., et al. (1983). Stressful events in prenatal life and bi- and homosexual men. *Experimental & Clinical Endocrinology, 81,* 83–87.

Douvan, E. & Adelson, J. (1966). *The Adolescent Experience.* New York: Wiley.

Draper, P. (1976). Social and economic constraints on child life among the !Kung. In R. B. Lee & I. DeVore (eds.), *Kalihari Hunter-Gatherers.* Cambridge, MA: Harvard University Press.

Draper, P., & Belsky, J. (1990). Personality development in evolutionary perspective. *Journal of Personality, 58,* 141–162.

Draper, P., & Harpending, H. (1988). A sociobiological perspective on the development of human reproductive strategies. In K. MacDonald (ed.), *Sociobiological Perspectives on Human Development.* New York: Springer-Verlag.

Drever, J. (1964). *A Dictionary of Psychology.* Middlesex, England: Penguin.

Dreyer, P. H. (1982). Sexuality during adolescence. In B. Wolman (ed.), *Handbook of Developmental Psychology.* Englewood Cliffs, NJ: Prentice-Hall.

Drickamer, L. C. (1974). Sexual maturation of female house mice: Social inhibition. *Developmental Psychobiology, 7,* 257–265.

Drigotas, S., & Udry, J. (1993). Biosocial models of adolescent problem behavior: Extension to panel design. *Social Biology, 40*, 1–7.

Driver, H. E. (1969). *Indians of North America.* Chicago: University of Chicago Press.

Dubowitz, H., et al. (1988). The changing American family. *Pediatric Clinics of North America, 35*, 1291–1311.

Dunbar, R.I.M. (1991). Functional significance of social grooming in primates. *Folia Primatologica, 57*, 121–131.

Durden-Smith, J., & deSimone, D. (1983). *Sex and the Brain.* New York: Arbor House.

Dwyer, J., & Mayer, J. (1968–1969). Psychological effects of variations in physical appearance during adolescence. *Adolescence, 3*, 353–380.

Dyer, G. (1985). *War.* New York: Crown Publishers.

Eder, D. & Kinney, D. (1995). The effect of middle-school extracurricular activities on adolescents' popularity and peer status. *Youth & Society, 26*, 298–324.

Ehrhardt, A. A., & Meyer-Bahlburg, H.F.L. (1981). Effects of prenatal sex hormones on gender-related behavior. *Science, 211*, 1312–1318.

Eibl-Eibesfeldt, I. (1979). *The Biology of Peace and War: Men, Animals, and Aggression.* New York: Viking.

———. (1989). *Human Ethology.* Hawthorne, NY: Aldine de Gruyter.

Einon, D. (1994). Are men more promiscuous than women? *Ethology & Sociobiology, 15*, 131–143.

Eitzen, D. (1975). Athletics in the status system of male adolescents: A replication of Coleman's *The Adolescent Society. Adolescence, 16*, 267–276.

Ekehammer, B. (1974). Sex differences in self-reported anxiety for different situations and modes of response. *Scandinavian Journal of Psychology, 15*, 154–160.

Ekehammer, B., Magnusson, D., & Ricklander, L. (1974). An interactionist approach to the study of anxiety: An analysis of an S-R inventory applied to an adolescent sample. *Scandinavian Journal of Psychology, 15*, 4–14.

Ekman, P. (1973). *Darwin and Facial Expression.* New York: Academic Press.

Ekman, P., & Friesen, W. V. (1986). A new pan-cultural expression of emotion. *Motivation & Emotion, 10*, 159–168.

Elder, G. H., Jr. (1968). *Adolescent Socialization and Personality Development.* Chicago: Rand McNally.

Elkind, D. (1978). Understanding the young adolescent. *Adolescence, 13*, 127–134.

Ellis, B. J. (1992). The evolution of sexual attraction: Evaluative mechanisms in women. In J. H. Barkow, L. Cosmides, & J. Tooby (eds.), *The Adapted Mind: Evolutionary Psychology and the Generation of Culture.* Oxford: Oxford University Press.

_____. (1998). Psychosocial antecedents of pubertal maturation in girls: Parental psychopathology, stepfather presence, and family and marital stress. *ASCAP, 11,* 5.

Ellis, B. J., & Symons, D. (1990). Sex differences in sexual fantasy: An evolutionary psychological approach. *Journal of Sex Research, 27,* 527–556.

Ellis, H. (1936). *Studies in the Psychology of Sex* (2 vols.). New York: Random House.

Ellis, H. D. (1975). Recognizing faces. *British Journal of Psychology, 4,* 409–426.

Ellis, L. (1982). Developmental androgen fluctuations and the five dimensions of mammalian sex. *Ethology & Sociobiology, 3,* 171–197.

_____. (1986). Evidence of neuroandrogenic etiology of sex roles from a combined analysis of human, nonhuman primate, and nonprimate mammalian studies. *Personality & Individual Differences, 7,* 519–551.

_____. (1995). Dominance and reproductive success among nonhuman animals: A cross-species comparison. *Ethology & Sociobiology, 16,* 257–333.

_____. (1996a). Theories of homosexuality. In R. C. Savin-Williams & K. M. Cohen (eds.), *The Lives of Lesbians, Gays, and Bisexuals: Children to Adults.* New York: Harcourt Brace.

_____. (1996b). The role of perinatal factors in determining sexual orientation. In R. C. Savin-Williams & K. M. Cohen (eds.), *The Lives of Lesbians, Gays, and Bisexuals: Children to Adults.* New York: Harcourt Brace.

Ellis, L. (ed.). (1993). *Social Stratification and Socioeconomic Inequality,* Vol. 1. New York: Praeger.

Ellis, L., & Ames, M. A. (1987). Neurohormonal functioning and sexual orientation: A theory of homosexuality-heterosexuality. *Psychological Bulletin, 101,* 233–258.

Ellis, L., et al. (1988). Sexual orientation of human offspring may be altered by severe maternal stress during pregnancy. *Journal of Sex Research, 25,* 152–157.

Ember, C. R. (1978). Myths about hunter-gatherers. *Ethnology, 17,* 439–448.

Erikson, E. (1968). *Identity: Youth and Crisis.* New York: Norton.

Essock-Vitale, S. M., & McGuire, M. T. (1985). Women's lives viewed from an evolutionary perspective, 2: Patterns of helping. *Ethology & Sociobiology, 6,* 155–173.

Eveleth, P. B. (1986). Timing of menarche: Secular trend and population differences. In J. B. Lancaster & B. A. Hamburg (eds.), *School-Age Pregnancy and Parenthood: Biosocial Dimensions.* New York: Aldine de Gruyter.

Eveleth, P. B., & Tanner, J. M. (1976). *Worldwide Variation in Human Growth.* Cambridge: Cambridge University Press.

Eysenck, H. J., & Wilson, G. (1979). *The Psychology of Sex.* London: Dent.

Faust, M. S. (1960). Developmental maturity as a determinant of prestige in adolescent girls. *Child Development, 31,* 173–184.

Fedigan, L. M. (1992). *Primate Paradigms: Sex Roles and Social Bonds.* Chicago: University of Chicago Press.

Feingold, A. (1994). Gender differences in personality: A meta-analysis. *Psychological Bulletin, 116,* 429–456.

Feldman, R., & Weisfeld, G. (1973). An interdisciplinary study of crime. *Crime & Delinquency, 19,* 150–162.

Fernald, A. (1992). Human maternal vocalizations to infants as biologically relevant signals: An evolutionary perspective. In J. H. Barkow, L. Cosmides, & J. Tooby (eds.), *The Adapted Mind: Evolutionary Psychology and the Generation of Culture.* New York: Oxford University Press.

Fields, A., & Walters, J. M. (1985). Hustling: Supporting a heroin habit. In B. Hanson et al. (eds.), *Life with Heroin: Voices from the Inner City.* Lexington, MA: D. C. Heath.

Fischer, C. S. (1977). *Networks and Places: Social Relations in the Urban Setting.* New York: Free Press.

Fisher, H. (1992). *Anatomy of Love: The Mysteries of Mating, Marriage, and Why We Stray.* New York: Fawcett Comumbine.

Fisher, W. A. (1986). A psychological approach to human sexuality: The sexual behavior sequence. In D. Byrne & K. Kelley (eds.), *Alternative Approaches to the Study of Sexual Behavior.* Hillsdale, NJ: Erlbaum.

_____. (1989). Understanding and preventing teenage pregnancy and sexually transmitted disease/AIDS. In J. Edwards et al. (eds.), *Applying Social Influence Processes in Preventing Social Problems.* Beverly Hills, CA: Plenum.

Fleming, A. S. (1990). Hormonal and experiential correlates of maternal responsiveness. In N. A. Krasnegor & R. S. Bridges (eds.), *Mammalian Parenting: Biochemical, Neurobiological, and Behavioral Determinants.* New York: Oxford University Press.

Flinn, M. V. (1988). Parent-offspring interactions in a Caribbean village: Daughter guarding. In L. Betzig, M. Borgerhoff Mulder, & P. Turke (eds.), *Human Reproductive Behavior.* London: Cambridge University Press.

Ford, C. S., & Beach, F. A. (1951). *Patterns of Sexual Behavior.* New York: Harper & Row.

Frank, E., & Anderson, C. (1979). Sex and the happily married. *The Sciences, 19,* 10–14.

Frankenhaueser, M. (1982). Challenge-control interaction as reflected in sympathetic-adrenal and pituitary-adrenal activity: Comparison between the sexes. *Scandinavian Journal of Psychology, 23* (Suppl. 1), 158–164.

Franz, C. E., McClelland, D. C., & Weinberger, T. (1991). Childhood antecedents of conventional social accomplishment in mid-life adults: A 36-year prospective study. *Journal of Personality & Social Psychology, 60,* 586–595.

Freedman, D. G. (1967). A biological view of man's social behavior. In W. Etkin (ed.), *Social Behavior from Fish to Man.* Chicago: University of Chicago Press.

_____. (1974). *Human Infancy: An Evolutionary Perspective.* Hillsdale, NJ: Erlbaum.

_____. (1979). *Human Sociobiology: A Holistic Approach.* New York: Free Press.

Friedl, E. (1975). *Women and Men: An Anthropologist's View.* New York: Holt, Rinehart & Winston.

Friesen, D. (1968). Academic-athletic-popularity syndrome in the Canadian high school society. *Adolescence, 3,* 39–52.

Frisch, R. E. (1983a). Fatness, puberty, and fertility: The effects of nutrition and physical training on menarche and ovulation. In J. Brooks-Gunn & A. C. Petersen (eds.), *Girls at Puberty: Biological and Psychosocial Perspectives.* New York: Plenum.

_____. (1983b). Comment on Anderson. *Current Anthropology, 24,* 32.

Frodi, A., & Lamb, M. E. (1978). Sex differences in responsiveness to infants: A developmental study of psychophysiological and behavioral responses. *Child Development, 49,* 1182–1188.

Fullard, W., & Reiling, A. (1976). An investigation of Lorenz's babyness. *Child Development, 47,* 1191–1193.

Fürer-Haimendorf, C. von (1967). *Morals and Merit.* London: Weidenfeld and Nicolson.

Furlow, F. B. (1996). The smell of love. *Psychology Today,* March/April, 38–45.

Furstenberg, F. (1988). Child care after divorce and remarriage. In E. M. Hetherington & J. Arasteh (eds.), *Impact of Divorce, Single Parenting, and Stepparenting on Children.* Hillsdale, NJ: Erlbaum.

Furstenberg, F., et al. (1983). The life course of children of divorce: Marital disruption and parental contact. *American Sociological Review, 48,* 125–129.

Furstenberg, F., Jr. (1976). The social consequences of teenage parenthood. *Family Planning Perspectives, 8,* 148–164.

Furstenberg, F., Jr., et al. (1987). Race differences in the timing of adolescent intercourse. *American Sociological Review, 52,* 511–518.

Gadpaille, W. J. (1980). Biological factors in the development of human sexual identity. *Psychiatric Clinics of North America, 3,* 3–20.

Gaffney, G. R., & Berlin, F. S. (1984). Is there hypothalamic-pituitary-gonadal dysfunction in paedophilia? A pilot study. *British Journal of Psychiatry, 145,* 657–660.

Galdikas, B. (1979). Orangutan adaptation at Tanjung Puting Reserve: Mating and identity. In D. A. Hamburg & E. R. McCown (eds.), *The Great Apes.* Menlo Park, CA: Benjamin/Cummings.

Gallup, G. G., Jr. (1986). Unique features of human sexuality in the context of evolution. In D. Byrne & K. Kelley (eds.), *Alternative Approaches to the Study of Sexual Behavior.* Hillsdale, NJ: Erlbaum.

Gangestad, S. W., & Thornhill, R. (1997). The evolutionary psychology of extrapair copulation: The role of fluctuating asymmetry. *Ethology & Sociobiology, 18,* 65–88.

Ganong, W. F. (1989). *Review of Medical Physiology,* (14th ed.). East Norwalk, CT: Appleton & Lange.

_____. (1997). *Review of Medical Physiology,* (18th ed.). Stamford, CT: Appleton & Lange.

Gantman, C. A. (1978). Family interaction patterns among families with normal, disturbed, and drug-abusing adolescents. *Journal of Youth & Adolescence, 7,* 429–440.

Garbarino, J., et al. (1978). The social maps of children approaching adolescence: Studying the ecology of youth development. *Journal of Youth & Adolescence, 7,* 417–428.

Gardner, E. G., & Thompson, G. G. (1963). *Investigation and Measurement of the Social Values Governing Interpersonal Relations Among Adolescent Youth and Their Teachers.* Washington, DC: U.S. Office of Education.

Garn, S. M., Pesick, S. D., & Petzold, A. S. (1986). The biology of teenage pregnancy: The mother and the child. In J. B. Lancaster & B. A. Hamburg (eds.), *School-Age Pregnancy and Parenthood: Biosocial Dimensions.* New York: Aldine de Gruyter.

Garn, S. M., Pesick, S. D., & Pinkington, J. J. (1984). The interaction between prenatal and socioeconomic effects on growth and development in childhood. In J. Borms et al. (eds.), *Human Growth and Development.* New York: Plenum.

Gaulin, S.J.C., & FitzGerald, R. W. (1986). Sex differences in spatial ability: An evolutionary hypothesis and test. *American Naturalist, 127,* 74–88.

Gautier-Hion, A., & Gautier, J.-P. (1985). Sexual dimorphism, social units and ecology among sympatric forest guenons. In J. Ghesquiere, R. D. Martin, & F. Newcombe (eds.), *Human Sexual Dimorphism.* London: Taylor & Francis.

Gerrard, M. (1987). Sex, sex guilt, and contraceptive use revisited: The 1980's. *Journal of Personality & Social Psychology, 52,* 975–980.

Ghiglieri, M. P. (1987). Sociobiology of the great apes and the hominid ancestor. *Journal of Human Evolution, 16,* 319–357.

Ginsburg, H. J. (1980). Playground as laboratory: Naturalistic studies of appeasement, altruism, and the omega child. In D. R. Omark, F. F. Strayer, and D. G. Freedman (eds.), *Dominance Relations: An Ethological View of Human Conflict and Social Interaction.* New York: Garland.

Ginsburg, M., & Miller, S. M. (1982). Sex differences in children's risk-taking behavior. *Child Development, 53,* 426–428.

Giovannoni, J., & Billingsley, A. (1970). Child neglect among the poor: A study of parental adequacy in families of their ethnic groups. *Child Development, 49,* 196–204.

Gladue, B. A., Green, R., & Hellman, R. E. (1984). Neuroendocrine response to estrogen and sexual orientation. *Science, 225,* 1496–1499.

Goethals, G. W. (1971). Factors affecting permissive and nonpermissive rules regarding premarital sex. In J. M. Henslin (ed.), *The Sociology of Sex: A Book of Readings.* New York: Appleton-Century-Crofts.

Gold, M., & Petronio, R. (1980). Delinquent behavior in adolescence. In J. Adelson (ed.), *Handbook of Adolescent Psychology.* New York: Wiley.

Goldberg, S., Blumberg, S. L., & Kriger, A. (1982). Menarche and interest in infants: Biological and social influences. *Child Development, 53,* 1544–1550.

Goldman, W., & Lewis, P. (1977). Beautiful is good: Evidence that the physically attractive are more socially skillful. *Journal of Experimental Social Psychology, 13,* 125–130.

Goldstein, H. (1971). Factors influencing the height of seven-year-old children: Results from the National Child Development Study. *Human Biology, 43,* 92–111.

Goldstein, M. J., et al. (1971). Experience with pornography: Rapists, pedophiles, homosexuals, transsexuals, and controls. *Archives of Sexual Behavior, 1,* 15.

Goodall, J. (1986). *The Chimpanzees of Gombe: Patterns of Behavior.* Cambridge, MA: Harvard University Press.

Goode, W. J. (1993). *World Changes in Divorce Patterns.* New Haven: Yale University Press.

Goodwin, C. (1980). Restarts, pauses, and the achievement of a state of mutual gaze at turntaking. *Sociological Inquiry, 50,* 272–302.

Gottesman, I. I. (1966). Genetic variance in an adaptive personality trait. *Journal of Child Psychology & Psychiatry, 7,* 199–208.

Gouldner, A. (1960). The norm of reciprocity. *American Journal of Sociology, 25,* 161–178.

Gove, W. R., Hughes, M., & Galle, O. R. (1979). Overcrowding in the home: An empirical investigation of its possible pathological consequences. *American Sociological Review, 44,* 59–80.

Grammer, K. (1992). Intervention in conflicts among children: Contexts and consequences. In A. H. Harcourt & F. de Waal (eds.), *Cooperation in Competition.* Oxford: Oxford University Press.

_____. (1996). The human mating game: The battle of the sexes and the war of signals. Paper presented at the Human Behavior and Evolution Society convention, Evanston, IL, June.

Grammer, K., & Thornhill, R. (1994). Human (*Homo sapiens*) facial attractiveness and sexual selection: The role of symmetry and averageness. *Journal of Comparative Psychology, 108,* 233–242.

Grant, V. W. (1976). *Falling in Love.* New York: Springer.

Granzberg, G. (1972). Hopi initiation rites: A case study of the Freudian theory of culture. *Journal of Social Psychology, 87,* 189–195.

———. (1973). The psychological integration of culture: A cross-cultural study of Hopi type initiation rites. *Journal of Social Psychology, 90,* 3–7.

Gray, J. (1971). Sex differences in emotional behaviour in mammals including man: Endocrine basis. *Acta Psychologica, 35,* 29–46.

Gray, J. A. (1987). *The Psychology of Fear and Stress.* Cambridge: Cambridge University Press.

Greenberger, E., & Steinberg, L. (1986). *When Teenagers Work: The Psychological and Social Costs of Adolescent Employment.* New York: Basic Books.

Greenberger, E., et al. (1980). Adolescents who work: Effects of part-time employment on family and peer relations. *Journal of Youth & Adolescence, 9,* 189–202.

Greenfield, P. M. (1974). What we can learn from cultural variation in child care. Paper presented at the 140th meeting of the American Association for the Advancement of Science, San Francisco, February.

Gregor, T. (1979). Short people. *Natural History,* February, 14–23.

Greif, E., & Ulman, K. (1982). The psychological impact of menarche on early adolescent females: A review of the literature. *Child Development, 53,* 1413–1430.

Gronlund, N. E. (1959). *Sociometry in the Classroom.* New York: Harper and Brothers.

Gronlund, N. E., & Anderson, L. (1957). Personality characteristics of socially accepted, socially neglected, and socially rejected junior high school pupils. *Educational Administration Supervision, 43,* 329–358.

Grossman, D. (1995). *On Killing: The Psychological Cost of Learning to Kill in War and Society.* Boston: Little, Brown.

Guthrie, R. D. (1976). *Body Hot Spots: The Anatomy of Human Social Organs and Behavior.* New York: Van Nostrand Reinhold.

Hall, G. S. (1904). *Adolescence.* New York: Appleton.

Hall, J. (1984). *Nonverbal Sex Differences: Communication Accuracy and Expressive Style.* Baltimore: Johns Hopkins University Press.

Hall, K. R. L., & DeVore, I. (1965). Baboon social behavior. In I. DeVore (ed.), *Primate Behavior: Field Studies of Monkeys and Apes.* New York: Holt, Rinehart and Winston.

Hamburg, B. A. (1986). Subsets of adolescent mothers: Developmental, biomedical and psychosocial issues. In J. B. Lancaster & B. A. Hamburg (eds.), *School-Age Pregnancy and Parenthood: Biosocial Dimensions.* New York: Aldine de Gruyter.

Hamburg, D. A. (1971). Crowding, stranger contact, and aggressive behaviour. In L. Levi (ed.), *Society, Stress, and Disease*. London: Oxford University Press.

Hamburg, D. A., Hamburg, B. A., & Barchas, J. D. (1975). Anger and depression in perspective of behavioral biology. In L. Levi (ed.), *Emotions—Their Parameters and Measurement*. New York: Raven Press.

Hamer, D. H., et al. (1993). A linkage between DNA markers on the X chromosome and male sexual orientation. *Science, 261*, 321–327.

Hamilton, E. (1971). *Sex Before Marriage*. London: Unwin.

Hamilton, J. B., & Mestler, G. E. (1969). Mortality and survival: Comparison of eunuchs with intact men and women in a mentally retarded population. *Journal of Gerontology, 24*, 395–411.

Hamilton, W. D. (1964). The genetical theory of social behavior, 1 and 2. *Journal of Theoretical Biology, 7*, 1–52.

Handlesman, C. D., Cabral, R., & Weisfeld, G. E. (1987). Sources of information and adolescent sexual knowledge and behavior. *Journal of Adolescent Research, 2*, 36–43.

Hanson, B., et al. (1985). *Life with Heroin: Voices from the Inner City*. Lexington, MA: Lexington Books.

Hanson, S. L., Myers, D. E., & Ginsburg, A. L. (1987). The role of responsibility and knowledge in reducing teenage out-of-wedlock childbearing. *Journal of Marriage & the Family, 49*, 241–256.

Hareven, T. K. (1984). Themes in the historical development of the family. In R. D. Parke (ed.), *Review of Child Development Research*, Vol. 7, *The Family*. Chicago: University of Chicago Press.

Harlow, H. F., & Harlow, M. K. (1962). Social deprivation in monkeys. *Scientific American, 287*, 136–146.

Harper, L. V. (1981). Offspring effects upon parents. In D. J. Gubernick & P. H. Klopfer (eds.), *Parental Care in Mammals*. New York: Plenum.

Harris, J. R. (1995). Where is the child's environment? A group socialization theory of development. *Psychological Review, 102*, 458–489.

Harris, M. (1974). *Cows, Pigs, Wars, and Witches: The Riddles of Culture*. New York: Random House.

_____. (1980). *America Now*. New York: Touchstone.

Harter, S. (1989). Causes, correlates, and the functional role of global self-worth: A life-span perspective. In J. Kolligian & R. Sternberg (eds.), *Perceptions of Competence and Incompetence Across the Life-Span*. New Haven: Yale University Press.

Hartup, W. W. (1974). Aggression in childhood: Developmental perspectives. *American Psychologist, 29*, 336–341.

_____. (1983). Peer relations. In P. Mussen (ed.), *Handbook of Child Psychology* (4th ed.). New York: Wiley.

_____. (1984). Peer relations. In M. E. Hetherington (ed.), *Carmichael's Manual of Child Psychology.* New York: Wiley.

Hartup, W. W., Glazer, J. A., & Charlesworth, W. R. (1967). Peer reinforcement and sociometric status. *Child Development, 38,* 1017–1024.

Harvey, P. H., & Bennett, P. M. (1983). Brain size, energetics, ecology, and life-history patterns. *Nature, 306,* 314–315.

Harvey, P. H., & Clutton-Brock, T. H. (1985). Life history variation in primates. *Evolution, 39,* 559–581.

Harvey, P. H., & Zammuto, R. M. (1985). Patterns of mortality and age at first reproduction in natural populations of mammals. *Nature, 315,* 318–329.

Hass, A. (1979). *Teenage Sexuality.* New York: Macmillan.

Hayes, C. (ed.) (1987). *Risking the Future: Adolescent Sexuality, Pregnancy, and Childrearing,* Vol. 1. Washington, DC: National Academy Press.

Hays, S. E. (1981). The psychoendocrinology of puberty and adolescent aggression. In D. A. Hamburg & M. B. Trudeau (eds.), *Biobehavioral Aspects of Aggression.* New York: Alan R. Liss.

Hazan, C., & Shaver, P. (1987). Romantic love conceptualized as an attachment process. *Journal of Personality & Social Psychology, 52,* 511–524.

Heckhausen, H. (1968). Achievement motive research: Current problems and some contributions towards a general theory of motivation. In W. J. Arnold (ed.), *Nebraska Symposium on Motivation,* Vol. 16. Lincoln: University of Nebraska Press.

Heiman, J. R. (1975). The physiology of erotica: Women's sexual arousal. *Psychology Today, 8,* 90–94.

Herbert, M. (1986). The pathology of human parental behaviour. In W. Sluckin & M. Herbert (eds.), *Parental Behaviour.* Oxford: Basil Blackwell.

Hess, E. H. (1977). *The Tell-Tale Eye.* New York: Van Nostrand Reinhold.

Hess, E. & Polt, J. M. (1960). Pupil size as related to interest value of visual stimuli. *Science, 132,* 349–350.

Hetherington, E. M. (1972). Effects of father absence on personality development in adolescent daughters. *Developmental Psychology, 7,* 313–326.

_____. (1993). An overview of the Virginia longitudinal study of divorce and remarriage with a focus on early adolescence. *Journal of Family Psychology, 7,* 39–56.

Hewlett, S. A. (1991). *When the Bough Breaks: The Cost of Neglecting our Children.* New York: Basic Books.

Hier, B. B., & Crowley, W. F. (1982). Spatial ability in androgen deficient men. *New England Journal of Medicine, 306,* 1202–1205.

Higham, E. (1980). Variations in adolescent psychohormonal development. In J. Adelson (ed.), *Handbook of Adolescent Psychology.* New York: Wiley.

Higley, J. D., & Suomi, S. J. (1986). Parental behaviour in non-human primates. In W. Sluckin & M. Herbert (eds.), *Parental Bahaviour.* Oxford: Basil Blackwell.

Hill, C., Rubin, Z., & Peplau, L. (1979). Breakups before marriage: The end of 103 affairs. In G. Levinger & O. Moles (eds.), *Divorce and Separation.* New York: Basic Books.

Hill, C. R., & Stafford, F. P. (1978). *Paternal Care of Children: Time Diary Estimates of Quantity, Predictability, and Variety.* Working paper series, Institute for Social Research, University of Michigan, Ann Arbor.

Hill, E. M., Young, J. P., & Nord, J. L. (1994). Childhood adversity, attachment security, and adult relationships: A preliminary study. *Ethology & Sociobiology, 15,* 323–338.

Hill, K. (1982). Hunting and human evolution. *Journal of Human Evolution, 11,* 522–544.

Hinde, R. A. (1987). *Individuals, Relationships, and Culture.* Cambridge: Cambridge University Press.

Hobhouse, L. T. (1924). *Morals in Evolution.* New York: Holt.

Hoffman, L. W. (1974). Effects of maternal employment on the child—A review of the research. *Developmental Psychology, 10,* 204–228.

_____. (1984). Work, family, and the socialization of the child. In R. D. Parke (ed.), *Review of Child Development Research,* Vol. 7, *The Family.* Chicago: University of Chicago Press.

Hokanson, J. E. (1970). Psychophysiological evaluations of the catharsis hypothesis. In E. I. Megargee & J. E. Hokanson (eds.), *The Dynamics of Aggression.* New York: Harper & Row.

Hokanson, J. E., Willers, K. R., & Koropsak, E. (1968). Modification of autonomic response during aggressive interchange. *Journal of Personality, 36,* 386–404.

Hold, B. (1976). Attention structure and rank specific behaviour in pre-school children. In M.R.A. Chance & R. R. Larsen (eds.), *Social Structure of Attention.* London: Wiley.

_____. (1977). Rank and behaviour: An ethological study of pre-school children. *Homo, 28,* 158–188.

_____. (1980). Attention-structure and behavior in G/wi San children. *Ethology & Sociobiology, 1,* 275–290.

Hold-Cavell, B.C.L. (1985). Showing-off and aggression in young children. *Aggressive Behavior, 11,* 303–314.

Holliday, M. A. (1978). Body composition and energy needs during growth. In F. Falker & J. M. Tanner (eds.), *Human Growth.* New York: Plenum.

Hoogland, J. L. (1982). Prairie dogs avoid extreme inbreeding. *Science, 215,* 1639–1641.

Hopwood, N. J., et al. (1990). The onset of human puberty: Biological and environmental factors. In J. Bancroft & J. M. Reinisch (eds.), *Adolescence and Puberty*. New York: Oxford University Press.

Horner, M. S. (1972). Toward an understanding of achievement-related conflicts in women. *Journal of Social Issues, 28,* 157–175.

Hotvedt, M. E. (1990). Emerging and submerging adolescent sexuality: Culture and sexual orientation. In J. Bancroft and J. M. Reinisch (eds.), *Adolescence and Puberty*. New York: Oxford University Press.

Hoyenga, K. B., & Hoyenga, K. T. (1979). *The Question of Sex Differences: Psychological, Cultural, and Biological Issues.* Boston: Little, Brown.

————. (1984). *Motivational Explanations of Behavior.* Monterey, CA: Brooks/Cole.

————. (1993). *Gender-Related Differences: Origins and Outcomes.* Boston: Allyn & Bacon.

Hrdy, S. B. (1981). *The Woman That Never Evolved.* Cambridge, MA: Harvard University Press.

Hrdy, S. B., & Carter, C. S. (1995). Hormonal cocktails for two. *Natural History,* December, 129.

Humphrey, N. K. (1976). The social function of intellect. In P.P.G. Bateson & R. A. Hinde (eds.), *Growing Points in Ethology.* Cambridge: Cambridge University Press.

Huntingford, F., & Turner, A. (1987). *Animal Conflict.* New York: Chapman & Hall.

Huston, T. L. (ed.) (1974). *Foundations of Interpersonal Attraction.* New York: Academic Press.

Hutt, C. (1972). *Males and Females.* Baltimore: Penguin.

Hyde, J. S., & DeLamater, J. (1997). *Understanding Human Sexuality* (6th ed.). New York: McGraw-Hill.

Hyman, H. H. (1942). *The Psychology of Status.* New York: Archives of Psychology.

Insel, T. R., & Carter, C. S. (1995). The monogamous brain. *Natural History,* August, 121–122.

Institute of Medicine (1975). *Legalized Abortion and the Public Health.* Washington, DC: National Academy of Sciences.

Isaacson, R. I. (1964). Relations between N-achievement, test anxiety, and curricular choices. *Journal of Abnormal & Social Psychology, 68,* 447–452.

Itard, J.M.G. (1932). *The Wild Boy of Aveyron.* New York: Century.

Izard, C. (1977). *Human Emotions.* New York: Plenum.

Jacklin, C. N., Maccoby, E. E., & Doering, C. H. (1983). Neonatal sex-steroid hormones and timidity in 6–18-month-old boys and girls. *Developmental Psychology, 16,* 163–168.

Jackson, L. A. (1992). *Physical Appearance and Gender: Sociobiological and Sociocultural Perspectives.* Albany, NY: SUNY Press.

Jacob, T. (1974). Patterns of family conflict and dominance as a function of age and social class. *Developmental Psychology, 10,* 21–24.

Jacobson, J. L., & Kriger, A. (1978). Interest in babies at the onset of puberty. Manuscript, Brandeis University.

Jankowiak, W. R., & Fischer, E. F. (1992). A cross-cultural perspective on romantic love. *Ethnology, 31,* 149–155.

Janson, C. H., & van Schalk, C. P. (1993). Ecological risk aversion in juvenile primates: Slow and steady wins the race. In M. E. Pereira & L. A. Fairbanks (eds.), *Juvenile Primates: Life History, Development, and Behavior.* New York: Oxford University Press.

Jardine, R., & Martin, N. G. (1983). Spatial ability and throwing accuracy. *Behavior Genetics, 13,* 331–340.

Jessor, R., & Jessor, S. (1977). *Problem Behavior and Psychological Development: A Longitudinal Study of Youth.* New York: Academic Press.

Johnson, C., Loxterkamp, D., & Albanese, M. (1982). Effect of high school students' knowledge of child development and child health on approaches to child discipline. *Pediatrics, 69,* 558–562.

Johnson, M. M. (1963). Sex role learning in the nuclear family. *Child Development, 34,* 315–333.

Johnston, E. E. (1974). Control of age at menarche. *Human Biology, 46,* 159–171.

Johnston, V., & Franklin, M. (1993). Is beauty in the eye of the beholder? *Ethology & Sociobiology, 14,* 183–199.

Jolly, A. (1985). *The Evolution of Primate Behavior* (2nd ed.). New York: Macmillan.

Jolly, C. (1970). The seed-eaters: A new model of hominid differentiation based on a baboon analogy. *Man, 5,* 5–26.

Jones, B., et al. (1972). Factors influencing the age of menarche in a low socioeconomic group in Melbourne. *Medical Journal of Australia, 2,* 533–535.

Jones, M. C. (1965). Psychological correlates of somatic development. *Child Development, 36,* 899–911.

Jones, M. C., & Bayley, N. (1950). Physical maturing among boys as related to behavior. *Journal of Educational Psychology, 41,* 129–148.

Jones, M. C., & Mussen, P. H. (1958). Self-conceptions, motivations, and interpersonal attitudes of early- and late-maturing girls. *Child Development, 29,* 492–501.

Jones, R. E. (1991). *Human Reproductive Biology.* New York: Academic.

Jones, S., Martin, R., & Pilbeam, D. (eds.) (1992). *Cambridge Encyclopedia of Human Evolution.* Cambridge: Cambridge University Press.

Julien, R. M. (1992). *A Primer of Drug Action.* New York: Freeman.

Jütte, A., Bernhard, F., and Grammer, K. (1998). Hormonal changes under-lying sexual responses in women and men. Paper presented at the convention of the International Society for Human Ethology, Burnaby, BC, Canada, August.

Kagan, J. (1970). The many faces of response. In P. Cramer (ed.), *Readings in Developmental Psychology Today.* Del Mar, CA: CRM Books.

Kagan, J., & Moss, H. A. (1962). *Birth to Maturity: A Study in Psychological Development.* New York: Wiley.

Kalat, J. W. (1992). *Biological Psychology* (4th ed.). Belmont, CA: Wadsworth.

Kallen, D., & Stephenson, J. (1982). Talking about sex revisited. *Journal of Youth & Adolescence, 11,* 11–24.

Kandel, D. (1978). Homophily, selection, and socialization in adolescent friendships. *American Journal of Sociology, 84,* 427–436.

Kanin, E. J., Davidson, K. R., & Scheck, S. R. (1970). A research note on male-female differentials in the experience of heterosexual love. *Journal of Sex Research, 6,* 64–72.

Katchadourian, H. (1977). *Biology of Adolescence.* San Francisco: Freeman.

Katz, M. M., & Konner, M. J. (1981). The role of the father: An anthropo-logical perspective. In M. E. Lamb (ed.), *The Role of the Father in Child Development.* New York: Wiley.

Kaufmann, J. H. (1967). Social relations of adult males in a free-ranging band of rhesus monkeys. In S. A. Altmann (ed.), *Social Communication Among Primates.* Chicago: University of Chicago Press.

Kay, J. H. (1997). *Asphalt Nation: How the Automobile Took Over America and How We Can Take It Back.* New York: Crown.

Keating, C. F. (1985). Gender and the physiognomy of dominance and at-tractiveness. *Social Psychology Quarterly, 48,* 61–70.

Keating, C. F., et al. (1981). Culture and the perception of social dominance from facial expressions. *Journal of Personality & Social Psychology, 40,* 615–626.

Kelley, K., et al. (1983). Facilitating sexual arousal via anger, aggression, or dominance. *Motivation & Emotion, 7,* 191–202.

Kemper, T. D. (1990). *Social Structure and Testosterone: Explorations of the Socio-Bio-Social Chain.*

Kendrick, D. T., & Keefe, R. C. (1992). Age preferences in mates reflect sex differences in reproductive strategies. *Behavioral & Brain Sciences, 15,* 75–133.

Kennedy, J. H. (1990). Determinants of peer social status: Contributions of physical appearance, reputation, and behavior. *Journal of Youth & Adoles-cence, 19,* 233–244.

Kephart, W. M. (1967). Some correlates of romantic love. *Journal of Mar-riage & the Family, 29,* 470–474.

Kerfoot, M. (1980). The family context of adolescent suicidal behavior. *Journal of Adolescence, 3,* 335–346.

Kessen, W. (1975). *Childhood in China.* New Haven: Yale University Press.

Kett, J. (1977). *Rites of Passage: Adolescence in America, 1790 to the Present.* New York: Basic Books.

Kim, F., Smith, P. K., & Palermiti, A. L. (1997). Conflict in childhood and reproductive development. *Ethology & Sociobiology, 18,* 109–142.

Kim, P., & Bailey, J. M. (1996). Butch or femme: Partner preferences of gay men and lesbians. Paper presented at the convention of the Human Behavior and Evolution Society, Evanston, IL, June.

Kimura, D. (1998). Biological contributions to sex differences in human cognition. Paper presented at the convention of the International Society for Human Ethology, Burnaby, BC, Canada, August.

Kinsey, A. C., et al. (1953). *Sexual Behavior in the Human Female.* Philadelphia: Saunders.

Kirkendall, L. A. (1961). *Premarital Intercourse and Interpersonal Relationships.* New York: Julian Press.

Kleiman, D. G. (1977). Monogamy in mammals. *Quarterly Review of Biology, 52,* 39–69.

Klissouras, V. (1984). Factors affecting physical performance with reference to heredity. In J. Borms et al. (eds.), *Human Growth and Development.* New York: Plenum.

Kolata, G. (1984). Puberty mystery solved. *Science, 223,* 272.

Kolb, B., & Whishaw, I. Q. (1990). *Fundamentals of Human Neuropsychology* (3rd ed.). New York: Freeman, 1990.

Konner, M. J., & Shostak, M. (1986). Adolescent pregnancy and childbearing: An anthropological perspective. In J. B. Lancaster & B. A. Hamburg (eds.), *School-Age Pregnancy and Parenthood: Biosocial Dimensions.* New York: Aldine de Gruyter.

Kotlar, S. L. (1965). Middle-class marital role perceptions and marital adjustment. *Sociology & Social Research, 49,* 283–294.

Kronk, L. (1993). Parental favoritism toward daughters. *American Scientist, 81,* 272–279.

Kuester, J., & Paul, A. (1989). Reproductive strategies of subadult Barbary macaque males at Affenberg Salem. In A. E. Rasa, C. Vogel, & E. Voland (eds.), *The Sociobiology of Sexual and Reproductive Strategies.* New York: Chapman & Hall.

Kulka, R. A., & Weingarten, H. (1979). The long-term effects of parental divorce in childhood on adult adjustment. *Journal of Social Issues, 33,* 50–78.

Kummer, H. (1971). *Primate Societies: Group Techniques of Ecological Adaptation.* Chicago: Aldine.

Kurdek, L. A., Blisk, D., & Siesky, A. E. (1981). Correlates of children's long-term adjustment to their parent's divorce. *Developmental Psychology, 17,* 565–579.

La Fontaine, J. S. (1985). *Initiation.* New York: Viking Penguin.

LaFrenière, P., & Charlesworth, W. R. (1983). Dominance, attention, and affiliation in a preschool group: A nine month longitudinal study. *Ethology & Sociobiology, 4,* 55–67.

Lamb, M. E. (1981). The development of father-infant relationships. In M. E. Lamb (ed.), *The Role of the Father in Child Development.* New York: Wiley.

Lancaster, J. B. (1984). Evolutionary perspectives on sex differences in the higher primates. In A. S. Rossi (ed.), *Gender and the Life Course.* New York: Aldine.

———. (1986). Human adolescence and reproduction: An evolutionary perspective. In J. B. Lancaster & B. A. Hamburg (eds.), *School-Age Pregnancy and Parenthood: Biosocial Dimensions.* New York: Aldine de Gruyter.

———. (1994). Human sexuality, life histories, and evolutionary ecology. In A. S. Rossi (ed.), *Sexuality Across the Life Course.* Chicago: University of Chicago Press.

Lancaster, J. B., & Lancaster, C. S. (1983). Parental investment: The hominid adaptation. In D. J. Ortner (ed.), *How Humans Adapt: A Biocultural Odyssey.* Washington, DC: Smithsonian Institution Press.

Landry, E., et al. (1986). Teen pregnancy in New Orleans: Factors that differentiate teens who deliver, abort, and successfully contracept. *Journal of Youth & Adolescence, 15,* 259–274.

Langlois, J. H., & Downs, A. C. (1979). Peer relations as a function of physical attractiveness: The eye of the beholder or behavioral reality? *Child Development, 50,* 409–418.

Langlois, J. H., & Roggman, L. A. (1990). Attractive faces are only average. *Psychological Science, 1,* 115–121.

Langlois, J. H., & Stephan, C. (1981). Beauty and the beast: The role of physical attractiveness in the development of peer relations and social behavior. In S. S. Brehm, S. M. Kassin, & F. X. Gibbons (eds.), *Developmental Social Psychology.* New York: Oxford University Press.

Lasch, C. (1977). *Haven in the Heartless World: The Family Besieged.* New York: Basic.

Lauer, C. (1992). Variability in the patterns of agonistic behavior of preschool children. In J. Silverberg & J. P. Gray (eds.), *Aggression and Peacefulness in Humans and Other Primates.* Oxford: Oxford University Press.

Laumann, E. O., et al. (1994). *The Social Organization of Sexuality: Sexual Practices in the United States.* Chicago: University of Chicago Press.

Laursen, B., & Ferreira, M. (1994). Does parent-child conflict peak at mid-adolescence? Paper presented at the Society for Research on Adolescence convention, San Diego, February.

Leach, P. (1989). *Your Baby and Child: From Birth to Age 5.* New York: Knopf.

LeDoux, J. E. (1994). Cognitive-emotional interactions in the brain. In P. Ekman & R. J. Davidson (eds.), *The Nature of Emotion: Fundamental Questions.* Oxford University Press.

_____. (1996). *The Emotional Brain: The Mysterious Underpinnings of Emotional Life.* New York: Simon & Schuster.

Lee, G. (1982). *Family Structure and Interaction: A Comparative Analysis* (2nd ed.). Minneapolis: University of Minnesota Press.

Lefkowitz, M. M., et al. (1977). *Growing Up to Be Violent: A Longitudinal Study of the Development of Aggression.* New York: Pergamon.

Lehrman, D. S. (1961). The presence of the mate and of nesting material as stimuli for the development of incubation behavior and for gonadotropic secretion in the ring dove. *Endocrinology, 68,* 507–516.

Lerner, R. M., & Foch, T. T. (1987). Biological-psychosocial interactions in early adolescence: An overview of the issues. In R. M. Lerner & T. T. Foch (eds.), *Biological-Psychosocial Interactions in Early Adolescence.* Hillsdale, NJ: Erlbaum.

Lesser, G. S. (1959). The relationship between various forms of aggression and popularity among lower-class children. *Journal of Educational Psychology, 50,* 20–25.

Lesser, G. S., & Kandel, D. (1969). Parent-adolescent relationships and adolescent independence in the United States and Denmark. *Journal of Marriage & the Family, 31,* 348–358.

Leutenneger, W., & Cheverud, J. (1982). Correlates of sexual dimorphism in primates. *International Journal of Primatology, 3,* 367–387.

LeVay, S. (1993). *The Sexual Brain.* Cambridge, MA: MIT Press.

Lidicker, W. (1980). The social biology of the California vole. *Biologist, 62,* 46–55.

Lindemann, C., & Scott, W. J. (1981). Wanted and unwanted pregnancy in early adolescence: Evidence from a clinic population. *Journal of Early Adolescence, 1,* 185–193.

Littlefield, C. H., & Silverman, I. (1991). Marital dissatisfaction following the death of a child: The influence of genetic factors at cause in the death. *Journal of Marriage & the Family, 53,* 799–804.

Livson, N., & Peskin, H. (1980). Perspectives on adolescence from longitudinal research. In J. Adelson (ed.), *Handbook of Adolescent Psychology.* New York: Wiley.

Logue, A. W. (1991). *The Psychology of Eating and Drinking: An Introduction* (2nd ed.). New York: Freeman.

Lombardi, J. R., & Vandenbergh, J. G. (1977). Pheromonally induced sexual maturation in females: Regulation by the social environment of the male. *Science, 196,* 545–546.

Lord, S. E., & Eccles, J. S. (1994). James revisited: The relationship of domain self-concepts and values to black and white adolescents' self-esteem. Paper presented at the Society for Research on Adolescence convention, San Diego, February.

Lorenz, K. (1966). *On Aggression.* New York: Harcourt Brace Jovanovich.

Louv, R. (1990). *Childhood's Future.* Boston: Houghton Mifflin.

Low, B. S. (1979). Sexual selection and human ornamentation. In N. A. Chagnon & W. Irons (eds.), *Evolutionary Biology and Human Social Behavior.* North Scituate, MA: Duxbury Press.

———. (1990). Fat and deception. *Ethology & Sociobiology, 11,* 67–74.

Low, B. S., Alexander, R. D., & Noonan, K. M. (1987). Human hips, breasts, buttocks: Is fat deceptive? *Ethology & Sociobiology, 8,* 249–257.

Luce, G. G. (1971). *Body Time: Physiological Rhythms and Social Stress.* New York: Pantheon.

Lueptow, L. B., Garovich, L., & Lueptow, M. B. (1995). The persistence of gender stereotypes in the face of changing sex roles: Evidence contrary to the sociocultural model. *Ethology & Sociobiology, 16,* 509–530.

Lutz, P. (1983). The stepfamily: An adolescent perspective. *Family Relations, 32,* 367–375.

Maccoby, E. E. (1966). Sex differences in intellectual functioning. In E. E. Maccoby (ed.), *The Development of Sex Differences.* Stanford: Stanford University Press.

Maccoby, E. E., & Jacklin, C. N. (1974). *The Psychology of Sex Differences.* Stanford: Stanford University Press.

MacDonald, K. (1989). The plasticity of human social organization and behavior: Contextual variables and proximal mechanisms. *Ethology & Sociobiology, 10,* 171–194.

Mackey, W. C. (1983). A preliminary test for the validation of the adult male-child bond as a species-characteristic trait. *American Anthropologist, 85,* 391–402.

———. (1996). *The American Father: Biocultural and Developmental Aspects.* New York: Plenum.

Magee, K., et al. (1970). Blindness and menarche. *Life Sciences, 9,* 7–12.

Magnusson, D., Stattin, H., & Allen, V. (1986). Differential maturation among girls and its relation to social adjustment in a longitudinal perspective. In P. Baltes, D. Featherman, & R. Lerner (eds.), *Life Span Development and Behavior,* Vol. 7. Hillsdale, NJ: Erlbaum.

Malson, L. (1964). *Wolf Children and the Problem of Human Nature.* New York: Monthly Review Press.

Mann, J. (1992). Nurturance or negligence: Maternal psychology and behavioral preference among preterm twins. In J. H. Barkow, L. Cosmides, & J. Tooby (eds.), *The Adapted Mind: Evolutionary Psychology and the Generation of Culture.* New York: Oxford University Press.

Manning, J. T. (1998). Developmental instability of the digits and predictors of spermatogenesis, testosterone, LH, and fecundity in men and women. Paper presented at the convention of the International Society for Human Ethology, Burnaby, BC, Canada.

Marcoen, A., & Brumagne, M. (1985). Loneliness among children and young adolescents. *Developmental Psychology, 21,* 1025–1031.

Marcoen, A., Goossens, L., & Caes, P. (1987). Loneliness in pre- through late adolescence: Exploring the contributions of a multidimensional approach. *Journal of Youth & Adolescence, 16,* 561–577.

Marenko, A. A. (1955). *The Road to Life.* Moscow: Foreign Languages Publishing House.

Margolin, L., & White, L. (1987). The continuing role of physical attractiveness in marriage. *Journal of Marriage & the Family, 49,* 21–27.

Marler, P. (1976). On animal aggression: The roles of strangeness and familiarity. *American Psychologist, 31,* 239–246.

Mascie-Taylor, C.G.N. (1991). Biosocial influences on stature: A review. *Journal of Biosocial Science, 23,* 113–128.

Masters, R. D., & McGuire, M. T. (eds.) (1994). *Neurotransmitter Revolution: Serotonin, Social Behavior, and the Law.* Carbondale: Southern Illinois University Press.

Masters, W. H., & Johnson, V. E. (1966). *Human Sexual Response.* Boston: Little, Brown.

Mathes, E. W. (1986). Jealousy and romantic love: A longitudinal study. *Psychological Reports, 58,* 885–886.

Mausner, B., & Coles, B. (1978). Avoidance of success among women. *International Journal of Women's Studies, 1,* 30–49.

Mazur, A. (1983). Hormones, aggression, and dominance in humans. In. B. Svare (ed.), *Hormones and Aggressive Behavior.* New York: Plenum.

————. (1985). A biosocial model of status in face-to-face primate groups. *Social Forces, 64,* 377–402.

Mazur, A., & Booth, A. (1998). Testosterone and dominance in men. *Behavioral & Brain Sciences, 21,* 353–397.

Mazur, A., Halpern, C., & Udry, J. R. (1994). Dominant-looking male teenagers copulate earlier. *Ethology & Sociobiology, 15,* 87–94.

Mazur, A., & Lamb, T. A. (1980). Testosterone, status, and mood in human males. *Hormones & Behavior, 14,* 236–246.

Mazur, A., Mazur, J., & Keating, C. (1984). Military rank attainment of a West Point class: Effects of cadets' physical features. *American Journal of Sociology, 90*, 125–150.

Mazur, A., et al. (1980). Physiological aspects of communication via mutual gaze. *American Journal of Sociology, 86*, 50–74.

McArthur, L. Z. (1982). Judging a book by its cover: A cognitive analysis of the relationship between physical appearance and stereotyping. In A. H. Hastorf & A. M. Isen (eds.), *Cognitive Social Psychology.* New York: Elsevier.

McArthur, L. Z., & Apatow (1983–1984). Impressions of baby-faced adults. *Social Cognition, 2*, 315–342.

McArthur, L. Z., & Berry, D. S. (1987). Cross-cultural agreement in perceptions of baby-faced adults. *Journal of Cross-Cultural Psychology, 18*, 165–192.

McCabe, V. (1984). Abstract perceptual information for age level: A risk factor for maltreatment? *Child Development, 55*, 267–276.

McCarrick, A. K., Manderscheid, R. W., & Silbergeld, S. (1981). Gender differences in competition and dominance during married-couples therapy. *Social Psychology Quarterly, 44*, 164–177.

McClelland, D. C. (1961). *The Achieving Society.* New York; Van Nostrand Reinhold.

———. (1971). *Motivational Trends in Society.* New York: General Learning.

McClintock, M. K. (1971). Menstrual synchrony and suppression. *Nature, 229*, 244–245.

McDougall, W. (1921). *An Introduction to Social Psychology.* Boston: Luce.

———. (1923). *Outline of Psychology.* New York: Charles Scribner's Sons.

McGhee, P. E. (1979). *Humor: Its Origins and Development.* San Francisco: Freeman.

McGraw, K. O. (1987). *Developmental Psychology.* New York: Holt, Rinehart & Winston.

McGrew, W. C. (1992). *Chimpanzee Material Culture: Implications for Human Evolution.* Cambridge: Cambridge University Press.

McGrew, W. C., & Feistner, A.T.C. (1992). Two nonhuman primate models for the evolution of human food sharing: Chimpanzees and Callitrichids. In J. H. Barkow, L. Cosmides, & J. Tooby (eds.), *The Adapted Mind: Evolutionary Psychology and the Generation of Culture.* New York: Oxford University Press.

McGuire, J. M. (1973). Aggression and sociometric status with preschool children. *Child Development, 36*, 542–549.

McGuire, M. T., Raleigh, M. J., & Brammer, G. L. (1984). Adaptation, selection, and benefit-cost balances: Implications of behavioral-physiological studies of social dominance in male vervet monkeys. *Ethology & Sociobiology, 5*, 269–277.

McKay, H. D. (1949). The neighborhood and child conduct. *Annals of the American Academy of Political & Social Science* January, 32–41.

McKenna, J. J., & Bernshaw, N. J. (1995). Breastfeeding and infant-parent co-sleeping as adaptive strategies: Are they protective against SIDS? In P. Stuart-Macadam & K. A. Dettwyler (eds.), *Breastfeeding: Biocultural Perspectives.* New York: Aldine de Gruyter.

McKeon, R. (ed.). (1941). *The Basic Works of Aristotle.* New York: Random House.

McLaughlin, D. K., & Lichter, D. T. (1997). Poverty and the marital behavior of young women. *Journal of Marriage & the Family, 59,* 582–594.

Mead, M. (1935). *Sex and Temperament in Three Primitive Societies.* New York: Mentor Book.

Mellen, S.L.W. (1981). *The Evolution of Love.* San Francisco: Freeman.

Michel, G. F., & Moore, C. L. (1995). *Developmental Psychobiology: An Interdisciplinary Science.* Cambridge, MA: MIT Press.

Miller, P. H. (1993). *Theories of Developmental Psychology.* San Francisco: Freeman.

Miller, P. Y., & Simon, W. (1980). The development of sexuality in adolescence. In J. Adelson (ed.), *Handbook of Adolescent Psychology.* New York: Wiley.

Miller, R. L. (1991). *The Case for Legalizing Drugs.* New York: Praeger.

Mitchell, A. K. (1983). Adolescents' experiences of parental separation and divorce. *Journal of Adolescence, 6,* 175–187.

Mitchell, G. (1981). *Human Sex Differences: A Primatologist's Perspective.* New York: Van Nostrand Reinhold.

Moerman, M. L. (1982). Growth of the birth canal in adolescent girls. *American Journal of Obstetrics & Gynecology, 143,* 528–532.

Moffitt, T., et al. (1992). Childhood experience and the onset of menarche: A test of a sociobiological model. *Child Development, 63,* 47–58.

Money, J., & Ehrhardt, A. A. (1972). *Man and Woman, Boy and Girl.* Baltimore: Johns Hopkins University Press.

Montemayor, R. (1986). Family variation in parent-adolescent storm and stress. *Journal of Adolescent Research, 1,* 15–31.

Montemayor, R., & Hanson, E. (1985). A naturalistic view of conflict between adolescents and their parents and siblings. *Journal of Early Adolescence, 5,* 23–30.

Mook, D. G. (1996). *Motivation: The Organization of Action.* New York: Norton.

Moore, M. (1985). Non-verbal courtship patterns in women: Context and consequences. *Ethology & Sociobiology, 6,* 237–247.

———. (1995). Courtship signals and adolescents: Girls just wanna have fun? *Journal of Sex Research, 31,* 319–328.

Morris, N. M., & Udry, J. R. (1980). Validation of a self-administered instrument to assess stage of adolescent development,. *Journal of Youth & Adolescence, 5,* 271–280.

Morris, N. M., et al. (1987). Marital sex frequency and midcycle female testosterone. *Archives of Sexual Behavior, 16,* 27–37.

Moyer, K. E. (1976). *The Psychobiology of Aggression.* New York: Harper & Row.

Munroe, R. H., Munroe, R. L., & Shimmin, H. S. (1984). Children's work in our cultures: Determinants and consequences. *American Anthropologist, 86,* 369–379.

Munroe, R. L., & Munroe, R. H., (1975). *Cross-Cultural Human Development.* Monterey, CA: Brooks/Cole.

Murdock, G. P. (1937). Comparative data on division of labor by sex. *Social Forces, 15,* 551–553.

_____. (1949). *Social Structure.* New York: Macmillan.

_____. (1965). *Culture and Society.* Pittsburgh: University of Pittsburgh Press.

_____. (1967). *Ethnographic Atlas.* Pittsburgh: University of Pittsburgh Press.

Murdock, G. P., & Provost, C. (1973). Factors in the division of labor by sex: A cross-cultural analysis. *Ethnology, 12,* 203–219.

Mussen, P. H., & Jones, M. C. (1957). Self-conceptions, motivations, and interpersonal attitudes of late- and early-maturing boys. *Child Development, 28,* 243–256.

Muuss, R. E. (1970). Puberty rites in primitive and modern societies. *Adolescence, 5,* 109–128.

Nag, M. G., Whitehead, N. F., & Peet, R. C. (1978). An anthropological approach to the study of the economic value of children. In D. Ortner (ed.), *How Humans Adapt: A Biocultural Odyssey.* Washington, DC: Smithsonian Institution.

Nash, J. (1978). *Developmental Psychology: A Psychobiological Approach.* Englewood Cliffs, NJ: Prentice-Hall.

Neill, S. R., St. J. (1983). Children's social relationships and education—An evolutionary effect? *Social Biology & Human Affairs, 47,* 48–55.

_____. (1985). Rough-and-tumble and aggression in schoolchildren: Serious play? *Animal Behaviour, 33,* 1380–1382.

Neimark, E. (1975). Intellectual development during adolescence. In F. Horowitz (ed.), *Review of Child Development Research* (Vol. 4). Chicago: University of Chicago Press.

Nielsen, F. (1994). Sociobiology and sociology. *Annual Review of Sociology, 20,* 267–303.

Nishida, T., & Hiraiwa-Hasegawa, M. (1987). Chimpanzees and bonobos: Cooperative relationships among males. In B. B. Smuts et al. (eds.), *Primate Societies.* Chicago: University of Chicago Press.

Nisbett, R. E. (1996). *Culture of Honor: The Psychology of Violence in the South.* Boulder: Westview Press.

Nottelmann, E. D., et al. (1990). Hormones and behavior at puberty. In J. Bancroft & J. M. Reinisch (eds.), *Adolescence and Puberty.* New York: Oxford University Press.

Numan, M. (1990). Neural control of maternal behavior. In N. A. Krasnegor & R. S. Bridges (eds.), *Mammalian Parenting: Biochemical, Neurobiological, and Behavioral Determinants.* New York: Oxford University Press.

Olson, C. F., & Worobey, J. (1984). Perceived mother-daughter relations in a pregnant and nonpregnant adolescent sample. *Adolescence, 19,* 781–794.

Olweus, D. (1984). Development of stable aggressive reaction patterns in males. In R. Blanchard & D. C. Blanchard (eds.), *Advances in the Study of Aggression.* Orlando, FL: Academic Press.

Omark, D. R., & Edelman, M. S. (1976). The development of attention structures in young children. In M.R.A. Chance & R. R. Larsen (eds.), *The Social Structure of Attention.* London: Wiley.

Omark, D. R., Omark, M., & Edelman, M. S. (1975). Formation of dominance hierarchies in young children: Action and perception. In T. Williams (ed.), *Psychological Anthropology.* The Hague: Mouton.

Ottenberg, S. (1994). Initiations. In P. K. Bock (ed.), *Handbook of Psychological Anthropology.* Westport, CT: Greenwood Press.

Paige, K. E. (1983). A bargaining theory of menarcheal responses in pre-industrial cultures. In J. Brooks-Gunn and A. C. Petersen (eds.), *Girls at Puberty: Biological and Psychosocial Perspectives.* New York: Plenum Press.

Paikoff, R., & Brooks-Gunn, J. (1991). Do parent-child relationships change during puberty? *Psychological Bulletin, 110,* 47–66.

Panksepp, J. (1993). Neurochemical control of moods and emotions: Amino acids to neuropeptides. In M. Lewis & J. M. Haviland (eds.), *Handbook of Emotions.* New York: Guilford.

Parish, T. S. (1981). The impact of divorce on the family. *Adolescence, 16,* 577–580.

Parisi, P., & de Martino, V. (1980). Psychosocial factors in human growth. In F. E. Johnston, A. F. Roche, and C. Susanne (eds.), *Human Physical Growth and Maturation: Methodologies and Factors.* New York: Plenum.

Parker, R., & Omark, D. R. (1980). The social ecology of toughness. In D. R. Omark, F. F. Strayer, and D. G. Freedman (eds.), *Dominance Relations: An Ethological View of Human Conflict and Social Interaction.* New York: Garland.

Passingham, R. E. (1982). *The Human Primate.* San Francisco: W. H. Freeman.

Patterson, G. R. (1982). *Coercive Family Processes.* Eugene, OR: Castalia Publishing.

Pearson, W., Jr., & Hendrix, L. (1979). Divorce and the status of women. *Journal of Marriage & the Family, 41,* 375–385.

Pellegrini, A., D. (1995). A longitudinal study of boys' rough-and-tumble play and dominance during early adolescence. *Journal of Applied Developmental Psychology, 16,* 77–93.

Peplau, L. A. (1976). Fear of success in dating couples. *Sex Roles, 2,* 249–258.

Peplau, L., Rubin, Z., & Hill, C. (1977). Sexual intimacy in dating relationships. *Journal of Social Issues, 33,* 86–109.

Pereira, M. E., & Altmann, J. (1985). Development of social behavior in free-living nonhuman primates. In E. S. Watts (ed.), *Nonhuman Primate Models for Human Growth and Development.* New York: Liss.

Perez-Reyes, M., & Falk, R. (1973). Follow-up after therapeutic abortion in early adolescence. *Archives of General Psychiatry, 28,* 120–126.

Perkins, D. F., & Lerner, R. M. (1995). Single and multiple indicators of physical attractiveness and psychosocial behaviors among young adolescents. *Journal of Early Adolescence, 15,* 269–298.

Perry, D. G., Perry, L. C., & Kennedy, E. (1992). Conflict and the development of antisocial behavior. In C. U. Shantz & W. W. Hartup (eds.), *Conflict in Child and Adolescent Development.* New York: Cambridge University Press.

Perry, J. S. (1971). *The Ovarian Cycle of Mammals.* Edinburgh: Oliver & Boyd.

Persky, H., et al. (1978). Plasma testosterone level and sexual behavior of couples. *Archives of Sexual Behavior, 7,* 157–173.

Peskin, H., & Livson, M. (1972). Pre- and postpubertal personality and adult psychological functioning. *Seminars in Psychiatry, 4,* 343–353.

Petersen, A. C., & Taylor, B. (1980). The biological approach to adolescence: Biological change and psychological adaptation. In J. Adelson (ed.), *Handbook of Adolescent Psychology.* New York: Wiley.

Petzel, S. V., & Cline, D. W. (1978). Adolescent suicide: Epidemiological and biological aspects. *Adolescent Psychiatry, 6,* 239–266.

Pfeiffer, E., & Verwoerdt, A. (1978). Middle life. In E. Palmore (ed.), *Normal Aging II.* Durham, NC: Duke University Press.

Pfeiffer, J. E. (1982). *The Creative Explosion: An Inquiry into the Origins of Art and Religion.* New York: Harper & Row.

Pierce, S. (1990). The behavioral attributes of victimized children. M.A. thesis, Florida Atlantic University.

Plomin, R. (1990). *Nature and Nurture: An Introduction to Human Behavioral Genetics.* Pacific Grove, CA: Brooks/Cole.

_____. (1994). *Genetics and Experience: The Interplay Between Nature and nurture.* Thousand Oaks, CA: Sage.

Plomin, R., DeFries, J. C., & McClearn, G. E. (1990). *Behavior Genetics: A Primer.* New York: W. H. Freeman.

Plomin, R., et al. (1994). Genetic contributions to measures of the family environment. *Developmental Psychology, 30,* 32–43.

Pollis, N. P., & Doyle, D. C. (1972). Sex-role status and perceived competence among first graders. *Perceptual & Motor Skills, 34,* 235–238.

Pond, C. M. (1977). The significance of lactation in the evolution of mammals. *Evolution, 31,* 177–199.

Popenoe, D. (1993). American family decline, 1960–1990: A review and appraisal. *Journal of Marriage & the Family, 55,* 527–555.

Powell, M. (1955). Age and sex differences in degree of conflict within certain areas of psychological adjustment. *Psychological Monographs, 69,* Whole No. 387.

Powers, S., & Wagner, M. (1984). Attributions for school achievement of middle school students. *Journal of Early Adolescence, 4,* 215–222.

Precourt, W. E. (1975). Initiation ceremonies and secret societies as educational institutions. In R. W. Brislin, S. Bochner, & W. J. Lonner (eds.), *Cross-Cultural Perspective on Learning.* New York: Wiley.

Preti, G., et al. (1986). Human axillary secretions influence women's menstrual cycles: The role of donor extract of females. *Hormones & Behavior, 20,* 474–482.

Pugh, G. E. (1977). *The Biological Origin of Human Values.* New York: Basic Books.

Pulkkinen, L. (1982). Self-control and continuity in childhood-delayed adolescence. In P. Baltes & O. Brim (eds.), *Life Span Development and Behavior.* Vol. 4. New York: Academic Press.

_____. (1987). Offensive and defensive aggression in humans: A longitudinal perspective. *Aggressive Behavior, 13,* 197–212.

Puterbaugh, G. (1990). *Twins and Homosexuality.* New York: Grand Publishing.

Putnam, R. D. (1996). The strange disappearance of civic America. *American Prospect,* Winter, 34–48.

Queen, S. A., Habenstein, R. W., & Quadagno, J. S. (1985). *The Family in Various Cultures.* New York: Harper & Row.

Rachman, S. J. (1978). *Fear and Courage.* San Francisco: Freeman.

Raine, A. (1998). Biosocial bases of violence. In F. S. Pearson & G. E. Weisfeld (eds.), *Proceedings of a Conference on Young Male Violence.* Detroit: Program on Mediating Theory & Democratic Systems, Working Paper Series, Wayne State University.

Rajecki, D. W., & Flannery, R. C. (1981). Social conflict and dominance in children: A case for a primate homology. In M. E. Lamb & A. Brown (eds.), *Advances in Developmental Psychology.* Vol. 1. Hillsdale, NJ: Erlbaum.

Rathus, S. A., Nevid, J. S., & Fichner-Rathus, L. (1997). *Human Sexuality in a World of Diversity* (3rd ed.). Boston: Allyn & Bacon.

Raynor, L. (1980). *The Adopted Child Comes of Age.* London: Allen & Unwin.

Reinisch, J. M. (1981). Prenatal exposure to synthetic progestins increases potential for aggression in humans. *Science, 211,* 1171–1173.

Reis, H. T., et al. (1982). Physical attractiveness in social interaction, 2: Why does appearance affect social experience? *Journal of Personality and Social Psychology, 43,* 979–996.

Reiter, E. O. (1986). The neuroendocrine regulation of pubertal onset. In J. B. Lancaster & B. A. Hamburg (eds.), *School-Age Pregnancy and Parenthood: Biosocial Dimensions.* New York: Aldine de Gruyter.

Rickel, A. U. (1989). *Teen Pregnancy and Parenting.* New York: Hemisphere.

Robertson, R. (1987). *Heroin, AIDS and Society.* London: Hodder & Stoughton.

Robins, L. (1978). Sturdy childhood predictors of adult antisocial behaviour: Replications from longitudinal studies. *Psychological Medicine, 8,* 611–622.

Robinson, J. E., & Short, R. V. (1977). Changes in breast sensitivity at puberty, during the menstrual cycle, and at parturition. *British Medical Journal, 1,* 1188–1191.

Rodin, J. (1977). Bidirectional influences of emotionality, stimulus responsivity, and metabolic events in obesity. In J. D. Maser & M.E.P. Seligman (eds.), *Psychopathology: Experimental Models.* San Francisco: Freeman.

Rohlen, T. P. (1983). *Japan's High Schools.* Berkeley: University of California Press.

Rohner, R. P. (1975). *They Love Me, They Love Me Not: A World-Wide Survey of the Effects of Parental Acceptance and Rejection.* New Haven: HRAF Press.

――――. (1976). Sex differences in aggression. *Ethos, 4,* 57–72.

Rose, R. M., Bernstein, I. S., & Gordon, T. P. (1975). Consequences of social conflict on plasma testosterone levels in rhesus monkeys. *Psychosomatic Medicine, 37,* 50–61.

Rosenblatt, P. C. (1974). Cross-cultural perspective on attraction. In T. L. Huston (ed.), *Foundations of Interpersonal Attraction.* New York: Academic.

Rosenblatt, P. C., & Unangst, D. (1979). Marriage ceremonies: An exploratory cross-cultural study. In G. Kurian (ed.), *Cross-Cultural Perspectives of Mate-Selection and Marriage.* London: Greenwood.

Rosenblum, L. A. (1971). The ontogeny of mother-infant relations in macaques. In H. Moltz (ed.), *The Ontogeny of Vertebrate Behavior.* New York: Academic Press.

Rosenblum, L. A., & Nadler, R. D. (1971). Ontogeny of male sexual behavior in bonnet macaques. In D. Ford (ed.), *Influence of Hormones on the Nervous System.* Basel, Switzerland: Karger.

Rosenthal, R., & DePaulo, B. M. (1979). Sex differences in eavesdropping in nonverbal cues. *Journal of Personality & Social Psychology, 37,* 271–285.

Rosenzweig, M. R., Leiman, A. L., & Breedlove, S. M. (1996). *Biological Psychology.* Sunderland, MA: Sinauer.

Rossi, A. (1987). Parenthood in transition: From lineage to child and self-orientation. In J. B. Lancaster et al. (eds.), *Parenting Across the Life Span: Biosocial Dimensions.* New York: Aldine de Gruyter.

Rowell, T. E. (1972). *The Social Behaviour of Monkeys and Apes.* New York: Penguin.

Rubenstein, D. I. (1993). On the evolution of juvenile life-styles in mammals. In M. E. Pereira & L. A. Fairbanks (eds.), *Juvenile Primates: Life History, Development, and Behavior.* New York: Oxford University Press.

Rubin, L. (1986). *Just Friends: The Role of Friendship in Our Lives.* New York: Harper.

Ruble, D. N. (1983). The development of social-comparison processes and their role in achievement-related self-socialization. In E. T. Higgins, D. N. Ruble, & W. W. Hartup (eds.), *Social Cognition and Social Development.* Cambridge: Cambridge University Press.

Rueter, M. A., & Conger, R. D. (1995). Interaction style, problem-solving behavior, and family problem-solving effectiveness. *Child Development, 66,* 98–115.

Rushton, J. P. (1988). Genetic similarity, mate choice, and fecundity in humans. *Ethology & Sociobiology, 9,* 329–333.

Russell, R. J. H., & Wells, P. A. (1987). Estimating paternity confidence. *Ethology & Sociobiology, 8,* 215–220.

Russell, S. T. (1994). Life course antecedents of premarital conception in Britain. *Journal of Marriage & the Family, 56,* 480–492.

Rutter, M., & Giller, H. (1983). *Juvenile Delinquency: Trends and Perspectives.* Harmondsworth, England: Penguin.

Rutter, M., & Rutter, M. (1993). *Developing Minds: Challenge and Continuity Across the Life Span.* New York: Basic Books.

Sabatelli, R. M., & Rubin, M. (1986). Nonverbal expressiveness and physical attractiveness as mediators of interpersonal perceptions. *Journal of Nonverbal Behavior, 10,* 120–133.

Sadalla, E. I., Kenrick, D. T., & Vershure, B. (1987). Dominance and heterosexual attraction. *Journal of Personality & Social Psychology, 52,* 730–738.

Saghir, M. T., & Robins, E. (1973). *Male and Female Homosexuality: A Comprehensive Investigation.* Baltimore: Williams & Wilkins.

Saltz, E., Dixon, D., & Johnson, J. E. (1977). Training disadvantaged preschoolers on various fantasy activities: Effect on cognitive functioning and impulse control. *Child Development, 40,* 367–380.

Sanders, S. A., & Reinisch, J. M. (1990). Biological and social influences on the endocrinology of puberty: Some additional considerations. In J. Bancroft & J. M. Reinisch (eds.), *Adolescence and Puberty.* New York: Oxford University Press.

Sanford, S., & Eder, D. (1984). Adolescent humor during peer interaction. *Social Psychology Quarterly, 47,* 235–243.

Santrock, J. W. (1996). *Adolescence.* Dubuque, IA: Brown & Benchmark.

Savin-Williams, R. C. (1976). An ethological study of dominance formation and maintenance in a group of human adolescents. *Child Development, 47,* 972–979.

———. (1982). A field study of adolescent social interactions: Developmental and contextual influences. *Journal of Social Psychology, 117,* 203–209.

———. (1987). *Adolescence: An Ethological Perspective.* New York: Springer-Verlag.

Savin-Williams, R. C., & Cohen, K. M. (1996). *The Lives of Lesbians, Gays, and Bisexuals: Children and Adults.* New York: Harcourt Brace.

Savin-Williams, R. C., & Demo, D. H. (1984). Conceiving or misconceiving the self: Issues in adolescent self-esteem. *Journal of Early Adolescence, 3,* 121–140.

Savin-Williams, R. C., & Small, S. A. (1986). The timing of puberty and its relationship to adolescent and parent perceptions of family interactions. *Developmental Psychology, 22,* 342–347.

Scanzoni, J. (1972). *Sexual Bargaining: Power Politics in the American Marriage.* Englewood Cliffs, NJ: Prentice-Hall.

Scarr, S., & McCartney, K. (1983). How people make their own environments: A theory of genotype-environmental effects. *Child Development, 54,* 424–435.

Scherer, K. R. (1984). On the nature and function of emotion: A component process approach. In K. R. Scherer & P. Ekman (eds.), *Approaches to Emotion.* Hillsdale, NJ: Erlbaum.

Schlegel, A. (1995). A cross-cultural approach to adolescence. *Ethos, 23,* 15–32.

Schlegel, A., & Barry, H., III (1980a). Adolescent initiation ceremonies: A cross-cultural code. In H. Barry III & A. Schlegel (eds.), *Cross-Cultural Samples and Codes.* Pittsburgh: University of Pittsburgh Press.

———. (1980b). The evolutionary significance of adolescent initiation ceremonies. *American Ethnologist, 7,* 696–715.

_____. (1991). *Adolescence: An Anthropological Inquiry.* New York: Free Press.

Schmitt, A., & Atzwanger, K. (1995). Walking fast—ranking high: A sociobiological perspective on pace. *Ethology & Sociobiology, 16,* 451–462.

Schnatz, P. T. (1985). Neuroendocrinology and the ovulation cycle—Advances and review. *Advances in Psychosomatic Medicine, 12, 7.*

Schreider, E. (1964). Recherches sur la stratification sociale des caractères biologiques. *Biotypologie, 26,* 105–135.

Schroeder, R., & Flapan, D. (1971). Aggressive and friendly behaviors of young children from two social classes. *Child Psychiatry & Human Development, 2,* 32–41.

Schultz, H. (1959). Tukuna maidens come of age. *National Geographic Magazine, 116,* 629–649.

Scott, E. C., & Johnston, F. E. (1982). Critical fat, menarche, and the maintenance of menstrual cycles. *Journal of Adolescent Health Care, 2,* 249–260.

Scott, E. M., Illsley, I. P., & Thomson, A. M. (1956). A psychological investigation of primagravidae: Maternal social class, age, physique and intelligence. *Journal of Obstetrics & Gynaecology of the British Empire, 63,* 338–343.

Scott, J. F. (1971). *Internalization of Norms.* Englewood Cliffs, NJ: Prentice-Hall.

Seccombe, K., & Lee, G. (1987). Female status, wives' autonomy, and divorce: A cross-cultural study. *Family Perspectives, 20,* 41–49.

Segal, N. L. (1988). Cooperation, competition, and altruism in human twinships: A sociobiological approach. In K. B. MacDonald (ed.), *Sociobiological Perspectives on Human Development.* New York: Springer-Verlag.

Segal, N. L., Weisfeld, G. E., & Weisfeld, C. C. (1997). *Uniting Psychology and Biology: Integrative Perspectives on Human Development.* Washington, DC: American Psychological Association.

Selye, H. (1956). *The Stress of Life.* New York: McGraw-Hill.

Sevenster, P. (1973). Incompatibility of response and reward. In R.A. Hinde & J. Stevenson-Hinde (eds.), *Constraints on Learning.* New York: Academic Press.

Shaffer, L. F., & Shoben, E. J., Jr. (1956). *The Psychology of Adjustment.* Boston: Houghton Mifflin.

Shanas, E. (1942). *Recreation and Delinquency.* Chicago: Chicago Recreation Commission.

_____. (1973). Family-kin networks in cross-cultural perspective. *Journal of Marriage & the Family, 35,* 505–511.

Shattuck, R. (1980). *The Forbidden Experiment: The Story of the Wild Boy of Aveyron.* New York: Farrar Straus Giroux.

Sheldon, W. H., Stevens, S. S., & Tucker, W. B. (1940). *The Varieties of Human Physique.* New York: Harper.

Shepher, J., & Tiger, L. (1978). Female hierarchies in a kibbutz community. In L. Tiger & H. Fowler (eds.), *Female Hierarchies.* Chicago: Beresford Book Service.

Sherif, M., & Sherif, C. W. (1953). *Groups in Harmony and Tension: An Integration of Studies on Intergroup Relations.* New York: Harper & Row.

_____. (1956). *An Outline of Social Psychology* (2nd ed.). New York: Harper & Row.

_____. (1964). *Reference Groups: Exploration into Conformity and Deviation of Adolescents.* New York: Harper and Row.

Short, R. V. (1981). Sexual selection in man and the great apes. In C. E. Graham (ed.), *Reproductive Biology of the Great Apes.* New York: Academic.

Shostak, M. (1981). *Nisa: The Life and Words of a !Kung Woman.* New York: Vintage.

Silbereisen, R., et al. (1989). Maturational timing and the development of problem behavior: Longitudinal studies in adolescence. *Journal of Early Adolescence, 3,* 247–268.

Silverberg, S. B. (1989). Parents as developing adults: The impact of perceived distance in the parent-adolescent relationship. Poster presented at the biennial meeting of the Society for Research in Child Development, Kansas City, MO, April.

Silverman, I., & Phillips, K. A. (1993). Effects of estrogen changes during the menstrual cycle on spatial performance. *Ethology & Sociobiology, 14,* 257–269.

Simmons, R. G., Blyth, D. A., & McKinney, K. L. (1983). The social and psychological effects of puberty on white females. In J. Brooks-Gunn & A. C. Petersen (eds.), *Girls at Puberty: Biological and Psychosocial Perspectives.* New York: Plenum.

Singer, B. (1985a). A comparison of evolutionary and environmental theories of erotic response, Part 1: Structural features. *Journal of Sex Research, 21,* 229–257.

_____. (1985b). A comparison of evolutionary and environmental theories of erotic response, Part 2: Empirical arenas. *Journal of Sex Research, 21,* 346–374.

Singh, D. (1993). Adaptive significance of female attractiveness: Role of waist-to-hip ratio. *Journal of Personality & Social Psychology, 65,* 293–307.

_____. (1995). Female judgment of male attractiveness and desirability for relationships: Role of waist-to-hip ratio and financial status. *Journal of Personality & Social Psychology, 69,* 1089–1101.

Singh, D., & Young, R. K. (1995). Body weight, waist-to-hip ratio, breasts, and hips: Role in judgments of female attractiveness and desirability for relationships. *Ethology & Sociobiology*, 16, 483–507.

Sluckin, A. M. (1980). Dominance relationships in preschool children. In D. R. Omark, F. F. Strayer, & D. G. Freedman (eds.), *Dominance Relations: An Ethological View of Human Conflict and Social Interaction*. New York: Garland.

Smith, D. S., & Hindus, M. S. (1975). Premarital pregnancy in America, 1640–1971: An overview and interpretation. *Journal of Interdisciplinary History*, 5, 537–570.

Smith, E. A. (1989). A biosocial model of adolescent sexual behavior. In G. R. Adams, R. Montemayor, & T. P. Gullotta (eds.), *Biology of Adolescent Behavior and Development*. New York: Sage.

Smith, G. (1985). Facial and full-length ratings of attractiveness related to the social interactions of young children. *Sex Roles*, 12, 287–293.

Smith, M. S. (1987). Modern childhood: An evolutionary perspective. In K. Ekberg & P. E. Mjaavatn (eds.), *Growing into a Modern World*. Trondheim, Norway: University of Trondheim.

Smith, P. K., & Thompson, D. (eds.). (1991). *Practical Approaches to Bullying*. London: David Fulton.

Smuts, B. (1985). *Sex and Friendship in Baboons*. Hawthorne, NY: Aldine de Gruyter.

Soltz, H. R., & Soltz, L. M. (1944). Adolescent problems related to somatic variation. In N. B. Henry (ed.), *Adolescence: 43rd Yearbook of the National Committee for the Study of Education, Part 1*. Chicago: University of Chicago Press.

Sommer, B. B. (1978). *Puberty and Adolescence*. New York: Oxford University Press.

Sones, G., & Feshbach, M. (1971). Sex differences in adolescent reactions towards newcomers. *Developmental Psychology*, 4, 381–386.

Sorensen, R. C. (1973). *Adolescent Sexuality in Contemporary America*. New York: World Publishing.

Spindler, G. D. (1970). The education of adolescents: An anthropological perspective. In D. Ellis (ed.), *Adolescents: Readings in Behavior and Development*. Hinsdale, IL: Dryden Press.

Spiro, M. E. (1979). *Gender and Culture: Kibbutz women revisited*. Durham, NC: Duke University Press.

Staffieri, J. R. (1967). A study of social stereotypes of body image in children. *Journal of Personality & Social Psychology*, 7, 101–104.

Stanley, H. M. (1898). Remarks on tickling and laughing. *American Journal of Sociology*, 9, 235–240.

Stapley, J. C., & Haviland, J. M. (1989). Beyond depression: Gender differences in normal adolescents' emotional experiences. *Sex Roles, 20,* 295–308.

Stattin, H., & Klackenberg, G. (1992). Discordant family relations in intact families: Developmental tendencies over 18 years. *Journal of Marriage & the Family, 54,* 940–956.

Steinberg, L. (1987). The impact of puberty on family relations: Effects of pubertal status and pubertal timing. *Developmental Psychology, 23,* 451–460.

_____. (1988). Reciprocal relation between parent-child "distance" and pubertal maturation. *Developmental Psychology, 24,* 122–128.

_____. (1996). *Adolescence.* 4th ed. New York: McGraw-Hill.

Steinberg, L. D., & Hill, J. P. (1978). Patterns of family interaction as a function of age, the onset of puberty, and formal thinking. *Developmental Psychology, 14,* 683–684.

Stephens, W. N. (1963). *The Family in Cross-Cultural Perspective.* New York: Holt, Rinehart & Winston.

Sternglanz, S. H., Gray, J. L., & Murakami, M. (1977). Adult preferences for infantile facial features. *Animal Behaviour, 25,* 108–116.

Steward, C. S., & Zaenglein-Senger, M. M. (1982). The parent-adolescent power contest. *Social Casework,* 457–464.

Stimson, G. V., & Oppenheimer, E. (1982). *Heroin Addiction: Treatment and Control in Britain.* London: Tavistock.

Stipek, D. (1995). The development of pride and shame in toddlers. In J. P. Tangney & K. W. Fischer (eds.), *Self-Conscious Emotions: The Psychology of Shame, Guilt, Embarrassment, and Pride.* New York: Guilford Press.

Stoddart, D. M. (1990). *The Scented Ape: The Biology and Culture of Human Odour.* Cambridge: Cambridge University Press.

Stoltz, H. R., & Stoltz, L. M. (1944). Adolescent problems related to somatic variation. In N. B. Henry (ed.), *Adolescence: Forty-Third Yearbook of the National Committee for the Study of Education.* Chicago: Department of Education, University of Chicago.

Straus, M., Gelles, R. J., & Steinmetz, S. K. (1980). *Behind Closed Doors: Violence in American Families.* New York: Doubleday.

Strayer, F. F., & Strayer, J. (1976). An ethological analysis of social agonism and dominance relations among preschool children. *Child Development, 47,* 980–989.

Strayer, F. F., & Trudel, M. (1984). Developmental changes in the nature and function of social dominance among young children. *Ethology & Sociobiology, 5,* 279–295.

Stuart-Macadam, P. (1995a). Biocultural perspectives on breastfeeding. In P. Stuart-Macadam & K. A. Dettwyler (eds.), *Breastfeeding: Biocultural Perspectives.* New York: Aldine de Gruyter.

_____. (1995b). Breastfeeding in prehistory. In P. Stuart-Macadam & K. A. Dettwyler (eds.), *Breastfeeding: Biocultural Perspectives.* New York: Aldine de Gruyter.

Sullen-Tullberg, B., & Moller, A. P. (1993). The relationship between concealed ovulation and mating systems in anthropoid primates: A phylogenetic analysis. *American Naturalist, 141,* 1–25.

Surbey, M. (1987). Anorexia nervosa, amenorrhea, and adaptation. *Ethology & Sociobiology, 8,* 47–61.

Surbey, M. K. (1990). Family composition, stress, and the timing of human menarche. In T. E. Ziegler & F. B. Bercovitch (eds.), *Socioendocrinology of Primate Reproduction.* New York: Wiley-Liss.

_____. (1998a). Developmental psychology and modern Darwinism. In C. Crawford & D. L. Krebs (eds.), *Handbook of Evolutionary Psychology: Ideas, Issues, and Applications.* Mahwah, NJ: Erlbaum.

_____. (1998b). Parent and offspring: Strategies in the transition at adolescence. *Human Nature, 9,* 67–94.

Svare, B., Bartke, A., & Macrides, F. (1978). Juvenile male mice: An attempt to accelerate testis function by exposure to adult female stimuli. *Physiology & Behavior, 21,* 1009–1014.

Symons, D. (1979). *The Evolution of Human Sexuality.* New York: Oxford University Press.

Tamashiro, R. T., (1979). Adolescents' concept of marriage: A structural-developmental analysis. *Journal of Youth & Adolescence, 8,* 643–652.

Tannenbaum, A. J. (1960). Adolescents' attitudes toward academic brilliance. Ph.D. dissertation, New York University. Cited in Coleman (1961).

Tanner, J. M. (1955). *Growth at Adolescence.* Oxford: Blackwell.

_____. (1962). *Growth at Adolescence* (2nd ed.). Oxford: Blackwell Scientific.

_____. (1975). Growth and endocrinology of the adolescent. In L. Gardner (ed.), *Endocrine and Genetic Diseases of Childhood* (2nd ed.). Philadelphia: Saunders.

_____. (1978). *Fetus into Man: Physical Growth from Conception to Maturity.* Cambridge, MA: Harvard University Press.

Tanner, N., & Zihlman, A. (1976). Women in evolution, Part I: Innovation and selection in human origins. *Signs: Journal of Women in Culture & Society, 1:* 585–608.

Teismann, M. W. (1975). Jealous conflict: A study of verbal interaction and labeling of jealousy among dating couples involved in jealous improvisations. Ph.D. dissertation, University of Connecticut.

Terman, L. M., & Miles, C. C. (1936). *Sex and Personality: Studies in Masculinity and Femininity.* New York: McGraw-Hill.

Tharp, R. G. (1963). Psychological patterning in marriage. *Psychological Bulletin, 60,* 97–117.

Thompson, L., & Joseph, A. (1944). *The Hopi Way*. Chicago: University of Chicago Press.

Thornhill, R., & Gangestad, S. W. (1994). Fluctuating asymmetry correlates with lifetime sex partner numbers and age at first sex in *Homo sapiens*. *Psychological Science, 5,* 297–302.

Thornhill, R., & Thornhill, N. (1983). Human rape: An evolutionary analysis. *Ethology & Sociobiology, 4,* 63–99.

Thrasher, F. M. (1926). *The Gang*. Chicago: University of Chicago Press.

Tiger, L. (1969). *Men in Groups*. New York: Random House.

Tiger, L., & Shepher, J. (1975). *Women in the Kibbutz*. New York: Harcourt Brace Jovanovich.

Tinbergen, N. (1951). *The Study of Instinct*. London: Oxford University Press.

_____. (1963a). On the aims and methods of ethology. *Zeitgeist für Tierpsychologie, 20,* 410–433.

_____. (1963b). The shell menace. *Natural History, 72,* 28–35.

Tobin-Richards, M. H., Boxer, A. M., & Petersen, A. C. (1983). The psychological significance of pubertal change: Sex differences in perceptions of self during early adolescence. In J. Brooks-Gunn & A. C. Petersen (eds.), *Girls at Puberty: Biological and Psychosocial Perspectives*. New York: Plenum.

Tocqueville, A. de (1835/1969). *Democracy in America*. Garden City, NJ: Anchor Books.

Tolan, P. H., & Lorion, R. P. (1988). Multivariate approaches to the identification of delinquency proneness in adolescent males. *American Journal of Community Psychology, 16,* 547–561.

Tolan, P. H., & Thomas, P. (1995). The implications of age of onset for delinquency risk, 2: Longitudinal data. *Journal of Abnormal Child Psychology, 23,* 157–181.

Tomkins, S. S. (1962). *Affect, Imagery and Consciousness*, Vol. 1: *The Positive Affects*. New York: Springer.

Tooke, R., Camire, L., & Poore, G. (1990). Sex differences in mating strategies involving intersexual and intrasexual deception. Paper presented at the convention of the Human Behavior and Evolution society, Los Angeles, August.

Townsend, J. M., Kline, J., & Wasserman, T. H. (1995). Low-investment copulation: Sex differences in motivations and emotional reactions. *Ethology & Sociobiology, 16,* 25–51.

Trent, K., & South, S. (1989). Structural determinants of the divorce rate: A cross-societal analysis. *Journal of Marriage & the Family, 51,* 391–404.

Trivers, R. L. (1971). The evolution of reciprocal altruism. *Quarterly Review of Biology, 46,* 35–57.

_____. (1972). Parental investment and sexual selection. In B. Campbell (ed.), *Sexual Selection and the Descent of Man, 1871–1971*. Chicago: Aldine.

_____. (1974). Parent-offspring conflict. *American Zoologist, 14,* 249–264.

_____. (1985). *Social Evolution*. Menlo Park, CA: Benjamin/Cummings.

_____. (1994). The new evolutionary genetics. Paper presented at the convention of the Human Behavior and Evolution Society, Ann Arbor, MI, June.

_____. (1997). Genetic basis of intrapsychic conflict. In N. L. Segal, G. E. Weisfeld, & C. C. Weisfeld (eds.), *Uniting Psychology and Biology: Integrative Perspectives on Human Development*. Washington, DC: American Psychological Association.

Trivers, R. L., & Willard, D. E. (1973). Natural selection of parental ability to vary the sex ratio of offspring. *Science, 179,* 90–91.

Tulkin, S. R., Muller, J. P., & Conn, L., K. (1969). Need for approval and popularity: Sex differences in elementary school children. *Journal of Consulting & Clinical Psychology, 33,* 35–39.

Turke, P. W. (1988). Helpers at the nest: Childcare networks on Ifaluk. In L. Betzig, M. Borgerhoff Mulder, & P. Turke (eds.), *Human Reproductive Behavior*. Cambridge: Cambridge University Press.

Turner, A. K. (1994). Genetic and hormonal influences on male violence. In J. Archer (ed.), *Male Violence*. London: Routledge.

Turner, J. C. (1982). Intergroup conflict and cooperation. In A. M. Colman (ed.), *Cooperation and Competition in Humans and Animals*. New York: Van Nostrand Reinhold.

Tzeng, M.-S. (1992). The effects of socioeconomic heterogamy and changes on marital dissolution of first marriages. *Journal of Marriage & the Family, 54,* 609–619.

Udry, J. R. (1988). Biological predispositions and social control in adolescent sexual behavior. *American Sociological Review, 53,* 709–722.

Udry, J. R., & Billy J. (1987). Initiation of coitus in early adolescence. *American Sociological Review, 52,* 841–855.

Udry, J. R., & Cliquet, R. L. (1982). A cross-cultural examination of the relationship between ages at menarche, marriage, and first birth. *Demography, 19,* 53–63.

Urberg, K. A., & Labouvie-Vief, G. (1976). Conceptualizations of sex roles: A life-span developmental study. *Developmental Psychology, 12,* 15–23.

Useche, B., Villegas, M., & Aizate, H. (1980). Sexual behavior of Colombian high school students. *Adolescence, 25,* 291–303.

Vandenbergh, J. G. (1969). Effect of the presence of a male on the sexual maturation of female mice. *Endocrinology, 81,* 345–356.

van den Berghe, P. L. (1979). *Human Family Systems: An Evolutionary View*. New York: Elsevier.

———. (1980). The human family: A sociobiological look. In J. S. Lockard (ed.), *The Evolution of Human Social Behavior.* New York: Elsevier.

van der Dennen, J.M.G. (1992). The sociobiology of behavioural sex differences, 2: Sex differences in sexual and aggressive behavioural systems. In J.M.G. van der Dennen (ed.), *The Nature of the Sexes: The Sociobiology of Sex Differences and the "Battle of the Sexes."* Groningen, The Netherlands: Origin Press.

van Gennep, A. (1909/1960). *The Rites of Passage.* Chicago: University of Chicago Press.

van Hooff, J.A.R.A.M. (1969). The facial display of the catarrhine monkeys and apes. In D. Morris (ed.), *Primate Ethology.* London: Weidenfeld & Nicolson.

Veith, J. L., et al. (1983). Exposure to men influences the occurrence of ovulation in women. *Physiology & Behavior, 31,* 313–315.

Vernon, M. D. (1969). *Human Motivation.* Cambridge: Cambridge University Press.

Vinovskis, M. A. (1986). Adolescent sexuality, pregnancy, and childbearing in early America: Some preliminary speculations. In J. B. Lancaster & B. A. Hamburg (eds.), *School-Age Pregnancy and Parenthood: Biosocial Dimensions.* New York: Aldine de Gruyter.

Vizedom, M. (1976). *Rites and Relationships: Rites of Passage and Contemporary Anthropology.* Beverly Hills, CA: Sage.

Voland, E., & Engel, C. (1990). Female choice in humans: a conditional mate selection strategy of the Krummhorn women (Germany, 1720–1874). *Ethology, 14,* 144–154.

Vrugt, A. (1987). The meaning of nonverbal sex differences. *Semiotica, 64,* 371–380.

Wagner, E., & Asarnow, R. (1980). The interpersonal behavior of preadolescent boys with high and low peer status. Manuscript, University of Waterloo. Cited in Hartup (1983).

Wallerstein, J. S., & Blakeslee, S. (1989). *Second Chances: Women and Children a Decade After Divorce.* New York: Ticknor & Fields.

Wallerstein, J. S., & Kelley, J. B. (1980). *Surviving the Breakup: How Children and Parents Cope with Divorce.* New York: Basic Books.

Walsh, A. (1993). Love styles, masculine/feminine physical attractiveness, and sexual behavior: A test of evolutionary theory. *Ethology & Sociobiology, 14,* 25–38.

Walters, J. R. (1987). Transition to adulthood. In B. B Smuts et al. (eds.), *Primate Societies.* Chicago: University of Chicago Press.

Ward, I. L., & Weisz, J. (1980). Maternal stress alters plasma testosterone in fetal males. *Science, 207,* 328–329.

Warren, M. P. (1980). The effects of exercise on pubertal progression and reproductive function in girls. *Journal of Clinical Endocrinology & Metabolism, 51,* 1150–1157.

_____. (1983). Physical and biological aspects of puberty. In J. Brooks-Gunn & A. C. Petersen (eds.), *Girls at Puberty: Biological and Psychosocial Perspectives.* New York: Plenum.

Warren, M. P., & Shortle, B. (1990). Endocrine correlates of human parenting: A clinical perspective. In N. A. Krasnegor & R. S. Bridges (eds.), *Mammalian Parenting: Biochemical, Neurobiological, and Behavioral Determinants.* New York: Oxford University Press.

Watts, D. P., & Pusey, A. E. (1993). Behavior of juvenile and adolescent great apes. In M. E. Pereira & L. A. Fairbanks (eds.), *Juvenile Primates: Life History, Development, and Behavior.* New York: Oxford University Press.

Watts, E. S. (1985). Adolescent growth and development of monkeys, apes, and humans. In E. S. Watts (ed.), *Nonhuman Primate Models for Human Grown and Development.* New York: Alan Liss.

Weatherley, D. (1964). Self-perceived rate of physical maturation and personality in late adolescence. *Child Development, 35,* 1197–1210.

Webster, M., & Sobieszek, B. (1974). *Sources of Self-Evaluation.* New York: Wiley.

Weisfeld, C. C. (1986). Female behavior in mixed-sex competition: A review of the literature. *Developmental Review, 6,* 278–299.

Weisfeld, C. C., & Weisfeld, G. E. (1996). Some correlates of marital satisfaction. Paper presented at the convention of the International Society for Human Ethology, Vienna, August.

Weisfeld, C. C., Weisfeld, G. E., & Callaghan, J. W. (1982). Female inhibition in mixed-sex competition among young adolescents. *Ethology & Sociobiology, 3,* 29–42.

Weisfeld, C. C., et al. (1983). The spelling bee: A naturalistic study of female inhibition in mixed-sex competition. *Adolescence, 18,* 695–708.

Weisfeld, G. E. (1980). Social dominance and human motivation. In D. R. Omark, F. F. Strayer, & D. G. Freedman (eds.), *Dominance Relations: An Ethological View of Human Conflict and Social Interaction.* New York: Garland.

_____. (1982). The nature-nurture issue and the integrating concept of function. In B. B. Wolman (ed.), *Handbook of Developmental Psychology.* Englewood Cliffs, NJ: Prentice-Hall.

_____. (1986). Teaching about sex differences in human behavior and the biological approach in general. *Politics & the Life Sciences, 5,* 36–43.

_____. (1990). Sociobiological patterns of Arab culture. *Ethology & Sociobiology, 11,* 23–49.

_____. (1993). The adaptive value of humor and laughter. *Ethology & Sociobiology, 14,* 141–169.

_____. (1994). Aggression and dominance in the social world of boys. In J. Archer (ed.), *Male Violence.* London: Routledge.

_____. (1997a). Discrete emotions theory with specific reference to pride and shame. In N. L. Segal, G. Weisfeld, & C. C. Weisfeld (eds.), *Uniting Psychology and Biology: Integrative Perspectives on Human Development.* Washington, DC: American Psychological Association.

_____. (1997b). Research on emotions and future developments in human ethology. In A. Schmitt et al. (eds.), *New Aspects of Human Ethology.* New York: Plenum Press.

_____. (1997c). Puberty rites as clues to the nature of human adolescence. *Cross-Cultural Research, 31,* 27–55.

Weisfeld, G. E., & Aytch, D. M. (1996). Biological factors in family violence. *Michigan Family Review, 2,* 25–39.

Weisfeld, G. E., & Beresford, J. M. (1982). Erectness of posture as an indicator of dominance or success in humans. *Motivation & Emotion, 6,* 113–131.

Weisfeld, G. E., & Berger, J. M. (1983). Some features of human adolescence viewed in evolutionary perspective. *Human Development, 26,* 121–133.

Weisfeld, G. E., & Billings, R. L. (1988). Observations on adolescence. In K. B. MacDonald (ed.), *Sociobiological Perspectives on Human Development.* New York: Springer-Verlag.

Weisfeld, G. E., Bloch, S. A., & Ivers, J. W. (1983). A factor analytic study of peer-perceived dominance in adolescent boys. *Adolescence, 18,* 229–243.

_____. (1984a). Possible determinants of social dominance among adolescent girls. *Journal of Genetic Psychology, 144,* 115–129.

Weisfeld, G. E., & Feldman, R. (1982). A former street gang leader re-interviewed eight years later. *Crime & Delinquency, 28,* 567–581.

Weisfeld, G. E., & Laehn, T. (1986). Eye gaze and posture as related to arrogation of a resource and dominant personality. Poster presented at the convention of the International Society for Human Ethology, Tutzing, West Germany, July.

Weisfeld, G. E., & Linkey, H. E. (1985). Dominance displays as indicators of a social success motive. In J. Dovidio & S. Ellyson (eds.), *Power, Dominance, and Nonverbal Behavior.* New York: Springer-Verlag.

Weisfeld, G. E., Omark, D. R., & Cronin, C. L. (1980). A longitudinal and cross-sectional study of dominance in boys. In D. R. Omark, F. F. Strayer, & D. G. Freedman (eds.), *Dominance Relations: An Ethological View of Human Conflict and Social Interaction.* New York: Garland.

Weisfeld, G. E., & Weisfeld, C. C. (1984). An observational study of social evaluation: An application of the dominance hierarchy model. *Journal of Genetic Psychology, 145,* 89–99.

Weisfeld, G. E., Weisfeld, C. C., & Callaghan, J. W. (1984b). Peer and self perceptions in Hopi and Afro-American third and sixth graders. *Journal of Genetic Psychology, 12,* 64–84.

Weisfeld, G. E., Weisfeld, C. C., & Segal, N. L. (1997). Final overview: Uniting psychology and biology. In N. L. Segal, G. E. Weisfeld, & C. C. Weisfeld (eds.), *Uniting Psychology and Biology: Integrative Perspectives on Human Development.* Washington, DC: American Psychological Association.

Weisfeld, G. E., et al. (1987). Stability of boys' social success among peers over an eleven-year period. In J. A. Meacham (ed.), *Interpersonal Relations: Family, Peers, Friends.* Basel, Switzerland: Karger.

Weisfeld, G. E., et al. (1992). Correlates of satisfaction in British marriage. *Ethology & Sociobiology, 13,* 125–145.

Werner, E. E. (1979). *Cross-Cultural Child Development.* Monterey, CA: Brooks/Cole.

Werner, E. E., & Smith, R. S. (1982). *Vulnerable but Invincible.* New York: McGraw-Hill.

Westoff, C. F., Calot, G., & Foster, A. D. (1983). Teenage fertility in developed nations: 1971–1980. *Family Planning Perspectives, 15,* 105–110.

White, L. K., & Booth, A. (1985). The quality and stability of remarriages: The role of stepchildren. *American Sociological Review, 58,* 689–698.

Whiting, B. B., & Edwards, C. P. (1973). A cross-cultural analysis of sex differences in the behavior of children aged three through 11. *Journal of Social Psychology, 91,* 171–188.

――――. (1988). *Children of Different Worlds.* Cambridge, MA: Harvard University Press.

Whiting, B. B., & Whiting, J.W.M. (1975a). *Children of Six Cultures: A Psycho-Cultural Analysis.* Cambridge, MA: Harvard University Press.

――――. (1975b). Task assignment and personality: A consideration of the effect of herding on boys. In W. W. Lambert & R. Weisbrod (eds.), *Comparative Perspectives on Social Psychology.* Boston: Little, Brown.

Whiting, J.W.M. (1968). Commentary. In R. B. Lee & I. DeVore (eds.), *Man the Hunter.* Chicago: Aldine.

Whiting, J.W.M., Kluckhohn, F., & Anthony, A. S. (1958). The function of male initiation ceremonies at puberty. In E. E. Maccoby, T. Newcomb, & E. Hartley (eds.), *Readings in Social Psychology.* New York: Holt.

Whiting, J.W.M., & Whiting, B. B. (1960). Contributions of anthropology to the methods of studying child-rearing. In P. Mussen (ed.), *Handbook of Research Methods in Child Development.* New York: Wiley.

_____. (1973). Altruistic and egoistic behavior in six cultures. *Anthropological Studies, 9,* 56–66.

Whitman, F. L. (1983). Culturally invariable properties of male homosexuality: Tentative conclusions from cross-cultural research. *Archives of Sexual Behavior, 12,* 207–226.

Whyte, W. F. (1943). *Street Corner Society.* Chicago: University of Chicago Press.

Widdowson, E. M. (1951). Mental contentment and physical growth. *Lancet, 1,* 1316–1318.

Wilkinson, G. S. (1984). Reciprocal food sharing in the vampire bat. *Nature, 308,* 181–184.

Williams, J. E., & Best, D. L. (1986). Sex stereotypes and intergroup relations. In S. Worchel & W. G. Austin (eds.), *Intergroup Relations.* Chicago: Nelson-Hall.

Williams, J. M., & White, K. A. (1983). Adolescent status systems for males and females at three age levels. *Adolescence, 18,* 381–389.

Willner, L. A., & Martin, R. D. (1985). Some basic principles of mammalian sex dimorphism. In J. Ghesquiere, R. D. Martin, & F. Newcombe (eds.), *Human Sexual Dimorphism.* London: Taylor & Francis.

Wilson, E. O. (1975). *Sociobiology: The New Synthesis.* Cambridge, MA: Harvard University Press.

Wilson, G. D. (1983). Finger-length as an index of assertiveness in women. *Personality & Individual Differences, 4,* 111–112.

Wilson, M., & Daly, M. (1985). Competitiveness, risk taking, and violence: The young male syndrome. *Ethology & Sociobiology, 6,* 59–73.

_____. (1992). The man who mistook his wife for a chattel. In J. H. Barkow, L. Cosmides, & J. Tooby (eds.), *The Adapted Mind: Evolutionary Psychology and the Generation of Culture.* New York: Oxford University Press.

Wilson, W. J. (1987). *The Truly Disadvantaged.* Chicago: University of Chicago Press.

Wolk, S., & Brandon, J. (1977). Runaway adolescents' perceptions of parents and self. *Adolescence, 12,* 175–187.

Wooley, S. C., & Garner, D. M. (1991). Obesity treatment: The high cost of false hope. *Journal of the American Dietetic Association, 91,* 1248–1251.

_____. (1994). Dietary treatments for obesity are ineffective. *British Medical Journal, 309,* 655–656.

Woolridge, M. W. (1995). Baby-controlled breastfeeding: biocultural implications. In P. Stuart-Macadam & K. A. Dettwyler (eds.), *Breastfeeding: Biocultural Perspectives.* New York: Aldine de Gruyter.

Worthman, C. M. (1993). Biocultural interactions in human development. In M. E. Pereira & L. A. Fairbanks (eds.), *Juvenile Primates: Life History, Development, and Behavior.* New York: Oxford University Press.

Wrangham, R. W. (1980). An ecological model of female-bonded primate groups. *Behaviour, 75,* 262–299.

Wrangham, R. W., et al. (eds.). (1994). *Chimpanzee Cultures.* Cambridge, MA: Harvard University Press.

Wylie, R. (1979). *The Self-Concept,* Vol. 2, *Theory and Research on Selected Topics.* Lincoln: University of Nebraska Press.

Yablonsky, L. (1966). *The Violent Gang.* New York: Macmillan.

Yalom, I. D., Green, R., & Fisk, N. (1973). Prenatal exposure to female hormones: Effect on psychosexual development in boys. *Archives of General Psychiatry, 28,* 554–561.

Yinon, Y., & Landau, M. (1987). On the reinforcing value of helping behavior in a positive mood. *Motivation & Emotion, 11,* 83–93.

Young, F. (1965). *Initiation Ceremonies: A Cross-Cultural Study of Status Dramatization.* New York: Bobbs-Merrill.

Zeifman, D., & Hazan, C. (1997). Attachment: The bond in pair-bonds. In J. A. Simpson & D. T. Kendrick (eds.), *Evolutionary Social Psychology.* Mahwah, NJ: Erlbaum.

Zelditch, M., Jr. (1955). Role differentiation in the nuclear family: A comparative study. In T. Parsons & R. F. Bales (eds.), *Family, Socialization and Interaction Process.* Glencoe, IL: Free Press.

Zeller, A. C. (1987). A role for children in hominid evolution. *Man, 22,* 528–557.

Zelnick, M., & Kantner, J. F. (1978). Contraceptive patterns and premarital pregnancy among women aged 15–19 in 1976. *Family Planning Perspectives, 10,* 135–142.

_____. (1979). Sex education and knowledge of pregnancy risk among U.S. teenage women. *Family Planning Perspectives, 11,* 355–357.

_____. (1980). Sexual activity, contraceptive use, and pregnancy among metropolitan area teenagers: 1971–1979. *Family Planning Perspectives, 12,* 230–237.

Zhou, J. (1995). A sex difference in the human brain and its relation to transsexuality. *Nature,* November 2, 68–70.

Ziegenhorn, L., & Schubiner, M. D. (1997). Depression, suicidality, peer status, and sex in adolescence. Poster presented at the American Psychological Association convention, Chicago, August.

Zivin, G. (ed.). (1985). *The Development of Expressive Behavior: Biology-Environment Interaction.* New York: Academic Press.

Author Index

Abelson, H., 253
Adams, G.R., 224, 233, 304, 307
Adelson, J., 242
Ågren, Greta, 139
Ahmad, Y., 51, 232
Ainsworth, M.D.S., 289
Aizate, H., 254
Albanese, M., 297
Alexander, R.D., 83
Algozzine, O., 222
Allen, C.D., 233
Allen, V., 236, 237
Alley, T.R., 199
Altmann, J., 122, 130, 131, 286
Amato, P.R., 36, 278, 290, 303, 305
Ames, M.A., 249
Anastasi, A., 8
Anderson, C., 70
Anderson, J.L., 6
Anderson, K., 276
Anderson, L., 215
Andersson, T., 237
Apatow, 199
Apte, M.L., 178
Aquilino, W.S., 305
Arafat, I.S., 194
Archer, J., 320
Argyle, M., 97, 201
Aries, P., 239
Aristotle, 19
Aro, H., 236
Asarnow, R., 214
Astone, N.M., 303
Åstrand, P.O., 160, 161
Atkinson, J.W., 59
Atzwanger, K., 265

Austin, C.R., 142
Aytch, D.M., 290, 298–99, 300

Babchuk, W.A., 202
Bacon, M., 304
Bailey, J. M., 247, 248, 249, 304
Baker, M.A., 165, 206, 255
Baker, R.R., 137, 145, 169, 172, 194, 195, 197, 254
Baldwin, J.D., 44, 168
Baldwin, J.I., 44
Bancroft, J., 112
Bandura, A., 292
Barber, A.P., 264
Barber, B.K., 288
Barber, N., 162, 195, 196, 218, 260, 264
Barchas, J.D., 48
Barchas, P.R., 48
Barkow, J.H., 52, 55, 81, 106, 217, 221, 275
Barnard, C.J., 264
Barnes, G.M., 290, 293
Barnlund, D.C., 225
Barry, H., III, 95, 104, 109, 112, 113, 114, 115, 116, 117, 118–19, 120, 121, 122, 123, 200, 285, 304
Bartoshuk, L.M., 16
Bateman, A.J., 171
Baumrind, D., 293
Bayley, N., 219
Beach, F.A., 158, 195, 245, 262, 264
Bean, J.W., 143
Beauchamp, G.K., 16
Becker, J.S., 142, 154, 190, 202, 207
Bellis, M.A., 137, 145, 169, 172, 194, 195, 197, 254, 255

378

Eggebeen, D., 290
Ehrhardt, A.A., 35, 37, 172, 173, 175, 176, 204, 250
Eibl-Eibesfeldt, I., 27, 34, 70, 84, 111, 114, 116, 117, 119, 162, 198, 199, 203, 227, 228, 260, 279, 291
Eicher, J.B., 233
Einon, D., 172
Eitzen, D., 215
Ekehammer, B., 205, 206
Ekman, P., 24
Elder, G.H., Jr., 218, 235, 288, 295
Elkind, D., 31
Ellis, B.J., 144, 252
Ellis, H., 142
Ellis, H.D., 66, 201
Ellis, L., 118, 151, 174, 176, 179, 180, 206, 245, 247, 248, 249
Ember, C.R., 92
Engel, C., 264
Erikson, E., 95
Essock-Vitale, S.M., 106
Eveleth, P.B., 121, 137, 267
Eysenck, H.J., 259

Falk, R., 272
Farrell, M.P., 290, 293
Faust, M.S., 234
Fedigan, L.M., 80
Feingold, A., 208
Feingold, D., 213
Feistner, A.T.C., 80, 81, 82, 83
Feldman, R., 213, 299, 301, 302
Fernald, A., 39, 40
Ferreira, M., 287
Feshbach, M., 242
Fichner-Rathus, L., 194, 203, 265, 273, 276, 306
Fields, A., 308
Fischer, C.S., 37, 101
Fisher, A.D., 267
Fisher, H., 37, 79, 81, 101, 277
Fisher, W.A., 273, 274
FitzGerald, R.W., 179–180
Flannery, R.C., 52
Flapan, D., 222
Fleming, A.S., 39, 191, 203

Flinn, M.V., 140, 287
Ford, C.S., 158, 195, 245, 263, 264
Fossett, M.A., 279
Foster, A.D., 216
Frame, C.L., 223
Frank, E., 70
Frankenhaueser, M., 240
Franklin, M., 260
Franz, C.E., 290
Freedman, D.G., 10, 71, 91, 167, 172, 205, 254
Friedl, E., 42, 69, 80, 89, 90, 91, 94, 100, 116, 124, 132, 277
Friesen, D., 24, 216
Frisch, R.E., 138, 141, 196
Frodi, A., 41, 222
Fullard, W., 205
Furlow, F.B., 165
Furman, W., 242
Furstenberg, F., 267, 305

Gadpaille, W.J., 246
Gaffney, G.R. 248
Galdikas, B., 83
Gallup, G.G., Jr., 247, 248
Gangestad, S.W., 218, 257
Ganong, W.F., 129, 148, 150, 154, 187, 189, 190
Gantman, C.A., 292
Garbarino, J., 105
Gardner, E.G., 226
Garn, S.M., 139, 267
Garner, D.M., 142, 238, 239
Gaulin, S.J.C., 179–180
Gelles, R.J., 291
Gerrard, M., 273
Ghiglieri, M.P., 78
Giller, H., 223, 224, 291, 293, 297, 298, 299, 301, 302, 303
Ginsburg, A.L., 292
Ginsburg, H.J., 52
Ginsburg, M., 174
Giovannoni, J., 102
Gladue, B.A., 247
Goethals, G.W., 94
Gold, M., 302
Goldberg, S., 205

Subject Index

expression of, 22, 24
vicarious, 27–28
See also Motivation
Endearment behavior, 200–202
Endocrine system
breast feeding, 190–192
female, 185–192
male, 147–158
menstrual cycling, 186–188
pregnancy and labor, 188–190
sex differentiation, 148–151, 185–186
See also Hormones
Endometrium, 187
Endorphins, 173
Environmental influences, 7–9, 77,
297–298
EPCs. *See* Extrapair copulations
Epigamic displays, 167
Erect posture, 52–53
Erotophobia, 273
Estrogens, 157–158, 185–187, 314
Estrus, 83
Ethnocentrism, 111–112
Ethogram, 4
Ethology, 4, 313–314
Evolutionary theory, 3, 8, 82, 313
Evolved behaviors, 5, 8
determining functions of, 13–17
identification of, 9–13
neural structures and, 11–12, 13
Exchange theories, 59
Exogamy, 84
Exploration, 42–43
Extended family, 101, 102
Extrapair copulations (EPCs), 91,
254–256, 281
Eyebrows, 162–163, 260
Eye contact, 53, 57

Facial expressions, 12, 13, 22, 24,
201–202
Facultative strategies, 135
Family conflict, 100–103, 284–287, 320.
See also Juvenile delinquency.
Fat, in females, 137, 195–197, 237–239,
259

Father, 41–42, 66–67, 303–304
father-daughter relationship, 287,
322–323
father-son relationship, 286–287
self-esteem and, 290–291
Father absence, 143–144, 246, 275, 276,
282, 285, 303
divorce and, 304–307, 322
juvenile delinquency and, 299,
303–304, 311
peer relations and, 303–304
promiscuity and, 304, 311, 320
Fearfulness, 42–43, 205–206
Female inhibition in mixed-sex
competition, 239–241, 244, 321
Femininity, 235–237, 257–260, 281
Fertility, 183
adolescent subfertility, 158,
268–269
female, 236
gonadarche, 155
male, 121–122
menarche, 120, 121, 126, 132, 137,
275, 319
puberty rites and, 121–123, 126
spermarche, 158, 182, 304
Fetal masculinization, 175–176, 204, 237,
249
Fitness, 16–17, 33
Fixed (modal) action patterns, 13
Flirtation, 70–71
Fluid intelligence, 30, 147
Follicle-stimulating hormone (FSH),
152, 154, 155, 182, 185
Follicular phase, 188
Food acquisition, 80–82, 83, 85
breast feeding, 16, 133, 190–192,
203–206, 207, 238, 319
maturation and, 131–132, 145
sexual dimorphism and, 133
Formal operational reasoning, 29–31,
147, 294
Friendships, 36, 211, 226, 241–244, 262,
315
FSH. See Follicle-stimulating hormone
Function, 13–17, 22, 313–314
development and, 16